Beyond the Persecuting Society

Beyond the Persecuting Society

Religious Toleration Before the Enlightenment

edited by
John Christian Laursen
and Cary J. Nederman

PENN

University of Pennsylvania Press

Philadelphia

Copyright © 1998 University of Pennsylvania Press
All rights reserved
Printed in the United States of America on acid-free paper

10 9 8 7 6 5 4 3 2 1

Published by
University of Pennsylvania Press
Philadelphia, Pennsylvania 19104-4011

Library of Congress Cataloging-in-Publication Data
Beyond the persecuting society : religious toleration before the Enlightenment / edited by
John Christian Laursen and Cary J. Nederman.
      p.   cm.
Includes bibliographical references and index.
    ISBN 0-8122-3331-X (alk. paper). — ISBN 0-8122-1567-2 (pbk. : alk. paper)
    1. Religious tolerance—History.   I. Laursen, John Christian.   II. Nederman, Cary J.
BR1610.B48   1997
291.1′772′09—dc21
                                                                          97-26795
                                                                          CIP

Contents

Acknowledgments

THE COMPILATION OF A COLLECTION of essays is necessarily a cooperative process, requiring the aid and good will of numerous individuals, especially the contributors. In addition to thanking them, the editors wish to recognize several persons without whom this project could not have come to fruition. In the early stages, Professor Edward Peters offered important advice as well as moral support. Jerome Singerman of the University of Pennsylvania Press lent expert guidance at each point in the editorial process. Professor Randolph Head cheerfully and efficiently translated Detlef Döring's chapter and wrote the introduction to Part II, both on short notice.

One of the most rewarding aspects of publishing a book is the opportunity to acknowledge and repay, by way of dedication, personal and scholarly debts to teachers and friends. The editors are, therefore, extremely gratified to dedicate this volume to the memory of George Armstrong Kelly, a scholar of remarkable range and insight and a teacher of genuine dedication and humanity, and to Kate Langdon Forhan, a fount of intellectual stimulation and an individual of uncommon strength.

General Introduction:
Political and Historical
Myths in the Toleration
Literature

John Christian Laursen and Cary J. Nederman

ISSUES OF TOLERANCE AND TOLERATION are surely high on anyone's agenda for thinking about politics and history today. What causes people to tolerate and what causes them to persecute each other? What are the benefits and drawbacks of each of these? How have they changed over time? What makes them change? It is our belief that scholarly studies of the sort collected in this volume can contribute to our collective understanding of these issues.

Before we begin substantive discussion, readers may already be wondering about the meaning of the words "tolerance" and "toleration."[1] We do not wish to advance tendentious definitions of these terms, but prefer to allow different nuances of meaning to emerge from the different contexts and the different approaches of our authors. The variety of meanings in ordinary language suggest something like Wittgensteinian "family resemblances" rather than some essentialist core meaning for the words. A key point here, to be fleshed out below, is that toleration was not one thing, not a juggernaut through history that had to emerge in order to bring about modernity. Rather, different theories and practices of toleration were contingent, often local, and, as we shall see, surprisingly widespread from early times.

Although a substantial literature on toleration already exists, it is also our belief that much of it perpetuates distortions. Some of these are based on large-scale interpretive theories of obviously political provenance. Others are less obviously political, and perhaps better described as historical errors. But all of them are best understood as myths. The chief thrust of this book is that there is no overstatement in saying that in medieval and early modern Europe the voices favoring and the actual practices of toleration were present, both in number and in variation, on a scale hitherto unappreciated. But we can only hear them when we have dispelled some of the dominant myths about those times. In the following introductory remarks, we will sketch how the essays in this volume help to explode some of these myths.

Let us begin with what we will call the Enlightenment stereotype. In recent years, the ideas and practices of toleration and tolerance have come under increasing attack. On the theoretical side, critics from the left have insisted that toleration of the wrong sorts of people and activities means complicity in repression.[2] Recent critics of the so-called "Enlightenment" have claimed that tolerance is no more than yet another ideology, and too narrowly Western, classist, and sexist at that.[3] At times, the critiques of toleration have seemed only too easy to explain. Throughout much of its history, criticism of tolerance has been little more than an excuse to justify persecution of one's enemies. But sometimes the critics have had a theoretical point that bears more weight. Critics show, rightly, that Enlightenment values are more ambiguous and less satisfactory than they have sometimes been made to appear. When a caricature of Cartesian rationalism, Lockean bourgeois "possessive individualism," and Kantian idealism is made to stand for the best of Enlightenment values, it is not too hard to see why many people would not have much confidence in them.

The simplest answer[4] to critics of this association of tolerance and toleration with Enlightenment values is to show that ideas and practices of tolerance and toleration were available and in use long before the Enlightenment. That is one of the chief roles of the present volume. Constant Mews on Abelard, Cary Nederman on John of Salisbury, and Gary Remer on Menahem Ha-Me'iri draw our attention to currents of tolerance in ideas and practices as far back as medieval times. Later chapters give us a variety of different variations on the theme from the Reformation of the sixteenth century through developments in the seventeenth century. And yet, curiously enough, the paradigmatic treatment of the matter, in the anglophone world at least, has been to start with John Locke, leap ahead to John Stuart Mill, and then discuss cases like Northern Ireland, Lebanon, or Bosnia.[5] This leads us to what we call the Locke obsession.

Over and over in the large Locke literature that great philosopher is featured as the inventor of modern toleration. This literature sometimes seems to feed on itself, and it shows no signs of abating. But if one can escape from the shackles of anglocentrism one discovers that Locke was neither very original in his argumentation nor very broad in his toleration. Catholics and atheists have never thought much of a toleration that excluded them. Only recently have those who discuss his work set it in the context of his early letter to Henry Stubbe of 1659 or his *First and Second Tracts on Government* of 1660–62, in which he advocates suppression of religious dissidents.[6] From many essays on Locke, one would never guess that major debates over toleration had taken place in England decades before he began to write, nor that he was familiar with those works.[7] One would never suspect that Locke's friend and host in the Netherlands, Philip van Limborch, had written on toleration, along with Adriaan van Paets, Pierre Bayle, and other authors—and all this before Locke began to compose his more famous *Letter on Toleration* in 1685.

Another common flaw in the Locke literature is the tendency to identify a single point as the heart of Locke's originality. One recent piece, otherwise very thoughtful, asserts that without "the multiple or plural self . . . toleration would not have been possible as a viable ideal in the context of early modern Europe."[8] A better approach, which juxtaposes Locke to Spinoza, Bayle, and Pufendorf, writes of four contemporary arguments for tolerance (private conscience vs. public exercise, tolerance as the lesser evil, attempts to establish a consensus about *fundamentalia*, and a broad palette of lesser incentives as an alternative to suppression) along with four conditions for toleration theory (acceptance of the idea that unity leads to violence rather than plurality leading to violence, the spread of travel literature and knowledge of other cultures, the rise of the *respublica literaria* and freedom of action, and spreading recognition of the right to association or to join groups), all of which contributed to Locke's theory.[9] The point is not only that Locke did not do it alone, but that he did not do it with one instrument. Throughout this volume, the variety of approaches will perhaps suggest that the medium is part of the message; toleration of multiple viewpoints is justified from multiple viewpoints.

Two of the essays in this volume do bear on Locke, but from uncommon perspectives. Richard Popkin's essay ranges widely over discourses of toleration in the seventeenth and eighteenth centuries without mentioning Locke's essays on toleration, but he does find a role for Locke's philosophy. Chris Laursen's essay on Pierre Bayle draws attention to some comparisons to Locke, pointing out that Locke may have borrowed ideas and learned from practices he observed during his stay in the Netherlands.

Beginning our discussion with reference to the Enlightenment and to Locke may give the impression that we fall into the same trap that so many have, of assuming that we owe toleration to philosophy. Too many treatments of the matter take the "great thinker" approach, according to which somebody said, "Let there be tolerance," and then it happened. Heiko Oberman has made the point that we need much more in the way of the social history of toleration in order to be able to understand the theories.[10] In this volume, we have made an effort to place studies of thinkers and studies of doers in juxtaposition, with the hope that this would stimulate reflection on the relationship between theory and practice. Randolph Head's study of Swiss villages and Frank Way's exploration of court records in colonial Massachusetts make it clear that in many places, toleration in practice came before anybody managed to theorize about it. Judging from the after-the-fact theorizing of Locke and others, Hegel may be right about the owl of Minerva.

Yet another distortion is the Inquisition cliché, according to which all of the medieval period and some of the early modern period are seen as an era of relentless persecution. We do not want to imply that all was sweetness and love, and indeed we have borrowed one element of the title of this volume from a valuable work which describes the formation of persecuting societies in medieval Europe.[11] But the monolithic conception of the Roman Church's reaction to heresy, embodied by the systematic extirpation of heretics through inquisitional procedures, is surely a political construct. Edward Peters has drawn our attention to the forces at work in the creation of the myth of "The Inquisition": "The myth was originally devised to serve variously the political purposes of a number of early modern political regimes, as well as Protestant reformers, proponents of religious and civil toleration, philosophical enemies of the civil power of organized religions, and progressive modernists; but the myth remained durable, widely adaptable, and useful, so that in time it came to be tightly woven into the fabric of modern consciousness."[12]

In fact, responses to religious reform varied as much within the Roman Church as they ever had. Just as systematic persecution enjoyed its Catholic advocates, so did doctrines of patient correction and instruction and even of open public debate find many supporters among those loyal to Rome. It is worth remembering that one of the great texts of opposition to

Spanish imperialism and persecution of the Indians, gleefully translated by Protestants all over northern Europe, was Bishop Bartolomé de Las Casas's *Brief Relation*, published in Seville in 1552 under official imprimatur. Joseph Lecler's now-classic book found many Catholic proponents of toleration throughout Europe in the sixteenth century.[13] Thomas Mayer's chapter in this volume on Cardinal Pole shows how a prominent Catholic thinker could be interpreted by his disciples as a proponent of toleration.

A related distortion gives the general impression that the voices of tolerance have always come from lonely souls crying in the dark. But on closer examination of the period from medieval times to the seventeenth century, proponents of toleration turn out to be more numerous and also more diverse in their approach than has often been acknowledged. On all sides, one can identify apostles of toleration battling with exponents of intolerance.

Another widespread myth has it that toleration went hand in hand with secularization. But some of the most insistent voices have always demanded toleration as a matter of religion. Remer's Ha-Me'iri was very much a Jewish thinker, defending toleration with Biblical categories. In Marion Leathers Kuntz's interpretation of Bodin, his tolerant position was based on a conception of multiple religious truths; in Popkin's view, Bodin's is a fundamentally Jewish view. In either case, his toleration is based on a genuinely religious world view. Detlef Döring's Pufendorf developed a distinctly Lutheran theory of expedient toleration. Laursen's Bayle is a sincere Calvinist. And, again, it should not be thought that toleration was merely an ideology of the persecuted Jews, Protestants, and other heterodox figures; we have already mentioned some of the Catholic supporters of toleration.

Another misunderstanding created by seeing the issue only in terms of winners and losers is the currently fashionable assumption that, whatever they might have tolerated inside Christian Europe, the early modern Europeans closed ranks in intolerance of non-Christians. We have already mentioned the heritage of engagement with Jewish and Islamic culture, which continued apace in the sixteenth and seventeenth centuries.[14] As Popkin's chapter shows, a perfectly good reason for toleration of Jews and Muslims was that such toleration created the conditions for a future salvation of their souls by conversion when the time is ripe. Arlen Feldwick and Cary Nederman add Aphra Behn's *Oroonoko* as an example of the role in the development of toleration played by the European "encounter" with different cultures in Africa and America.

Another set of chapters in this volume explores the crucial phenomena of almost-tolerationist theory and practice. Much of the debate in the sixteenth and seventeenth centuries was couched in terms of defining the minimum *fundamentalia* that could unite all Christians. An influential book and series of articles by Mario Turchetti has drawn a sharp distinction between "concordance," or the policy of seeking agreement among all the warring parties, and a truer tolerance, which allows each party to go his or her own way.[15] One of his claims is that the only writer of the sixteenth century with the wider view of tolerance was Sebastian Castellion.[16] One of the chapters in this book takes issue with that claim. Kuntz shows how Bodin's *Dialogue of the Seven* expressed a genuine toleration. Her exploration of Bodin makes him an unconscious inheritor of the dialogic style of Abelard.

Interestingly, Döring's chapter on Pufendorf tends to confirm Turchetti's most general point, which is that many a writer who might appear to call for toleration was playing only a temporary, tactical game. Döring shows that a major figure in seventeenth-century toleration theory, often credited with a theory of true tolerance,[17] in fact never wanted more than concordance. Döring's careful exposition is based on generally neglected materials such as Pufendorf's letters and minor writings.

Many of the chapters in this volume make it clear that toleration research must consider Europe as a whole (and for that matter, the known world) in order to understand the history of toleration from a cosmopolitan point of view. Too often, the history of toleration has been written as national history. Books such as Jordan's *History of Toleration in England*, Vivanti's *Political Wars and Religious Peace in France*, and Kot's *Socinianism in Poland* are undoubtedly valuable, but they too often play down the larger international contexts.[18] After all, Robinson cited Grotius, Aubert de Versé answered Hobbes and Spinoza, Van Paets wrote on the problems of toleration in England, and many a peacemaker, such as Hugo Grotius and Jan Comenius, were hounded from one country to another. In this volume, for example, Mayer's study of Pole's network of supporters from Hungary to Italy brings out the point that theories and ideas crossed many a political boundary. Laursen's study draws on Bayle's discussion of figures ranging from Savonarola in Italy to Kotterus in Germany to Pierre Jurieu in the Netherlands. In this sense, this volume aspires to supplement heroic efforts at cosmopolitan history such as Lecler's *Toleration and the Reformation*.[19]

It is sometimes forgotten that theories of toleration were not always expressed in serious tracts with prosaic titles like "A Tract on Toleration." A recent editor of Fernão Mendes Pinto's *Travels* of 1569–78 (first published in 1614) argues that Mendes Pinto's irony and satire amounted to an appeal for toleration.[20] The *Menippean Satire* of Leroy, Gillet, and Pithou, another effort to sap the strength of persecutorial convictions, was first published in 1594 and reissued more than once. The Huguenot Denis Veiras's contribution was the use of utopian literature to send a message in favor of tolerant attitudes.[21] The chapter in this volume on Aphra Behn by Feldwick and Nederman gives an example of drama, poetry, and fiction pressed into service as vehicles for the dissemination of practices and attitudes of toleration.

Mention of Aphra Behn leads us to the role of the rise of deism and atheism in the theory and practice of toleration. Many voices were accused of deism or atheism, especially in the seventeenth century, but it has been much debated as to when genuine atheism actually came into being. Recent work has ingeniously suggested that atheism was the natural product of so many fighting faiths, each drawing atheistic conclusions from the principles of its opponents.[22] The chapter on Behn shows how her rhetoric drew on the deist tradition in England. The wide-ranging chapter by Popkin attributes a substantial current in toleration theory to the deists. Students of Locke will not really know what Locke meant by excluding atheists from toleration (and what Bayle meant by including them, in most of his works) until they understand what deism and atheism meant in his time.

We have tried to avoid some of the above-mentioned errors by casting a wide net for original and novel approaches to toleration in theory and practice before the Enlightenment. One of the chief purposes of this volume is to encourage readers to expand their horizons in thinking about the origins and problems of toleration. We shall be drawing attention to political actors and political thinkers who have not been seen or heard in most of the contemporary discussion of toleration theory. We shall also be drawing attention away from the standard models of England for toleration, France for civil war, and Spain for the Inquisition. After all, variations on the theme of each of these factors can be found in each of these countries.

Contemporary discussions of tolerance[23] often turn on questions of toleration or persecution of lifestyles, gender or sexual orientations, ethnic groups, and so forth, and the connections to religious tolerance and persecution may not be immediately obvious. But there does not seem to be much doubt that in Europe the ideas and practices of tolerance and toleration were developed with reference to religion.[24] One does not need tolerance in matters that do not provoke much dispute and persecution within a community. Religion, and specifically Christianity, created the most significant such disputes in the European world from the time of the Roman empire, and accordingly the chapters in this book focus on the nexus between religion and persecution in the period from the twelfth century to the late seventeenth century. But that does not mean that the ideas, practices, and strategies discussed below cannot be applied by analogy to more recent forms of difference and persecution. One of the purposes of this book is to provide a catalog of tools for confronting persecution in its recent forms as well.

For heuristic purposes, this volume is divided into three sections: one on the medieval period, one on the "long" sixteenth century, and one on the seventeenth century. Each section begins with an introduction to the major events of the period and to the contextual background of the theories and practices of toleration that emerged in that period. These introductions draw attention to the contributions of each of the chapters in the book.

It should be kept in mind that, rather than describing a unilinear progression from darkness to light, from persecution to toleration, from all that was old and backward to all that is new and modern, the essays in this volume tell a different story. It is not the "Whig" history of inevitable liberal democratic progress toward what we are today. When we speak of "paths to toleration" we are making it clear that tolerance and toleration have come in many forms, in many practices and theories. This may in fact be a good thing. In the face of contemporary persecutions and intolerance, we can take comfort that we are not necessarily sliding backwards into darkness. Then we can ransack the history of the theories and practices of tolerance and toleration in order to develop new tools for contesting persecution in its contemporary forms.

Notes

1. Although semantic distinctions can be made between "tolerance" and "toleration," we will not make any technical distinction between these terms, but rather rely on the context for any differences in meaning. Sometimes we will repeat "tolerance and toleration" in order to indicate that we mean to pick up the largest range of ordinary meanings.

2. These charges can often be traced back to Robert Paul Wolff, Barrington Moore, Jr., and Herbert Marcuse, *A Critique of Pure Tolerance* (Boston: Beacon Press, 1968).

3. See, for example, Roger Crisp, "Communitarianism and Toleration," in

John Horton and Peter Nicholson, eds., *Toleration: Philosophy and Practice* (Aldershot: Avebury, 1992), 108–25; Kirstie McClure, "Difference, Diversity, and the Limits of Toleration," *Political Theory* 18 (1990): 361–91.

4. Another answer would be to follow Christine Korsgaard: "According to an old quip, Christianity has not been tried and found too difficult, but rather has been found too difficult and so not tried. Despite some currently popular claims about the bankruptcy of the Enlightenment, I believe that this is true of Enlightenment ideals." "A Note on the Value of Gender-Identification" in Martha C. Nussbaum and Jonathan Glover, eds., *Women, Culture and Development: A Study of Human Capabilities* (Oxford: Oxford University Press, 1995), 402.

5. Typical examples are Susan Mendus, *Toleration and the Limits of Liberalism* (London: Macmillan, 1989); Susan Mendus and David Edwards, eds., *On Toleration* (Oxford: Clarendon Press, 1987); John Horton and Susan Mendus, eds., *Aspects of Toleration: Philosophical Studies* (London: Methuen, 1985); Nick Fotion and Gerard Elfstrom, *Toleration* (Tuscaloosa: University of Alabama Press, 1992); Glenn Tinder, *Tolerance and Community* (Columbia: University of Missouri Press, 1995). See also John Horton and Susan Mendus, eds., *John Locke—A Letter Concerning Toleration in Focus* (London: Routledge, 1991).

6. See the Introduction to David Wootton, ed., *Political Writings of John Locke* (New York: Penguin, 1993), 32ff. Wootton's volume reprints Locke's early letters and essays.

7. For a survey of these debates, see William K. Jordan, *The Development of Religious Toleration in England*, 4 vols. (Cambridge, Mass.: Harvard University Press/London: Allen and Unwin, 1932–1940; reprint Gloucester, Mass.: Peter Smith, 1965).

8. Ingrid Creppell, "Locke on Toleration: The Transformation of Constraint," *Political Theory* 24 (1996): 202. Creppell also asserts that Locke argued "unequivocally" in favor of toleration (216), although she later recognizes that he denied toleration to Catholics and atheists (note 41).

9. Horst Dreitzel, "Gewissensfreiheit und soziale Ordnung. Religionstoleranz als Problem der politischen Theorie am Ausgang des 17. Jahrhunderts," *Politische Vierteljahresschrift* 36 (1995): 3–34.

10. Heiko A. Oberman, "The Travail of Tolerance: Containing Chaos in Early Modern Europe" in Ole Peter Grell and Robert W. Scribner, eds., *Tolerance and Intolerance in the European Reformation* (Cambridge: Cambridge University Press, 1996), 13–31.

11. Robert Ian Moore, *The Formation of a Persecuting Society: Power and Deviance in Western Europe, 950–1250* (Oxford: Blackwell, 1987). Our chapters show that Moore's conclusion from the details of cases of persecution to an overarching persecutory mentality could be balanced by the extrapolation of an antipersecutory mentality. However, we would prefer not to risk such tendentious social-psychological claims, and content ourselves with the local and particular established by each chapter. On this strategy, see David Nirenberg, *Communities of Violence: Persecution of Minorities in the Middle Ages* (Princeton, N.J.: Princeton University Press, 1996), esp. 5ff.

12. Edward Peters, *Inquisition* (New York: Free Press, 1988), 1–2.

13. Joseph Lecler, S.J., *Histoire de la tolérance au siècle de la Réforme* (Paris: Albin Michel, 1992 [orig. 1955]); English translation: *Toleration and the Reformation* (New York: Association Press, 1960). The reader of this marvelous work soon learns to discount for the Catholic bias of the author, which manifests itself in drawing attention to the intolerant side of Protestant heroes and unearthing at least one forgotten Catholic tolerationist for every Protestant tolerationist — surely both useful services even if they may amount to distortion.

14. See, recently, Gül A. Russell, *The "Arabick" Interest of the Natural Philosophers in Seventeenth-Century England* (Leiden: Brill, 1993) and Alison P. Coudert, *The Impact of the Kabbalah in the Seventeenth Century* (Leiden: Brill, 1994).

15. Mario Turchetti, *Concordia o tolleranza? Francois Bauduin (1520–1573) e i Moyenneurs* (Geneva: Droz, 1984); "Religious Concord and Political Tolerance in Sixteenth- and Seventeenth-Century France," *Sixteenth Century Journal* 22 (1991): 15–25.

16. Thomas Mayer points out that a forthcoming study will challenge this point, claiming that Castellion only sought concordance. See below.

17. See, e.g., Simone Zurbuchen, *Naturrecht und naturliche Religion: Zur Geschichte des Toleranzproblems von Samuel Pufendorf bis Jean-Jacques Rousseau* (Wurzburg: Königshausen & Neumann, 1990).

18. Jordan, *The Development of Religious Toleration in England*; Corrado Vivanti, *Lotte politica e pace religiosa in Francia fra Cinque e Seicento* (Torino: Einaudi, 1963); Stanislaw Kot, *Socinianism in Poland: The Social and Political Ideas of the Polish Anti-Trinitarians in the Sixteenth and Seventeenth Centuries*, trans. Earl Morse Wilbur (Boston: Starr King Press, 1959 [orig. 1932]).

19. See note 13.

20. Fernão Mendes Pinto, *The Travels of Mendes Pinto*, ed. and trans. Rebecca D. Catz (Chicago: University of Chicago Press, 1989), xv.

21. Denis Veiras, *The History of the Sevarites or Sevarambi* (London, 1675; French edition, 1677–79; German edition 1689).

22. Alan Charles Kors, *Atheism in France, 1660–1730* (Princeton, N.J.: Princeton University Press, 1989).

23. See, for example, David Heyd, ed., *Toleration: An Elusive Virtue* (Princeton, N.J.: Princeton University Press, 1996).

24. And they often still are matters of religion. See, for example, the following exchange: Anna Elisabetta Galeotti, "Citizenship and Equality: The Place for Toleration," *Political Theory* 21 (1993): 585–605; Norma Claire Moruzzi, "A Problem with Headscarves: Contemporary Complexities of Political and Social Identity," Anna Elisabetta Galeotti, "A Problem with Theory: A Rejoinder to Moruzzi," and Norma Claire Moruzzi, "A Response to Galeotti," all in *Political Theory* 22 (1994): 653–79; and Levent Köker, "Political Toleration or Politics of Recognition," *Political Theory* 24 (1996): 315–20.

PART I

THE MEDIEVAL
BALANCE

Introduction: Discourses and Contexts of Tolerance in Medieval Europe

Cary J. Nederman

Beyond the Persecuting Society

The choice to begin narrating the history of toleration in Europe with the Latin Middle Ages may seem a highly contentious one. After all, the most common impression of medieval life among scholars is perhaps best summed up by the title of R. I. Moore's influential study of secular and ecclesiastical conformity during the High Middle Ages: *The Formation of a Persecuting Society*.[1] As Preston King bluntly states, "Christians . . . persecuted dissident sects. No Christian writer during the Middle Ages can readily be described as an opponent of intolerance."[2] Henry Kamen is even more succinct: "The Middle Ages had not tolerated dissent."[3] In unqualified form, however, the case that medieval Europe was purely and simply a "persecuting society" is too much a caricature to be deserving of uncritical acceptance.[4]

Moore and others may be correct in observing increasing efforts during the course of the Middle Ages to impose and extend control on Europeans both as political subjects and as faithful Christians.[5] But this is not to say that such efforts were uniformly successful. Indeed, the evidence suggests that persecution did not halt dissent and in some instances may have only hardened the resolve of dissidents. This is true at all levels of medieval society: theologians and philosophers did not forgo reading Aristotle because the Church proscribed many of his teachings; peasant Cathar heretics did not surrender their beliefs even when a crusade was preached against them; kings and princes did not lay down their claims to political autonomy in secular (and even some spiritual) matters simply because the pope anathematized them. The centralized power whose rhetoric is so rigorously documented by Moore was often still too frail in practice to realize the claims made by and for it. In some parts of Europe, such as Spain, these realities would generate centuries of peaceful coexistence among divergent religions. In the Spanish context, not merely Christians of diverging stances but non-Christians alongside Christians were the focus of tolerant practices.

Of course, it is one matter to say that diversity was too entrenched in fact to be effectively suppressed by medieval institutions and quite another to assert that toleration was upheld as a matter of principle. As Kamen notes, "Liberalism in religion is not the same thing as tolerance."[6] Yet here and there in the Middle Ages one does find advocates of the view that toleration is something of value beyond merely pragmatic considerations. Ironically, a similar attitude toward toleration seems to emerge, if only on the fringes, within both the dominant and the minority cultures of medieval Europe. A somewhat unorthodox, although still respected, Christian thinker such as Peter Abelard, the twelfth-century theologian and philosopher, could propose that open dialogue, even among people of apparently incommensurable viewpoints, is necessary in order to achieve truth. On Constant Mews's account, Abelard's *Dialogue Between a Christian, a Jew and a Philosopher* is a demonstration (in method as much as in substance) that the pursuit of knowledge cannot be detached from the inclusion of diverse viewpoints in the process of discussion. Truth, or at least its comprehension by mere mortal beings, is open-ended and constantly subject to renewed inquiry.

Abelard's position demonstrates significant congruence with ideas expressed in the work of the Jewish thinker Ha-Me'iri, writing in the context of fourteenth-century Provence. Like their Christian counterparts, the Jews of medieval Europe held intolerant views toward other religions, a fact whose significance has perhaps not been fully appreciated. But, as Gary Remer reveals, Ha-Me'iri developed an innovative theory of why Jews should tolerate Christians in certain matters. Contact with uncivilized, barbarian religions, Ha-Me'iri reasoned, was surely what sacred writings meant to proscribe. But for him Christianity, being now a civilized religion, was exempt from this prohibition. Ha-Me'iri thus resists the demonization of the oppressor that oppressed groups sometimes readily embrace.

In sum, the conventional wisdom about the role of tolerance in the Latin Middle Ages requires some modification. If one examines the historical record, it turns out to be less than surprising that opportunities for and pockets of toleration abounded throughout medieval Europe. But a full appreciation of this observation requires, first of all, examination of the background against which theories and practices of toleration emerged during the first fifteen hundred years of the Christian era.

The Roads from Rome

To achieve an understanding of persecution and toleration in European society, we must turn initially to the predecessor culture of ancient Greece and Rome. For the Greeks and the early Romans, religion was effectively indistinguishable from civic ritual and political identity. The priest was a public official, often selected in the same way as other magistrates. Piety was expected of the citizen not in order to promote some further moral or religious vision of the good but as a useful aid in the conduct of public business. As Cicero observed in *De legibus*, "Who will deny that such beliefs are useful when he remembers how often oaths are used to confirm agreements, how important to our well-being is the sanctity of treaties, how many persons are deterred from crime by fear of divine punishment, and how sacred an association of citizens becomes when the immortals partake of it either as judges or as witnesses?"[7]

The expansionism of the great empires of the classical Mediterranean world was wholly consonant with this outlook. Since religion was so closely tied to a particular civic identity, there was no pretense of universalism; submission to an imperial power did not require replacing one's own deities by the gods of the conquering city. The municipal system, perfected by the Romans, permitted newly vanquished territories a measure of autonomy (under the watchful eye of imperial authorities) that extended to religious rituals and practices. The only stipulation was that the provincials in addition made sacrifice to the approved deities of Rome—an unproblematic request to a pantheist or a religious pluralist. In the most extreme case—that of the Jews—Rome proved even able to tolerate non-worship of its cult, provided the unbelievers were prepared to pray to their own God for the sake of the Emperor. Although the Roman establishment was by no means fond of the peculiar beliefs and rites of Judaism, the antiquity of that religion earned its adherents the respect and forbearance of authorities.

It is popularly supposed that Christianity afforded an exception to the general pattern of sufferance of religious difference that characterized the ancient Western world. Christianity is said to be a faith both persecuted and persecuting. But this statement requires some qualification. While the persecution of Christians occurred throughout the imperial period, it was seldom conducted on a systematic basis coordinated by central authorities (the Great Persecution of 303–312 was exceptional in this regard).[8] Rather, persecution of Christians happened in a sporadic and localized manner, and was sometimes even discouraged by imperial officials who sympathized with persons accused of holding Christian beliefs. To the modern mind, perhaps the most horrifying aspect of Roman persecutions was the nature of the charge: merely to be "Christian," rather than to commit some definite action, was sufficient to be prosecuted for a capital crime.

It must be recognized, however, that this harshness stemmed from the very odd character of Christian belief when judged by Roman standards: it was universalistic and exclusivist. That is, the Christian faith claimed validity for all people at all times and in all places, and it was unwilling to accommodate other deities or the public rites associated with the Roman cults. Indeed, Roman society regarded Christianity as atheistic, in the precise sense that its adherents refused to "pay cult to the gods." And while such a refusal may have been tolerable in the case of the Jews, whose religion was venerable and who did not shirk from serving the Empire, it was deemed dangerous when it involved a conscious break with tradition and outright hostility to imperial authority. There is every reason to suppose that Christians themselves did much to incur Roman wrath and intensify their own victimization. The Christian penchant for martyrdom was often realized by clear provocation of Roman officials, as Christians flaunted themselves in gratuitous acts of disobedience and disruption.

The fourth century was a watershed in the history of Christianity, which moved rapidly from a proscribed faith to an officially protected and subsidized sect. Yet the public privileging of Christian religion cannot be equated with the state-sanctioned imposition of strict orthodoxy in the lands under the control of the Roman Empire. Beyond the myriad practical problems involved with eliminating paganism and heretical Christian movements, Christianity's universalistic and exclusivist elements were tempered by biblical teachings about charity, patience, non-violence, and the like. Jesus had advocated preaching and example as the appropriate techniques for disseminating his message. The employment of Church-endorsed state compulsion to enforce Christian conformity fit uncomfortably with scriptural lessons that advocated personal free choice and commended turning the other cheek in response to one's enemies. As early as the end of the fourth century, St. Augustine grappled with the issue of whether he should call on the resources of the Roman state to assist him in suppressing the Donatist heresy. Although Augustine ultimately embraced persecution and intolerance as the only practicable solution to the persistence and strength of Donatism, he did so only as a last resort, after nearly a decade of promoting less extreme measures. As he later explained in one of his letters,

It seemed to certain of the brethren, of whom I was one, that although the madness of the Donatists was raging in every direction, yet we should not ask of the emperors to ordain that heresy should absolutely cease to be, by sanctioning a punishment on all who wished to live in it; but that they should rather content themselves with ordaining that those who either preached the Catholic truth with their voice, or established it by their study, should no longer be exposed to the furious violence of the heretics.[9]

These are hardly the words of a man to whom intolerance came easily. In his initial view, at least, the role of the state should be strictly limited to the protection of peaceful persons from religiously-motivated attacks, in other words, a function essentially consistent with publicly approved toleration. In open debate with Donatists, Augustine even attacked those among his own Church who sought to persecute heretics, citing scripture in support of a policy of patient correction, forbearance and prayer.[10] Persecution, he says, is "the work of evil men" who do not comprehend the nature of the faith to which they pretend.

The Fine Medieval Balance

Although Augustine's dramatic change of heart is perhaps the best documented case of a Church Father brought to pursue a program of intolerance in the face of seemingly intractable heresy, his situation was surely not unique. The official status of Latin Christianity and the growing intersection of the powers and the interests of ecclesiastical magistrates and secular rulers meant that throughout the late Roman and medieval periods political authority was available to enforce orthodox faith.[11] It is easy to be so dazzled by tales of the Crusades and stories of inquisitional procedures (formal or informal), however, that one neglects the mundane realities of Christian Europe in the millennium after St. Augustine. Chief among these realities was the sheer diversity of religious life, which simmered near the surface of sanctioned Roman Christendom. Most important perhaps were the regional and even local differences of belief arising from the imposition of a literate, text-based religion on an illiterate, custom-based population. In order to make Christian doctrine comprehensive, it was often imbued or admixed with elements of traditional "pagan superstition." (One might plausibly question whether it is even possible to speak of the vast mass of the medieval European populace as recognizably Christian at all in the substance of their faith.) Except in rare instances where such popular belief broke out into full-fledged heresy—as in the case of the Cathars—we know far too little about the content of the versions of Christianity practiced in the parish to form hard and fast judgments.[12] But evidence suggests that one of the greatest frustrations of the ecclesiastical hierarchy was the difficulty of ensuring that orthodoxy was disseminated to and adopted by the body of the Christian faithful.

The Roman Church had only slightly more success in regulating public differences of opinion among Christian teachers and scholars, theologians prominent among them. The medieval intelligentsia were in fact permitted reasonably wide latitude in debating fundamental issues concerning the faith, whatever our uninformed impressions may be. This becomes especially apparent after about 1000, when the pace of academic debate picks up rapidly. By the turn of the twelfth century, one can find profound disagreements among Christian theologians about important metaphysical questions which touched on both the divine nature and the nature of God's creations.[13] Only the most obdurate thinkers and the most extreme positions were threatened with official condemnation, and then the decision to proscribe certain doctrines seems to have been as much the result of petty academic and ecclesiastical rivalries and jealousies as of any intrinsic danger posed by the ideas themselves. If never quite formally institutionalized, freedom of intellectual inquiry into matters of central concern to orthodoxy seems to have been remarkably well preserved by the medieval Church, both before and after the rise of universities.

Such respect for intellectual investigation was perhaps reinforced by the Church's attitude toward the study of the writings of non-Christians, especially of pagan antiquity.[14] Already in patristic times there had been considerable discussion about whether the words and ideas of unbelievers could possibly contribute anything to the deepening of the Christian faith. Were not such uninspired texts corrupt and useless for salvation? St. Jerome cautioned against the unbridled use of pagan writings on the grounds that they were tainted with the stain of worldliness. Jerome was echoing a concern that Tertullian had articulated (albeit more dramatically) two centuries earlier: "What is there in common between the philosopher and the Christian, between the pupil of Hellas and the pupil of Heaven?"

But the lack of forbearance toward pagan thought professed by Tertullian and Jerome did not ultimately prevail. It was rather St. Augustine's position, stated in his widely influential treatise, *De doctrina christiana*, that guided future generations of Christian scholars. Augustine, who possessed an excellent classical education, drew an analogy between pagan learning and the Egyptian gold taken by the Israelites in their flight described in Exodus. Just as the Hebrews were justified in removing the gold from an "unjust possessor" and converting it to righteous uses, so the Christian intellectual may rightfully seize upon those elements of non-Christian teaching that are of assistance to him in the work of spreading the gospel.[15] Thus Augustine counseled the study of a range of pagan philosophical, literary, historical, and rhetorical texts to improve the pedagogical and evangelical skills of Christian preachers and authors.

The Augustinian outlook predominated during the Latin Middle Ages. Even those medieval churchmen such as St. Bonaventure who were deeply suspicious of extensive reliance on the ideas of the pagan classics never proposed prohibition of their circulation entirely. No one questioned that a Plato or an Aristotle, a Cicero or a Seneca, a Virgil or even an Ovid, could teach the Christian scholar a great deal. Indeed, it was deemed senseless to shun pagans simply because they had the misfortune to be born prior to the Christian era and thus to have missed the opportunity to receive the word of Jesus (although some suspected that Plato's thought must have enjoyed at least a little direct divine inspiration). Ecclesiastical authorities generally moved to proscribe pagan doctrines only in cases where they directly conflicted with such established and fundamental tenets of Christian faith as the finite nature of creation or the eternity of the soul. And even then there was no concerted attempt to suppress the classical texts harboring such ideas.

Perhaps the greatest measure of intellectual forbearance during the Latin Middle Ages stemmed from the open dissemination of Islamic learning. Islam posed a challenge to medieval Christianity different from that of pagan antiquity: Islam was a vital religious force with which the Christian West had repeatedly clashed over the salvation of souls. That Christians and Muslims were capable of coexisting in relative proximity is demonstrated by the circumstances of Spain. But no medieval Christian would have dreamed of living in complete equality with Muslims in the heart of Europe, just as no Muslim was likely to have accorded similar toleration to a Christian. At the same time, however, the Church did permit scholars to study the writings of their Islamic counterparts, especially commentaries on the pagan classics.[16]

Unlike Christianity, Islam had maintained a vigorous intellectual life, stimulated by the ancient Greek philosophers as well as its own doctrines, throughout the Middle Ages: Islamic scholars read Greek, translated pagan texts into Arabic, and produced voluminous commentaries and original studies. It was largely through contact with Islam, in turn, that the Latin West renewed its acquaintance with the learning of the ancient Greek world. In this process, not only original texts were translated into Latin (sometimes from an Arabic intermediary rather than directly from Greek), but also a large body of related Islamic literature. In certain cases, Islamic writings were mistakenly thought to be the genuine work of Greek antiquity (as in the case of the pseudo-Aristotelian *Secreta secretorum*), but more often Latin readers were fully aware of the Islamic provenance of a text, as in the instance of the writings of Avicenna (Ibn Sina) and Averroes (Ibn Rusd), both of whom were revered in the West. Indeed, Averroes quickly earned the title The Commentator for his authoritative textual analysis of the corpus of The Philosopher, Aristotle. It is perhaps not too great an exaggeration to say that Islam played a major role in shaping the way Latin Christendom assimilated and embraced the wisdom of the ancients from the twelfth century onward. The intellectual importance of Islam in the Latin West is hardly compatible with an attitude of intransigence and indiscriminate intolerance toward all infidels.

Of course, one might say that the toleration accorded to Islam was "merely theoretical," since the ideas promoted by Islamic texts were just as disembodied in the Christian West (at least outside Spain) as the teachings of the ancient pagans. That is, one might suspect that there is an important distinction between permitting a few Christian scholars to read non-Christian writings and an officially Christian society's ability to live on a daily basis with people who practice a non-Christian faith. But even if this is so, we must remember that Christianity throughout the Middle Ages did coexist in just such fashion with another prominent religion, Judaism. Judaism was as much an anomaly in medieval Europe as it had been during the ascendency of the Roman Empire. Jewish communities existed in many European cities, and though their members lacked rights identical to those of Christians, the common image of medieval Jews as under constant threat of pogrom or expulsion is now regarded as overdrawn. Medieval Jewry may have been reviled and despised, but it played a vital and ineliminable role in the social, economic, and intellectual life of the Middle Ages.[17]

Thus, while they were never integrated into the mainstream of Latin society, the Jews could not be entirely expunged from it either. They formed a stable presence in the Latin world, their numbers fluctuating at about the same rate as the general European population. Some of the explanation for this situation must be referred to the historical resilience displayed by Jewish communities, their ability to adapt to circumstance. But much of the reason for the perpetuation of Judaism in Western Europe rests with Christianity itself. The Jews, of course, enjoyed a special place in the history of the Christian religion, inasmuch as Christianity styled itself as the fulfillment of traditional Judaic prophecies. From the patristic era onward, it was argued that forbearance toward Jewish communities by Christianity was justified by their function as witnesses to the law of the Old Testament as well as by the scriptural promise of Jewish conversion at the end of the world. While this was hardly sufficient to halt popular expressions of anti-Semitism, it did afford to the Jewish faith a sort of formal (albeit limited) toleration, the significance of which should not be disparaged. If the incidence of intolerance toward the Jews was on the rise during the later Middle Ages, as has been documented, this may well have been due to the erosion of ecclesiastical influence over secular government rather than the result of pressure brought to bear on temporal authorities by the Church.

Reform and Heresy

Thus far we have dealt with challenges to Christianity from outside the pale — Islam, Judaism, pagan philosophy. But what of dissonant voices within Christianity? It was long supposed that the Roman Church was an unwavering fount of monolithic faith and guidance until Martin Luther and his fellow reformers tumbled the structure. But the past several decades of historical revision have made us aware of the unwavering medieval desire for reform, expressed in any number of movements, from the Cluniac push for reform in "head and members" to the Franciscan glorification of evangelical poverty as a clerical ideal to the conciliarist agenda pursued by ecclesiological reformers in the age of the Council of Constance.[18] Heresy can thus sometimes be properly characterized as reforming sentiment that has found itself in political disfavor with the institutional Church authorities.

No one denied, of course, the right of the Church to identify those who stood outside its true beliefs and to exclude them by act of excommunication.[19] But some medieval thinkers were prepared to mitigate the consequences of a declaration of excommunication. Marsiglio of Padua, for instance, proposed in his *Defensor Minor* (c. 1340) that excommunication ought to be a spiritual penalty only, cutting the excommunicate off from the sacraments but not from everyday economic and social relations with the faithful. Marsiglio's argument for this view is decidedly pragmatic: it is to the detriment of believers, as well as excommunicates, when they are not able to engage in marketplace exchanges that will benefit both parties.[20] Such a division between the economic and the religious/moral realms, while perhaps most clearly drawn by Marsiglio, grew more common over the course of the later Middle Ages.

Of course, most heretics were relatively unconcerned about the condition of human beings in the present world. Rather, they believed that the Church itself had become corrupt and that their mission was to restore the faithful to some higher or more primal purity away from which the degraded priesthood had led them. Heretical sects generally claimed to enjoy privileged access to the revealed word of God, setting their followers in direct opposition to the established Church.[21] The Church responded to the charges of heretics, arguing for its own special relationship to Christ derived from its historical patrimony stemming from St. Peter. But even ecclesiastical loyalists were critical of many of the practices which they perceived the Church to sanction. The twelfth-century English churchman (and eventual bishop of Chartres) John of Salisbury reports his personal complaint to the reigning pope, Adrian IV, that the entire ecclesiastical hierarchy, including the Roman curia, stood validly accused of extortion, corruption, venality, and a multitude of other crimes.[22] John goes on in his *Policraticus* to defend the liberty of inferiors to criticize their superiors, at least if their motives for correction and improvement are pure. As Cary Nederman's essay in this volume argues, John's teaching derives directly from his dedication to the skeptical method of the New Academy, knowledge of which he gleaned from Cicero and various Christian interpreters and critics.

In sum, it is simply incorrect to conflate the Church's war on heresy with the stifling of all religious dissent. The urge to reform enjoyed a venerable lineage within ecclesiastical circles, and criticism of the practices of churchmen was widely regarded as worthy of forbearance. The questioning of religious dogma was, without question, more problematic. As Peter Abelard discovered, the price to be paid for too inquisitive and too open a mind was subjection to recurrent charges of heterodoxy before church councils. But such cases were the extreme. In general, the line between calling for reform of ecclesiastical practices and questioning central articles of faith was sufficiently blurred to permit a wider band of debate than is often supposed. If medieval Christendom was not an entirely open society, when judged in terms of post-Enlightenment standards, neither was it the closed and monolithic "persecuting society" that it has been portrayed.

Notes

1. Robert Ian Moore, *The Formation of a Persecuting Society: Power and Deviance in Western Europe, 950–1250* (Oxford: Blackwell, 1987).

2. Preston King, *Toleration* (London: Allen and Unwin, 1976), 73.

3. Henry Kamen, *The Rise of Toleration* (New York: McGraw-Hill, 1967), 18.

4. Only a very few, primarily European scholars have recognized this. In particular, see Klaus Schreiner, "Toleranz," in Otto Bruner, Werner Conze, and Reinhart Koselleck, eds., *Geschichtliche Grundbegriffe* (Stuttgart: Klett-Cotta, 1990), 6: 445–605.

5. In addition to Moore, see Mark R. Cohen, *Under Cross and Crescent: The Jews in the Middle Ages* (Princeton, N.J.: Princeton University Press, 1994); Jeffrey Richards, *Sex, Dissonance and Damnation: Minority Groups in the Middle Ages* (London: Routledge, 1990); and David Nirenberg, *Communities of Violence: Persecution of Minorities in the Middle Ages* (Princeton, N.J.: Princeton University Press, 1996).

6. Kamen, *The Rise of Toleration*, 8.

7. Cicero, *De legibus*, ed. C. W. Keyes (Cambridge, Mass.: Harvard University Press, 1928), 2.10. For a comprehensive summary of Cicero's views on religion, see G. E. M. de Ste Croix, "Why Were the Early Christians Persecuted?" in M. I. Finley, ed., *Studies in Ancient Society* (London: Routledge and Kegan Paul, 1974), 245–48.

8. For what follows, I have drawn heavily on de Ste Croix's essay, along with the "Amendment" by A. N. Sherwin-White and the "Rejoinder" by de Ste Croix, all published in Finley, ed., *Studies in Ancient Society*, 210–62; and W. H. C. Frend, *Martyrdom and Persecution in the Early Church: A Study of a Conflict from the Maccabees to Donatus* (Oxford: Clarendon Press, 1965).

9. St. Augustine, *Political Writings*, ed. Henry Paolucci (Chicago: Regnery, 1962), 219–20.

10. Ibid., 184–89.

11. On this point, see Kamen, *The Rise of Toleration*, 12–17.

12. Whatever the faults of its scholarship, Emmanuel Leroy Ladurie's *Montaillou: Promised Land of Error* (New York: Random House, 1974) gives a fascinating glimpse into the everyday beliefs of one Cathar village, and tells us much about the failure of orthodox Christianity to permeate the peasant population of Europe, even in the fourteenth century.

13. See Constant J. Mews, "Philosophy and Theology 1100–1150: The Search for Harmony," in Françoise Gasparri, ed., *Le XIIe siècle: Mutations et renouveau en France dans la première moitié du XIIe siècle* (Paris: Le Léopard d'Or, 1995), 159–203 and Janet Coleman, "The Science of Politics and Late Medieval Academic Debate," in Rita Copeland, ed., *Criticism and Dissent in the Middle Ages* (Cambridge: Cambridge University Press, 1996), 181–214.

14. The following paragraphs draw on Charles Norris Cochrane, *Christianity and Classical Culture* (Oxford: Oxford University Press, 1957).

15. St. Augustine, *On Christian Doctrine*, trans. D. W. Robertson, Jr. (Indianapolis: Bobbs-Merrill/Library of Liberal Arts, 1958), 2.40.

16. On this process, see M. R. Dod, "Aristoteles Latinus," in Norman Kretzmann, Anthony Kenny, and Jan Pinborg, eds., *The Cambridge History of Later Medieval Philosophy* (Cambridge: Cambridge University Press, 1982), 45–79.

17. The account contained in this and the following paragraph is especially indebted to Kenneth R. Stow, *Alienated Minority: The Jews of Medieval Latin Europe* (Cambridge, Mass.: Harvard University Press, 1992). See also the studies contained in Vivian B. Mann, Thomas F. Glick, and Jerrilynn D. Dodds, eds., *Convivencia: Jews, Muslims, and Christians in Medieval Spain* (New York: George Braziller, 1992).

18. Steven Ozment, *The Age of Reform, 1250–1550: An Intellectual and Religious History of Late Medieval and Reformation Europe* (New Haven, Conn.: Yale University Press, 1980).

19. Elisabeth Vodola, *Excommunication in the Middle Ages* (Berkeley: University of California Press, 1986).

20. See Cary J. Nederman, "Liberty and Toleration: Freedom of Conscience in Medieval Political Thought," *Vital Nexus* 1 (July 1995): 43–58 and "Tolerance and Community: A Medieval Communal Functionalist Argument for Religious Toleration," *Journal of Politics* 56 (November 1994): 901–18.

21. See Robert Ian Moore, *The Origins of European Dissent* (New York: St. Martin's, 1977).

22. John of Salisbury, *Policraticus*, trans. Cary J. Nederman (Cambridge: Cambridge University Press, 1990), 6.24, pp. 131–36.

Peter Abelard and the Enigma of Dialogue

Constant J. Mews

PETER ABELARD (1079–1142) IS OFTEN remembered as a victim of persecution. Punished by castration in 1117 following his affair with Heloise, then accused of heresy at the Council of Soissons in 1121 and again by Bernard of Clairvaux at the Council of Sens in 1140, Abelard has long been considered a forerunner of the cause of toleration in the West. At one stage in his career, he contemplated going to live in Muslim territory, where he thought he would be made more welcome than in Christendom. Abelard lived at a time of unusual interest by some Latin scholars in the non-Latin world, even though strong forces were afoot to re-assert Latin orthodoxy in Europe and the Middle East.[1] His *Dialogue of a Philosopher with a Jew and a Christian* or *Collationes* has been seen by some as a plea for intellectual toleration.[2] Is this too idealistic a perspective? Was he rejecting a contemporary trend toward exclusion of the outsider, or did he in fact participate in that movement Anna Sapir Abulafia has identified as the Christianization of reason in the twelfth century, by which Christian thinkers found reasons for proving that Jews and pagans were blind to the truth?[3] In order to assess Abelard's contribution to the idea and practice of religious toleration, we need to relate his *Dialogus* both to his other writings and to those of his contemporaries, for whom dialogue was often a technique for asserting the truth rather than for engaging in a listening exercise.

The Dialogue of a Philosopher with a Jew and a Christian

Abelard's *Dialogus* comprises two separate conversations, one of a philosopher with a Jew, the other of a philosopher with a Christian, introduced by a prologue in which Abelard describes how he saw in a dream that he was asked by three individuals to adjudicate their debate about which path to take to supreme truth. When he asked their identity, they replied that they were pursuing the worship of one God "serving him variously in faith and way of life" (5–7; Payer, 19).[4] The philosopher explained that he had long pursued truth with philosophical reasoning, and that he had turned to moral philosophy, "which is the end of all disciplines and which I have judged to be tasted above all other things" (20–21; Payer, 20). He asked what both Jews and Christians taught about the supreme good and the supreme evil. Having found Jews foolish and Christians mad, he sought a rational conclusion to their debate. With no little self-confidence, Abelard had the philosopher praise his own skill and capacity both in philosophical and divine matters, demonstrated through "that wonderful work of the *Theologia* which envy could neither tolerate nor has been able to destroy, but which it has made more glorious by persecution" (50–52; Payer, 21–22). The prologue concludes with Abelard's recollection of an adage, in fact a remark of Augustine:

No teaching, as one of our own remembers, is so false that it does not contain some truth; I also consider that no disputation is so frivolous, that it does not provide some lesson. As the greatest of the wise said at the very beginning of his Proverbs [1:5], *by hearing a wise person will be wiser, an intelligent person will acquire the art of guidance*, and James the apostle [1:19], *Let every man be quick to listen, but slow to speak*. (68–78; Payer, 23; Payer's emphasis)[5]

Abelard was reminding his audience that the roots of toleration were to be found in the wisdom of Jewish and Christian tradition. The two dialogues which follow serve to instruct the reader in the underlying validity of Augustine's dictum. The discussion is not a report of an actual exchange between three parties but an extended argument about the foundations of ethics and the nature of good and evil.

Perhaps the biggest problem confronting any student of the *Dialogus* is lack of scholarly agreement about its date. This question relates to the broader issue of its interpretation. The traditional argument that Abelard wrote the *Dialogus* in his final years at Cluny (1140–42) derives from the claim that it is incomplete, and that therefore it must have been interrupted by his death. The second debate concludes with a lengthy dissertation by the Christian on the nature of the supreme good, but leaves space for further discussion:

Unless I am mistaken, I have said enough for the present to have shown these things, namely how the name of "good" is to be understood when it is taken simply for a good thing, or when it is applied to the occurrences of things, or to what are expressed by propositions. If there is anything left which you think should be questioned further because it related to inquiry into the supreme good, you are permitted to introduce it or hurry on to what remains. (3422–28; Payer, 169)[6]

While it is certainly true that in the surviving text of the *Dialogus* the Christian never delivers his response to the philosopher's exposition of how the supreme good was to be reached, there is no reason to assume that Abelard's death was to blame for the lack of a conclusion. Textual evidence suggests that it belongs to any time in the period 1125–33, perhaps before he had left the community of students that had gathered around his oratory dedicated to the Paraclete and certainly before he had prepared the *Theologia "Scholarium"* in the early 1130s.[7] At the end of the first conference, Abelard intervenes as a judge only to assert that he wishes to defer judgment, as he prefers to learn from arguments, so that he may become wiser by listening (1165–71; Payer, 71). The absence of adjudication is pedagogical technique. Abelard wants the reader to form his own judgment in the debate, exactly as he wanted the reader of the *Sic et Non* to evaluate for himself opposing views of the Church Fathers about a wide range of questions about Christian doctrine.[8]

The closing speech of the Christian introduces a certain element of finality to the *Dialogus*, even though no third party intervenes. In the first conference Abelard had set up the debate between the Jew and the philosopher, not to establish the superiority of one position over the other, but in order to elucidate the rationale for Jewish observance of the Law as well as the arguments from reason as to why it was not essential to submit to the obligations of the Law. In the second conference he investigated the relationship between the discipline of ethics, concerning how the supreme good was to be attained, and divinity, concerning the supreme good itself:

What you [the philosopher] are accustomed to call ethics, that is morals, we call divinity, giving it that name from what is aimed at being understood, namely God, while your name comes from those things through which it is reached, that is good moral behaviour, which you call virtues. (1265–69; Payer, 76)

Abelard allows the philosopher to present ethical teaching arrived at through natural reason before the discussion moves to a consideration of the supreme good, in which the Christian becomes the dominant voice. It is not clear whether he meant the Christian to present his own version of how the supreme good was to be attained. Having delivered his reflection from the standpoint of reason through the voice of the philosopher, Abelard uses the persona of the Christian to deliver his own reflection that, while we may call something good or evil because of some advantage or disadvantage to us, true goodness is an attribute of God alone, who allows all things to happen for a good reason, even if the cause is unknown to us. The fact that the final speech concludes in the same way as the *Historia calamitatum*, with the prayer "Thy will be done," suggests that Abelard never intended to take the *Dialogus* beyond this point.

The Tradition of Philosophical Dialogue

Although the idea of presenting separate but related dialogues of a philosopher with a Jew and then of a philosopher with a Christian had no immediate literary precedent, the genre of the philosophical dialogue as a means of developing one's ideas had been popularized in the late eleventh century by Anselm of Canterbury (1033–1109). Comparing Abelard's *Dialogus* with dialogues influenced by St. Anselm enables us to appreciate the extent of Abelard's originality. The format Anselm adopted in his early treatises, the *De veritate*, *De casu diaboli*, *De libertate arbitrio*, and *De grammatico* (composed c. 1080–85), was that of master and disciple, modeled on the early dialogues of Augustine.[9] Anselm had established the value of discussing issues "from reason alone," but he was not concerned with eliciting ideas from different points of view. The questioner in a dialogue simply served to bring out the inherent logic of Anselm's conclusion for an audience who shared the same assumptions about the pursuit of truth.[10]

Shortly before Anselm was enthroned as archbishop of Canterbury in September 1093, Gilbert Crispin, abbot of Westminster from 1085 to 1117 and a former pupil of Anselm, sent him a copy of a *Disputatio Iudei et Christiani*. Gilbert's dialogue came to enjoy great popularity in the twelfth century. The work is presented as the outcome of conversations Gilbert had with a Jew from Mainz, involved in building activity at Westminster.[11] It begins in a way that recalls Abelard's own *Dialogus*, with a description of how Gilbert was led to an inn where he came across two philosophers "of great fame, but following different paths," engaged in disputation on the worship of the one God. From the outset, Gilbert emphasized the spirit of tolerance in which the discussion was conducted: "As often as we got together we soon had a conversation in a friendly spirit about the Scriptures and our faith."[12] Gilbert had the Jew open the debate by invoking tolerance as an ideal: "Since Christians claim that you are learned in letters and ready with the faculty of speaking, I should like you to deal with me in a tolerant spirit."[13] The specific speeches Gilbert attributed to the Jew are too laden with careful argument and quotation to represent the actual words the Jew might have used. It is nonetheless significant that Gilbert should consciously distance himself from traditional anti-Jewish invective.

Gilbert wanted to formulate a convincing argument from reason by which he could justify the doctrine of the incarnation. Because of its sinful nature, mankind was unable to effect its own redemption. A God-man was thus logically necessary. Such ideas show strong similarities to those of St. Anselm, who came to England from Bec in September 1092.[14] It has a continuation in the *Disputatio cum gentili*, a dialogue between a Christian and a Gentile.[15] As Sapir Abulafia has observed, although Crispin may have introduced the figure of the Gentile to raise objections to Christian doctrine from reason alone (objections essentially similar to those of the Jew), he was unable to refrain from justifying his argument by reference to scripture.[16] Dialogue for Gilbert Crispin as for Anselm meant demonstration of the rightness of one point of view. The *Disputatio* concluded with the Gentile abandoning the discussion. His place was then taken by a disciple willing to learn, rather than argue about the truth of the doctrine of the Trinity. Gilbert drew his arguments from those of St. Anselm in his treatise against Roscelin, the nominalist theologian who became Abelard's teacher.[17]

A similar dialogue structure is employed in a little studied *Disputatio* between a Christian and a Gentile attributed to St. Anselm, not included within Schmitt's edition of the *Opera Omnia*.[18] It opens with a question from an imaginary Gentile: "I want to learn why the divine majesty humbled himself to beyond the sufferings of mortal nature, to accept the shame of the cross. I do not want this to be proved by the authority of your scriptures, in which I do not believe, but, if it has been done rationally, I want a reason for this event."[19] The Gentile's role is to extract from the Christian a rational argument why it should be that God became man in the way that he did, so ignominiously on the cross. The Christian argues that Christ's death was not shameful but rather a rational and fitting event: "Christ did what was fitting, nothing other than to say that he did what he ought. This is the way of speaking about everything which God does. He does what he must, that is what is fitting for him, not because he is obliged by any debt demanded by anyone."[20] The final statement of the Gentile is an abject admission of the logic of the Christian's argument: "I admit that until now I have erred, and I acknowledge in heart and mouth that Christ is truly God and the author and healer of true salvation."[21] As in the closing section of Gilbert Crispin's disputation, the Gentile is then transformed into a "faithful disciple." In this case he questions his teacher about why God wanted to be honored by the sacraments and ceremonies which are read about in the Old Testament, and why they were replaced in the Christian church. This very Anselmian *Disputatio* concludes with an exhortation of the Master to the disciple to remain illumined by the light of Christ. Dialogue here was disputation to establish the truth of Christian doctrine against the error of the unbeliever.[22]

Although not developed with the same sophistication as in the *Cur Deus homo*, the underlying argument of this *Disputatio* is the same: given the sinfulness of man, unable to restore himself by his own efforts, the only person who could redeem mankind was someone who was sinless, in other words a man who was also God. The Christian tries to follow the instruction of the Gentile not to argue from the authority of the scriptures, but he finds it difficult to avoid falling into the occasional scriptural phrase. Twice he alludes to the formula "Unless you believe, you shall not understand" (Isaiah 7:9, as quoted by Augustine).[23] Like the dialogues of Gilbert Crispin, this *Disputatio* (a lost work of St. Anselm?) vindicates the rightness of one point of view. While Anselm had established a new point of departure for theological debate in insisting that all such enquiry had to be based on "reason alone," rather than on written authority which might not be acceptable to all parties, he never questioned fundamental Augustinian assumptions about the sinfulness of man and the priority of faith over understanding. Rational enquiry was confined by tight parameters. Anselm perceived Jews, pagans, indeed anyone suspected of being a nonbeliever (including dialecticians like Roscelin of Compiègne), as threatening the Christian community.[24] Rational argument did not necessarily make for greater tolerance.

Roscelin himself justified his search for a rational explanation of the Trinity on the ground that Jews and pagans (Muslims) both defended their faith, so Christians should do the same.[25] Shortly after disputing with St. Anselm in England in 1092, Roscelin obtained a canonry at the Angevin stronghold of Loches, where the young Peter Abelard happened to arrive at about the same time.[26] Studying in the Loire valley under a master who had acquired notoriety in monastic circles through controversy with St. Anselm, Abelard was exposed to very different attitudes from those promulgated by the abbot of Bec, now archbishop of Canterbury. From Roscelin, Abelard imbibed a sense of hostility toward intellectual persecution, even though he subsequently distanced himself from particular doctrines of his teacher on logic and theology.

At the time that the first Crusade was called in 1095, there was little consensus among educated Latin thinkers about the extent to which one could learn from non-Latin culture. There was more sympathy among some intellectuals for rational Arab wisdom than for Jewish tradition. Medical works had been translated from Arabic into Latin by Constantine the African, a monk of Monte Cassino.[27] Orderic Vitalis reports that in 1100 a Moorish doctor, versed in pagan medicine and philosophy, saved the life of the young prince Louis after an attempt to poison him, purportedly at the instigation of his step-mother, Queen Bertrada.[28] Adelard of Bath, who studied at Tours in 1107, was so enamored of Arab learning that he traveled East (certainly to Salerno, perhaps also further) to study under Arab masters, whom he praised for teaching "through the leadership of reason."[29] Works translated from Arabic by Adelard were known to Thierry of Chartres, from whom Abelard once tried to learn mathematics.[30] At the same time, Adelard's collaborator, Petrus Alfonsi, who brought many stories of Arab wisdom to the attention of the Latin West, composed inflammatory and very popular *Dialogi contra Iudaeos* between a Christian and a Jew, which used quotations from the Talmud to refute Jews with as much vigor as Gilbert Crispin.[31] Abelard's approach to exploring dialogue was rather different.

The Role of the Philospher in Abelard's Dialogus

The major difference between Abelard's *Dialogus* and the dialogues of Crispin and the Anselmian *Disputatio* lies in the prominence accorded the role of the philosopher. Rather than using the philosopher to elucidate the rightness of the Christian position, Abelard has him elicit truth from different points of view. By not placing the Jew and the Christian together in the same dialogue, Abelard replaced overt refutation with more subtle analysis. In the first conference, the Jew explains the reasons behind the ceremonies and observances of Jewish tradition, while the philosopher presents arguments against the necessity of following the precepts of the Law. The second conference permitted Abelard to explore the interconnection between the study of ethics, the prime concern of the philosopher, and that of divinity, the concern of the Christian. Abelard identified the insight each of the three figures could contribute, while explaining what he saw as the limitations of Judaism.

The method Abelard employed directly extends principles laid out in his preface to the *Sic et Non* ("Yes and No"). In that work, Abelard gathered together apparently contradictory statements from the Fathers of the Church about Christian doctrine, prefaced by advice on the methodology students should follow: "Since amidst a great profusion of words many sayings of the saints seem to be not only different from each other, but even mutually contradictory, it is not rash for judgment to be made about them, through whom the world itself will be judged."[32] Judgment must not be hasty. The student needed to be aware of being confused by unfamiliar forms of expression or of differing possible meanings of the same words. It was rash for someone to make a judgment about the meaning or understanding of another, given that hearts and thoughts were known to God alone. The preface to the *Sic et Non* was a plea for tolerance in debate about ecclesiastical tradition, argued above all from the authority of Augustine. The intelligent reader had to learn to sift out falsehood and error from the truth of what others had to say. Abelard complained that many pronouncements of the Fathers were delivered "more from opinion rather than from truth." Contradictions were to be resolved by appreciating the diversity of circumstance and intention in which apparently opposing statements were made. No one was to be convicted of being a liar who said something through ignorance rather than duplicity. Had not Augustine said, "Have charity, and do whatever you will"? Whoever spoke sincerely and not fraudulently was free from being guilty of falsehood.

The preface to the *Sic et Non* voiced a plea to move beyond rash judgment to considered reflection of the words used. The essence of wisdom lay in a spirit of enquiry: "The first key to wisdom is defined as persistent and frequent questioning. . . . By doubting we come to enquiry; by enquiry we perceive truth. As the Truth itself says, 'Seek and you shall find, knock and it will be opened to you' (Mt 7:7)."[33] Abelard invoked scripture to support a principle he had already formulated in his *Dialectica*. Questioning was a tool of dialectical inquiry, the science of investigating truth: "he who asks, expresses his own doubt, so that he may attain the certitude which he does not yet have."[34] He cited the example of Christ himself, who sat and asked questions of the elders in the Temple at twelve years of age, even though he was the embodiment of perfect wisdom.

In the *Dialogus* Abelard introduced his reader to a much wider range of views than those raised in the *Sic et Non*. His concern was with nothing less than supreme good and evil and how that supreme good was to be attained. The figure with whom he identified from the outset was the philosopher, who had devoted his life to investigating truth by philosophical reasoning and was now applying himself to moral philosophy, "the end of every discipline." He is interested not in the theory of toleration, but in rational dialogue as necessary for the pursuit of truth. The enemy was religious dogmatism.

The First Conference: The Philosopher and the Jew

The philosopher opens the first conference by observing that religious faith tends to be influenced more by upbringing than by blood or reason. It seemed absurd for believers to be so attached to one way of thinking that they considered all others as condemned by God, and refused to advance in asking questions about their faith. The Jew recognizes the truth of this observation, maintaining that it was all the more necessary for individuals as adults to follow the counsel "of reason rather than opinion" (174–83; Payer, 29). Abelard's presentation of the Jew as an intelligent, reflective commentator differed markedly from the stereotype in most Jewish-Christian dialogues. His sympathy for the position of the Jews in society is evident in a long, frequently quoted description of the practical problems they faced in society. He has the Jew make many perceptive remarks about the role of written Law. How else could any society be governed without a written Law (223–91; Payer, 31–33)? The philosopher sympathized with the Jew's plight, but asked whether the written Law imposed any greater advantage than the natural Law, observed by the patriarchs before the time of Abraham. The Jew's subsequent explanation of circumcision emphasized its social function as well as interior significance. It provided a way of keeping one people apart from the gentiles so that they would not be corrupted by association. Observance of the Law provided an opportunity for sanctification. The Jew rebutted the conventional criticism that observance of the Law conferred only material reward (738–97; Payer, 53–55). Its ultimate command was the perfect love of God and of neighbor. Abelard was raising the argument that the essence of the Jewish Law was the same as the natural law of the philosopher, the precept of perfect love. The Jew puts forward an ethical position, one with which Abelard sympathized: "For every virtue of the mind, the true love of God and of man is sufficient" (831–42; Payer, 57–58).

The philosopher's criticism relates not to this fundamental principle, identified as the core teaching shared by the two parties, but to the Jew's imposition of additional precepts. His argument turns on the narrowness of the Jewish Law, rather than the underlying ethical principle. God was also the God of the uncircumcised patriarchs, like Enoch and Noah, whose life was happier for not having a written Law. Why was it necessary to add additional precepts? The philosopher's critique of the Law resembles that of St. Paul in the Epistle to the Romans, but here it is made not from the standpoint of faith in Christ but from reason. His interpretation of scripture demonstrates the importance of a contrite heart rather than righteous actions. Ritual uncleanness cannot be identified with sin. What had a nocturnal emission of semen or menstruation to do with sinfulness? The philosopher's discussion of sin here is relatively simplistic. He makes the contrast between obvious sins, like murder and adultery, and ritual transgressions, but does not define sin itself except as the fruit of a perverse will. Sin was remitted simply by a contrite heart. Abelard's discussion of sin here has none of the subtlety of the *Scito teipsum* ("Know Thyself," or *Ethics*), written in the late 1130s. In that work Abelard argued that the will to sin was not itself sinful, only the deliberate consent to such a will.[35] When he composed the first conversation of the *Dialogus*, he was not concerned with the psychological and moral questions raised by Heloise in her letters to him, issues he was initially unwilling to confront in his first two letters to Heloise.

The Second Conference: The Philosopher and the Christian

Like so many of his educated contemporaries, Abelard was more favorably disposed to the arguments of the philosopher than to those of the Jew. This attitude was already evident in the second book of the *Theologia christiana*, added to his original treatise on the Trinity to provide further argument for reliance on pagan philosophers: "We seem not forced by any reason to despair about the salvation of such gentiles, instructed before the arrival of the Saviour not by any written Law; according to the Apostle [Rom 2:14–15], they did those things of the Law naturally; they were themselves the Law, showing the work of the Law written in their hearts, providing a witness for them in their own conscience."[36] Writing then in a flush of enthusiasm for the moral teaching of the ancient philosophers (which he contrasted with current monastic behavior), Abelard was not particularly interested in discussing the nature of sin. Rather, he wanted to demonstrate the validity of pagan philosophical insight for Christian reflection on the nature of the supreme good, which was God. The moral precepts of the Gospels he saw as no more than a reform of the natural law followed by the philosophers. He had also pursued this theme in his *Soliloquium*, an early internal dialogue in which he referred back to an "exhortation" (perhaps incorporated into the second book of the *Theologia christiana*) as proving that "philosophers are especially in fellowship with Christians not so much in name as in actual fact."[37] When preparing the *Theologia "Scholarium"* in the early 1130s, Abelard removed the lengthy ethical excursus incorporated into the second book of the *Theologia christiana*, perhaps because he had already given ethics separate treatment in the *Dialogus*.

The philosopher and the Christian agree on the relationship between ethics and divinity. Ethics concentrates on the path to the desired end, while divinity examines the supreme good itself, namely God. To the philosopher's request for a definition of "true ethics," the Christian replies that it should establish where the supreme good is and by what path it is to be reached (1280–82; Payer, 76). Other disciplines, like grammar and dialectic, lie far below the grand subject matter of the supreme good, even though they may prepare the way, introducing us to "the ladies-in-waiting," rather than the *domina* herself. Abelard uses the subsequent dialogue to advance a case for identifying Christianity as a truly rational religion, as well as to criticize those who consider that Christian faith precludes rational enquiry. Again these are not matters which are disputed by the Christian. The philosopher commends Christian preaching for its capacity to engage in rational debate, but insists that its teaching should not be accepted through faith alone.

The philosopher's criticism of those "who seek solace for their lack of skill" in the saying of Pope Gregory, "Faith has no merit for which human reason offers proof," closely echoes a theme Abelard reinforced in the revised introduction to the second book of the *Theologia "Scholarium."* This widely known saying of Gregory could easily be interpreted as asserting that the subject matter of faith was beyond rational discussion. In the original version of the treatise on the Trinity, it had been one of a number of quotations Abelard had used against Roscelin of Compiègne. By the time Abelard was writing the *Dialogus* and preparing the *Theologia "Scholarium,"* he had to defend his rational discussion of belief against those who were throwing the same argument against himself. He pointed out that if this saying of Gregory meant that there could be no rational inquiry into faith, there would logically be no place for the Christian to provide any kind of response or criticism relating to a matter of faith (1376–94; Payer, 81).[38]

The Christian in the *Dialogus* is fully in accord with the complaints of the philosopher about those who refuse to reason about their beliefs. Abelard is arguing for the cause of rational discussion. He uses the philosopher to put the argument he had raised in the prologue to the *Sic et Non* to criticize blind reliance on the judgments of others as authoritative, but in stronger terms: "In every philosophical disputation authority is thought to hold last place or no place at all to such an extent that it is shameful for those who trust in their own powers and scorn the refuge of another's wealth, to adduce arguments based on judgment of a matter [extrinsic judgment], namely on authority" (1413–17; Payer, 83). An argument based "on judgment of a matter" (*a rei judicio*) had been considered by Boethius to be weak because the orator had not constructed it for himself. Abelard insisted on applying to matters of faith the principle of questioning all authoritative statements. By demonstrating that this was common ground to the philosopher and the Christian, he was endeavoring to make his readers accept the rational necessity for such a principle, as he had argued in the second book of the *Theologia christiana*.

He then moved to presenting the philosopher's understanding of the virtues, followed by the Christian's commentary on the same subject. The philosopher interprets virtue as acquired through self-control: "a good will strengthened into habit can be called virtue" (1555–56; Payer, 90). This Aristotelian *habitus* theory of virtue as an acquired disposition was to become a significant theme in twelfth-century ethical thought.[39] The philosopher then presents the Stoic position that there can be no increase in beatitude without an increase in virtue, an assertion countered by the Christian locating supreme happiness not in this world but in the life to come. Whereas the philosopher sees virtues to be desired and vices avoided for their own sake, the teaching of Christ presents a better reason for pursuing virtue and avoiding vice. The philosopher suggests that there may simply be different names given to the goal of this beatitude: pleasure by Epicurus, the kingdom of heaven by Christ. Is not the intention of living justly the same for all people (1687–1720; Payer, 96–97)?

When the Christian accuses the philosopher of holding the idea that all good men are equally good and all the guilty equally guilty, following lengthy citation from Cicero's *De officiis*, the philosopher points to the teaching of Augustine that charity includes all the virtues under one name (1793–1823; Payer, 101–2). This prompts the Christian to argue that the presence of virtue in one individual does not mean that it is fully operative to the same degree as in another. The philosopher's teaching is not so much contradicted as clarified. A virtuous action to which one is obliged by precept is not the same as one (like virginity) not required by precept (1909–14, quoting 1 Cor 7:25; Payer, 105–6). No one who has virtue perishes, but not all are equal in virtue.

The philosopher's discussion of virtue in the *Dialogus* represents Abelard's first sustained treatment of the issue, certainly pre-dating that of the *Scito teipsum*. Virtue, he teaches, is an acquired habit of the mind, achieved through personal effort. His comment that chastity is not a virtue if no struggle is involved against concupiscence had particular relevance in Abelard's personal situation. The philosopher's exposition had none of the subtlety of the *Scito teipsum*, although some of its themes are hinted at. Some things are good and bad in themselves, like virtues and vices; others are indifferent, but are said to be good and bad by the intention by which they were done (1992–2030; Payer, 109–11). Although the framework for the philosopher's fourfold analysis of the virtues (prudence, justice, courage, and temperance) is based on a traditional source, Cicero's *De inventione*, there is considerable originality to the way he rearranges them. Abelard had the philosopher emphasize the role of justice (quoting examples given in the *Theologia christiana*) and the pre-eminence of the will in determining moral goodness.[40] Ciceronian themes are thus presented in an original way.

In the last section of the *Dialogus*, Abelard turned his attention back to the nature of the supreme good, the subject on which the Christian has the most to say. The discussion begins with his identification of what the philosopher believes about good and evil: that the supreme good is a future life of supreme happiness, the supreme evil that of perpetual punishment. Abelard uses both the philosopher and the Christian as mouthpieces for his argument. At stake is the thorniest issue in any providential view of the world: how can supreme evil be reconciled to supreme good? Abelard's resolution turns on careful distinction of the way in which words are used. To say that something is good is not the same as saying that it is a good thing. His distinction of the different ways *bonus* can be used is one he had made in his *Dialectica*.[41] A term's meaning is dependent on the usage to which it is put. Applied to the mystery of suffering, the philosopher observes that a punishment may be good because it is just, but this did not mean that we could say that it is a good thing. The punishment of man cannot be worse than the fault which makes a man evil (2324–50, 2437–46; Payer, 125, 128–29). The unhappiness of the wicked is self-inflicted. There may be great variety in beatitude, in proportion to each individual's mode of understanding. Once the philosopher accepts the argument that the supreme good or evil of man is that by which he becomes better or worse,

the Christian moves to identifying the supreme good with the vision of
God. Distinctions between substance and accident made by a philosopher
apply only to the material realm, not to the heavenly (2557–2603; Payer,
133–35).

The Platonic aspect of this final section of the *Dialogus* has never attracted as much commentary as his logical or ethical writings, but it dis-
closes the same sense of an ideal beyond language which pervades Abelard's
thought. In the incomplete fifth book of the *Theologia christiana* Abelard
had begun to sketch out his doctrine of God, argued from reason rather
than from authority. The closing section of the *Dialogus* was similarly con-
ceived as a natural theology, worked out from rational principles in dialogue with a philosopher. This was the goal to which the philosopher was
moving in his ethical theory, although he had to turn to the Christian for
a full picture of the goal. Only in this final section does Abelard introduce
the notion of grace, not in the context of accomplishing virtue, but as the
means through which God is present—as the sun fills the world with light
(2744–57; Payer, 141).

The thrust of Abelard's final discussion was to reject any notion that
Christian teaching about movement or place (like the bodily ascension of
Christ into the heavens at the right side of the Father, or hell itself) had
a physical meaning (2767–877; Payer, 142–47). Descriptions of hell in the
Old and New Testaments cannot be taken literally, as they refer to the perpetual torment souls suffered in their consciences. If one followed "the
common opinion of almost everyone" that the damned were placed in
the same fire, how could there be any gradation in punishment? Suffering
comes about not through any common substance but from the nature of
those punished (3026–61; Payer, 153–54).

The discussion of the reward of the good and the punishment of the
damned is followed by what the Christian admits is a most difficult task,
the definition of good and evil. A good thing is something which does not
have the effect of impeding the advantage of anything, something evil is
the opposite (3153–56; Payer, 158). Good and evil cannot be used to refer
to absolutes, as the same action can be good or evil, depending on the intention in the mind. There is properly no such thing as a good action, but
an action done well, with a good intention. Judas' betrayal of Jesus was bad
because of Judas' bad intention, while God's action of delivering up Jesus
was good because it happened for a different reason. This led Abelard to
argue that everything that happens is done for a rational reason, known to
God, a theme with which he had concluded the *Theologia "Scholarium."* It

might be good for an evil thing to exist, even though that evil could not be good (3220–70, 3381–82; Payer, 161–63, 167–68).

The Dialogus *and the Ideal of Toleration*

Modern notions of religious toleration should not be read back into the *Dialogus*. Abelard is never explicitly concerned in his writings with the right of alternative groups in society to hold dissenting views. Like St. Anselm and Gilbert Crispin, Abelard was laying out a rational framework for Christian doctrine. Nonetheless, there was a profound difference in perspective between Abelard's *Dialogus* and earlier disputations. Anselm and Gilbert Crispin never questioned traditional assumptions about the sinfulness of human nature. In the *Cur Deus homo* Boso had disagreed with the notion that the devil enjoyed any legitimate rights over mankind, but had never questioned the reality of this bondage. Abelard's initial assumption in the *Dialogus*, as in every version of the *Theologia*, was that human beings are not flawed by original sin. The ethical precepts of the Jewish Law are fundamentally the same as those of the natural law observed by the philosopher. Philosophical reflection on ethics is ultimately in harmony with Christian reflection on the supreme good.

Perhaps the most significant difference between Abelard's *Dialogus* on one hand and the disputations of Gilbert Crispin and St. Anselm (or attributed to him) on the other lies in their contrasting subject matter. From the time in the early 1090s that Roscelin emphasized the necessary distinction between God the Father and God the Son, both Anselm and Gilbert Crispin were preoccupied with proving the rightness of the doctrine of the incarnation, against rational doubt. Abelard was primarily concerned not with proving Jews wrong, but with understanding the supreme good and how that supreme good should be reached. In terms of existing dialogue literature, this was a novel perspective. By drawing attention to the common ground that was the goal of the philosopher, the Jew, and the Christian, Abelard avoided the customary arguments generated by the uniqueness of the Christian claim. Such inquiry provided a better starting point for discussion of ethical precepts. Abelard's theological investigations similarly centered around the supreme good and its three-fold attributes of power, wisdom, and benignity as glimpsed by gentile philosophers, rather than the doctrine of the incarnation in particular. He started to develop his ideas about pagan ethical philosophy at about the same time as he freed himself from obligation to the abbot of St. Denis. In the *Dialogus* Abelard was able to take those ethical reflections much further in the form of debates of a philosopher with a Jew and with a Christian. He wanted to show that dialectical technique could become open-ended, in order to evaluate the common ground of different religious traditions and challenge Christians to move away from rigidly confrontational attitudes.

While Abelard has the philosopher present a theory of ethics and the Christian a vision of the supreme good as the focus of ethical discussion, he does not have the Christian comment on the path to be taken to the supreme good. The traditional explanation offered for this, that Abelard must have died before he could complete the work, is difficult to reconcile with the evidence for an early date discussed above. Abelard may not yet have fully worked out his own understanding of Christian ethics when he wrote the *Dialogus*. Many of the issues about the Law and circumcision Abelard raised in the first conference are themes he discussed at much more length in his commentary on St. Paul's Epistle to the Romans, written while he was working on the *Theologia "Scholarium."* In that commentary Abelard tackled the issues of sin and grace so conspicuously absent from the *Dialogus*. In his account of the redemption in that commentary on Paul, he expanded on the idea (introduced tentatively in the *Cur Deus homo*) that the Devil enjoys no legitimate dominion over man. We are redeemed by the word and example of Christ, which prompts mankind to the true love of God.[42] This theory of the redemption took for granted the ethical principles laid out in the *Dialogus*.

In his position as abbot of St. Gildas from 1127 and as spiritual director to the nuns of the Paraclete from 1129, Abelard was obliged to develop his understanding of Christian doctrine. Certainly, by the 1130s, when he had resumed teaching on the Mont Sainte-Geneviève, Abelard had developed his own distinctive interpretation of the redemptive action of Christ. His lectures from the period are recorded in various collections of his *sententiae* about faith in God, the incarnation and redemption, the sacraments and charity.[43] Abelard transformed the *Theologia christiana* into the *Theologia "Scholarium"* in the 1130s so as to place his discussion of the supreme good within this wider framework. When he was writing his commentary on Romans, he already had in mind ideas which he was reserving for his *Ethics* or *Scito teipsum*. While the *Dialogus* has none of the Christological reflection of the commentary on Romans or the psychological subtlety of that later work, it anticipates themes about the priority of natural law and the role of intention developed in these two later works.

The Enigma of Dialogue

Although it may be tempting to read Abelard's *Dialogus* as an early manifesto of religious toleration between a Jew, a philosopher, and a Christian, it is not the record of a discussion between historical individuals. Jolivet's suggestion that the picture Abelard has drawn there of the philosopher may have owed something to reports he had heard of a Muslim philosopher, Ibn Badadya (Avempace, d. 1138), cannot be sustained. Even if Abelard had thought of taking flight in Muslim territory in a moment of depression, too much should not be made of a passing allusion made by the Jew that the philosopher was of the seed of Ishmael. The philosopher is someone who has rejected the path of revelation, and considers the Jews "foolish" and the Christians "insane" (29; Payer, 21). He is an imaginary figure with whom Abelard identifies, as he strives to work out an ethical path to the supreme good, argued in relation to the role of the Jewish Law, the natural law of the philosopher, and Christian understanding of God as the supreme good. He was only imagining a situation of philosophical tolerance in order to debate the nature of truth and how it could be reached. The paradox of his position was that while he insisted there was a supreme truth to which all rational men were devoted, he was unwilling to come to a firm conclusion about what he thought.

A guiding thread in the *Dialogus*, as indeed through all Abelard's writing, is confidence in the power of rational discussion. He questions all attempts to impose belief by force: "Heretics are more to be coerced by reason than by power, since, according to the authority of the holy fathers, the faithful, for whom all things co-operate for the good (Rom 8:28), exercized by their disputations, are made more watchful and cautious."[44] In the *Historia calamitatum*, Abelard expressed only contempt for those who preached what they did not understand through their reason, a hostility to unreasoning belief that he developed further in his *Theologia "Scholarium."*[45] The very first question discussed in the *Sic et Non* is whether faith was to be supported by reason. Criticism leveled at his endeavor to understand Christian doctrine through examples and analogies from secular philosophy motivated him to find many patristic texts which showed that assertions qualified as "Christian tradition" were not as fixed as many Christians thought.

Abelard's confidence in the capacity of rational discussion to arrive at greater understanding of any subject, whether it be theology, ethics, or whatever, reflects a particular fascination with the process of dialogue. His

reputation in dialectic turned not so much on the brilliance of his writing as on his ability to counter an argument in public disputation. This
is the image Goswin remembered when he recounted to his biographer
how he, the young Goswin, had dared to challenge the supreme master of
dialectic at the public school of the abbey of Sainte-Geneviève (sometime
around 1110). Goswin also recalled a conversation about the nature of hon-
esty he had with the stubborn Abelard, when Abelard was incarcerated at
the abbey of St. Medard after being found guilty of preaching heresy at the
Council of Soissons (1121).[46]

Abelard tended to be remembered by his critics as a master of disputation who never grew beyond his early gifts in dialectic. Certainly his skill in
argument made a negative impression on those who could not understand
what he was saying. It is a mistake, however, to think that he saw dialectic
as an end in itself. There was a Platonic idealism in his conviction that it was
a tool in the service of truth. In his first major work of theology about God
as a Trinity of persons, Abelard transferred ideas about the artificial nature
of all language to theological concepts. No linguistic statement could ever
define the totality of understanding, known ultimately only to God.

The *Dialogus* demonstrates how Abelard constructed his argument in
the form of an ongoing dialogue. His philosophy of language militated
against identifying any "final solution." The lack of a firm conclusion to
this treatise is not an accident due to external circumstances beyond Abelard's control, but a characteristic of his thought. He observed in his *Theologia "Scholarium"* that he was not expounding the truth, but "the sense of
our opinion."[47] More controversially, he defined faith as "the estimation
of things not apparent to the senses," in accord with a theme he had developed in the *De intellectibus* ("On Understandings"), that an estimation
(*existimatio*) of something was not the same as an understanding, which
conferred certitude.[48] He did not deny the existence of truth, only our capacity to give it final definition.

The *Sic et Non* is like the *Dialogus* in being an invitation to thought
rather than a finished work. Judgment on the questions under debate is
left to the reader, rather than imposed by Abelard himself. The closest we
can get to judgments delivered by Abelard on these questions are the various surviving collections of his *sententiae* recorded by students on matters
of faith, the sacraments, and charity. The very fluid nature of these "sentences," each manuscript of which tends to be different from another, testi-
fies to Abelard's unwillingness to deliver a final resolution of any question.
The same lack of resolution applies to the *Theologia*, a treatise he kept on
revising for over twenty years.[49]

The open-ended quality of Abelard's thought contrasts sharply with that of many of his contemporaries. Anselm of Laon and William of Champeaux were celebrated for delivering definitive "sentences" on a wide range of doctrinal questions being debated by students. They did not introduce into discussion of theology or ethics anything like the wide range of texts and ideas Abelard was willing to debate when dealing with these questions. Abelard was engaged in the same underlying program as St. Anselm and Gilbert Crispin, to lay out a rational framework vindicating the authority of Christian doctrine, but he was prepared to enter more into dialogue than into disputation with those who were not Christians. His sympathies were more with the idealized Gentile philosopher he constructed in his mind than with the rational Jew, whose arguments he still considered limited in nature.

Abelard's correspondence with Heloise can also be seen as a dialogue, albeit one in which Abelard was initially unwilling to engage. When Abelard wrote the *Historia calamitatum*, he was full of admiration for the ascetic virtue of pagan philosophers and claimed that he had contemplated living in a "pagan" society where there was greater toleration than in Christendom. The fact that it was addressed to a male friend struck Heloise as an alarming sign that there were severe constraints to his capacity to enter into dialogue with a woman with whom he had once had a sexual relationship. It is a measure of his personal evolution that, after Heloise had urged him to respond more fully to her requests, Abelard discussed in his *Scito teipsum* the psychology of sexual temptation and the difference between temptation and sin, issues never raised in the *Dialogus*. In that work, he was interested simply in the ideal of virtue, based on natural law. As in classical tradition, philosophical dialogue was a male affair. His analysis of ethics can be seen as providing discussion missing from the end of the *Dialogus*. Abelard now defined sin not as a wrong will as in the *Dialogus* and the commentary on Romans, but as consent to a wrong will in contempt of God. By the time he wrote the treatise he called "Know Yourself," Abelard had acquired a greater degree of self-knowledge.

Perhaps the most expressive articulation of Abelard's attitude to diversity occurs in his didactic poem, the *Carmen ad Astralabium*, addressed to his son. Given that Astralabe was born around 1117, the poem must belong to the final years of Abelard's life. The poem provides a moving summation of Abelard's wisdom, although it has never attracted the sort of critical attention devoted to his early writings on dialectic. In one passage, he raises the theme of the diversity of beliefs in a way that recalls the

opening of the *Dialogus*. The solution Abelard offers his son is to emphasize that only contempt for God, not ignorance, is truly sinful:

The world is divided among so many sects
that what may be the path of life is hardly clear.
Because the world harbors so many conflicting dogmas,
each makes his own, by way of his own background.
In the end, no one dares rely on reason in these things,
while he wants to live in some kind of peace with himself.
Each person sins only by having contempt for God—
only contempt can make this person guilty.
One does not have contempt if one does not know what is to be done,
unless not knowing is due to one's own fault.
Sins abandon you more than you abandon them,
if, when you cannot do more harm, you repent.
There are those who so much delight in past sins
that they never truly repent of them.
Rather, the sweetness of that pleasure may be so great
that no satisfaction for it has any weight.
Because of this comes the frequent complaint of our Heloise,
by which she often says to me what she says to herself:
"If I cannot be saved without repenting
of what I committed in the past, there is no hope for me.
The joys of what we did are still so sweet
that what pleased greatly gives help by being recalled."
One who tells the truth does not strain in telling it:
What is hard is first fabricating falsehood, then speaking.[50]

When Abelard wrote the *Dialogus*, he was not preoccupied at all with sin.
In the *Carmen*, he admits openly that it was Heloise who caused him to
be preoccupied with the issue. She had rebuked Abelard for looking at
her so much in terms of virtue that he had not recognized the reality of
her situation. Before he resumed contact with Heloise, Abelard had been
fascinated by the example of male pagan philosophers because their virtuous lives contrasted so sharply with the lives of Christian monks. Through
rational inquiry into Jewish and Christian tradition he thought that one
could arrive at an understanding of the truth sought by philosopher and
Christian alike. When he wrote the *Carmen* to Astralabe, he put more emphasis on practical wisdom and the search for inner peace. His image of
reason was still based on a male philosophical ideal, which subtly excluded
the anguished insight of Heloise.

Abelard touched most fully on the ethics of sexual relationships in his
Scito teipsum. As if responding to Heloise, he explained to his readers that

one could not sin through ignorance and that sin lay not in an evil will but in consent to an evil will in contempt of God. This definition provoked new controversy in 1140. Abelard's refutation of the idea that mankind was held in any legitimate bondage to the devil, an argument raised in St. Anselm's *Cur Deus homo*, struck Bernard as denying the reason Christ came to redeem man. He considered Abelard's thought dangerously open-ended. In his eyes, Abelard was "a monk without a rule, a prelate without responsibility, an abbot without discipline, who argues with boys and consorts with women."[51] Bernard's powerful rhetoric about the dangers of disputation illustrates well the fear such discussion generated. Ironically, Abelard had moved beyond the technique of disputation when exploring the common ground of philosophical, Jewish, and Christian perspectives on truth. Bernard did not appreciate that Abelard's version of disputation involved greater respect for alternative perspectives on the supreme good and how it was reached.

Not all Abelard's critics relied on such emotive language to express their criticism. Peter Lombard was a more assiduous critic who read the *Theologia "Scholarium"* with far more care than Bernard of Clairvaux and quoted many passages from the work with great accuracy.[52] Conscious of the need to provide teachings based on critical assessment of a wide range of disputed questions, he composed a vast treatise which provided firm answers to far more issues than Abelard had raised.[53] The Lombard was not afraid to question many of the arguments Abelard had put forward, such as the claim that divine truth had been perceived through reason by pagan philosophers.[54] The cautious judgments of Peter Lombard were more attuned to the needs of ecclesiastical authority in the second half of the twelfth century than Abelard's reflective self-questioning in the *Dialogus*. Certainly the Lombard's synthesis illustrates the powerful urge of a clerical class to systematize Christian doctrine in the twelfth century and thus impose a framework of orthodoxy in Latin Europe. Systematization was a response to much greater questioning in society. Abelard shared in this process by which Christian faith was identified as wholly consistent with reason, but he was critical of dogmatic attitudes toward those outside the Christian dispensation. In this sense he did defend values of religious toleration. Abelard's critics considered that he was questioning too much and wished to define a fixed conclusion to theological enquiry. In more ways than one, the problem with Abelard's dialogue was that it had no end.

Notes

1. Jacques Monfrin, ed., *Pierre Abélard: Historia calamitatum* (Paris: Vrin, 1959), 97–98; translated by Betty Radice, *The Letters of Abelard and Heloise* (Harmondsworth: Penguin, 1974), 94. The growing pressure toward establishing social and religious conformity in this period is analyzed by Robert Ian Moore, *The Formation of a Persecuting Society: Power and Deviance in Western Europe, 950–1250* (Oxford: Blackwell, 1987).

2. Rudolf Thomas, ed., *Petrus Abaelardus: Dialogus inter Philosophum, Judaeum et Christianum* (Stuttgart-Bad Canstatt: Friedrich Frommann Verlag, 1970); Pierre J. Payer, trans., *Peter Abelard: A Dialogue of a Philosopher with a Jew and a Christian* (Toronto: Pontifical Institute of Mediaeval Studies, 1979). A new edition and translation of the work is being prepared by Giovanni Orlandi and John Marenbon. Rheinwald's 1831 edition of the work was reprinted by Jacques-Paul Migne, Patrologia Latina [PL] 178: 1609–82. The rubric *Dialogus Petri Baiolardi* is added to one of two twelfth-century MSS of the work (Vienna MS, Oesterreichische Nationalbibliothek cvp 819), although the title *Collationes* is given in the Balliol College MS 296 (mid-fourteenth century). Abelard himself referred to the second discussion of the *Dialogus* as a *collatio* (see below, n.7). The term *Dialogus* will be maintained for consistency with earlier editions. It was the term used by a twelfth-century reader of the work, who composed an essay on the supreme good which follows it in the Vienna MS (see below, n.8). Aryeh Graboïs invokes the notion of "intellectual tolerance" when comparing it to a Jewish dialogue written in Spain at this time, "Un chapitre de tolérance intellectuelle dans la société occidentale au XIIᵉ siècle: le «Dialogus» de Pierre Abélard et le «Kuzari» d'Yehuda Halévi," in René Louís and Jean Jolivet, eds., *Pierre Abélard-Pierre le Vénérable: Les courants philosophiques, littéraires et artistiques en Occident au milieu du XIIᵉ siècle* (Paris: CNRS, 1975), 641–52; Graboïs defends his use of the notion of tolerance in conference discussion with Rudolf Thomas, recorded on p. 653.

3. *Christians and Jews in the Twelfth-Century Renaissance* (London: Routledge, 1995), 89–91, 124–25.

4. References to the *Dialogus* are to the line number of Thomas's edition and the page number of Payer's translation. While translations of the *Dialogus* are my own, I am frequently indebted to Payer's felicitous phraseology. Giovanni Orlandi pointed out that Thomas tends to follow readings of the Vienna MS, even though those are sometimes palpably inferior to those of the Balliol MS (consigned by Thomas to an apparatus), "Per una nuova edizione del Dialogus di Abelardo," *Rivista Critica di Storia della Filosofia* 34 (1979): 474–94. Three seventeenth-century transcriptions of the *Dialogus*, all based on the Balliol MS, have no independent value, but testify to a revival of interest in Abelard's ideas, even during the civil war; see my comments in the introduction to *Theologia "Scholarium" [TSch]*, *Petri Abaelardi Opera Theologica III*, Corpus Christianorum Continuatio Mediaeualis [CCCM] 13 (Turnhout: Brepols, 1987), 258–61.

5. Augustine, *Libri duo quaestionum evangeliorum* 2.40, PL 35: 1354.

6. Rheinwald created the impression that the work broke off incomplete by

concluding his edition with a set of dots, not present in the original MS: *licet te subinferre vel ad reliqua festinare.......* . Unaware that the text in the Balliol MS concludes at exactly the same point, Samuel Martin Deutsch considered that a faulty manuscript was to blame for the unfinished state of the work, *Peter Abälard: Ein kritischer Theologe des zwölften Jahrhunderts* (Leipzig: S. Hirzel, 1883), 451.

7. See my "On Dating the Works of Peter Abelard," *Archives d'Histoire Doctrinale et Littéraire du Moyen Age* 52 (1985): 73–134, especially 105–26. Abelard alludes to the last part of the second conference of the *Dialogus* in his *Expositio in Haemeron* (PL 178: 768A), which survives in three different recensions. Whereas Abelard refers nowhere in the *Dialogus* to texts unique to *TSch* (prepared in the 1130s), he does make specific allusion (1497–1503; Payer, 87) to the second book of his *Theologia christiana [Tchr]*, ed. Eligius M. Buytaert, CCCM 12 (Turnhout: Brepols, 1969), composed 1121–27. A little earlier (1458–77; Payer, 85–86), he cites two passages from Augustine about dialectic in exactly the same slightly inaccurate way as in the earlier recension of the *Tchr* II.117 [*R*, not *CT*], ed. Buytaert, CCCM 12: 184–85, not in the improved way characteristic of *TSch* II.19, ed. Buytaert-Mews, CCCM 13: 415 and in Letter 13 (critical of someone ignorant of dialectic), ed. Edmé Smits, *Peter Abelard: Letters IX–XIV* (Groningen: distributed by Bouma, 1983), 272, drafted in the early 1130s. In the earlier *Theologia "Summi boni" [TSum]* II.5, ed. Buytaert-Mews, CCCM 13: 116, Abelard's misquotation had been even more inaccurate.

8. In one of the two twelfth-century manuscripts of the *Dialogus*, the work has been copied alongside the *Sic et Non*; in the Vienna MS it is followed by a reflection of a teacher to a student on the nature of the supreme good, responding to questions raised in the *Dialogus*, ed. Edward A. Synan, "The Exortacio Against Peter Abelard's *Dialogus inter Philosophum, Iudaeum et Christianum*," in J. Reginald O'Donnell, ed., *Essays in Honor of Anton Charles Pegis* (Toronto: PIMS, 1974), 176–92.

9. Franciscus Salesius Schmitt, ed., *Sancti Anselmi Opera*, 6 vols. (Edinburgh: Thomas Nelson, 1946–61), 1: 146–276.

10. Anna Sapir Abulafia makes this point in an excellent article, "St. Anselm and Those Outside the Church," in David Loades and Katherine Walsh, eds., *Faith and Identity: Christian Political Experience*, Studies in Church History, Subsidia VI (Oxford: Blackwell, 1990), 11–37.

11. Edited by Anna Sapir Abulafia and Gillian R. Evans, *The Works of Gilbert Crispin Abbot of Westminster*, Auctores Britannici Medii Aevi (London: British Academy, 1986), 8–53; see also her studies: "The 'ars disputandi' of Gilbert Crispin, Abbot of Westminster (1085–1117)," in C. M. Cappon, ed., *Ad fontes: Opstellen aangeboden aan Professor Dr. C. van de Kieft* (Amsterdam: Verloren, 1984), 139–52; "An attempt by Gilbert Crispin, abbot of Westminster, at rational argument in the Jewish-Christian debate," *Studia Monastica* 26 (1984): 55–74; *Christians and Jews*, 77–81.

12. *Disputatio* 4, *Works of Gilbert Crispin*, ed. Abulafia and Evans, 9.

13. *Disputatio* 4, *Works of Gilbert Crispin*, ed. Abulafia and Evans, 10.

14. Richard W. Southern suggested that Gilbert both profited from Anselm's company in 1092/93 and prompted Anselm to think further about that subject, "St.

Anselm and Gilbert Crispin, Abbot of Westminster," *Mediaeval and Renaissance Studies* 3 (1954): 78–115.

15. The work, which survives in only a single manuscript, was first edited by Clement C. J. Webb, "Gilbert Crispin, Abbot of Westminster: Dispute of a Christian with a Heathen Touching the Faith of Christ," *Mediaeval and Renaissance Studies* 3 (1954): 55–77; *Works of Gilbert Crispin*, ed. Abulafia and Evans, 61–87.

16. Anna Sapir Abulafia, "Jewish-Christian Disputations and the Twelfth-Century Renaissance," *Journal of Medieval History* 15 (1989): 105–25.

17. I have edited a hitherto unnoticed draft of this treatise, dating from Anselm's first months in England in 1092, in "St. Anselm and Roscelin: Some New Texts and Their Implications. I. The *De incarnatione uerbi* and the *Disputatio inter christianum et gentilem*," *Archives d'Histoire Doctrinale et Littéraire du Moyen Age* 58 (1991): 55–97.

18. It occurs within a larger corpus of Anselmian texts than the corpus preserved at Bec or Canterbury, which includes a hitherto unpublished draft of part of the *De incarnatione Verbi*, a judgment about marriage, and copies of secret letters of Pope Pascal II to Henry I, quoted by Eadmer but not preserved in most MSS of the letters of Anselm. I have provided a provisional transcription in "St. Anselm and Roscelin: Some New Texts and Their Implications," 86–98, from British Library MS, Royal 5.E.xiv (s. xiii) and argue that this dossier was compiled separately from the more official collection of Anselm's writing compiled at Christ Church, Canterbury. The *Disputatio* is incomplete in the London MS, as in a sizable number of related fourteenth-century manuscripts, mostly from the West country. A complete version survives in three twelfth-century MSS: Hereford Cathedral MS O.I.xii; Berlin, Staatsbibliothek Preussische Kulturbesitz theol. lat. fol. 276 (from Maria Laach); and Cambridge, Cambridge University Library Gg.V.34 (written at the abbey of St Werburgh, Chester, whose community was visited by Anselm in 1092–93); see Colin Gale, *Delivered to the Devil? St. Anselm and His Circle on the Consequences of the Fall* (Cambridge University, Faculty of History, 1993), 33–37.

19. Ed. Mews, 86: "Maiestas divina cur ad dolores mortalis nature insuper et usque ad opprobria crucis se humiliauit, uellem addiscere. Quod quidem ex auctoritate uestrarum scripturarum nolo [mistakenly printed as *uolo*] michi probari, cui non credo, sed si rationabiliter factum est, huius rei rationem quero."

20. Ed. Mews, 95: "Quod dicitur: fecit quod decuit, nichil aliud est dicere quam fecit quod debuit. Secundum hanc formam loquendi dicitur de omnibus que facit Deus. Facit quod debet, id est quid eum decet, non quia obligatus sit ullo debito ab aliquo exigendo."

21. Ed. Mews, 95: "Fateor me hoc usque errasse, et Christum uerum Deum et uere salutis auctorem et reparatorem corde et ore contestor."

22. Sapir Abulafia identifies its author as Pseudo-Anselm in "Christians Disputing Disbelief: St. Anselm, Gilbert Crispin, and Pseudo-Anselm," in Bernard Lewis and Friedrich Niewöhner, eds., *Religionsgespräche im Mittelalter*, Wolfenbütteler Mittelalter-Studien IV (Wiesbaden: Harrassowitz, 1992), 131–48 and *Christians and Jews*, 85–87, 104–5, 156 n.4. Its relationship to other Anselmian writings needs further study. The absence of any explicit refutation of the legitimacy of the

devil's power over man, comparable to Boso's argument, argues against the idea that the *Disputatio* is based on a complete version of the *Cur Deus homo*. The Gentile does not articulate Boso's explicit rejection of the rights of the devil, although he does say that the devil does not "deserve" to have power over man (*Disputatio*, ed. Mews, 86). Part of the *Disputatio* (ed. Mews, 90) explicitly addresses the question raised by Roscelin, why the incarnation should not have involved all three persons, not an issue raised in the *Cur deus homo*.

23. Ed. Mews, 90: "Si credere uolueris quod impossibile tibi uidetur, ipso Christo adiuuante in ueritate esse comprobabis. Scriptum est enim: *Nisi credideritis non intellegitis*. . . . Hoc est quod iam dixi, et nunc iterum dico: *Nisi credideritis, non intelligitis*." Cf. *Cur Deus homo*, Commendatio operis, ed. Schmitt 2: 40 (alluding to Augustine, *Sermo* 91, PL 38: 571). It was also cited in a Commentary on the Apostle's Creed attributed to Augustine, but in fact by Rufinus, *Commentarius in Symbolum Apostolorum* 4, ed. Manlius Simonetti, CCSL 20 (Turnhout: Brepols, 1961), 136. This is not a phrase cited by Gilbert Crispin, according to the scriptural concordance provided by Abulafia and Evans.

24. This is the implication of an analogy he once provided for his monks: the Jews and pagans lived in the Devil's territory outside a city in which Christians lived, who could only seek refuge within the keep of the city's castle, where the monks lived; *De humanis moribus per similitudines* 75–76, ed. Richard W. Southern and Franciscus Salesius Schmitt, *Memorials of St. Anselm*, Auctores Britannici Medii Aevi 1 (Oxford: Oxford University Press, 1969), 66–67, commented on by Abulafia, "St. Anselm and Those Outside the Church" (n.10 above).

25. Reported by St. Anselm, *Epistola de incarnatione verbi* 2, ed. Schmitt, 2: 10.

26. Joseph Reiners, ed., *Der Nominalismus in der Frühscholastik. Ein Beitrag zur Geschichte der Universalienfrage im Mittelalter. Nebst einer neuen Textausgabe des Briefes Roscelins an Abaelard*, Beiträge zur Geschichte der Philosophie des Mittelalters [BGPM] 8.5 (Münster, 1910), 63.

27. The most recent survey of Constantine's writing and influence has been edited by Charles Burnett and Danielle Jacquart, *Constantine the African and 'Aku ibn al-'abbas ak-magusi: The Pantegni and Related Texts* (Leiden: Brill, 1994).

28. Orderic Vitalis, *Ecclesiastical History* xi.9, ed. and trans. Marjorie Chibnall (Oxford: Oxford University Press, 1969), 6: 50–52.

29. *Quaestiones naturales*, ed. Martin Müller, BGPM 31 (1934): 11: ". . . a magistris Arabicis ratione duce didici." See Marie-Thérèse d'Alverny, "Translations and Translators," in Giles Constable and Robert L. Benson, eds., *Renaissance and Renewal in the Twelfth Century* (Oxford: Clarendon Press, 1982), 421–62, esp. 440–43 and Jean Jolivet, "The Arabic Inheritance," in Peter Dronke, ed., *A History of Twelfth-Century Western Philosophy* (Cambridge: Cambridge University Press, 1988), 113–48.

30. Charles Burnett summarizes information about these and other translations of the period in his chapter "Scientific Speculations" in Dronke, ed., *History of Twelfth-Century Western Philosophy*, 151–76; see also the studies in Burnett, ed., *Adelard of Bath: An English Scientist and Arabist of the Early Twelfth Century*, Warburg Institute Studies and Texts 14 (London: Warburg Institute, 1987). Abelard's

attempt to learn from Thierry is related in a humorous anecdote, which I discuss in "In Search of a Name and Its Significance: A Twelfth-Century Anecdote About Thierry and Peter Abaelard," *Traditio* 44 (1988): 175–200.

31. J. V. Tolan, *Text as Tool: Petrus Alfonsi and His Medieval Readers* identifies sixty-three manuscripts of the *Dialogi* (compared to thirty-four for Crispin's *Disputatio*). Abelard's *Dialogus* by contrast survives in only three medieval manuscripts.

32. Blanche Boyer and Richard McKeon, eds., *Peter Abailard: Sic et Non* (Chicago-London: University of Chicago Press, 1976–77), 89.

33. *Sic et Non*, Pref., ed. Boyer-McKeon, 103: "Haec quippe prima sapientiae clavis definitur assidua scilicet seu frequens interrogatio. . . . Dubitando quippe ad inquisitionem venimus; inquirendo veritatem percipimus. Iuxta quod et Veritas ipsa *Quaerite* inquit *et invenite, pulsate et aperietur vobis.*"

34. Lambert Marie De Rijk, ed., *Petrus Abaelardus: Dialectica*, 2d ed. (Assen: Van Gorcum, 1970), 153: "Qui autem querit, dubitationem suam exprimit, ut certitudinem quam nondum habet, consequatur."

35. David E. Luscombe, ed., *Peter Abelard's Ethics* (Oxford: Clarendon Press, 1971), 14.

36. *Tchr* II.19, ed. Buytaert, CCCM 12: 141.

37. Charles Burnett, ed., "Peter Abelard «Soliloquium»," *Studi Medievali* 3ª ser. 25.2 (1984): 889 (859–94): "Quam quidem exhortationem quisquis legerit, videbit philosophos non tam nomine quam re ipsa Christianis maxime sociatos."

38. *TSch* II.46–47, ed. Buytaert-Mews, CCCM 13: 431.

39. Among the isolated comments of Aristotle on virtue available prior to the translation of the *Ethics*, see *Categories* 8b25, ed. Lorenzo Minio-Paluello, *Aristoteles Latinus* (Bruges-Paris: Desclée, De Brouwer, 1961), 63, as well as the remark of Boethius, *De divisione* (PL 64: 885B): "Virtue is an excellent habit of the mind." Abelard's role in the development of these ideas has been emphasised by Cary J. Nederman in numerous studies, notably "Nature, Ethics, and the Doctrine of 'Habitus': Aristotelian Moral Psychology in the Twelfth Century," *Traditio* 45 (1989–90): 87–110. Marcia Colish observes that Anselm of Laon employed the traditional definition, while Abelard developed it in a more Aristotelian sense, *Peter Lombard*, 2 vols. (Leiden: Brill, 1994), 476–77.

40. John Marenbon, "Abelard's Ethical Theory: Two Definitions from the *Collationes*," in Haijo Jan Westra, ed., *From Athens to Chartres: Neoplatonism and Medieval Thought, Essays in Honour of Édouard Jeauneau* (Leiden: Brill, 1992), 301–15.

41. *Dialectica*, ed. De Rijk, 116.

42. *Commentaria in Epistolam ad Romanos*, ed. Eligius Marie Buytaert, CCCM 11 (Turnhout: Brepols, 1969), 113–18.

43. The most important of these sentence collections have been edited, very imperfectly, by Sandro Buzzetti, *Sententie magistri Petri Abelardi (Sententie Hermanni)* (Florence: La Nuova Italia Editrice, 1983). I present my arguments for rejecting Ostlender's hypothesis that these sentences were written by a certain Hermannus in "The *Sententiae* of Peter Abelard," *Recherches de Théologie Ancienne et Médiévale* 53 (1986): 130–84, summarized in the introduction to the edition of the *Theologia "Scholarium*," CCCM 13: 221–26. In *Peter Lombard*, 51 n.43, Marcia Col-

ish accepts Ostlender's hypothesis, without presenting any substantive proof for her statement that opinions in these *Sententiae* differ in some respects from teachings of Abelard. She refers back to David Luscombe's *The School of Peter Abelard* (Cambridge: Cambridge University Press, 1969), without appreciating the historiography of this debate or realizing that Luscombe has himself since acknowledged that the *Sententiae* "represents the teaching given by Abelard to students," in "The School of Peter Abelard Revisited," *Vivarium* 30 (1992): 128 (127–38). Her reference in that footnote to my comments in CCCM 13 needs to be completed with reference to my fuller discussion on 221–26. Ostlender's hypothesis that the sentence collections had been compiled by other individuals than Abelard had been questioned by Artur Landgraf in relation to the *Sententiae Parisienses* in the introduction to *Ecrits théologiques de l'école d'Abélard* (Louvain: Spicilegium Sacrum Lovaniense, 1934). Colish cites the *Sententiae Parisienses* as the work of a disciple "who rushed to his support" (*Peter Lombard*, 295), even though Landgraf explicitly defends the idea that it is a record of Abelard's lectures in its introduction.

44. *Tchr CT* IV.74-b, ed. Buytaert, CCCM 12: 299, transferred into *TSch* II.41, ed. Buytaert-Mews, CCCM 13: 427.

45. *Historia calamitatum*, ed. Monfrin, ll. 699–701; cf. *TSch* II, 1–61, ed. Buytaert-Mews, CCCM 13: 406–38.

46. *Vita Goswini*, ed. Richard Gibbons (Douai, 1620), reprinted in *Recueil des historiens des Gaules et de la France*, vol. 14 (Paris, 1877), 442–48.

47. *TSch* Pref. 5, ed. Buytaert-Mews, CCCM 13: 314.

48. *De intellectibus* 24–27, ed. Patrick Morin, *Des intellections* (Paris: Vrin, 1994), 42–44.

49. Colish observes that "he was one of those academics constitutionally incapable of finishing anything he started," *Peter Lombard*, 48, a claim that does a manifest injustice to the works which are complete (the treatises on logic, the epistolary treatises, the liturgical writing, the commentary on Romans, the *Theologia* "'*Summi boni*,'" etc.).

50. This translation follows the edition of the passage by José M. A. Rubingh-Bosscher, *Peter Abelard: Carmen ad Astralabium* ll. 363–84 (Groningen: privately published, 1987), 127. Dronke edits and translates this passage (following a MS which reads *cultus* for *mundus* in l.363) in *Abelard and Heloise in Medieval Testimonies*, 14–15, 43, reprinted in *Intellectuals and Poets in Medieval Europe*, Storia e Letteratura 183 (Rome: Edizioni di Storia e Letteratura, 1992), 257, 279–80. Rubingh-Bosscher, *Carmen*, 97–102, puts forward strong arguments for accepting the attribution to Abelard given in a number of MSS of the poem. This passage occurs in Recension I, represented by four manuscripts, ranging in date from the early to the late thirteenth century.

51. Bernard, *Ep.* 332 to Cardinal G., ed. Jean Leclercq, *Sancti Bernardi Opera*, vol. 8 (Rome: Editiones Cistercienses, 1977), 271: "Disputantem cum pueris, conversantem cum mulierculis."

52. I have been able to document the remarkable accuracy with which Peter Lombard cites passages from the *Theologia "Scholarium"* in the introduction to my edition, CCCM 13: 264–67, bearing out the truth of the comment of John of Cornwall that Lombard was always reading Abelard's *Theologia* and drew ideas from

Abelard, Nikolaus Häring, "The Eulogium ad Alexandrum Papam tertium of John of Cornwall," *Mediaeval Studies* 13 (1951): 265. There is a strong possibility that one manuscript of the *Theologia* was used to list books belonging to Peter Lombard, one which also happens to contain a thirteenth-century copy of John of Cornwall's *Eulogium* (CCCM 13: 244–45).

53. For a comparison of the attitude of Peter Lombard and Robert of Melun to Peter Abelard, see my study "Orality, Literacy and Authority in the Twelfth-Century Schools," *Exemplaria* 2 (1990): 475–500. On the urge to systematization in scholasticism, see Richard W. Southern, *Scholastic Humanism and the Unification of Europe* (Oxford: Blackwell, 1995), 1: 6–13.

54. Colish observes that Lombard expresses in this respect the orthodox consensus of his time, *Peter Lombard*, 259.

2

Toleration, Skepticism, and the "Clash of Ideas": Principles of Liberty in the Writings of John of Salisbury

Cary J. Nederman

THE DEVELOPMENT OF IDEAS of religious toleration in early modern Europe has been commonly and closely associated with the rise of the philosophical movement of skepticism.[1] As Preston King explains, there appears to exist a

> symbiotic relationship . . . between *tolerance* and *scepticism*. The tolerance involves an antipathy towards certain ideas combined with the conviction that one should not exclude from consideration that they may be correct; the scepticism involves the approval of (meaning agreement with) certain ideas combined with the conviction that one should not exclude from examination arguments which might prove those views mistaken. . . . *Tolerance*, although it begins with a negative assessment conjoined with a suspended negative act, always involves *scepticism*, conceived as a positive assessment conjoined with a suspended positive act.[2]

Although an automatic connection between skeptical and tolerant stances has been convincingly challenged on historical grounds by some recent scholarship,[3] it remains the case that skepticism often supported principles of toleration toward religious differences in the early modern world. A wide range of thinkers, from Sebastian Castellio and Jean Bodin in the sixteenth century to Voltaire in the eighteenth, reasoned that the recognition of human fallibility in matters of religion must entail a program of tolerance and respect for dissenting points of view.

Of course, philosophical skepticism itself was by no means an invention of early modern thought. Versions of the skeptical thesis had been popular in pagan antiquity and had been disseminated (via critics such as St. Augustine as well as proponents such as Cicero) without a break in medieval and Renaissance Latin Christendom.[4] But it has been generally (if somewhat uncritically) assumed that the Christian reception of ancient skepticism was of a largely negative character—a straw man against whom to reaffirm the absolute indubitability of God's revelation and of the moral and metaphysical truths flowing therefrom. This was the position adopted by St. Augustine in his polemic *Contra Academicos*, which sought to refute the methodological skepticism that had been championed by Cicero and other adherents to the Academic School. The supposedly unquestioned acceptance of Augustine's attack on the skeptical position by medieval thinkers has been taken as a virtual article of faith. As Richard Tuck remarks, "At the back of many people's minds is a rough history of the modern world in which the dissolution of strongly held beliefs (typically, the relatively unified Christianity of the Middle Ages) was a precondition for extending toleration to men who would once have been attacked as heretics."[5] Hence the presumption runs that, while medieval Europe was familiar with skepticism, a skeptical outlook could not have been embraced to such an extent as to generate the principles from which toleration (understood as something like a defensible right to freedom of inquiry, conscience, and dissent) might be admitted. The corollary to this claim is that only "progressive" or "unorthodox" figures in later medieval and Renaissance philosophy (such as William of Ockham) were able to develop a skeptical stance with regard to knowledge or truth claims—and then without direct reference to ancient accounts of skepticism.[6]

The present paper challenges all such complaisant, modernist assumptions about the absence of a clear understanding of the relationship between skeptical and tolerant attitudes among thinkers of medieval Christendom. I will focus on the work of the twelfth-century churchman John of Salisbury, who is recognized to be one of the most prominent medieval champions of the moderate skepticism of the New Academy that had been promoted by Cicero.[7] I have argued elsewhere that John's political theory (especially his famed conception of the body politic) entails a compelling defense of liberty of thought and speech (and hence of forbearance and toleration) in a wide range of moral matters.[8] My claim in the following essay is that John's position is directly tied in his work to his advocacy of

Ciceronian skepticism as the appropriate stance to be adopted by the wise person when confronted with complex and difficult philosophical issues. After summarizing John's position regarding personal liberty of conscience and expression, I shall examine his interpretation of the Academic School and shall argue that this leads to a defense of *de jure* freedom to dispute and dissent in those matters about which rational minds may disagree. Surprisingly—at least to those who maintain an ingrained prejudice against the possibility of intellectual and religious diversity during the Middle Ages— John defends *on principle* a remarkably extensive right on the part of wise individuals to uphold differing points of view about issues of fundamental importance.

John on Liberty

Without question, John of Salisbury maintained a central role for human liberty in his moral and political thought.[9] The force of his claims made on behalf of such liberty is evident in his *Policraticus* (composed between 1156 and 1159). John defends there a conception of open personal expression that is vast even judged by far later standards. He counsels a doctrine of "patience" for the opinions and deeds of others that becomes difficult to distinguish from toleration.

The best and wisest man is moderate with the reins of liberty and patiently takes note of whatever is said to him. And he does not oppose himself to the works of liberty, so long as damage to virtue does not occur. For when virtue shines everywhere from its own source, the reputation of patience becomes more evident with glorious renown.[10]

The patient man respects the liberty of others to state their own honest opinions, and he attempts to improve himself by patiently regarding his fellows. "The practice of liberty . . . displeases only those who live in the manner of slaves" (*Policraticus*, 7.25 [176]). Free men are reciprocally tolerant of the freedom of others, even when they are the objects of criticism. John praises the Romans for "being more patient than others with censure," since they adhered to the principle that "whoever loathes and evades [criticism] when fairly expressed seems to be ignorant of restraint. For even if it conveys obvious or secret insult, patience with censure is among wise men far more glorious than its punishment" (7.25 [179]). The *Policraticus* supports this claim in characteristic form with numerous *exempla* of wise people who spoke their minds straightforwardedly and of wise rulers who permitted such free expression to occur.

At one level, John's praise of liberty of thought and speech reflects his conception of decorum and "civility": the refined person permits civilized speech in his presence, and such speech may involve personal criticism and admonitions. But more is at stake than simple good manners. John posits an intimate relationship between liberty and morality.

[Virtue] does not arise in its perfection without liberty, and the loss of liberty demonstrates irrefutably that virtue is not present. And therefore anyone is free according to the virtue of their dispositions, and, to the extent that one is free, the virtues are effective (7.25 [176]).

Freedom makes virtue possible, for no one who is unfree (i.e., unable to make decisions for oneself) can ever be counted as capable of moral action. A virtuous (and also presumably a vicious) act is one that an individual has intentionally chosen to do, and thus for which one can be held responsible. But no such intentional choice is possible in the absence of liberty; the slave merely does as he is told, so that it is his master who must bear the blame for his conduct.

John therefore denies that it is possible to achieve virtue through coercive means. Enforced virtuous actions are not really virtuous at all and do more harm than good to subjects. It is for this reason that he condemns the immoderation (and immorality) of zealous rulers who compel their subjects to perform good deeds and who excessively punish evildoers (4.9 [53–54]).[11] But does this not imply the view that "every man has the right to go to hell in his own way"?[12] By no means. While John upholds that there must be a realm of personal discretion in decision-making with which no one may interfere, he also insists that patient endurance of the liberty of others must be matched by a liberty of critical speech. John asserts that "it is permitted to censure that which is to be equitably corrected" (7.25 [180]). If we may not properly force people to do good, then we must equally be respected and tolerated when we point out the error of their ways. In other words, if you are free to do wrong, then I must also be free to correct or reprove you. John emphasizes this point: "Liberty . . . is not afraid to censure that which is opposed to sound moral character . . . . Man is to be free and it is always permitted to a free man to speak to persons about restraining their vices" (7.25 [175, 180]). The *Policraticus* indeed practices what it preaches. John describes an encounter between himself and

Pope Adrian IV, in which he had recounted to the pontiff all the evils that were commonly ascribed to the Roman Church and curia (6.24 [132–35]). Moreover, John does not shy from lamenting at great length the many sins and vices committed by priests, monks and members of the ecclesiastical hierarchy.[13] In fact, John claims that his liberty to censure is not merely a privilege: "It is not necessary to obtain confirmed permission for such remarks which serve the public utility" (7.25 [180]). Freedom to speak one's mind about the ills of society, whether spiritual or temporal, parallels the legitimate liberty to act without restraint (1.5).

Of course, the toleration of liberty proposed by John is by no means unlimited. He asserts that the "vices" of individuals which we ought to endure, if we are unable to correct them through free speech, must be distinguished from "flagrant crimes," that is, "acts which one is not permitted to endure or which cannot faithfully be endured" (6.26 [140]). Similarly, he acknowledges that statements made "rashly," that is, without respect for the persons to whom they are addressed and with the intent of harming another's reputation, are deserving of censure and condemnation (7.25 [176–77, 179]). The intent must be pure for liberty of action and expression to be tolerated; manifestly irreligious or dishonorable conduct and words have no claim on our patience. Still, the individual is afforded a remarkably large realm of personal freedom not simply in private but as a part of one's public role and perhaps even responsibility.

The political ramifications of John's doctrine of liberty become especially evident when we turn to his well-known conception of the body politic. The *Policraticus* articulated a complex and influential version of the organic metaphor for the political community whose full statement occupies two books and over two hundred pages of text.[14] John compares the ruler to the head, the counselors to the heart, the various administrators and officials to the several organs and limbs, and the peasants and artisans to the feet (5.2 [66]).[15] Central to this analogy is the construction of civil order on the principle of the social division of labor along with rejection of the strictly hierarchical values of the Platonic polis (the outlines of which John would have been familiar with via the opening section of the *Timaeus*).[16] John designed his body politic as a system of harmonious cooperation based on reciprocal interdependence and social and political inclusion.

The recognition and toleration of personal liberty is crucial to the successful operation of the political organism. John insists that all the relations between the members of the community ought to be governed according to a principle consistent with reciprocity. Adapting the advice of Terrence in regard to the treatment of the evils of one's spouse, he proposes that "the vices of princes and subjects ought to be either endured or removed" (6.26 [140]). Now, John points out that "removal" here does not imply coercion or punishment. Rather, according to his interpretation, " 'Removing' is meant in the sense of correction. . . . What cannot be removed is to be endured" (6.26 [140]). John thus argues that we ought to attempt to restore erring members of the body politic to the path of virtue, but that, so long as their vices do not disturb the material or spiritual well-being of the whole, they are to be tolerated when they cannot be convinced of their errors. This principle entails both of the aspects of liberty discussed previously: it involves not only the freedom to speak to people about their vices, but also the liberty to act, at least within the limits of public order.

Several implications follow from the general principle of liberty and toleration espoused in the *Policraticus*. First, the ruler must carefully respect the liberty of his subjects. Indeed, John's famous distinction between the true prince (or king) and the tyrant turns on his doctrine of liberty. By definition, "the prince fights for the laws and the liberty of the people; the tyrant supposes that nothing is done unless the laws are cancelled and the people are brought into servitude" (8.17 [191]). The good ruler will necessarily govern so as to promote the liberty of subjects: liberty "has spurred on all outstanding princes; and none has ever trampled on liberty except for the manifest enemies of virtue" (7.25 [176]). It is perhaps for this reason that John places the prince under the strict dictates of law (4.2 [30–31]), since "laws were introduced in support of liberty" (7.25 [176]). That is, law assures men that they will not be subject to the arbitrary will of a ruler and thus that they will be free to act within the fixed and equitable restraints imposed by legal standards.

One consequence of this legally (as well as morally) assured liberty is that a measure of public criticism of superiors, even rulers and priests, must be permitted. John takes great pains to distinguish between "high treason" (*crimen majestas*) and proper free expression. "High treason" has the express purpose of separating the head from its members, and thus of violating the reciprocity which is vital to the life of the body politic. Such an attack on the head is a violation of the whole (6.25 [137]). John enumerates all the deeds that count as cases of high treason, citing copious legal texts in support of his definition (6.25 [138–39]). But it is noteworthy that liberty of conscience, construed as public criticism of the ruler, is excluded as an example of traitorous activity. For this reason, John insists that he is exempt from the charges that he himself is committing high treason by criticizing the bad morals and frivolities of princes and courtiers: "I myself will not be accused unfairly by anyone of having presumed against the authority of the prince" (6.26 [139–40]). Of course, just as princes (and indeed all people) must endure those vices that cannot be corrected in their fellow human beings, so subjects must tolerate the vices of their superiors.

> Even if the ruler is too loose in the virtues of his office, still he has to be honored; and . . . subjects, whom we have said to be the feet and members, should exhibit subservience to him in every way, so long as his vices are not pernicious. For, even if he is afflicted with vices, he is to be endured as one with whom rests the hopes of the provincials for their security. (6.24 [132])

But note that such "subservience" is not slavery. The liberty to speak openly to superiors about their vices in hopes of achieving correction cannot be suppressed by a ruler without the enslavement of his subjects, at which point he ceases to be merely vicious and commits a flagrant crime against the body politic. The liberty of the individual members is the lifeblood of the political organism, and is violated only by the tyrant. The proper response of the good ruler is illustrated by the *Policraticus*'s account of the reply of Pope Adrian IV to John's own honest and stinging criticisms of the papal curia: "The pontiff laughed and congratulated such great candor, commanding that whenever anything unfavorable about him made a sound in my ears, he was to be informed of this without delay" (6.24 [135]). Free speech, even of a highly critical nature, is always welcomed at the court of the good ruler.

The Medieval Academy

It might be objected, however, that John's functional or communal defense of personal liberty constitutes an insufficient basis for a full-blooded theory of toleration, inasmuch as it does not include some rights-based conception of individual liberty of conscience or belief.[17] To adopt terminology suggested by Hans Guggisberg, John's position reflects a "politico-pragmatic" or perhaps an "economic" vision of toleration, rather than a "theologico-philosophical" one.[18] Lacking firm principles on which an individual may claim a right to exercise liberty apart from direct considerations of some moral or public good, it might be argued, John's account of tolerance remains susceptible to the charge that it permits a political authority to revoke the exercise of liberty when deemed incompatible with standards of virtue or the perceived needs of the community.

Regardless of whether such a charge is warranted (and I personally do not think it is), I contend that the idea of toleration proposed in the *Policraticus* in fact possesses a compelling philosophical grounding, yielding a *right* of dissent quite apart from communal considerations. The locus of this foundation is to be discovered in John's abiding dedication to the teachings of the Academic School of philosophy, espoused in several works by Cicero available during the Latin Middle Ages. Cicero's defense of a version of Academic philosophy known as the "New Academy" (sometimes filtered through his Christian critics Augustine and Lactantius) was the primary brand of skepticism with which medieval thinkers were familiar. In a number of his mature writings (including *De natura deorum*, *De officiis*, and the two versions of the *Academica*), Cicero professed a moderate skepticism regarding matters in which probability rather than dogmatic certitude seemed the best course.[19] Cicero thus distanced himself from the more radically skeptical method of the so-called "Old Academy," which denied that anything whatsoever could be known with certainty.

The fundamentals of Ciceronian skepticism are too well known to require lengthy rehearsal.[20] Cicero succinctly states his guiding principle in the Prologue to *De natura deorum*:

The philosophers of the Academy have been wise in withholding their consent from any proposition that has not been proved. There is nothing worse than a hasty judgment, and nothing could be more unworthy of the dignity and integrity of a philosopher than to adopt a false opinion or to maintain as certain some theory which has not been fully explored and understood.[21]

As Cicero explains in the *Academica*, this is not to deny the *possibility* of the human mind attaining truth (*pace* the Old Academy), but only to insist that the criteria for knowing truth and falsity are not inborn or intuitive and that the senses can be deceptive.[22] Cicero's skepticism hence has the character of anti-dogmatism, not of absolute doubt.

John of Salisbury clearly understood this difference between a moderate and a complete skeptical stance. In his early didactic poem *Entheticus de dogmate philosophorum* (the second section of which, containing a discussion of the Academy, may have been written while he was studying in Paris during the 1130s and 1140s, but was probably not finished any later than 1155),[23] he chides the radically skeptical Academic view that "the human race is deprived of light" (*Entheticus*, l. 1138). Instead, he prefers the alternate position of the more enlightened Academic that one should

hesitate in all things except those which are proved by living reason. . . . These things, he declares, are known; he passes doubtfully on other things, of which more certainty is to be had from experience. For the usual course of events makes probable what you always see under a similar pattern. Yet, since it sometimes happens otherwise, these things are not sufficiently certain, and yet not without evidence. What he, therefore, affirms to be true, he thinks to be necessary; for the rest, he says "I believe" or "I think it to be." (ll. 1144, 1147–54)

Thus John clearly recognizes the epistemological underpinnings of the rival versions of skeptical philosophy. This fact has been missed, for instance, by Charles Schmitt, who, concentrating only on the later *Policraticus*, concludes that John "really gives us little detail regarding those aspects—e.g., sense deception or the fallibility of normally accepted logical doctrine—which were central to ancient writings on skepticism. . . . On the whole, . . . his treatment has little philosophical sophistication."[24] On the contrary, if John in his later writings did not dwell on these epistemological issues, it is only because he had previously acknowledged and examined them in the *Entheticus*.

John's expression of admiration for temperate Academic skepticism reinforces another of the key themes of his work: *modestia* or *moderatio*. He was a convinced adherent to an Aristotelian-tinged doctrine that virtue necessarily consists in the mean, and that moderation in all things is therefore the most valid standard for judging human thought and action.[25] As John points out in the *Entheticus*, the Academic stance is consonant with "a modest mind . . . that no one may accuse it of being guilty of falsehood; it thus tempers all words with qualifiers, so that it should always be rightly credible" (ll. 1161–62). John stresses that the possessors of such a modest mind "restrain their words according to condition, time, cause, and manner, [and] they avoid speaking with too much simplicity" (ll. 1161–62). Academic moderation results in rhetorical as well as intellectual humility, if not caution, consistent with the virtuous mean.

John's later work on the current state of scholastic education, the *Metalogicon* (probably written between 1157 and 1159), reiterates the Academic position articulated in the *Entheticus*. He repeatedly proclaims his explicit commitment to the philosophical program of the New Academy. In the Prologue, he announces, "Being an Academic in matters that are doubtful to the wise person, I cannot swear to the truth of what I say.

Whether such propositions may be true or false, I am satisfied with probable certainty."[26] John again distances his own version of skepticism from more radical views that deny the possibility of knowing truth (or at any rate, very many truths) (*Metalogicon*, 4.31). But he admits that, even if truth is susceptible to human comprehension, the process of achieving knowledge is troublesome. Echoing a remark by Cicero in the *Academica*, John observes, "It is difficult to apprehend the truth, which (as our Academics say) is as obscure as if it lay at the bottom of a well" (2.13). Although he demonstrates some sympathy for St. Augustine's criticisms in *Contra Academicos* of Ciceronian skepticism (2.13), John returns often in the *Metalogicon* to Cicero's methodological injunction against embracing insufficiently substantiated truth-claims too hastily in the quest for knowledge. Indeed, a main theme of the *Metalogicon* might aptly be characterized as the refutation of the arid argumentation that occurred among the Parisian teachers of his time as a result of their unwillingness to renounce their rigid formulae and fixed dogmas.

Skepticism in the Policraticus

John of Salisbury's most extensive discussion and use of the Ciceronian New Academy occurs not in the *Entheticus* or the *Metalogicon*, however, but in the *Policraticus*. And as we shall see, he appeals to Academic philosophy there in ways that are crucial for establishing the principles of his theory of toleration. The *Policraticus* once again contains repeated self-identification of its author with the teachings of the Academy, its Prologue echoing the words of the *Metalogicon*:

In philosophy, I am a devotee of Academic dispute, which measures by reason that which presents itself as more probable. I am not ashamed of the declarations of the Academics, so that I do not recede from their footprints in those matters about which the wise person has doubts.[27]

Indeed, this point is raised to the level of an evaluative standard in Book Seven of the *Policraticus*, which contains a lengthy recounting of the major schools of Greco-Roman philosophy, the stated aim of which is to discover the valuable lessons in each approach as well as to demonstrate the limitations inherent in all of them (7.1 [148–49]).

The treatment of the Academic School is given pride of place, opening Book Seven's critical history of pagan philosophy. Even as he admits his own devotion to the Academy, John stresses the divide that exists within the School between an extreme skepticism which proclaims the utter fallibility of the human mind and his own moderate Ciceronian stance. In this connection, he offers a kind of *reductio* argument against the radically skeptical position:

> Yet I do not say that all those who are included under the name of Academic have upheld the rule of modesty, since even its basic creed is in dispute and parts of it are open as much to derision as to error. . . . If the Academic is in doubt about each thing, he is certain about nothing. . . . But he possesses uncertainty about whether he is in doubt, so long as he does not know for certain that he does not know this doubt itself (7.2 [150]).

Extreme doubt, which refuses any criteria for knowledge, leads to a vicious circle in which the doubter must doubt even his own uncertainty and must thereby admit at least of the possibility of attaining valid knowledge about certain matters. Radical skepticism cannot even attain to the mantle of philosophy, John says, for the philosopher's love of wisdom requires the admission that one may know what is true (even if this is difficult to achieve) (7.2 [151–52]).

By contrast, John's moderate skepticism, consciously modelled on the lessons of Cicero, accepts that there are three reliable foundations for knowledge: faith, reason, and the senses (7.7 [153–56]). Thus it does not behoove the philosopher to question his faith in the existence of God, nor the certainty of certain postulates of mathematics, nor a number of other first principles which "one is not permitted to doubt, except for those who are occupied by the labors of not knowing anything" (7.7 [154]). It might seem, then, that John's skepticism is not so very skeptical after all, in the sense that he seems willing to countenance as certain a wide range of knowledge-claims stemming from a number of different sources. But this turns out not to be the case. John in fact generates an extremely lengthy list of "doubtful matters about which the wise person is not convinced by the authority of either faith or his senses or manifest reason, and in which contrary claims rest on the support of some evidence" (7.2 [152]). The topics subject to doubt which John enumerates include major issues of metaphysics and cosmology (such as the nature of the soul and the body, time and place, and the status of universals), ethics (the unity of the virtues, the nature of virtue and vice, legal and moral duties and punishments), natural science (magnitude, friction, the humors, geography), and even theology (free will and providence, punishment of sin, angels, what can be asked of

God by human beings) (7.2 [152–53]).[28] The entire list goes on in Webb's critical edition of the *Policraticus* for 24 lines, and is clearly meant to be illustrative rather than inclusive. In sum, John opens up to doubt and dispute an extraordinarily broad array of topics which for him are by no means settled and are thus appropriate for philosophical discourse.

In confronting all such debatable subjects, John counsels adherence to the Academic method, since "the Academics have doubts regarding these matters with so much modesty that I perceive them to have guarded diligently against the danger of rashness" (7.2 [153]). Unique among all schools of philosophy, the Academy resists the temptation to replace open discussion of uncertain matters with prematurely closed dogma. In John's view, the moderate skepticism of the New Academy alone defends the liberty of inquiry that he evidently regards to be necessary to the quest for truth.

From Skepticism to Toleration

Although the *Policraticus* does not return to the epistemological bases of intellectual fallibility that John had addressed in the *Entheticus* and *Metalogicon*, it clearly takes for granted that the human mind is furnished with only weak powers for comprehending truth. Hence John rejects the Augustinian claim that even Cicero's moderate skepticism "piles up darkness from some hidden source, and warns that the whole of philosophy is obscure, and does not allow one to hope that any light will be found in it."[29] Indeed, in a surprising twist John attempts to enlist Augustine himself in support of those who evince Academic doubt: "Even our Augustine does not assail them, since he himself somewhat frequently employs Academic moderation in his works and propounds many matters as ambiguous which would not seem to be in question to another arguing with greater confidence and just as safely" (7.2 [152]). On John's reading, Augustine practiced the Academic method even while he excoriated it in principle. The validity of this interpretation aside, John seeks any evidence whatsoever to bolster his own view that "mortals can know very little," as he puts it in the *Entheticus* (l. 1142).

This epistemological premise stands at the philosophical core of John's approach to human liberty and toleration. As we have seen, John believes that both personal virtue and good political order assume extensive freedom of choice and expression, and that such freedom must be respected and indeed protected by other individuals as well as by the healthy public body. But why is such freedom necessary at all? The answer must lie with the fallibility of human intellect: since we cannot be certain in many matters connected with human goodness and earthly well-being what the correct action may be, we must extend tolerance to persons who have different conceptions of goodness and who seek to realize them in different ways. If there were some sure standard for the moral or public good, which could be known and imposed infallibly, respect for liberty would not be necessary. But because such matters are difficult to ascertain and subject to debate, due to the nature of the human mind itself, John requires the exercise of forbearance. And this not only applies in the case of toleration in political affairs, but encompasses freedom of inquiry in the full range of philosophical and theological matters detailed above.

John himself is aware of the connection between his Academy-influenced skepticism and the necessity for a wide band of free judgment and expression. In prefacing his critical history of philosophy contained in Chapter Seven, wherein he seeks to trace the "footprints of philosophers," John explains the operative principle of the Academic School:

> If these inquiries seem to approach formal philosophy, the spirit of investigation corresponds to Academic practices rather than to the plan of a stubborn combatant, so that each is to reserve to oneself freedom of judgment in the examination of truth (*in examinationem veri suum cuique iudicium liberum reservetur*), and the authority of writers is to be considered useless whenever it is subdued by a better argument. (*Policraticus*, 7.Prologus [147–48])

The approach of the Academy requires that in all matters not settled beyond reasonable doubt it is the force of the evidence alone that should prevail. Authorities themselves should not be granted superior wisdom if a more cogent viewpoint opposes them. Likewise, the determination of what position seems most plausible or defensible *lies with the individual*. In view of his skeptical predilections, John raises the priority of individual judgment to a universal principle, not susceptible to revocation in the manner of a privilege conceded by some external authority.

That John recognized this implication of his adherence to the Academy is signaled by his statement on more than one occasion in the *Policraticus* that freedom of judgment is a *ius*, a right that pertains to human beings. Now, the history of rights language during the Middle Ages is a tangled one, much debated in present scholarship, and I cannot begin to address it here.[30] But, at minimum, the medieval understanding of *ius* entailed acknowledgment of a fixed and defensible sphere of activity whose exercise is independent of external infringement or control. This seems to be precisely what John has in mind when insisting upon the *right* of free inquiry and determination: "The Academy of the ancients bestows upon the human race the leave that each person by his right (*suo iure*) may defend whatever presents itself to him as most probable" (2.22).[31] Or, as he remarks in another passage, "It is a very ancient rule of the Academics that each person may of his own right (*suo iure*) defend that which presents itself to him as most probable" (7.6). The source of this right is surely neither political or (except indirectly) divine; it is not granted from above and therefore subject to limitation or removal. Rather, one's right to assert one's freedom to form one's own judgments apparently derives from the fallible nature of the human mind and the uncertain character of many knowledge-claims. It is, in short, a result of the human predicament.

In John's reference to the "right" of persons, then, we encounter the philosophical roots of the toleration that he advocates elsewhere in the *Policraticus*. For if we each enjoy a right to draw conclusions and construct arguments regarding those matters open to rational disagreement, then it follows that others (regardless of their status or power) likewise have a duty to respect our thoughts even if they do not endorse them. At times, John of Salisbury approaches the position embraced by another English probabilist, John Stuart Mill, seven hundred years later. In *On Liberty*, Mill had commented,

There is the greatest difference between presuming an opinion to be true because, with every opportunity for contesting it, it has not been refuted, and assuming its truth for the purpose of not permitting refutation. Complete liberty of contradicting and disproving our opinion is the very condition which justifies us in assuming its truth.[32]

In the *Policraticus*, likewise, John remarks that, regarding unsettled issues, "one is free to question and doubt, up to the point where, from a comparison of views, truth shines through as though from the clash of ideas (*quasi quadam rationum collisione*)" (7.8 [160]). Such a statement suggests that John understood very well the implications of his skeptical philosophy: the quest for truth in matters of practical as well as philosophical import demands the maintenance of openness and dissent. It is the responsibility of the wise person, not to mention the wise ruler or prelate, to uphold and defend the grounds of public debate. The realization of truth is hampered, not aided, by the suppression of divergent positions and the persecution of their adherents.

Conclusion

Of course John of Salisbury was no John Stuart Mill. Many of the issues Mill regarded as contestable would have fallen under John's rubric of those things known to be true according to faith, reason, or the senses.[33] Yet the example of John of Salisbury demonstrates that a philosophically mature defense of toleration of free thought and debate, based on a probabilistic conception of knowledge, did not have to await the dawn of the Renaissance, let alone the Enlightenment. The materials of Ciceronian Academic skepticism, deployed by an author of John's moderate intellectual temperament, afforded a theoretically cogent starting point for the maximization of intellectual liberty and the enshrined protection thereof. This should dispel any lingering suspicions that the mythical monolith of medieval Christian orthodoxy was so hegemonic as to render a principled concept of toleration unthinkable. Not only was dissent in many forms a fact of life throughout the Middle Ages, but some medieval people at least realized that the persecution of philosophical differences was a retrograde policy if one's goal was discovery of the truth.

The work of John of Salisbury thus deserves an honored place in the complex story of how ideas of tolerance and liberty came to coexist peacefully with the unifying demands of Christian religion. But it should be kept in mind that John's accomplishment is less singular than we might wish to claim. He was simply one among many people during the High and Late Middle Ages who sought to make room for reasoned discussion regarding those matters about which rational minds can and do disagree. He may have gone further than most of his near contemporaries in examining the philosophical precepts on the basis of which such toleration could be defended. But the skeptical spirit in which John conducted this enterprise was in many ways the spirit of his times.

Notes

1. See, for example, Quentin Skinner, *The Foundations of Modern Political Thought*, 2 vols. (Cambridge: Cambridge University Press, 1978), 2: 245–49 and Karl Popper, "Toleration and Intellectual Responsibility," in Susan Mendus and David Edwards, eds., *On Toleration* (Oxford: Clarendon Press, 1987), 17–18.

2. Preston King, *Toleration* (London: Allen and Unwin, 1976), 120; for the full argument, see pp. 122–31.

3. The two most prominent examples are Richard Tuck, "Scepticism and

Toleration in the Seventeenth Century," in Susan Mendus, ed., *Justifying Toleration: Conceptual and Historical Perspectives* (Cambridge: Cambridge University Press, 1988), 21–35 and Alan Charles Kors, *Atheism in France, 1650–1729*, Vol. I: *The Orthodox Sources of Disbelief* (Princeton, N.J.: Princeton University Press, 1990).

4. A brief history of the diffusion of skepticism in the pagan and early Christian worlds is provided by Charles Schmitt, *Cicero Scepticus: A Study of the Influence of the* Academica *in the Renaissance* (The Hague: Martinus Nijhoff, 1972), 5–42. Also see John Christian Laursen, *The Politics of Skepticism in the Ancients, Montaigne, Hume, and Kant* (Leiden: Brill, 1992), 14–32 and R. J. Hankinson, *The Sceptics* (London: Routledge, 1995).

5. Tuck, "Scepticism and Toleration in the Seventeenth Century," 21.

6. Schmitt, *Cicero Scepticus*, 9. For a critical examination of alleged Ockhamist skepticism, see John F. Boler, "Intuitive and Abstractive Cognition," in Norman Kretzmann, Anthony Kenny, and Jan Pinborg, eds., *The Cambridge History of Later Medieval Philosophy* (Cambridge: Cambridge University Press, 1982), 469–75.

7. See Schmitt, *Cicero Scepticus*, 36–38; Birger Munk-Olsen, "L'humanisme de Jean de Salisbury, un Ciceronien au 12e siècle," in Maurice de Gandillac and Edouard Jeauneau, eds., *Entretiens sur la Renaissance du 12ᵉ siècle* (Paris: Mouton, 1968), 53–83; and Edouard Jeauneau, "Jean de Salisbury et la lecture des philosophes," in Michael J. Wilks, ed., *The World of John of Salisbury* (London: Blackwell, 1984), 77–108.

8. Cary J. Nederman, "Liberty and Toleration: Freedom of Conscience in Medieval Political Thought," *Vital Nexus* 1 (July 1995): 44–49.

9. Cary J. Nederman, "The Aristotelian Doctrine of the Mean and John of Salisbury's Concept of Liberty," *Vivarium* 24 (1986): 128–42.

10. John of Salisbury, *Policraticus*, ed. C. C. J. Webb, 2 vols. (1909; reprinted New York: Arno Press, 1979), 7.25 (pp. 176–77). The Webb edition will soon be replaced with one by K. S. B. Keats-Rohan, the first volume of which has now appeared (Turnhout: Brepols, 1993). Unfortunately, since virtually all the citations from the *Policraticus* in the present paper are from its later books, I have been compelled to use Webb's edition. Translations throughout are my own, sometimes derived from my published partial translation of the *Policraticus* (Cambridge: Cambridge University Press, 1990), in which case I have given a page reference parenthetically.

11. Coincidentally, he makes the same charge in his letters against Thomas Beckett; see Cary J. Nederman, "Aristotelian Ethics and John of Salisbury's Letters," *Viator* 18 (1987): 171–72.

12. A position he rejects explicitly at *Policraticus* 8.9 when he attacks the Roman tribune who once proclaimed in a speech that there is no value to "liberty if it is not permitted to those who desire to ruin themselves by luxury." Such "liberty" would have been regarded by John to be instead "license"; see Nederman, "The Aristotelian Doctrine of the Mean and John of Salisbury's Concept of Liberty," 139.

13. For a summary of these criticisms, see Cary J. Nederman and Catherine Campbell, "Priests, Kings and Tyrants: Spiritual and Temporal Power in John of Salisbury's *Policraticus*," *Speculum* 66 (July 1991): 579–80, 584–86.

14. For a full appraisal of John's version of the organic metaphor, see Tilman Struve, "The Importance of the Organism in the Political Theory of John of Salisbury," in Wilks, ed., *The World of John of Salisbury*, 303–17 and Cary J. Nederman, "The Physiological Significance of the Organic Metaphor in John of Salisbury's *Policraticus*," *History of Political Thought* 8 (Summer 1987): 21–23.

15. John compares the priesthood to the soul, which he does not count among the "parts" of the body strictly speaking. Hence the political body is, narrowly speaking, a secular organism.

16. See Paul Edward Dutton, "*Illustre civitatis et populi exemplum*: Plato's *Timaeus* and the Transmission from Calcidius to the End of the Twelfth Century of a Tripartite Scheme of Society," *Mediaeval Studies* 45 (1983): 79–119.

17. On this point, see Gordon J. Schochet, "John Locke and Religious Toleration," in Lois G. Schwoerer, ed., *The Revolution of 1688–1689: Changing Perspectives* (Cambridge: Cambridge University Press, 1992), 150–51 and Hans R. Guggisberg, "The Defense of Religious Toleration and Religious Liberty in Early Modern Europe: Arguments, Pressures, and Some Consequences," *History of European Ideas* 4 (1983): 36.

18. Ibid., 37.

19. On the details of Cicero's teachings in these works, see Paul MacKendrick, *The Philosophical Books of Cicero* (London: Duckworth, 1989), 114–30, 169–84. Medieval knowledge of the works containing Cicero's skepticism is examined by Schmitt, *Cicero Scepticus*, 33–42 and Mary A. Rouse and Richard H. Rouse, "The Medieval Circulation of Cicero's 'Posterior Academics' and the *De finibus bonorum et malorum*," in *Authentic Witnesses: Approaches to Medieval Texts and Manuscripts* (Notre Dame, Ind.: University of Notre Dame Press, 1991), 61–98.

20. In addition to MacKendrick's work cited in note 40, see Olof Gignon, "Cicero un die griechische Philosophie," in Hildegard Temporini, ed., *Aufsteig und Niedergang der Römischen Welt*, I (*Von den Anfängen Roms bis zum Ausgang der Republik*) (Berlin: Walter de Gruyter, 1973), 4: 226–61; Neal Wood, *Cicero's Social and Political Thought* (Berkeley: University of California Press, 1988), 58–61; Woldemar Görler, "Silencing the Troublemaker: *De legibus* I.39 and the Continuity of Cicero's Scepticism," in J. G. F. Powell, ed., *Cicero the Philosopher* (Oxford: Clarendon Press, 1995), 85–114; and John Glucker, "*Probabile, Veri Simile*, and Related Terms," in ibid., 115–44.

21. Cicero, *De natura deorum*, ed. Harris Rackham (London: Heinemann, 1933), I.l.

22. Cicero, *Academica*, ed. Harris Rackham (London: Heinemann, 1933), II.76–98.

23. Rodney M. Thomson, "What is the *Entheticus*?" in Wilks, ed., *The World of John of Salisbury*, 300; Jan van Laarhoven, ed., *John of Salisbury's Entheticus Maior and Minor*, 3 vols. (Leiden: Brill, 1987), 1: 50–51; Cary J. Nederman and Arlene Feldwick, "To the Court and Back Again: The Origins and Dating of the *Entheticus de Dogmate Philosophorum* of John of Salisbury," *Journal of Medieval and Renaissance Studies* 21 (Spring 1991): 129–45.

24. Schmitt, *Cicero Scepticus*, 37–38.

25. In addition to articles cited in notes 9 and 11 above, see Cary J. Nederman, "Knowledge, Virtue and the Path to Wisdom: The Unexamined Aristotelianism of John of Salisbury's *Metalogicon*," *Mediaeval Studies* 51 (1989): 268–86.

26. John of Salisbury, *Metalogicon*, ed., J. B. Hall and K. S. B. Keats-Rohan (Turnhout: Brepols, 1991), Prologus; see also 2.20, 4.7.

27. *Policraticus*, Prologus (7); see also 2.22, 7.Prologus (148), and 7.2 (152).

28. For a shorter list in the same vein, see Prologus (7).

29. St. Augustine, *Contra Academicos*, III.4.30.

30. For a sample of the debate, see Richard Tuck, *Natural Rights Theories: Their Origin and Development* (Cambridge: Cambridge University Press, 1979) and Brian Tierney, "Origins of Natural Rights Language: Texts and Contexts, 1150–1250," *History of Political Thought* 10 (1989): 615–46.

31. Interestingly, immediately following this statement, John refers to "Paripateticus Palatinus," that is, Peter Abelard, for an example of how logical probability poses important issues of individual judgment. John, who studied with Abelard at Paris, may well have taken his thought as a model for his own belief in intellectual freedom and forbearance. See the paper by Constant Mews in the present volume for an examination of Abelard's ideas about toleration and free intellectual inquiry.

32. John Stuart Mill, *On Liberty*, ed. E. Rapaport (Indianapolis: Hackett, 1978), 18.

33. John would seem susceptible to Mill's somewhat scathing dismissal: "Strange it is that men should admit the validity of the arguments for free discussion, but object to their being 'pushed to the extreme'. . . . Strange that they should imagine that they are not assuming infallibility when they acknowledge that there should be free discussion of all subjects which can possibly be *doubtful*, but think that some particular principle or doctrine should be forbidden to be questioned because it is so *certain*, that is, because *they are certain* that it is certain" (*On Liberty*, 20).

3

Ha-Me'iri's Theory of Religious Toleration

Gary Remer

GENERAL STUDIES OF THE HISTORY of religious toleration, like William K. Jordan's *The Development of Religious Toleration in England*, Joseph Lecler's *Toleration and the Reformation*, and Henry Kamen's *The Rise of Toleration*, have almost uniformly examined only the ideas of Christian advocates of toleration.[1] Consequently, factors that have been specifically significant to the development of Christian theories of toleration, such as "the division between church and state" or "liberty of conscience," have been widely accepted as if naturally linked to generic "toleration."[2] Although the Christianization of "toleration" is understandable—as the historical development of religious toleration in the West was promoted, primarily, by and for Christians—the result is that non-Christian justifications of toleration have been overlooked. For example, the analysis of Jewish contributions to religious toleration have largely been limited to Baruch Spinoza's *Tractatus Theologico-Politicus* (1670) and Moses Mendelssohn's *Jerusalem* (1783), works whose ideas, arguably, derive less from Jewish sources than from the dominant philosophies of the period.[3] By contrast, the Halakhic (Jewish legal) defense of religious toleration contained in the writings of Menaḥem ben Solomon Ha-Me'iri (1249–1316), Provençal scholar and commentator of the Talmud, is virtually unknown among scholars interested in the general history of religious toleration.[4]

In this chapter, I examine Ha-Me'iri's theory of religious toleration. I demonstrate that a uniquely Jewish theory of religious toleration was developed during the Middle Ages. In addition, I also show what it means to speak of a Jewish, as opposed to a Christian, theory of religious toleration. In the section entitled "Toward a Conception of a Jewish Theory of Religious Toleration," I explore some of the elements that distinguish a Jewish theory of religious toleration from its Christian counterpart. I argue that "toleration" must be understood contextually, through the interplay of the religion's specific assumptions and historical environment. Then, in the section entitled "Ha-Me'iri: The Status of Contemporary Gentile Religions," I examine the substance that forms the basis of Ha-Me'iri's theory of toleration: his Halakhic analysis of the Talmudic regulations and prohibitions concerning idolaters. Here I explicate the Jewish legal concepts Ha-Me'iri used, adapted, and developed to distinguish between the gentiles of the past, to whom the Talmudic restrictions applied, and the present-day gentiles, whose Halakhic position was superior to that of the ancient gentiles. I also contrast Ha-Me'iri's view of the Halakhic status of gentiles with the views of his rabbinic contemporaries. Finally, in the conclusion, entitled "Ha-Me'iri's Halakhic Innovations as a Theory of Toleration," I suggest that, when taken together, Ha-Me'iri's Halakhic innovations constitute a theory of religious toleration. Although these innovations had immediate practical implications, which Ha-Me'iri acknowledged, their greater importance, for toleration, lies in the new attitude toward gentiles that they represent.

Toward a Conception of a Jewish Theory of Religious Toleration

What does it mean to speak of a Jewish theory of religious toleration? Because toleration is defined contextually, to understand the meaning of Jewish toleration would require an inquiry into the context of Jewish ideas and historical events. The contextual basis of toleration becomes clearer by first looking at the better-known Christian example, in which the meaning of toleration is shaped, partly, by Christianity's religious assumptions. For example, Christianity's emphasis on doctrine over practice is important for the development of its theory of religious toleration. The religious crime par excellence in Christianity is heresy, which is defined as doctrinal deviation.[5] Since they still claimed to be Christians, heretics were viewed as an insidious, corrupting force within the body of the faithful who should be exterminated.[6] In early Christianity, heretics differed from the orthodox, primarily, in their beliefs about the nature of the Trinity.[7] Likewise, it was doctrine again that, fundamentally, divided Roman Catholics from Protestants and Protestants from each other: Luther split with the Catholic Church over "free will" and the efficacy of good works, and Protestants disagreed with Catholics and among themselves about the nature of the bread and wine in the Eucharist. As Christian religious intolerance focused on the persecution of the doctrinally deviant, Christian toleration emphasized the acceptance of heterodoxy. The influence of this conception of toleration can even be found in the U.S. Supreme Court's interpretation of the First Amendment's free exercise of religion clause. Rejecting the Mormon claim that polygamy was a religious duty, the Court declared in *Reynolds v. U.S.* that "Congress was deprived of all legislative power over mere opinion, but was left free to reach actions. . . ."[8] The Court reflects here the Christian assumption that religious toleration means greater protection of religious beliefs than of religious practices.

Christian toleration is shaped by other characteristically Christian assumptions. For example, *"Nulla salus extra Ecclesiam"* ("there is no salvation outside the Church") is a principle that was accepted by the authorities of the ancient and medieval Roman Catholic Church and, during the Reformation, by Protestants and Catholics alike.[9] Because those outside the Church are damned, Christians have seen it as their responsibility to convert the whole world to Christianity. And what if non-Christians refuse to "see the light"? Although Christian orthodoxy directed the full force of persecution against Christian heretics or apostates, it did not abjure coercion against those who were never Christians. The consequence of believing a people to be damned, as Jean-Jacques Rousseau observed, is that "they must absolutely be either brought into the faith or tormented."[10] St. Thomas Aquinas, in refusing toleration to most non-Christians, partially confirms Rousseau's observation. According to Aquinas, "Unbelievers although they sin by their rites may be tolerated either because a greater good may come of it or some evil may be avoided." Such is the case, he explains, with the Jews, who display to Christians the "rites which once prefigured the true faith." In contrast, "the rites of other unbelievers that have no truth or usefulness in them are not to be tolerated unless to avoid some evil."[11] Moreover, the theoretical toleration of the Jews did not prevent Church leaders, like Pope Innocent III, from justifying discrimination against the Jews, "the sons of crucifiers, against whom His blood still cries out to the ears of the Father." Nor did the principle of toleration prevent some Christian jurists from defending the freedom of rulers to expel Jews at will: "While no private person is entitled to molest them, a prince is allowed to do so, because since the death of Christ they have become our slaves. . . . If he is entitled to sell them, how much more should he be able to expel them!"[12]

Another distinctly Christian concept is the division between church and state. Since Christ, two levels of authority were recognized on earth: a temporal authority, with its powers of compulsion against those who commit social wrongs; and a spiritual authority, which is provided with spiritual means only, to lead humankind to salvation. Each of these institutions receives its authority from God, and, therefore, Christians are obligated to obey both. In Christ's words, "Render therefore unto Caesar the things which are Caesar's; and unto God the things which are God's" (Matt. 22:21). The religious duty to obey magistrates applied even to pagan states, since all magistrates receive their authority from God (Romans 13:1).[13] After Christianity became the sole official religion of the Roman Empire and pagan worship was banned, the state and church were viewed as functional parts of a greater *Respublica christiana*. Nevertheless, the dualism of church and state still continued, and this dualism profoundly affected the evolution of Christian toleration. It is doubtful that Locke and Jefferson could have developed their arguments for religious liberty without the antecedent Christian assumptions about church and state. The liberal argument that membership in the state is distinct from membership in the church and, therefore, that the state should not persecute its citizens for their religious beliefs, has its roots in the Christian theological tradition.

The interplay of a religion's concepts and historical circumstances determines the character of that religion's toleration. Therefore the meaning of Christian toleration is determined not only by Christianity's religious assumptions, but also by its historical conditions. And because historical conditions have varied over time, the meaning of Christian toleration likewise has changed. For example, before Christians acquired the coercive apparatus of the Roman state, toleration would have referred to the willingness of Christian churches to accept dissenting persons or groups into their communities; excommunication was the full extent of intolerance available at that point. By contrast, after the Roman Empire became Christian, toleration would have concerned refraining from physical compulsion. The historical specificity of toleration can again be seen in the post-Reformation period. One kind of toleration can be found in the Peace of Augsburg (1555), which gave German princes the right to decide the religion of their territories—so long as it was either Lutheran or Catholic. Although there could only be one religion within each territory and dissenters would have to leave or conform, the Peace of Augsburg implicitly rejected the previous proposition, accepted by Catholics and Lutherans, that heretics could not be tolerated anywhere. Another type of toleration can be seen in the Renaissance humanists' call for a broader, more comprehensive church. Sixteenth- and seventeenth-century humanists argued that religious dissenters who disagree on nonessentials, but accept the fundamentals of faith, should be allowed to retain their differences and remain within the church. This strategy, they hoped, would reunite Christians divided by the Reformation.[14] In late seventeenth-century England, however, the humanists' proposal was termed "comprehension," because it sought to include or "comprehend" Nonconformists within the Established church. At that time, "toleration," as opposed to "comprehension," meant the state's toleration of Christian denominations outside the Established church.

As in the Christian case, the meaning of Jewish religious toleration depends on the relationship between religious assumptions and historical circumstances. The differences between Jewish and Christian religious assumptions point up the distinctness of their theories of toleration. For example, in contrast to Christianity, Judaism emphasizes practice over doctrine, or what is sometimes referred to as orthopraxy over orthodoxy.[15] The anonymous author of the *Sefer Ha-Ḥinukh* (composed c. 1307) voices this principle when he states that "the heart is drawn by actions" and not vice versa.[16] Rabbi Yehuda Ha-Levi likewise emphasizes actions in his *Sefer Ha-Kozari* (c. 1140). In this classic of medieval Jewish philosophy, the pagan king of the Khazars is impelled to search for the true religion because of a recurring dream in which he is told by an angel: "Your way of thinking [or 'intention'] is pleasing in God's eyes, but your way of acting is not."[17] Ha-Levi's point is that a proper philosophy or good intentions are insufficient. Therefore, the Khazar king engages an Aristotelian philosopher, a Christian, a Muslim, and a Jew in philosophical dialogue, to compare their religions. According to Ha-Levi, the king, convinced of Judaism's truth, ultimately converts to Judaism, along with many of his Khazar subjects.

This Jewish stress on action shapes the meaning of toleration within Judaism. For Judaism, toleration relates more to forbidden actions than to heretical ideas. Halakha rarely sanctions the use of force against persons or groups because of their beliefs per se, but because of their actions. Thus for Judaism idolatry, not heresy, is the exemplar of religious treason. The sin of the "idolater" is the *act* of worshiping false gods. The heretic, by contrast, *believes* deviant doctrines. And while Halakha does not ignore the gravity of the heretic's sin, the continual lack of consensus about defining the Jewish articles of faith ensured that "heresy" would remain more a theoretical category than an actually punishable offense.[18] Historically, Jews have agreed about the performance of *mitzvot*, the divine commandments, but have disagreed about dogmas. Thus Jews have universally accepted their biblical credo, the Shema ("Hear, O Israel, the Lord our God, the Lord is One"[Deuteronomy 6:4]), as a rejection of idolatry, yet they have clashed on the theological meaning of the verse: the "One" of the medieval rationalist Maimonides (1135–1204) and the "One" of the sixteenth-century Kabbalist Isaac Luria (1534–1572) are incompatible.[19] Similarly, although Maimonides maintains that monotheism without a belief in divine incorporeality is heresy, his contemporary, Ra'avad of Posquieres (1125–1198), dissents: "Why does [Maimonides] call such a person a heretic, when there have been greater and better men than he who followed this opinion because of what they saw in Scripture?"[20]

Unlike Christianity, Jewish law does not deny salvation to those outside its religion and does not aspire to the conversion of all persons. Thus Maimonides writes: "Anyone who accepts the seven precepts [of the Noahide laws, to which gentiles are expected to adhere[21]] and is careful to follow them—this person is a righteous gentile and has a portion in the world-to-come."[22] Halakha does not demand, or permit, the persecution of gentiles for the "sin" of not being Jewish. The meaning of Jewish "toleration" vis-à-vis gentiles, therefore, is more expansive than that of Christian toleration in relation to non-Christians.

Judaism also differs from Christianity in its unity of religious and secular realms. Throughout the Middle Ages and beyond, however, this difference had little impact on the development of toleration in the two religions. Although the Christian division between church and state would eventually develop into a genuine separation of realms that would allow for religious toleration, before the seventeenth century it was a distinction without real meaning for toleration, since church and state worked together to punish religious dissenters.[23] In contrast, Judaism, despite its unity of realms, was not as actively intolerant as Christianity. It *could not* be, because Jews, since the destruction of the Second Commonwealth in 70 C.E., lacked the coercive apparatus of the state that Christianity had.[24] This irony raises the question of historical conditions. The meaning of toleration in Judaism depends on the institutional means available to the community. The most extreme tool of coercion against religious dissenters that was available to medieval Jewry was communal excommunication,[25] and the Jewish community had no legitimate means of coercion to punish gentiles for religious crimes.[26] Nevertheless, Jewish intolerance of idolatrous gentiles could exist. In the next section, I discuss the forms this intolerance could take and Ha-Me'iri's approach to dealing with these forms of intolerance.

Ha-Me'iri: The Status of Contemporary Gentile Religions

Rabbi Menahem Ha-Me'iri's reputation as one of the greatest Jewish scholars of his period finds support in the comprehensive scope of his works on Halakha and the Talmud, biblical interpretation, customs, ethics, and philosophy. In *Bet Ha-Behirah* (written between 1287 and 1300), his monumental exposition of the Talmud, Ha-Me'iri combines a broad review of German, French, Provençal, Catalonian, and Spanish rabbinic opinions with his own Halakhic determinations. In addition, Ha-Me'iri displays, in *Bet Ha-Behirah* and other works, a profound knowledge of philosophy, both Jewish and Aristotelian, that is reminiscent of Maimonides. Ha-Me'iri's similarity to Maimonides is more than coincidental. Ha-Me'iri is viewed as a primary exponent of the Maimonidean tradition, and he adheres to Maimonides's philosophical rationalism in his views of man's purpose, God, the afterlife, prophecy, and the meaning of the divine commandments.[27]

Despite Ha-Me'iri's fidelity to the Maimonidean tradition, he broke with his intellectual progenitor on the status of non-Jewish religions. For Maimonides, non-Jewish faiths lacked legitimacy as bona fide religions. Christianity, according to Maimonides, was clearly idolatrous, and Islam, while not idolatrous, was, nevertheless, a false religion.[28] Maimonides believed that Judaism was the sole true religion because it alone was the product of divine revelation. Ha-Me'iri, by contrast, accorded gentile faiths religious legitimacy. Ha-Me'iri could maintain this position because he, unlike Maimonides, did not define the legitimacy of religions solely by their origins in revelation. As Judaism contains within it practical and doctrinal elements that could have developed without prophecy or revelation, other religions could have developed along these lines as well. Of course, Ha-Me'iri explains, Judaism stands above all other religions because "our perfect Torah has come to perfect us by all kinds of perfections."[29]

This difference between Maimonides and Ha-Me'iri is not simply theoretical; it has practical implications, particularly in the case of Christianity. If a religion is considered idolatrous, then the Talmudic-based, discriminatory rules governing commercial relations with, and the legal status of, idolaters take effect. The classic example of these rules is the prohibition on conducting business with idolaters on their holidays. The prohibition's rationale is that gentiles will be more likely to thank their gods on festivals for any profits earned, and Jews will be indirectly responsible for these acts of idolatry.[30] Maimonides believes that Christianity, as an idolatrous religion, is subject to these regulations and that Jews are, therefore, forbidden to engage in business on Sundays, as well as on other Christian holidays.[31] Ha-Me'iri, however, denies that these regulations apply to Christians.

Ha-Me'iri, however, was not the only Halakhic scholar to deny the contemporary relevance of the Talmudic rules against idolaters. There existed a longstanding contradiction between the Halakhic requirements and the accepted practice of medieval Jewish communities.[32] As the extant rabbinic literature of the Middle Ages demonstrates, the Jews of Germany and France ignored the Talmudic prohibition and engaged in business as usual with gentiles on Christian holy days. Their reason for doing so was pragmatic: they needed to engage in commerce to earn a livelihood. Although it was painless enough for Maimonides, living in a predominately Islamic society, to accept these restrictions,[33] consenting to these restrictions in Christian countries would have been burdensome. Therefore the rabbis of predominately Christian countries felt obligated to justify popular practice and explain why the Talmudic law did not apply. In medieval Germany, Halakhic explanations varied. It was argued by some rabbis (Ra'avan, Rabbi Isaac Or-Zarua) that most contemporary gentiles practice their religion as a kind of prejudice accepted from their forefathers, without any genuine feeling or understanding.[34] Another rabbi (Rashi) argued that refusing to conduct business with Christians on their festivals may engender hostility against the Jews, poisoning the good social relations that Jewish communities needed for their survival. Finally, one rabbi (Rabbenu Tam) maintained that the original Talmudic regulation only pertained to commerce in animals and other foods that would themselves be offered in idolatrous services.[35]

Although Ha-Me'iri was only one of a number of medieval rabbis to justify the popular disregard for Halakhic prohibitions regarding gentiles, he was unique in presenting a principled argument for the legitimacy of contemporary gentile religions. As Jacob Katz argues, the other rabbinic explanations were of an ad hoc nature. They were intended to reconcile the contradiction between Halakhic theory and popular practice, but they were not concerned with removing the stigma of idolatry from Christianity. "The first and only one in the Middle Ages whose Halakhic distinction between idolatry and contemporary religions is based on a principled theological conception is Rabbi Menaḥem Ha-Me'iri."[36] Like his peers, Ha-Me'iri's justification of practice is based on the Halakhic tradition; yet he expands this tradition by creating new concepts to distinguish present-day religions from their idolatrous forerunners. This mixture of tradition and innovation can be seen in his explication of the Talmudic rules relating to idolaters.

For purposes of analyzing Ha-Me'iri's views, Moshe Halbertal divides the Halakha governing gentiles into three areas.[37] The first area comprises prohibitions against commerce with gentiles because such contacts may, indirectly, support idolatrous rituals or may enable Jews to benefit from idol worship. Ha-Me'iri contends that these rules no longer apply to today's gentiles; they only applied to the earlier, idolatrous nations. The Talmudic prohibitions in this first area are: the above-discussed ban on trading with idolaters on their holidays;[38] the prohibition against trading with gentiles when the profits are taxed to support idolatrous rituals;[39] the prohibition against selling to gentiles materials used in idolatrous rituals, like incense;[40] the ban on renting a house to gentiles, lest they bring idolatry into it;[41] the prohibition against benefiting from the wine of gentiles as a safeguard against benefiting from wine actually used in idolatry;[42] and the prohibition against oversociability with gentiles.[43]

The second area of laws governing gentiles concerns the gentile's Halakhic rights and obligations. According to the Talmud, the legal and personal status of gentiles is inferior to that of Jews.[44] For example, gentiles are obligated to compensate Jews fully for any damage their animals cause to Jewish property; Jews, however, are exempted from compensating gentiles for the same type of damages. In this case, and others in this second area of laws, Ha-Me'iri equates the Halakhic position of contemporary gentiles with Jews.[45] Other laws in which the Talmud vests Jews with superior legal status include the obligation to return lost property;[46] the obligation to save lives;[47] the prohibition against overcharging;[48] punishment for murder;[49] permission to break the Sabbath laws in cases where life is endangered;[50] permission to teach children and to lodge animals;[51] and permission to sell weapons.[52] Finally, according to the Talmud, it is forbidden to "show [idolaters] grace," which includes praising any of their qualities or giving them presents. As with the previous laws, Ha-Me'iri limits this prohibition to the ancient idolaters, excluding present-day gentiles.[53]

The third area of laws governing gentiles consists of laws intended to hinder intermarriage. These laws sometimes achieve their goal by indirectly restricting the social relations between Jews and gentiles by regulations on food and drink: forbidding Jews to eat food (made with kosher ingredients, but) baked by non-Jews; or prohibiting Jews to drink the wine of non-Jews. Here Ha-Me'iri leaves all the prohibitions intact and does not distinguish between ancient idolaters and the gentiles of his own day.[54] Because Ha-Me'iri's position in these laws is the same as that of his contemporaries, this third area of laws will not be discussed further.

In analyzing Ha-Me'iri's language in the first two areas of law, Halbertal finds that Ha-Me'iri uses different terms and concepts in each of the areas. In the first area, Ha-Me'iri relies on the traditional Halakhic distinction between idolatry and non-idolatry. In ancient times, gentile worship was idolatrous, and therefore the Talmud prohibited trade with gentiles that might indirectly support idolatry; in his own period, gentiles were no longer idolatrous, and, therefore, Ha-Me'iri maintained that those Talmudic regulations were no longer in effect.[55] Ha-Me'iri upheld this position, even though his own version of the Talmud stated that Christians were idolaters. He explained away this offending passage as referring not to Christians but to ancient Babylonian sun worshipers from the times of Nebuchadnezzar.[56]

In the second area of law, concerning the gentiles' Halakhic rights and duties, Ha-Me'iri coins a new set of terms: *"umot ha-gedurot be-dar'khey ha-datot"* (nations bound by the ways of religion) and *"umot she-enan gedurot be-dar'khey ha-datot"* (nations not restricted by the ways of religion); the former are not discriminated against by Halakha, while the latter are.[57] The closest traditional Halakhic analogue is the *"ger toshav"* (resident alien), a gentile who has accepted the seven Noahide laws.[58] Ha-Me'iri, however, would have had technical reasons to reject *"ger toshav"* for a new Halakhic concept. According to Maimonides, "a *ger toshav* is only accepted when the Jubilee [Leviticus 25:10] is in effect." But the Jubilee, a year occurring at the end of a fifty-year cycle, when slaves go free and the land is returned to its original owners, has long ceased to be practiced.[59] In addition, the law of *ger toshav*, even when in effect, requires the individual gentile to obligate himself to observe the Noahide laws.[60] Thus a gentile was not presumed to be a *ger toshav* unless there was specific knowledge of the gentile's acceptance of the Noahide Laws. Ha-Me'iri, however, wanted a Halakhic concept that referred not to the individual but to the community, and where belonging to the community was prima facie evidence of its members' commitment to the Noahide laws.[61] Ha-Me'iri met these criteria with his neologism, "nations bound by the ways of religion."

Ha-Me'iri's distinction between the two areas of law is plausible. Because the first area deals with a Jew's indirect support for idolatry, the relevant question is whether the gentile merchant's religion is idolatrous or not. Therefore Ha-Me'iri speaks in terms of idolatry and non-idolatry and determines that Christianity is non-idolatrous. (A Halakhic consensus already existed about Islam, which Maimonides had previously declared to be non-idolatrous.) The second area, by contrast, concerns a non-Jew's Halakhic rights and obligations. Because this area of law treats such issues as whether a gentile can be sold weapons or whether he can be entrusted with a Jew's children, or even animals, the question for Ha-Me'iri is whether or not the gentile belongs to a moral, lawful religion (nation). In this Halakhic domain, Ha-Me'iri wishes to draw a line between "law-abiding nations and lawless nations—between barbarity and civilization."[62] Therefore Ha-Me'iri speaks here not of "non-idolatrous" and "idolatrous nations" per se, but of "nations bound" and "nations unrestricted by the ways of religion," and he finds that contemporary gentile peoples adhere to law and morality, or at least aspire to.

Notwithstanding his linguistic distinctions, Ha-Me'iri links the "nations bound by the ways of religion" to "non-idolatrous religions." For Ha-Me'iri, morality presupposes belief in God and its corollary, the renunciation of idolatry. Thus, he writes, all those "who possess no religion and do not yield to the fear of the divine, but offer incense to the heavenly hosts and worship idols, do not care about any sin."[63] Idolaters, to Ha-Me'iri's mind, lack any conception of divine reward and punishment; therefore they cannot be considered "bound by the ways of religion."[64] Ha-Me'iri's conviction that belief in God/rejection of idolatry is a prerequisite to being a "nation bound by the ways of religion" is less theological than practical. He is not overly discriminating about the religion's metaphysical beliefs. For example, he does not require that the religions of his day adhere to a strict unitary conception of God. If he had, Christianity would have failed. Instead, gentile religions had to recognize a transcendental, incorporeal deity, which holds humanity accountable for its actions. Without such a conception of God, people could not be trusted to act morally.[65] The result of this theological laxity is that Ha-Me'iri granted Christianity greater legitimacy than did any of his contemporaries. Nevertheless, in subordinating theology to morality Ha-Me'iri does not depart from the Jewish norms; rather, he reflects the earlier-stated principle that Judaism emphasizes practice over doctrine.

Conclusion: Ha-Me'iri's Halakhic Innovations as a Theory of Toleration

It is almost impossible to speak of Jewish religious toleration of deviant Jews during the Middle Ages and the centuries following. Historically, Jewish law has shown little tolerance of Halakhic deviancy by Jews.[66] Idolatry by Jews, according to Halakha, is a capital offense, and heretics, when autonomous Jewish communities existed, could be banned by their communities. That these or other punishments were rarely carried out was due more to historical circumstances—the lack of Jewish sovereignty and power, divisions within the Jewish community, the need to protect the integrity of the community against a hostile environment, and so on—than to any commitment to toleration. By contrast, the question of tolerating gentiles was different; Halakha accepts that gentiles can attain salvation without converting to Judaism. Therefore, if gentiles satisfy the minimal Halakhic demands made on them—the Noahide laws—they are to be tolerated. Through the ages, however, most gentiles were not viewed as meeting Halakha's minimal requirements because their religions, including Christianity, were characterized as idolatrous. While they could not be persecuted so long as Jews lacked sovereignty in the Holy Land, there were Jewish laws that restricted commerce with them and accorded them an inferior Halakhic status because of their perceived idolatry-cum-barbarism. Although these laws did not involve violence, as did Christian laws against heretics, they were still intolerant. They denied non-Jews legitimacy as full, or at least trustworthy, persons, and they equated contemporary gentile religions with the ancient Near Eastern cults, which were to be shunned, if not extirpated. Most of these prohibitions and discriminatory rules were ignored in practice, and this practice was widely justified by different medieval rabbis. But Ha-Me'iri's justification differs from those of his contemporaries because it was principled.

Unlike other rabbinic justifications, Ha-Me'iri's was not stated narrowly, designed to concede the minimum. The other Halakhic authorities permitted commerce with Christians on their festivals because it was prudent or because of a technical argument about the specific items the Talmud included in its prohibition against trade. Some authorities even came as close as suggesting that Christians were not idolaters because of their religious ignorance. But none of these arguments stated, as did Ha-Me'iri, that Christianity was not idolatry. By contrast, Ha-Me'iri's justification was stated as a broad principle: there is a line between the idolatry, lawlessness, and immorality of the ancient religions, and the belief in God, law-abidingness, and morality of contemporary religions.

Consistent with my claim that Jewish toleration relates to action, Ha-Me'iri's arguments had practical consequences. For example, Ha-Me'iri abandoned the accepted Talmudic law that Jews may rightfully possess property received through a gentile's loss or error—so long as this acquisition did not lead to a desecration of God's name. In these matters, Ha-Me'iri equates "the nations bound by the ways of religion" to Jews. Thus, he writes: "We do not favor ourselves in legal cases."[67] Another instance in which Ha-Me'iri broke with accepted practice is the Halakha of overcharging. Maimonides confirms the Halakhic status quo when he writes that the law of overcharging does not apply to gentiles because the Torah limits this law to "brothers" (Leviticus 25:14), and the gentile is not considered a brother to the Jew.[68] Ha-Me'iri, however, maintains that it is forbidden to overcharge "anyone who is bound by the religious ways" because this person, unlike the gentile idolater, is a brother to the Jew.[69] Finally, Ha-Me'iri's most radical departure from conventional Halakha is in the case of Jews who forsake their religion for another. According to the Talmud, Jewish apostates can be killed.[70] Ha-Me'iri, however, interprets "apostates" as meaning Jews who have abandoned all religion, not Jews who have formally converted to another religion. "An apostate to idolatry," Ha-Me'iri writes, "is in the category of heretics [who can be physically harmed]." But this can be said only of

those for whom the name "Israel" can still be applied, because [such a person] who frees himself [of Judaism's laws] and desecrates the [Jewish] religion deserves the most serious punishment, for he becomes a heretic and like a person without religion. But anyone who has completely left the community and has become a member of another religion is considered by us as a member of the religion he has joined in all matters except the laws of divorce, marriage, and the like, . . . and thus my teachers ruled.[71]

Although Ha-Me'iri claims here that he was following his teachers' decisions, his ruling on Jewish apostates is sui generis in the extant Halakhic writings.[72]

The practical differences between Ha-Me'iri and his rabbinic con-

temporaries were relatively limited.[73] But these differences and the novel
Halakhic concepts on which they were based reflected a changed attitude
toward gentiles, one that emphasized the values Judaism shared with contemporary non-Jewish religions. This perception of fellowship is seen in
Ha-Me'iri's language: Ha-Me'iri sometimes refers to the gentile from the
"nations bound by the ways of religion" as a "brother," a term previously
reserved for fellow Jews.[74] This sense of brotherhood is at the root of Ha-
Me'iri's theory of religious toleration. Halbertal supports this view when
he writes that "Ha-Me'iri's religious tolerance derives from the recognition
of a religious domain common to Jews, Christians and Moslems."[75] Thus
for Ha-Me'iri the Jew who converts to Christianity still remains within
the broader communion of monotheistic faiths. Anyone who has rejected
all religion, however, stands outside the pale of civilized society and can
therefore be punished with the harshest penalties.

In grounding his theory of toleration on the brotherhood of the
monotheistic religions, Ha-Me'iri appears to foreshadow Nicholas of Cusa
(1401–1464), Marsilio Ficino (1433–1499), and Pico della Mirandola (1463–
1494), who base their Christian theories of toleration on the harmony of
Christianity, Judaism, and Islam.[76] The similarities between Ha-Me'iri and
the Christian thinkers, however, are largely superficial. For Cusa, Ficino,
and Mirandola, the harmony of faiths is found in the common metaphysical truths shared by the different religions. As Nicholas of Cusa writes:
" 'This Good, between ourselves, we call God, when we speak of it. As
to the ways of approaching it, Moses described one. . . . This way Christ
illuminated and perfected. . . . And it is this same way which Moham-
med tried to make more accessible to all.' "[77] For Ha-Me'iri, in contrast,
the fellowship of religions is not based on the truths shared by the three
monotheistic faiths, but on the common functional role the monotheistic
religions fulfill in creating peaceful and orderly societies. If Ha-Me'iri had
tried to build a bridge between Judaism and the other religions based on
their common truths, he would have undoubtedly failed.[78] Christianity, in
particular, with its doctrines about the Incarnation and Trinity, would have
remained an alien, "idolatrous" religion. Ha-Me'iri could find common
ground with Christianity because he minimized the particulars of Christian theology, emphasizing instead its more practical side. Although the
Christian conception of the divinity contains some errors, from the Jewish perspective, Christians, like Jews, saw God as omnipotent, omniscient,
and punishing the bad and rewarding the good. These religious beliefs,

Ha-Me'iri thought, were sufficient to forge and sustain ethical societies and moral institutions.

I would like to thank Rabbi Binyamin Tabory and Professor Moshe Halbertal for their helpful comments.

Notes

1. William K. Jordan, *The Development of Religious Toleration in England*, 4 vols. (London: Allen and Unwin, 1932–1940; reprint Gloucester, Mass.: Peter Smith, 1965); Joseph Lecler, *Toleration and the Reformation*, trans. T. L. Westow, 2 vols. (New York: Association Press, 1960); Henry Kamen, *The Rise of Toleration* (London: World University Library, 1967). The same Christian focus is also found in edited collections of essays. For example, of the twenty-nine substantive chapters in *Persecution and Toleration*, ed. William Eugene Shiels (Oxford: Blackwell, 1984), only three focus on non-Christian cases of toleration and persecution: the classical pagans, the nineteenth-century Yoruba of western Africa, and the Soviet Union, 1945–1964.

2. See, for example, John Rawls, *A Theory of Justice* (Cambridge, Mass.: Harvard University Press, 1971), 221–26; David A. J. Richards, *Toleration and the Constitution* (New York: Oxford University Press, 1986), 67–68, 133–36.

3. Spinoza was excommunicated by the Jewish community of Amsterdam for his heterodoxy (1656). As for Mendelssohn, in the first part of *Jerusalem*, where he develops his general case for religious toleration, he "spoke as a philosopher of the Enlightenment, very much in the spirit of John Locke." Michael A. Meyer, *The Origins of the Modern Jew: Jewish Identity and European Culture in Germany, 1749–1824* (Detroit: Wayne State University Press, 1967), 50.

4. Discussions of Ha-Me'iri's religious toleration have mostly appeared in Hebrew-language essays, addressed to scholars of Jewish studies.

5. For a discussion of the meaning of heresy in Christianity, see Edward Peters, ed., *Heresy and Authority in Medieval Europe: Documents in Translation* (Philadelphia: University of Pennsylvania Press, 1980), chapter 1.

6. Comparing heresy to forgery, which was then a capital offense, St. Thomas Aquinas argued that the heretic's crime was worse than the forger's: "It is, indeed, far more serious to pervert the faith which ensures the life of the soul than to counterfeit money which is only necessary for our temporal needs." *Summa theologiae*, II-II, q. 11, a. 3.

7. For Docetism Christ's human body was merely an illusion and the passion and resurrection were also illusory; whereas for Sabellianism the Father and Son were so closely identified that it maintained that the Father suffered the passion with the Son; and associated with Sabellianism, Dynamic Monarchianism claimed that Jesus was a superior human being chosen by the preexistent Christ and imbued with divine powers. Peters, *Heresy and Authority in Medieval Europe*, 23.

8. *Reynolds v. United States*, 98 U.S. 145 (1878).

9. Desiderius Erasmus, *Inquisitio de Fide: A Colloquy by Desiderius Erasmus Roterodamus 1524*, ed. with an Introduction and Commentary by Craig R. Thompson (Hamden, Conn.: Archon Books, 1975), 101–2.

10. Jean-Jacques Rousseau, *The Collected Writings of Rousseau*, vol. 4: *Social Contract*, ed. Roger D. Masters and Christopher Kelly, trans. Judith R. Rush, Roger D. Masters, and Christopher Kelly (Hanover, N.H.: University Press of New England, 1994), 223.

11. St. Thomas Aquinas, *Summa theologiae*, II-II, q. 10, a. 11.

12. Salo Wittmayer Baron, *A Social and Religious History of the Jews* (New York: Columbia University Press, 1965), 9: 36–37, 8.

13. Lecler, *Toleration and the Reformation*, 1: 18–22. Pope Gelasius I recognized the division of spheres when he wrote, at the end of the fifth century: " 'There are two powers that rule *this* world, the sacred authority of the bishops and the royal power.' " Cited in ibid., p. 66.

14. On the humanist theory of religious toleration, see Gary Remer, *Humanism and the Rhetoric of Toleration* (University Park: Pennsylvania State University Press, 1996).

15. "Judaism as a historic entity was not constituted by its set of beliefs. . . . Judaism as a specifically defined entity existing continuously over a period of three thousand years was not realized in philosophy, literature, art, or anything other than halakhic living." Yeshayahu Leibowitz, *Judaism, Human Values, and the Jewish State*, ed. Eliezer Goldman, trans. Eliezer Goldman et al. (Cambridge, Mass.: Harvard University Press, 1992), 6–7.

16. *Sefer Ha-Ḥinukh*, ed. Haim Dov Chavel (Jerusalem: Mosad Ha-Rav Kook, 1973–74), 73.

17. Yehuda Ha-Levi, *The Kosari of R. Yehuda Halevi*, trans. Yehuda Even Shmuel (Tel-Aviv: Dvir, 1972), 1.

18. Halakhic literature distinguishes between several types of heretic: *min*, *apikoros*, *kofer*, and *mumar*. Maimonides writes, of heretics, that they are denied a portion in the world-to-come and should be killed. Nevertheless, heresy is not as emphasized in Halakhic sources as is idolatry, and the more typical Halakhic reaction to heretics is to forbid discourse with them, rather than to counsel killing them. Further, "Jews never organized a central agency to define heresy and establish procedures to judge and punish heresy." See Maimonides, *Mishneh Torah*, Sefer Ha-Mada, Hilkhot T'shuva, 3: 6–9; ibid., Sefer Ha-Mada, Hilkhot Avodat Kokhavim, 10: 1, 2: 5; ibid., Sefer Shoftim, Hilkhot Mamrim, 3: 3; *Encyclopaedia Judaica*, s.v., "heresy."

19. Leibowitz, *Judaism, Human Values, and the Jewish State*, 9.

20. See Maimonides, *Mishneh Torah*, Sefer Ha-Mada, Hilkhot T'shuva, 3: 7; and comments in Ra'avad, "Hassagot Ha-Ra'vad [Critical Comments of Ra'avad]."

21. The seven precepts of the Noahide law are (1) courts must be established; prohibitions against (2) blasphemy, (3) idolatry, (4) murder, (5) sexual immorality, (6) robbery, and (7) the eating of a torn limb of a living animal. On the Noahide laws, see *Babylonian Talmud*, Tractate Sanhedrin, 56a–b; David Novak, *The Image*

of the Non-Jew in Judaism: An Historical and Constructive Study of the Noahide Laws (New York and Toronto: Edwin Mellen Press, 1983).

22. Maimonides, *Mishneh Torah*, Sefer Shoftim, Hilkhot M'lakhim, 8: 11. See also ibid., Sefer Ha-Mada, Hilkhot T'shuva, 3: 5. Maimonides qualifies this statement, however, by limiting salvation only to those gentiles who adhere to the seven precepts "because the Holy One, blessed be He, commanded [the precepts] in the Torah and made them known to us by Moses." Maimonides, however, excludes from salvation gentiles who base their observance of the Noahide precepts on reason, not revelation. Elsewhere, however, Maimonides takes a more tolerant position, extending salvation to gentiles "who have achieved a proper knowledge of the Creator and have corrected their souls to act ethically." Here Maimonides does not cite his proviso that righteous gentiles must act out of a belief in the divine revelation to Moses.

The principle that righteous gentiles have a share in the world-to-come was widely accepted after Maimonides, not only in Maimonidean but even in Ashkenazic circles, usually without Maimonides' limiting condition. By the late eighteenth century, Moses Mendelssohn declared that belief in the salvation of righteous gentiles was a central tenet of Judaism—to be contrasted with the Christian doctrine that there is no salvation outside the church. On the development of the principle "righteous gentiles have a share in the world-to-come," see Jacob Katz, "Sh'losha Mishpatim Apologeti'im Be-Gilgulehem [Three Apologetic Sentences in Their Metamorphoses]," *Zion* 23–24 (1958–59): 174–81.

23. It was the Church's duty to excommunicate the heretic and to deliver him "to the secular tribunal to be exterminated thereby from the world by death." *Summa theologiae* II-II, q. 11, a. 3.

24. The establishment of the State of Israel raises questions of the relationship between the religious and secular spheres. From the perspective of some Orthodox Jews in and outside of Israel, Judaism's unity of religious and secular spheres should mean that the Jewish state should exercise coercive power over religious issues. Most Israeli as well as non-Israeli Jews, however, argue that Israel is not, and should not become, a theocracy. This issue, however, will not be addressed in this chapter.

25. See *Encyclopaedia Judaica*, s.v., "heresy."

26. Had there been a Halakhic Jewish state during the Middle Ages, some gentiles might have been subject to persecution. Maimonides writes that, when Jews have achieved political power in the Holy Land, "it is forbidden to tolerate idolaters in our midst." Maimonides, *Mishneh Torah*, Sefer Ha-Mada, Hilkhot Avodat Kokhavim, 10: 6.

27. Consistent with the Maimonidean school, Ha-Me'iri "held that the ultimate destiny of man was intellectual insight into the essence of God." Jacob Katz, *Exclusiveness and Tolerance: Studies in Jewish-Gentile Relations in Medieval and Modern Times* (Oxford: Oxford University Press, 1961; reprint ed., Westport, Conn.: Greenwood Press, 1980), 119. For a full account of Ha-Me'iri's debt to Maimonides, see Moshe Halbertal, "R. Menahem Ha-Me'iri: Ben Torah Le-Hokhma [Menahem Ha-Me'iri: Talmudist and Philosopher]," *Tarbiz* 63 (1993): 67–81.

28. See Maimonides, *Igeret Teman*, chapter 1; Maimonides, *Mishneh Torah*,

Sefer Ha-Mada, Hilkhot Avodat Kokhavim, 9: 4; Ibid., Sefer K'dushah, Hilkhot Ma'akhalot Asurot, 11: 7; Jacob Katz, "*Sovlanut Datit Be-Shitato Shel Rabbi Menaḥem Ha-Me'iri Be-Halakha U-Be-Philosophia* [Religious Toleration in the Method of Rabbi Menaḥem Ha-Me'iri in Halakha and Philosophy]," *Zion* 18 (1953): 24, n. 49.

29. Katz, *Exclusiveness and Tolerance*, 119–20; Katz, "*Sovlanut Datit*," 24. On Ha-Me'iri's legitimation of non-Jewish forms of worship, contra Maimonides, see Gerald Blidstein, "Maimonides and Me'iri on the Legitimacy of Non-Judaic Religion," in Leo Landman, ed., *Scholars and Scholarship: The Interaction Between Judaism and Other Cultures* (New York: Yeshiva University Press, 1990), 27–35.

30. *Babylonian Talmud*, Tractate Avodah Zarah, 2a; Maimonides, *Mishneh Torah*, Sefer Ha-Mada, Hilkhot Avodat Kokhavim, 9: 1. In the Land of Israel, there is an additional prohibition of doing business for three days before idolaters' holidays.

31. Maimonides, *Mishneh Torah*, Sefer Ha-Mada, Hilkhot Avodat Kokhavim, 9: 4. Not only Maimonides but the Talmud itself (in the original, uncensored version of Tractate Avodah Zarah) included Christians in the prohibition against dealing with idolaters on their festivals. See Katz, *Exclusiveness and Tolerance*, 25, n. 2.

32. Katz, "*Sovlanut Datit*," 16–17.

33. Maimonides lived in Moslem Spain, Morocco, and Egypt. On the acceptance of the Talmudic restrictions in Moslem countries, see Israel Ta-Shma, "*'Y'mei-Edehem' Perek B'Hitpathut Ha-Halakha B'ymei Ha-Benai'im* ['Their Festivals' A Chapter in the Development of Halakha in the Middle Ages]," *Tarbiẓ* 47 (1977–78): 208.

34. Ibid., 202–3. A similar argument is made (Rashi)—concerning the Talmudic proscription against deriving monetary benefit from the wine of gentiles— "that gentiles today are not well-versed in the nature of idolatry." Katz, "*Sovlanut Datit*," 16, n. 4. See also David Novak, *Jewish-Christian Dialogue: A Jewish Justification* (New York: Oxford University Press, 1989), 44–53.

35. Ta-Shma, "*Y'mei Edehem*," 203–4. Although Ha-Me'iri resembled the German rabbis in trying to reconcile Halakha and practice, the situation in Provence differed from that of Germany. In Provence, Jews were able to use Muslims as intermediaries in their commerce with Christians before or on Christian festivals. The Jews of Provence, therefore, were generally unaware of the more lenient attitude of German rabbis toward such trade. In light of these conditions, Ta-Shma argues, Ha-Me'iri's position appears especially pathbreaking. Ibid., 206–9.

36. Katz, "*Sovlanut Datit*," 18. See also Katz, *Exclusiveness and Tolerance*, 118.

37. Halbertal, "Menaḥem Ha-Me'iri," 102–4.

38. Menaḥem Ha-Me'iri, *Bet Ha-Beḥirah* (hereafter cited as *BH*) on Tractate Avodah Zarah, ed. Abraham Sofer (Jerusalem: Kedem, 1970–71), 4, 9.

39. Ibid., 27–28.

40. Ibid., 32.

41. Ibid., 48.

42. Ibid., 214.

43. *BH* on Tractate Gitin, ed. Kalman Schlesinger (Jerusalem: Brodie, 1963–1964), 257–58.

44. Many of these laws could not be applied in the Middle Ages because they presuppose Jewish sovereignty.

45. *BH* on Tractate Bava Kama, ed. Kalman Schlesinger (Jerusalem: Brodie, 1963), 122.

46. *BH* on Tractate Bava Mezia, ed. Kalman Schlesinger (Jerusalem: Mekize Nirdamim, 1959), 100.

47. *BH* on Tractate Avodah Zarah, 59–60. The Talmud does not obligate the Jew to be a "good Samaritan" toward the gentile. Ha-Me'iri argues that, in contemporary religions, Jews are obligated to act as "good Samaritans" to both Jews and gentiles.

48. *BH* on Tractate Bava Mezia, 219.

49. *BH* on Tractate Sanhedrin, ed. Abraham Sofer (Jerusalem: Kedem, 1965), 226–27.

50. *BH* on Tractate Yoma, ed. Yosef Klein (Jerusalem: Makhon Ha-Talmud Ha-Yisraeli Ha-Shalem, 1974–75), 212. When a Jew's life is endangered, the Sabbath laws must be broken. However, when an idolater's life is in jeopardy, the Sabbath laws must not be broken.

51. Jews were not permitted to entrust idolaters with teaching Jewish children or lodging the animals of Jews because idolaters are suspected of sexual immorality. *BH* on Tractate Avodah Zarah, p. 39.

52. Ibid. The Talmud prohibits the selling of weapons to gentiles. The rationale behind this ban is that gentiles are suspected of murder (or homicidal tendencies). Ha-Me'iri argues that this rule applies only to the idolatrous nations of old.

53. *Babylonian Talmud*, Tractate Avodah Zarah, 20a. This Talmudic prohibition is based on Deuteronomy 7: 2, where the Israelites are commanded to "show no mercy" to the idolatrous nations of Canaan. The Talmudic prohibition is based on the similarity between the Hebrew word for showing mercy (*te-ḥa-nem*) and grace (*ḥen*). See *BH* on Tractate Avodah Zarah, p. 46.

54. *BH* on Tractate Avodah Zarah, 132, p. 59. See Katz, "*Sovlanut Datit*," 21, 27–28.

55. Halbertal, "Menaḥem Ha-Me'iri," 105–6.

56. Ha-Me'iri reinterprets the Hebrew/Aramaic term for Christian, "*nozri*." *BH* on Tractate Avodah Zarah, p. 4; Katz, *Exclusiveness and Tolerance*, 123.

57. Halbertal argues ("Menaḥem Ha-Me'iri," 106–7, 109) that Ha-Me'iri is strict in his linguistic usage, distinguishing between the terms used in the first and second areas of law. Closer analysis of the individual cases shows, however, that while Ha-Me'iri generally uses a distinct terminology for each area, he does not always do so. For example, when discussing the prohibition against oversociability with gentiles (first area), Ha-Me'iri writes that "the nations bound by the ways of religion [language of second area] and belief in the existence, unity, and power of God—despite their errors in a few matters, according to our faith—have no place in these matters [that is, the Talmudic prohibition does not apply to them]." *BH* on Tractate Gitin, 258.

58. Maimonides, *Mishneh Torah*, Sefer K'dushah, Hilkhot Isurei Bi'ah, 14: 7; ibid., Hilkhot Ma'akhalot Asurot, 11: 7.

59. Maimonides, *Mishneh Torah*, Sefer Ha-Mada, Hilkhot Avodat Kokhavim,

10: 6; ibid., Sefer K'dushah, Hilkhot Isurei Bi'ah, 14: 8. Maimonides bases himself on Rabbi Shimon ben Elazar's view, stated in the *Babylonian Talmud*, Tractate Arakhin, 29a. "The Jubilee was only in effect during the days of the First Temple when all twelve tribes of Israel enjoyed political sovereignty in the Land of Israel." Novak, *Images of the Non-Jew in Judaism*, 15.

60. Maimonides, *Mishneh Torah*, Sefer Ha-Mada, Hilkhot Avodat Kokhavim, 10: 6. Maimonides based himself on *Babylonian Talmud*, Tractate Avodah Zarah, 64b. See also Katz, "*Sovlanut Datit*," 25.

61. Ephraim E. Urbach, "*Shitat Ha-Sovlanut Shel R. Menaḥem Ha-Me'iri—M'korah U-Migb'loteha*" (The System of Toleration of Rabbi Menaḥem Ha-Me'iri: Its Origins and Limitations), in I. Etkes and Yosef Salmon, eds., *Perakim be-Toldot Ha-Ḥevra Ha-Yehudit B'ymei Ha-Beinai'im U-Be'et Ha-Ḥadasha Mukdashim Le'Y. Katz [Jacob Katz Jubilee Volume]* (Jerusalem: Hotsa'at seferim ash Y. L. Magres, ha-Universitah ha-'ivrit, 1980), 38; Jacob Blidstein, "*Y'ḥaso shel R. Menaḥem Me'iri Le-Nokhri-Ben Apologetika Le-Hapnama* [Me'iri's Attitude to Gentiles—Between Apologetics and Internalization]," *Zion* 51 (1986): 157.

62. Halbertal, "Menaḥem Ha-Me'iri," 107.

63. *BH* on Tractate Avodah Zarah, 39.

64. Halbertal, "Menaḥem Ha-Me'iri," 109.

65. Ibid., 114, 116; Katz, *Exclusiveness and Tolerance*, 120–21; Novak, *Image of the Non-Jew in Judaism*, 352.

66. In more recent times, the concept of "*tinok she-nishba*," or "a captured infant," has been used to argue that Jews who were not raised Halakhically observant (that is, the vast majority of Jews today) are not responsible for their heretical ideas because they, like the kidnaped infant who was raised by gentiles, cannot be expected to know better. Maimonides uses this argument regarding the Karaites, medieval Jewish heretics who denied the authority of the Oral Law: "The children and future generations of those who have gone astray, who have been corrupted by their parents and who have been born among the Karaites and raised according to their ideas, are like an infant who has been imprisoned and raised among them; he does not quickly accept the ways of [God's] commandments because he is like a person who has been subjected to force. And even though he eventually hears that he is a Jew and sees Jews and their religion—he is like a person under compulsion, as he was raised according to their errors." Maimonides, *Mishneh Torah*, Sefer Shoftim, Hilkhot Mamrim, 3: 3. Moreover, Rabbi Avraham Yeshayahu Karelitz (1878–1953)—the "Ḥazon Ish"—has argued that the extirpation of heretics was permitted only in times when God's activities in the world were visible, but in a period, like today, where they are hidden, "it is incumbent on us to bring [the heretics] back with the bonds of love." See Abraham Isaiah Karelitz, *Ḥazon Ish*, Yoreh Deah, Hilkhot Sh'ḥitah, 2: 16.

67. Jacob Katz, "*Od Al 'Sovlanuto Ha-Datit Shel R. Menaḥem Ha-Me'iri'* [More on the 'Religious Toleration of R. Menaḥem Ha-Me'iri']," *Zion* 46 (1981): 245; *BH* on Tractate Bava Kama, 330, 122. Also see Blidstein, "*Y'ḥaso*," 154–55.

68. Maimonides, *Mishneh Torah*, Sefer Kinyan, Hilkhot M'khirah, 13: 7.

69. *BH* on Bava Mezia, 219. See also Blidstein, "*Y'ḥaso*," 155–57, where Blidstein raises the possibility of textual error in our version of Ha-Me'iri's statement.

70. *Babylonian Talmud*, Tractate Avodah Zarah, 26b.

71. *BH* on Tractate Horayot, ed. Abraham Sofer (Jerusalem, 1957), 275. See also *BH* on Tractate Avodah Zarah, p. 61; Katz, "Sovlanut Datit," 27.

72. Ibid.; *BH* on Tractate Horayot, 275, n. 8.

73. Katz argues that by adhering to established usage, Ha-Me'iri did not follow the implications of his position. For example, Ha-Me'iri could have, consistent with his stand, rejected Halakhic prohibitions relating to the articles of gentile worship and the segregative aspects of dietary laws, but he did not. Katz attributes this reticence to the likelihood that Ha-Me'iri never overcame his aversion to other religions and their symbols. Katz, *Exclusiveness and Tolerance*, 125–26, 127–28; *Sovlanut Datit*, 22–23, 28–29; *Od Al Sovlanuto*, 245.

74. Blidstein, "Y'haso," 155–57, 160–61.

75. Halbertal, "Menahem Ha-Me'iri," 113.

76. Lecler, *Toleration and the Reformation*, 1: 107–13.

77. Cited in ibid., 108.

78. Halbertal contrasts Ha-Me'iri's tolerance based on the common functional roles shared by the religions with Maimonides's intolerance based on testing the metaphysical truth of religions. Halbertal, "Menahem Ha-Me'iri," 113–14.

PART II

THE
LONG SIXTEENTH
CENTURY

Introduction: The Transformations of the Long Sixteenth Century

Randolph C. Head

DEFINING TOLERATION AS A primarily philosophical issue might lead one to miss the important shifts that the changing religious and social context of the medieval and early modern periods brought about. Efforts to provide universal principles that allow us to discern every possible configuration of tolerance—efforts that often result in categorizing both medieval and early modern Europeans as extraordinarily intolerant—can thus obscure two important conclusions from the historical record. First, *practices* usefully characterized as "tolerant" were as much a part of everyday life during this period as were widespread intolerance or persecution, and second, at a different level of analysis, the religious changes of the sixteenth century required contemporaries (and require modern analysts) to consider carefully exactly what they meant by "toleration."

The period known as the "long sixteenth century" forms a coherent era with regard to these issues. Beginning with the Italian wars and Columbus's journeys in the 1490s, the era included the backward-looking decades of the early seventeenth century, and came to an end with the politico-religious crises between 1620 and 1640: the Thirty Years' War (Europe's last major "religious" war), the English Revolution, and the breaking of the French Protestant movement with the fall of La Rochelle in 1630. The decisive development that changed views about religious toleration during this "long century" was the breakdown of the western church's hegemony. Over the course of the Protestant Reformation, theoretical unity in the Latin West gave way not only to four "magisterial" faiths—the post-Tridentine Catholic, the Lutheran, the Reformed or Calvinist, and the Anglican—but also to strong sectarian movements ranging across a wide spectrum from the quietist Anabaptists and the communitarian Hutterites to millenarian revolutionaries such as Thomas Müntzer. No part of Western and Central Europe was untouched by this process, which forced entirely new views and practices of toleration on a wide variety of Europeans.

It is important to remember, as earlier sections of this book have shown, that Europe was not totally religiously homogeneous even before the early sixteenth century. Medieval Europeans had confronted religious diversity in at least three forms: heretics, Jews, and infidels. Each of these confrontations provided possible models for coping with the separate faiths that developed within Christian Europe itself, later on. In addition, medieval Christian practice and doctrine itself varied considerably among village populations as well as among contentious intellectuals. Nevertheless, the conceptual unity of the "corpus christianum," the body of all orthodox Latin Christians ruled by orthodox rulers, provided the framework for reacting to dissent or difference throughout the Middle Ages.[1] The collapse of this deeply-felt unity set the stage for the very different conflicts of the Reformation era. No longer was active dissent confined to a few marginal conventicles or to small Jewish populations: instead, activist clergy and their political supporters on all sides insisted on the sole validity of their versions of Christianity, and increasingly used both powerful propaganda and outright coercion to suppress large minorities or even majorities who disagreed. Yet at the same time, Catholics and various kinds of Protestants continued to live cheek-by-jowl in much of Europe, trading, marrying, and conversing with adherents of other views. The failure of either the papacy or the princes to suppress Luther's supporters in Germany and the rapid growth of the Reformed movement in autonomous Switzerland utterly transformed what toleration meant in daily practice.[2]

The effect of the Reformation on European understanding of toleration was not simple. On the one hand, growing differences, which became more and more clearly expressed in widely disseminated controversial literature, created new reasons for persecution and new tools for carrying it out. The prevalence of formal "confessions of faith"—a phenomenon of little importance during the Middle Ages—made it possible to ferret out dissidents by means of oaths or public confessions of obedience to the dominant church. Meanwhile, the pervasive sense of crisis that accompanied the religious split created strong moral and psychological incentives to root out the new "heresies" or the old "papism." One consequence was increasing levels of religious violence: state sponsored violence, such as the St. Bartholomew's Day massacre of 1572, was accompanied by popular riots and renewed pogroms as communities vainly sought to restore their spiritual purity,[3] a process culminating in the widespread destruction of the Thirty Years' War. Yet the very success of the new churches, on the other hand, meant that Catholics and Protestants often had little choice but to "tolerate" each other (in the limited sense of enduring an evil until it could be alleviated), especially in regions such as the Holy Roman Empire, where a patchwork of mixed adherences developed after 1555.

This situation leads to the second important point about sixteenth-century toleration: new conditions produced new thinking. Moreover, the changing (and limited) forms of toleration sixteenth-century intellectuals were willing to accept can reveal to modern readers the complexity and ambivalence of all toleration in actual practice. Today tolerance is sometimes equated with pluralism or at least with open-minded acceptance of multiple value systems, but scarcely anyone argued such positions during the Reformation. Rather, toleration remained more closely connected to the Latin root of the concept: "tolerare" suggests grudging and temporary acceptance of an unpleasant necessity. Marion Leathers Kuntz's article in this volume argues that Jean Bodin, late in the century, could use musical metaphors to defend the harmony of multiple paths to religious truth—but even he would probably have rejected the notion that the truth itself might be multiple. Similarly, early modern skeptics focused on the imperfection of human knowledge, rather than arguing for a diversity of religious truths per se. On the whole, learned opinion shared Martin Luther's view that he could not "imagine any reason to excuse toleration to God. The children may be dirty, but the bath at least must be pure, and not polluted."[4]

Still, Christianity itself provided a cogent set of arguments in favor of forbearance if not approval of religious dissent. Most important was the notion that the Christian's conscience could and should not be forced in matters of faith. This view provided the foundation for a strong and consistent eirenic tradition that opposed overt religious persecution throughout the century. Many thinkers in this tradition, such as the Dutch Spiritualist Dirk Volckertzoon Coornhert, the Englishman Thomas Starkey, and the Hungarian Andras Dudic looked to the mild-mannered views of Desiderius Erasmus, who had argued that little good ever came from the "forcing of consciences" in religious matters.[5] In a series of pamphlets that began after Geneva's execution of Michael Servetus, the Calvinist theologian

Sebastian Castellio combined eirenic and skeptical views to create some of
the earliest explicit arguments for religious toleration to appear during the
sixteenth century. His *Advice to a Desolate France* combined modest skepticism about sinful humans' ability to be certain about true doctrine with a
repeated emphasis on the Golden Rule and the spiritual dangers of forcing
men's consciences. Excommunication, he claimed, was the only scriptur-
ally sanctioned form of religious coercion, whereas violent enforcement
of doctrine produced only division and ruin.[6] For his troubles, Castellio
came under investigation by the magistrates in Basel, where he lived, and
possibly escaped a heresy trial only through his premature death—this despite the fact that Basel quietly tolerated more religious variation within
its walls than did many other cities.[7] Castellio's later unpublished tract on
The Art of Doubting may have reflected his despair at his contemporaries'
quick turn to violence in religious disputes.[8]

As Castellio's ideas demonstrate, even those few intellectuals who
openly called for tolerance during this period argued within the same
framework as their persecuting opponents: toleration in this world, even
if desirable, was a temporary phenomenon that would end at the latest on
Judgment Day. The question of how to treat religious dissidents—whether
infidels, Jews, or heretics, since these categories remained fundamental—
was fundamentally a tactical one, a question of means rather than of ends.
Many of the most prominent advocates of refraining from persecution,
as Mario Turchetti has observed, hoped that good will and forebearance
would bring about "concord," the peaceful reunification of the Christian
churches under true doctrine. As he points out about the Colloquy of
Poissy in 1561: "Its prime purpose was concord: each party tried to convert
the other to its own faith."[9] Lucien Febvre argued over a half century ago
that the question of atheism in the sixteenth century is "mal posée"—and
I would argue that the same applies to genuine pluralism.[10]

A desire for concord did not necessarily imply the toleration of dissent. In contrast to the Jews, who despite many lapses on the part of
Christians usually enjoyed the privilege of forming their own congregations, few sixteenth-century magistrates countenanced alternate Christian
worship unless they were powerless to prevent it. Only where political
pressures or economic interest made a dissident community's presence un-
avoidable did rulers try to find ways to cope with their presence—that is,
to tolerate them. Conversely, the loudest calls for religious toleration came
from those in the minority or excluded from political power—though such
calls were all too often forgotten when a group managed to achieve political dominance.

In a few places, the way Jews had been tolerated in the Middle Ages provided the norm for new versions of religious toleration through the sixteenth century.[11] Just as the Venetian Jews could live and worship only in the Ghetto, so German Protestants there had their own closed quarter, the Fondaco de Tedeschi, and even Muslim merchants had a closed district reserved for their use.[12] That Venice's magistrates considered this no more than a distasteful necessity is illustrated by their treatment of local Christian dissidents, who could expect swift repression if their activities came to the state's attention.[13] Elsewhere in Italy, dissidents from the Catholic church such as Bernardino Ochino also defended toleration, but soon found themselves driven into exile.[14] Even very modest efforts to conduct an open debate over the current issues could be dangerous, as Cardinal Giovanni Morone found: he was tried by the Roman Inquisition under suspicion of "protecting heretics" because of his connections to irenic Italian thinkers.[15] Far to the north, Hamburg—another great trading city—tolerated Calvinists, Jews, and other dissidents in neighboring Altona, even as magistrates and urban mobs ensured that the city itself remained religiously pure.[16] Dutch cities managed their considerable religious diversity in the late sixteenth century in a comparable way, by confining dissident worship to a domestic "private sphere" that the magistrates in some towns tolerated as long as no public evidence of dissent from the Calvinist public church occurred.[17] As is so often the case, necessity made political authorities philosophically inventive, resulting in various forms of toleration by segregation.

In much of Europe, such a response was not feasible, however. Where religious parties were closely balanced, or where the minority party could call on powerful friends nearby, other forms of de facto toleration evolved. The most important laboratory for working out religious coexistence in the first half of the sixteenth century was the Holy Roman Empire. After mid-century, France and the Netherlands became key battlegrounds in the struggle between toleration and overt persecution. Wherever such arguments took place, however, an important proviso must be remembered: although the doctrinal distinctions among Catholics, Lutherans, and Calvinists were essentially clear by the end of the 1530s, the adoption of clear denominational attitudes by the larger population, especially outside the cities, was much slower if it happened at all.[18] It is true that large numbers of people occasionally took action to "defend their faith," but this should not lead us to assume that they understood that faith exactly as Luther or the Pope did. Only recently have close studies of cities and villages begun to reveal how the population was tolerant, and how it was not—as opposed to the much better documented opinions of magistrates and clergymen.[19]

The rapid growth of the Evangelical movement in Germany in the 1520s, defended as it was by powerful political patrons, made some degree of forebearance part of the picture from the very beginning. As early as 1526 at the Diet of Speyer, each sovereign entity within the Empire was empowered to allow whatever it could "justify to God and his Imperial Majesty"—a formula sufficiently open-ended to allow the continued rapid spread of Luther's ideas. A few years later in Switzerland, the stalemate between Catholic and Reformed cantons, which emerged after Zwingli's defeat and death at the battle of Kappel in 1531, led to formal recognition of the Confederation's religious division:

First of all, with regard to God's word, since no one should be compelled to faith, the cantons and their dependents should not be compelled; and concerning the areas that are ruled jointly, if these have abolished the Mass and burned or destroyed the images, they shall not be punished; but where the Mass and other ceremonies are still practiced, they shall not be sent nor compelled to accept any [Reformed] ministers.[20]

By establishing the legal basis for two coexisting churches and forms of worship, the Peace of Kappel institutionalized limited religious toleration only a decade after Zwingli began preaching the Reformed faith in Zurich.[21] Relatively calm toleration of this sort lasted throughout the sixteenth century in parts of Switzerland, as my essay on Graubünden (Chapter 6 below) illustrates, but its lack of ideological underpinnings also meant that it could collapse rapidly when circumstances changed.

In Germany in the 1530s and '40s, meanwhile, various temporary resolutions delayed the imposition of Imperial mandates against heresy as long as efforts to resolve the split between Protestants and Catholics continued. After the failure of the Colloquy of Regensburg (1541), which satisfied neither Luther nor the Pope because of its moderation, Emperor Charles V turned to military force, and defeated the Protestants in 1547. Even then, he sought a "concordant" solution in the Augsburg Interim of 1548. The very name illustrated Charles's intention to allow temporary concessions until voluntary unity could be reestablished at a general council of the Church. In the event, the political threat of Habsburg dominance in Germany caused a shift in alliances that renewed the war and the religious stalemate, and the Religious Peace of Augsburg in 1555 recognized each sovereign's right to choose one of the two authorized confessions—the

Lutheran and the Catholic. The Augsburg agreement of 1555 also created a number of officially bi-confessional cities, where working out harmonious coexistence remained a key problem during the succeeding decades.[22]

The Religious Peace in Germany established a form of religious toleration far from modern ideals, of course. Freedom of choice in religion was conceded only to sovereign princes and magistrates, whereas subjects gained only the much more limited privilege of free emigration if they could not accept their ruler's choice. Only two faiths enjoyed even this limited protection, which was to cause great difficulty when Calvinism spread into Germany after the 1560s. And as events during the Thirty Years' War would show, committed believers on all sides saw the 1555 compromise as a temporary expedient rather than as a just and permanent resolution to the religious conflict. Nevertheless, it proved remarkably durable—not, perhaps, because of its philosophical clarity or fundamental justice, but because it accurately reflected the reality of sixteenth-century German politics and society. Such a limited form of toleration required neither approval of the other side's view or any weakening of one's own convictions. What it did do was spare Germany from religious war and from massive religious coercion for nearly sixty years—no small accomplishment when one compares Germany to the rest of Europe.

Voices calling for forbearance during the search for concord were not absent elsewhere, of course. Yet neither in Spain, England, nor France did such voices gain much hearing during the sixteenth century. In Spain, a strong monarchy possessed effective means of repression. The Inquisition, its methods refined in the pogrom against converted Jews between 1485 and the 1530s, ensured that evangelical movements remained extremely limited in their reach.[23] Indeed, most evidence suggests that orthodoxy was never challenged in Spain: early enthusiasm for Erasmian views never turned seriously anti-Papal, and the state's sense of mission as the bastion against the infidel and the Jews seems to have penetrated far into the population. In England, too, an activist state dominated questions of religious policy throughout the century, so that toleration remained limited to temporary forbearance in the hope of converting dissidents to the current orthodoxy. Not all clerics and statesmen believed that coercion would be effective, as Thomas Mayer illustrates for the circle around Cardinal Reginald Pole, but even a hint of threat to the dominant creed brought out the full force of an engaged state—Catholic under Mary, Protestant under Elizabeth—to defend its doctrine and its right to control the church.

The situation in France was more complex. Although the evangelical movement there lacked the early support among peasantry that it had in Germany, it spread after 1550 among the urban population and among influential professionals. Eventually it also drew strong noble support growing out of the Erasmian intellectual currents of the 1520s and '30s. The other key difference from Germany was the relative strength of the monarchy. The famous slogan "one faith, one law, one king" certainly appealed to the Habsburg Emperors of Germany as much as to the Valois Kings of France, but the latter had far better means to make it a reality. It was only the unexpected weakness of the monarchy after the sudden death of Henri II in 1559 that made open religious dissent possible at all in France.

When Protestantism did come out into the open in France after 1560, reinforced by the intellectual and organizational tools provided by John Calvin, the resulting conflicts quickly spun out of control. The doctrinal issues became entangled with an extended family struggle to control the monarchy, and leadership of the Reformed movement slipped from urban preachers and journeymen to the princes of the realm and the leading officers of the state. These circumstances produced a situation that was the exact inverse of the German one: rather than coming from the individual territories, the call for toleration in France emanated from those closest to the Crown, who feared that intractable religious division would destroy the monarchy itself. The most celebrated voice calling for coexistence was that of Chancellor Michel de l'Hôpital, but his individual ideas were less crucial than the structure of the situation: long after his dismissal, it was royalists who argued that only the separation of religious from political conflict could save France. More than three decades of war eventually proved them right, and Henri IV brought the "politique" line of thought to fruition with the Edict of Nantes in 1598. At a time when religious coexistence was coming under renewed stress in Germany, France finally established a precarious balance.

The form of toleration produced in France was both narrower and broader than the German solution. Lacking the constitutional underpinnings that the Peace of Augsburg enjoyed, the Edict of Nantes embodied an act of royal grace that could be withdrawn at the king's will. Protestantism was tolerated in the narrow sense of grudging forbearance, and this only in limited regions. Yet at the same time the Edict went further: not only could its protections be enjoyed by individuals in much of France, but the King also established balanced courts of arbitration specifically empowered to resolve cases of friction between the confessions. Despite such provisions, relations between Catholics and Protestants remained tense, especially after the assassination of Henri IV in 1610.

Finally, before turning to the consequences of these various situations for sixteenth-century theories about toleration, we should consider two havens of de facto toleration in later sixteenth-century Europe: the Dutch Republic and Eastern Europe, especially Poland. The Polish case is simpler to explain, though it stands as important proof that relatively harmonious coexistence was possible among Christian creeds. In Poland, a weak and often absentee monarchy faced a strong nobility and towns with close ties to the German world. By late in the century, the magisterial creeds from further west had all established or sustained their hold on parts of the population, so that Catholics, Lutherans, and Calvinists could not avoid dealing with one another. More surprisingly, radical refugees fleeing from bitter persecution elsewhere also found a haven and supporters in Poland. Best known are the Socinians, followers of Fausto Socini who rejected the Trinity, and who followed the eirenic line in claiming that violence had no place in religious debate.[24] In 1573, the Polish king was forced to accede to the Confederation of Warsaw, which provided Catholics, Lutherans, Calvinists, and even Anti-Trinitarians with some protection from overt persecution, leading to a brief "golden age" of religious toleration. Changing political winds, however, doomed Polish tolerance to be a temporary phenomenon that collapsed during the seventeenth century, when the Crown joined with the Jesuit order to impose post-Tridentine Catholicism from above.

Refugees from persecution in Western Europe found refuge in other Eastern European kingdoms as well: German radicals established themselves in Moravia and Transylvania, where they enjoyed protection from powerful lords for economic as well as spiritual reasons, while Calvinism spread among the Bohemian and Hungarian nobility. In 1568, the Transylvanian Diet capped several decades of increasingly tolerant legislation with the Decree of Torda, which protected four separate western Christian denominations, along with limited tolerance of Eastern Orthodoxy.[25]

In the Netherlands, the institutionally weak and distant sovereign—after 1553 King Philip II of Spain—never regained control after political insurgency joined forces with a potent though narrow Calvinist movement. The entire history of the Dutch revolt cannot be covered here, but the result was a publicly Calvinist state in the north whose magistrates never made Calvinism the exclusive state religion. Despite continual importuning from the devout and their clergy, the Dutch Republic became home not only to a thriving Jewish community (many of them refugees from the Iberian persecutions) but also to quiet but stable Anabaptist and Catholic communities who could count on tacit toleration as long as they kept their worship firmly in the "private" sphere.[26] Given the oligarchic republican government interested above all in stability and Dutch trade links to every part of Europe and beyond, neither political nor economic forces encouraged systematic persecution of religious minorities; moreover, by the end of the sixteenth century, voices were heard that explicitly defended open toleration on economic grounds.[27]

An uneasy combination of principle, prudence, and practicality thus underlay the practice of religious toleration in many parts of Europe during the sixteenth century. The schism of orthodoxy led to situations where practice rapidly outstripped the conceptual apparatus available to contemporary political and social theorists. It was political realities that turned the difficult situation in Germany before 1555 to de facto toleration, for example, not the efforts of eirenically-minded intellectuals. Each side fervently claimed to possess the sole religious truth, and smeared its opponents not merely as misguided but also as actively demonic, yet circumstances required them to live together, often in very close quarters. This required toleration, rather than approval or open-mindedness. Because the social theory of the sixteenth century lacked ways to conceptualize the friendly coexistence of communities that were divided on questions of fundamental importance, ironically, Western Europeans eventually developed both practical and finally theoretical models of toleration. The dynamics of Reformation and Counter-Reformation illustrate with special vividness that tolerance is most important precisely where the parties involved cannot even begin to resolve their differences.

Notes

1. On the beginnings of systematic persecution, see the work of Robert Ian Moore, especially his *The Formation of a Persecuting Society: Power and Deviance in Western Europe, 950–1250* (Oxford: Blackwell, 1987). The magisterial survey is Malcolm Lambert, *Medieval Heresy: Popular Movements from the Gregorian Reform to the Reformation* (Oxford: Blackwell, 1992).

2. For an introduction and articles covering much of Europe on this issue during the sixteenth century, see Ole Peter Grell and Bob Scribner, eds., *Tolerance and Intolerance in the European Reformation* (Cambridge: Cambridge University Press, 1996).

3. Natalie Zemon Davis, "The Rites of Violence," in *Society and Culture in Early Modern France* (Stanford, Calif.: Stanford University Press, 1975). On St. Bartholomew's Day, see Barbara Diefendorf, *Beneath the Cross: Catholics and Huguenots in Sixteenth-Century Paris* (Oxford: Oxford University Press, 1991).

4. Cited by Winfried Schulze, " 'Ex dictamine rationis sapere': Zum Problem der Toleranz im Heiligen Römischen Reich nach dem Augsburger Religionsfrieden," in Michael Erbe et al., eds., *Querdenken: Dissens und Toleranz im Wandel der Geschichte* (Mannheim: Palatium Verlag, 1996), 226.

5. On Coornhert, see Jonathan Israel, *The Dutch Republic: Its Rise, Greatness and Fall, 1477–1806* (Oxford: Clarendon Press, 1995), 97–99 and the citations there; on Starkey and Dudic, see Thomas Mayer's essay, Chapter 7, below.

6. *Conseil à la France désolée* (1562), translated by Wouter Valkhoff as *Advice to a Desolate France* (Shepherdstown: Patmos Press, 1975).

7. Hans Guggisberg, "Sebastian Castellio and the German Reformation," in Hans R. Guggisberg and Gottfried G. Krodel, eds., *The Reformation in Germany and Europe: Interpretations and Issues* (Gütersloh: Gütersloher Verlagshaus, 1993), 325–43.

8. *De arte dubitandi et confidendi, ignorandi et sciendi*, ed. Elisabeth Feist Hirsch (Leiden: Brill, 1981).

9. Mario Turchetti, "Religious Concord and Tolerance in Sixteenth- and Seventeenth-Century France," *Sixteenth Century Journal* 22 (1991): 17.

10. Lucien Febvrè, *The Problem of Unbelief in the Sixteenth Century: The Religion of Rabelais*, trans. Beatrice Gottlieb (Cambridge, Mass.: Harvard University Press, 1982).

11. See Robert Bonfil, "Aliens Within: The Jews and Antijudaism," in Thomas A. Brady, Jr., Heiko A. Oberman, and James D. Tracy, eds., *Handbook of European History, 1400–1600* (Leiden: Brill, 1994), 1: 263–302.

12. There is an extensive literature on the Venetian Jews. See, e.g., Benjamin Ravid, "The Religious, Economic and Social Background and Context of the Establishment of the Ghetti of Venice," in Gaetano Cozzi, ed., *Gli Ebrei e Venezia, secoli XIV–XVIII* (Milan: Edizioni Communità, 1987), 211–60.

13. John Martin, *Venice's Hidden Enemies: Italian Heretics in a Renaissance City* (Berkeley and Los Angeles: University of California Press, 1993).

14. Ochino's eirenic views and opposition to the use of violence in religious debates are found in his *Dialogi XXX in duos libros* of 1563, after his exile.

15. See most recently Massimo Firpo, *Inquisizione romana e controriforma: studi sul cardinal Giovanni Morone e il suo processo d'eresia* (Bologna: Il Mulino, 1992).

16. Joachim Whaley, *Religious Toleration and Social Change in Hamburg, 1529–1819* (Cambridge: Cambridge University Press, 1985).

17. Israel, *Dutch Republic*, 369, 372–77. The way the Dutch used the public/private distinction to tolerate dissenting practice is currently being studied by Benjamin Kaplan, "Towards a Social History of Religious Toleration in Early Modern Europe" (Paper read at the Sixteenth Century Studies Conference, San Francisco, Oct. 28, 1995).

18. The reception of Reformation and Catholic Reformation ideas and practices by the broader population is one of the key foci of current research. An excel-

lent summation, is in Geoffrey Parker, "Success and Failure During the 1st Century of the Reformation," *Past and Present* no. 136 (1992): 43–82.

19. This topic is the subject of much current research, for example Gregory Hanlon, *Confession and Community in Seventeenth-Century France: Catholic and Protestant Coexistence in Aquitane* (Philadelphia: University of Pennsylvania Press, 1993); Marc Forster, *The Counter-Reformation in the Villages: Religion and Reform in the Bishopric of Speyer, 1560–1720* (Ithaca, N.Y.: Cornell University Press, 1992).

20. Translated from the "Zweiter Kappeler Landfrieden 1531," in Ernst Walder, ed., *Religionsvergleiche des 16. Jahrhunderts* (Bern: Herbert Lang, 1945), 5.

21. This toleration was limited in several ways: most important, *individuals* gained no protection against coercion within the separate cantons—as vividly illustrated by the persecution of Anabaptists in Zurich in the later 1520s.

22. On these cities, see esp. Paul Warmbrunn, *Zwei Konfessionen in Einer Stadt: Das Zusammenleben von Katholiken und Protestanten in den paritätischen Reichsstädten Augsburg, Biberbach, Ravensburg, und Dinkelsbühl von 1548 bis 1648* (Wiesbaden: Franz Steiner, 1983).

23. Henry Kamen's *The Rise of Toleration* (New York: McGraw-Hill, 1967), covers the situation for Spain, arguing for some *de facto* tolerance there.

24. A survey in Janusz Tazbir, *Geschichte der polnischen Toleranz* (Warsaw: Verlag Interpress, 1977). See also Michael Müller, "Protestant Confessionalisation in the towns of Royal Prussia and the practice of religious toleration in Poland-Lithuania," in Grell and Scribner, eds., *Tolerance*, 262–81.

25. Described by Ágnes R. Várkonyi, "Pro quiete regni—For the Peace of the Realm: The 1568 Law on Religious Tolerance in the Principality of Transylvania," *Hungarian Quarterly* (Hungary) 34 (1993): 99–112. See more generally the chapters by Katalin Péter and Jaroslav Pánek in Grell and Scribner, eds., *Tolerance*, 249–61, 231–48 respectively.

26. For an example see Benjamin Kaplan, *Calvinists and Libertines: Confession and Community in Utrecht, 1578–1620* (Oxford: Clarendon Press, 1995).

27. See Erich Hassinger, "Wirtschaftliche Motive und Argumente für religiöse Duldsamkeit im 16. und 17. Jahrhundert," *Archiv für Reformationsgeschichte* 49, 1/2 (1958): 226–45.

4

"Heretics be not in all things heretics": Cardinal Pole, His Circle, and the Potential for Toleration

Thomas F. Mayer

IN THE EARLY 1530S, WRITING HIS "Dialogue Between Pole and Lup-set," Thomas Starkey ascribed the apparently tolerant sentiment "heretics be not in all things heretics" to his patron Reginald Pole (1500–1558). After Starkey left his service, Pole became a leading opponent of Henry VIII, cardinal, nearly successful candidate for pope, papal legate, and archbishop of Canterbury under Mary I.[1] Later, another of Pole's dependents, Andras Dudic, became known as one of the most famous sixteenth-century defenders of toleration.[2] Dudic, along with Pole's client Gianbattista Binardi and Starkey, also tried to create an image of Pole in accord with such opinions. That they did raises several problems. It might have been mere coincidence that three of Pole's satellites put forward such views, just as it will always be open to question to what degree Starkey, Dudic, and Binardi accurately represented their patron, especially in light of recent studies which demonstrate the conflicted nature of patron-client relations in the Renaissance.[3] A partial answer to the first difficulty is that Pole, to an unusual degree, was a composite construction, created through intensive interaction with his household of true believers.[4]

But Starkey's, Dudic's, and Binardi's views raise another, more serious problem. Do even they, much less those of their patron, reflect a belief in toleration? Mario Turchetti maintains that nearly all sixteenth-century advocates of leniency to those with whom they disagreed, except for Sebastian Castellio, favored reunifying Christianity without resorting to force, not permanently tolerating disparate viewpoints.[5] (I shall refer to this attitude by the terms "concordance" and "concordant.") Turchetti's special subject, François Baudouin, certainly did not see Pole as tolerant, lumping him with the notoriously vehement Albert Pighe.[6] Yet the fact that Pighe, despite valiant efforts, failed to attach himself to Pole (or any of Pole's allies) may give a first clue to Pole's position, as on the other hand do the comparatively subtle criticisms of John Calvin against certain prelates at Trent who knew the truth "but yet having nothing in order to resist manfully" did not follow it, or the stark attacks of Francesco Negri and Pierpaolo Vergerio, both converts to Protestantism and violent critics of Pole.[7]

Finding himself for much of his career uncomfortably suspended between various political and religious positions, Pole reacted by leaving his lines of communication as open as the good rhetorician he was could. Given his eminence in the mid-sixteenth century, and the strength of his "party," a large space for dialogue resulted, not only with Protestants but within the Catholic church. Unlike many of Pole's contemporaries who could sometimes talk a good line about some kind of toleration if circumstances made it impossible for them to enforce their views, Pole in practice took an unusually lenient line on heresy even when he had virtually full religious authority in England in the last four years of his life. In the light of the present state of the question, it would be strange indeed to find any kind of opening toward toleration in the Catholic church, but had Pole's tenure in England coincided with Pius IV's papacy, which followed shortly after Pole's death, the opening for dialogue, even embryonic toleration, could have been quite large.

What were Pole's views? There has been much disagreement about whether Starkey's statement reflected them, Starkey's, or some combination. Starkey was undoubtedly close enough to the notoriously taciturn Pole to have heard him discourse more than once. They had probably met at Oxford in the early 1520s, and Starkey remained in Pole's household as they moved about Europe off and on until his return to England in late 1533. Thereafter they remained in touch, right up to Starkey's death in 1538, at which point Pole was about to be declared a traitor.[8] Despite this extended period of contact between Pole and Starkey, for our purposes paternity matters less than the proper interpretation of the dictum. The real question is whether it reflects a tolerant, as opposed to a concordant, attitude to heresy.[9] If the possibility of toleration is predicated on allowing the existence of more than one truth, then it did not. Pole and Thomas Lupset, Starkey's other interlocutor, were debating whether scripture should be put into the vernacular. Pole strongly urged the utility to ordinary people of both an English liturgy and Bible (not to mention canon law).[10] Lupset objected that these were Lutheran tenets, and just look what a mess they have made. Were we to follow their lead, we would soon see as many errors in England as in "Almayn." Pole replied:

fyrst you schal be sure of thys I wyl not folow the steppys of Luther whose juge-ment I estyme veray lytyl, & yet he & hys dyscypullys be not so wykkyd & folysch that in al thyngys they erre, heretykys be not in al thyngys heretykys, wherefor I wyl not so abhorre theyr heresye that for the hate therof I wyl fly from the truth, I alow thys maner of saying of servyce not bycause they say & affyrme hyt to be gud & laudabul but bycause the truth ys so as hyt apperyth to me.[11]

The most important point here is that Pole believed in the unity of truth. Heretics might discover it, but it remained a single truth nonetheless. Such a notion of truth obtained throughout the "Dialogue," which, like most such blueprints of the ideal commonwealth, claimed to embrace a single vision of felicity, at least some of the time.

A crucial ambiguity undercuts many of the apparent implications of Pole's emphasis on a unitary truth: were laws or men to rule? Despite the elaborate constitutional structures Starkey designed, full of interlocking councils intended to force the rulers to virtue, the work ultimately took a Pauline twist and concluded (more or less) that the law was insufficient. This time Lupset got the big speech:

Whether yet al thes ordynance ye or al the powar of law be abul to bryng man to thys perfectyon I somewhat dowte, for as much as the perfectyon of man stondyth in reson & vertue, by the wych he both knowyth that wych ys truth & gud & also hath wyl stabyl & constant purpos to folow the same, not compelllyd by feare of any payne or punnyschement, nor yet by any plesure or profyt alluryd therto, but only of hys fre wyl & lyberty wyth prudent knolege & perfayt love movyd.

Pole agreed, adding that the law was "the pegadoge of chryst" and a means to prepare humans to achieve perfect knowledge. That, however, came only from Christ and was, as Lupset put it, "only the worke of god." Pole again agreed that to attain perfection "we must use other mean than cyvyle ordynance . . . & as nere as we may folow the exampul of our mastur chryst, the wych by no compulsyon instytute hys law, nor by any drede of fear of any thyng." Christ's original means were "exampul of lyfe, & exhortacyon" which meant ensuring good preaching and circulating translations of Eras-mus. As Pole concluded, once good preachers had been provided for, and the Bible, Christ's law, and worship services put into English, "then I thynke schortly yu schold see more frute of the gospel then we have, you schold see wyhtin few yerys men wyth love dow such thyng as now they can not be brought to be no mannys law." Nevertheless, Pole reiterated that "fere of punnyschment & payne" and "desyre of honest plesure & profyt by law prescrybyd" came first, to be replaced gradually by action undertaken out of love of virtue and of Christ.[12] Thus it seems that no one could be compelled to salvation, but at the same time, the means which made salvation accessible—preaching and education—could indeed be dictated. There is slippage here, which may produce an opening toward toleration. Put into Pole's mouth, it contributed to an image of *his* tolerance.[13]

It may not be accidental that Starkey laid so much emphasis on Erasmus at the moment of this maneuver. Although his attitude changed over time and was probably always concordant rather than tolerant, it was possible to read some of Erasmus's works as leaning in the direction of toleration.[14] *Inquisitio de fide* offers perhaps the clearest instance. This dialogue between the characters Aulus and Barbatius, written as late as 1524 but before Erasmus's celebrated dispute with Luther over the will, transparently defended Luther (and by implication other "heretics") by arguing that belief in Christianity required only adherence to a very simple creed.[15] Above all, Barbatius (Luther) professed not to believe in "holy church," defining the church instead as "the body of Christ, that is, a universal assemblage of all those throughout the world who agree in the evangelic faith." Aulus pressed him on the point, and Barbatius defended himself by reference to Cyprian's explication of the creed (even though Erasmus knew the work not to be by Cyprian). Instead of any visible church, which, no matter how many good men it contained, could still be corrupted, Barbatius adhered to the "communion of the saints." That church was "no other than the belief in one God, one gospel, one faith, one hope, a joining in one spirit and the same sacraments," the last of which then disappeared from the discussion. Aulus concluded that Barbatius was as orthodox as his opponents, and let Barbatius persuade him to come to lunch to reason further. Aulus was a little concerned that he would be seen in the company of a heretic, but Barbatius convinced him, on the authority of Paul, that "nothing is more holy than to favor heretics." Aulus returned to his original pose of physician to Barbatius, but it would have been difficult to avoid the conclusion that the sick man not only did not require healing, but had done as much for Aulus as Aulus for him.

However much Starkey may have drawn on Erasmus, his example was probably more important to Dudic, who has been called the last important Hungarian Erasmian.[16] However that may be, in the late 1560s Dudic developed a position which came about as close as was possible in the sixteenth century to a demand for toleration. Already in 1568 Dudic had called on the emperor to allow "liberty of conscience" in Poland.[17] Sometime between then and 1572 he translated pseudo-Themistius, *Oratio XII, ad Valentem de religionibus* with a commentary which bluntly stated "no one may impose his opinion" about religion on any one else, and "each religion has its own rationale, as do all arts and all sciences." Yet Dudic also likened each religion to a component of an army and rooted his views in a neo-Platonic idea of charity, which probably means that he was after a new synthesis, and thus believed at bottom in concordance.[18]

One of the most important episodes in the sixteenth-century debate came in Dudic's dispute with Calvin's successor in Geneva, Theodore de Bèze, in the wake of the cases of Miguel Servetus (whom Calvin had had burned for heresy), Bernardino Ochino, and others.[19] Dudic's letter of 1 August 1570 is famous.[20] It opened with the same question Dudic had put earlier. How could one locate the true church, "about the possession of which there are now so many, so various, so sharp combats, and such a bloody dispute?" It was arrogance, Dudic several times argued, to claim sole access to truth, and worse to arm the people for religious wars. As he did frequently, Dudic pointed to the lengthy consensus behind the Catholics in wondering whether the Church could have survived for so long in what Bèze and others called darkness. Had not Christ promised to be with his church forever? If true Christians were identified by their works, what to make of all the cruelty and bloodshed practiced by Bèze and his allies? "Could you not be compared to ambushes laid for princes in a republic?" Reformed preaching, which led to such bloodshed, had helped little to uncover the truth. Surely the church had troubles with heretics, but "who might these disturbers of the Church, and destroyers of unity be?"

How to arrive at the mean? What to do when no judge could be found? Scripture, which everyone read by his own lights, could not fill that role. The fathers and church councils? Perhaps, but Dudic attacked Bèze's "inconstancy" in fleeing from those fathers who condemned his beliefs, and said Bèze knew perfectly well that the councils were against him. Dudic called the church "a fortress common to all" (a possible echo of Erasmus's emphasis on the common good), which Dudic nevertheless wished to be very careful about identifying. Not only various rulers but "whole nations" had tried to appropriate it in the name of "liberty of conscience." Returning to the question of consensus, Dudic denied Bèze's claim to superior philological ability as a guarantee of truth, again because there were so many possible leaders in it. Why follow Bèze more than another? Dudic willingly conceded the gifts Bèze immodestly claimed, but even so the Catholics might have been better still at languages, and could certainly read church history more carefully. Besides, deeds, not words, counted, and Bèze and his followers had not exactly distinguished themselves on that score, having killed so many men, disturbed so many cities, and "taught magistrates to be butchers." War was not the Christian magistrate's appropriate response to dissent. Dudic had no wish to defend Catholicism, but he admired the Roman church's "wonderful order" and readiness to do battle. Fighting it was like fighting Cadmus's constantly-renewed warriors.

Truth was still a unity for Dudic, but he could see no reason to privilege any one sect's apprehension of it over another's. All the issues between Bèze and the Catholics were and would remain "sub judice." The "Ebionites" in Transylvania and Poland were as likely to have found the truth as Bèze, or the Catholics, for that matter. Adapting the "if it walks like a duck" argument, Dudic pointed out that the reformed churches could easily be charged with usurping the prerogatives of the holy see; both obviously relied on excommunication. And a king, their preferred religious authority, could degenerate as easily as a pope. Yes, some rites needed modification, but differences among Catholics over them were small by comparison with Protestant variations, a point Dudic made at length. Although he insisted on the need for unity, which makes his "tolerant" attitude appear more "concordant," Dudic still rejected the persecution of heretics, because it disagreed with the doctrine of predestination, was more a matter of law than gospel, and violated John 18: 31, which forbade killing of any kind. It did no good to claim that magistrates actually did the killing, since anyone acting through another to commit a crime was equally guilty of it. Dudic closed by proudly admitting that he had not chosen his church, perhaps leaving the implication open that he never would.

It had taken Dudic a long time to get to this position, "concordant" if the tale were ever told, but "tolerant" *rebus sic stantibus*.[21] As a young man Dudic had spent about eighteen months in Pole's household in England, and the experience made a great impact on him. If I am right, he was very quickly promoted to a position of great responsibility, since it is likely that he was the principal author/copyist of Pole's strangest work, "De reformatione ecclesiae."[22] In 1556 Dudic extravagantly praised Pole together with their mutual friend Paolo Manuzio for their "true religion of Christ, by whom I was confirmed in the faith and by whose examples I was invited to spend life piously and holily."[23] About five years later, while at the council of Trent, Dudic repaid Pole's hospitality by engaging, along with Binardi, in a translation and adaptation of Ludovico Beccadelli's life of Pole.[24] Dudic continued to admire Pole right up to the end of his life, nearly thirty years later, long after he had definitively gone over to the Reformations, proposing a study of Pole as a model for a series of biographies of men "whom our age raises to the level of the fathers [of the church]."[25]

The question of Dudic's motives in adapting Beccadelli has long been debated, but virtually nothing has been said about Binardi, whom Dudic lauded in the preface to the *Vita Reginaldi Poli*. Dudic said he had asked Binardi for help because of his own artistic failings, and he went on to emphasize how much substance Binardi had contributed, in addition to having "polished" "totam hanc Poli effigiem."[26] Binardi had been one of the most central figures in Pole's English household because he had custody of Pole's writings and knew English. He enjoyed enough success to attract the envy of at least two competitors after his return to Italy.[27] His attitude has proven very difficult to reconstruct. For one thing, not much is known of Binardi's time in England until its very end. For another, if we can trust Ludovico Castelvetro, he busied himself turning works dictated by Pole in Italian into good Latin, including *De sacramento*, Pole's attack on Thomas Cranmer, his predecessor as archbishop of Canterbury.[28] Finally, Castelvetro called Binardi a persecutor.[29] This is more than a little ironic, since Binardi was among the very few to take Castelvetro's side in his literary dispute with Annibale Caro, well after Castelvetro had become a notorious heretic.[30]

The dearth of information about Binardi, beyond these possibly suggestive but contradictory tidbits, combined with the disagreements about Dudic's leanings and intentions, make it all the more interesting that whatever their inclinations may have been, they did not much affect the re-working of Beccadelli's original on the score of Pole's lenient attitude to heresy.[31] True, Dudic and Binardi emphasized much more than Beccadelli had the degree to which Pole combatted heresy in England, and cut out Pole's own relations with Marcantonio Flaminio, which Beccadelli had used as a major illustration of Pole's manner of dealing with heretics. Instead, they substituted the laconic "and certainly he [more than] once proved that this means of dealing with heretics is the most appropriate means." But they agreed with Beccadelli about "this means," no matter how many times employed.

He [Pole] truly, when perhaps he had fallen in with anyone, whom he understood to be in the grip of any false opinion, abhorring from the doctrine of the church, did not attack him with sharp accusations and certain inhumane reproofs, but he would admonish gently and in a friendly way, and so attempt to lead back to health. For, those who were neither public, nor contumacious, nor obstinate heretics, he thought ought to be so treated.[32]

To whatever degree reworked, the image of Pole is even more markedly concordant, with fully "tolerant" practical implications, than Starkey's had been more than thirty years earlier.

So much for the image. Before turning to test the views of Starkey, Dudic, and Binardi against Pole's practice, we may be able to get a little closer to his theory. Pole made his most explicit statement at Trent about how to treat heretics, the touchstone in discussions of toleration, unsurprisingly in the course of the debate over justification. Just before he left the council, he argued that Lutheran works on the subject should be read dispassionately. The principle "Luther said it, therefore it is false" had to be rejected. Whatever was good in such books should be kept and a *via media* sought which would lead to the truth.[33] Most of Pole's formal works, even those with promising contents, say very little. His tirade against Henry VIII, *Pro unitatis ecclesiae defensione* [*On the unity of the church*] (1536), made the obligatory point that heretics distorted the meaning of scripture, and praised John Fisher and Thomas More for having written against heresy.[34] Perhaps this is not the most likely of texts in which to seek a "soft" line. The sprawling manuscript of "De reformatione ecclesiae" appears to offer more hope, despite being well nigh unintelligible because of its at least eleven more or less independent versions, some now nearly illegible, as well as almost impossible to date.[35] Pole went on at length about the church's problems (variously blamed on the bishops and, later, on "the people") but never raised questions of heresy, except perhaps obliquely by stressing the need for discipline.[36] In a sermon prepared for delivery to the synod Pole held in London in 1555, he upbraided the clergy for giving an opening to heretics by their covetousness, and proposed as a remedy for heresy no more than instruction in good doctrine.[37] This was an exceptionally mild proposal.

But in what was probably a set of instructions to one of his subordinates in the archbishopric of Canterbury, probably the person or persons in charge of dealing with heretics, Pole spelled out a remarkably lenient approach.[38] Almost immediately Pole offered a definition of a heretic which comes close to that ascribed to him by Beccadelli, Dudic, and Binardi.

Merely holding a heretical opinion was not enough, unless one adopted it of one's own judgment and defended it obstinately, and after one had been better informed. Pole wished heretics would argue that they had been led astray by their leaders, which might well mean that they could be spared the consequences once those leaders' opinion was condemned. Heretics' confidence in their own reasoning powers was what got them into trouble, but any who blamed their beliefs on their bishop were to be spared. Instead of appealing to reason, Pole clung to the test of "paternity," or tradition. Any heretic, like Cranmer, who could not point out the father of his idea was to be condemned. Pole did not have much patience—heretics were to be admonished only once or twice before being condemned—but they had at least some chance to come around.[39]

It must be more than coincidence that Pole's position here is nearly identical to the strongest case Dudic put in favor of what has been taken to be toleration: the Catholics at least could still point to consensus over time, to tradition. Since Pole's stance cannot be safely called any more than concordant (or perhaps no more than lenient), this must raise some questions about exactly what Dudic claimed. Unlike the later Dudic, of course, Pole thought he knew what the true church was, but he had earlier had his problems with that church and would again. As his instructions about penitent heretics already indicate, Pole's practice leaned toward de facto toleration.

That was certainly the way his first life-writers put the point. Even the second set, who found the most notorious instance of his dealings with suspected heresy an embarassment, still emphasized that he had dealt leniently with *some* heretics. Beccadelli was more forthright in presenting Pole's relations with Flaminio as an example of his *mansuetudo*. Flaminio led a contingent of Juan de Valdés's followers into Pole's household shortly after he moved to Viterbo as papal legate in 1541. Although there is room for reservations on the specifics of this point, Massimo Firpo's contention that Flaminio meant to convert Pole's household into the foremost Valdesian cell in Italy underscores the attraction it exercised.[40] As the *processi* against Pole's friends Giovanni Morone and Pietro Carnesecchi reveal, a large number of Pole's intimates held heterodox religious views, more than a few of which could be traced to Flaminio.[41]

Eventually Flaminio's close ties to Pole would help to put Pole under a cloud of quasi-official accusations of heresy emanating from Paul IV, the former Gianpietro Carafa. By at least 1550 the future pope had become deeply suspicious of Pole's "seducer" Flaminio, going so far as to visit his deathbed to be sure he died a good Christian. Both Pole and Beccadelli, however, defended Pole's relation to Flaminio by claiming that Pole had taken Flaminio under his protection in an effort to save him.[42] Be that as it may, Flaminio used Pole's patronage as an opportunity to help write the most famous product of the Italian Reformation, *Il Beneficio di Cristo*.[43] Pole and his wider circles, including Morone and Cardinal Contarini, who shortly after Flaminio joined Pole engaged in a more public effort to recuperate a group of heretics in Modena (including Castelvetro), thought very highly of the book.[44]

The *Beneficio* quickly found its way onto the Index of Prohibited Books and Pole seems to have come under Carafa's suspicion even more quickly.[45] But the opening represented by Pole's patronage of Flaminio did not close as soon as historians have thought: Pole and Carafa, although engaging in a fierce duel, left the conclave of Julius III in 1550 as members of still more or less the same group of reformers.[46] The impact of Pole's attitude to heresy during his nearly decade-long intimacy with Flaminio comes out most clearly in his attempts to prevent the council of Trent from dealing first with doctrine, in order not to offend the emperor, who was then deep in negotiations with his Lutheran subjects. Pole failed in this, as he did in the first round of discussion of doctrine over justification. This episode resulted in his infamous flight from the council, which he had earlier defined in what has been called an "ecumenical" way in line with his generally concordant views.[47]

When Pole returned to England in late 1554, he took charge of a concerted effort to return the country to Roman obedience. Although his successor as archbishop of Canterbury called him a "butcher," Pole generally stayed away from persecution.[48] John Foxe, one of the most successful of Protestant martyrologists, who thus had a special incentive to look for martyr-making enemies, offered what amounts to an encomium of Pole. Foxe could not avoid noting that Pole was a papist, but "none of the bloody and cruel sort of papists," not only because he restrained "Bloody" Edmund Bonner, the bishop of London, but also because of his "solicitous writings" to Cranmer, not to mention his own difficulties with Paul IV. All this "notwithstanding, the pomp and glory of the world carried him away to play the papist thus as he did."[49] Foxe implicitly concluded that only circumstances prevented Pole from at least practical toleration.

Pole undoubtedly prevented some of Bonner's worst excesses, at one point refusing to allow him to put on an enormous auto-da-fé.[50] In another famous instance, Pole treated the prominent Protestant John Cheke with great leniency, sufficient to persuade him to recant.[51] Cheke was deeply grateful.[52] Whoever besides Bonner may have been responsible for the sanguinary side of the Marian Reformation, the list of suspects should not include Pole. Once again, leniency does not, any more than concordance, mean toleration, but it may perhaps be counted as a practical step toward it.

The grossest apparent exception to this pattern in Pole's practice is the treatment of Cranmer. Jasper Ridley, David Loades, and A. G. Dickens all agree that Pole badly abused Cranmer, although neither Loades nor Dickens goes to the lengths Ridley did to inculpate Pole in a plot to destroy him, for which there is no evidence.[53] The fact that Foxe equated Pole's behavior to that of Cheke and Cranmer suggests that bias speaks through Ridley's interpretation much more than do the sources, and versions of both pieces of direct evidence for Pole's attitude passed through Foxe's hands. They are a pair of letters to Cranmer, one a lengthy polemical treatise and the other a fragment of November 1555.[54] Not much has been said about the first, except to compare it implicitly to the second, which has been called "bitter" (Ridley) and "cold, furious and abusive" (Loades). By the standards of sixteenth-century controversial writing, however, neither the treatise, *De sacramento*, nor the letter is excessively vicious, even when they both blame the entire subversion of Henry VIII on Cranmer, and the treatise also laid to his charge murder and a long list of other crimes. In *De sacramento*, Pole distinguished his much more stringent private views from his public stance as legate, and devoted at least some sections of the treatise to trying to persuade Cranmer more or less calmly. Pole had some reservations about sending the work to Cranmer, because he had heard that it would not prove effective, but concluded that grace was always possible while life lasted.[55] A similar if even more restrained attitude came out in Pole's instructions cited above. They presented Cranmer as merely the obvious example of a heretic who could not furnish a complete tradition for his Eucharistic views, from the early church right through to the immediate past.[56]

Pole was never directly involved in Cranmer's protracted trial, degradation and execution. He did, however, send Pedro de Soto, one of his most trusted agents, to reason with the imprisoned Cranmer after his trial in Oxford, and de Soto continued to be involved almost until the end.[57] Likewise, the man who finally persuaded Cranmer to produce an acceptable recantation, Juan de Villagarcia, a Spanish Dominican and then Regius professor of theology at Oxford, was a client of Pole's close spiritual ally, Bartolomé Carranza, and linked to Pole's household as well.[58] The view one takes of their actions will almost certainly depend on the attitude one takes to the whole proceeding, but there can still be no doubt that they acted much more moderately than Bonner or Henry Cole (also, it is true, a sometime dependent of Pole).

Thus it seems that even in the case of Cranmer, Pole still managed to take a more lenient, concordant stance than most of his associates or his queen. To say this is not to claim any special sanctity for Pole. Even the young Calvin could nearly adhere to concordance in the first edition of *The Institutes of Christian Religion*.[59] Rather, I mean to extend to Pole an argument about the anabaptists, and in particular their pacifism, or refusal to use force on their own or any one else's behalf.[60] Far from an entrenched principle right from the start, pacifism *became* a hallmark of most anabaptists once efforts to impose their views—the usual sixteenth-century attitude—had failed. That is, principle arose from force of circumstances. Then again, neither pacifism nor toleration could have arisen had the linguistic and conceptual resources to fill the opening created by circumstances not existed. I have suggested above that Pole's suspended position helped generate his concordant behavior, and that Pole and some of his allies, reflecting on those circumstances, made a virtue of necessity and assigned to Pole a firm belief in concordance. This was not yet toleration, but the continuing interaction between the concept of concordance and circumstances like Pole's marked a major drift toward it.

Three major consequences follow from this examination of Pole's case. First, potentially anyone finding him- or herself in circumstances like his might have come to ideas like his. Therefore, since Protestants did not monopolize such circumstances, the roots of toleration did not grow exclusively among them.[61] Second, Pole's perfectly typical case can serve as a reminder that a distinction between theory and practice is not very helpful in the Renaissance, especially in ethical matters, as Nancy Struever has recently argued.[62] Third, Pole illustrates the more general point that it is perhaps impossible to find a coherent theory of toleration then, as it sounds a salutary warning that any attempt to isolate such a theory may be doomed. But when have historians *found* a coherent anything, as opposed to inventing one? R. G. Collingwood notoriously attacked "scissors-and-paste" or "philogical" history for its incapacity to say anything interesting about the past precisely because that approach denied the active role of the historian's mind in its re-enactment. In other words, the meaning, the coherence of the past is unavoidably a product of the historian's efforts to understand.

That must be as true of the history of toleration as of any other facet of human experience.[63]

Notes

1. *Thomas Starkey: A Dialogue Between Pole and Lupset*, ed. Thomas F. Mayer, Camden Fourth Series 37 (London: Royal Historical Society, 1989), 90. My editorial symbols have been omitted throughout. For Starkey and Pole, see Thomas F. Mayer, *Thomas Starkey and the Commonweal: Humanist Politics and Religion in the Reign of Henry VIII* (Cambridge: Cambridge University Press, 1989), passim. There is no adequate biography of Pole, but see Dermot Fenlon, *Heresy and Obedience in Tridentine Italy: Cardinal Pole and the Counter-Reformation* (Cambridge: Cambridge University Press, 1972) and Martin Haile (pseud. of Marie Hallé), *The Life of Reginald Pole* (London: Pitman, 1911). I am at work on a new life. In the meanwhile, see my summary articles in David A. Richardson, ed., *Dictionary of Literary Biography* 132 (Detroit: Gale Research, 1993) and Hans J. Hillerbrand et al., eds., *Oxford Encyclopedia of the Reformation* (New York: Oxford University Press, 1996).

2. Domenico Caccamo, *Eretici italiani in Moravia, Polonia e Transilvania (1558–1611). Studi e documenti*, Corpus Reformatorum Italicorum, ed. Luigi Firpo and Giorgio Spini (Florence and Chicago: Sansoni and the Newberry Library, 1970), 116 called the necessity of toleration Dudic's "fundamental thesis."

3. Diana Robin, *Filelfo in Milan: Writings, 1451–1477* (Princeton, N.J.: Princeton University Press, 1991), introduction.

4. For a sketch of some of Pole's relations with his clients, see Thomas F. Mayer, "Nursery of Resistance: Reginald Pole and his Friends," in Paul A. Fideler and Mayer, eds., *Political Thought and the Tudor Commonwealth: Deep Structure, Discourse and Disguise* (London: Routledge, 1992), 50–74 and "When Maecenas Was Broke: Cardinal Pole's 'Spiritual' Patronage," *Sixteenth Century Journal* 27 (1996): 419–35.

5. Mario Turchetti, *Concordia o tolleranza? François Bauduin (1520–1573) e i "moyenneurs"* (Geneva: Droz, 1984), 591–95. Turchetti argues that everyone besides Castellio who expressed tolerationist views, above all Erasmus, did so for tactical reasons. J. Wayne Baker's current work would remove the exception for Castellio.

6. Turchetti, *Concordia o Tolleranza?*, 136, drawing a contrast between Pole, Pighe and others, and Martin Bucer.

7. Mayer, *Starkey*, 264 for Pighe and Pole. I would now stress Pighe's failure to get anything worthwhile out of Pole. John Calvin, *Acta synodi Tridentinae cum antidoto*, in *Opera Omnia* (Braunschweig: C. A. Schwetske, 1863–1900, 59 vols.), vol. 7 (Corpus Reformatorum, vol. 35), col. 386. Paolo Simoncelli, *Il caso Reginald Pole: Eresia e santità nelle polemiche religiose del Cinquecento* (Rome: Edizioni di Storia e Letteratura, 1977), 54–55 and 58–59 for Negri, and passim for Vergerio.

8. Mayer, *Starkey*, chap. 8.

9. This was William K. Jordan's opinion. *The Development of Religious Tol-*

eration in England, Vol. 1, *From the Beginning of the English Reformation to the Death of Queen Elizabeth* (Cambridge, Mass.: Harvard University Press/London: Allen and Unwin, 1932; reprint Gloucester, Mass.: Peter Smith, 1965), 60–61. Jordan was typical in baldly claiming that the *Dialogue*'s implicit argument in favor of toleration was "probably" Starkey's own.

10. Starkey, *Dialogue*, 141 for the law.

11. Starkey, *Dialogue*, 89–90.

12. Starkey, *Dialogue*, 137–41.

13. See Thomas F. Mayer, "Faction and Ideology: Thomas Starkey's *Dialogue*," *Historical Journal* 28 (1985): 1–25, 19 for the argument that Starkey could not have gone too far afield of Pole's views if he hoped to keep his patronage.

14. See most recently Gary Remer, "Dialogues of Toleration: Erasmus and Bodin," *Review of Politics* 56 (Spring 1994): 305–36.

15. I cite Robert Adams's translation, Desiderius Erasmus, *The Praise of Folly and Other Writings* (New York and London: W. W. Norton, 1989), 219–22. The Latin text is Desiderius Erasmus, *Opera Omnia* (Amsterdam: North-Holland, 1972), 1, part 3: 371–74.

16. Agnes Rióok-Szalay, "Erasmus und die ungarischen Intellekutellen des 16. Jahrhundert," in August Buck, ed., *Erasmus und Europa* (Wiesbaden: Harassowitz, 1988; Wolfenbüttler Abhandlungen zur Renaissanceforschung, 7), 125–26. For Dudic's biography, see Caccamo, *Eretici italiani*, 110ff.

17. Caccamo, *Eretici italiani*, 117n.

18. Caccamo, *Eretici italiani*, 122, and Pierre Costil, *André Dudith, humaniste hongrois 1533-1589: Sa vie, son oeuvre et ses manuscrits grecs* (Paris: Les Belles Lettres, 1935), 348 for the likely date.

19. For discussion, see Massimo Firpo, *Il problema della tolleranza religiosa nell'età moderna dalla riforma protestante a Locke* (Turin: Loescher, 1978), 97–98, where Dudic's argument is identified with Castellio's. Partial Italian translations of the two most important letters appear on 130–33. Cf. also Costil, *Dudith*, 339–51. Cf. the next note for the bibliography of Dudic's letter.

20. *Correspondance de Théodore de Bèze*, ed. Hippolyte Aubert, Alain Dufour, Claire Chimelli, and Béatrice Nicollier (Geneva: Droz, 1983), 11: 226–48, with more accurate bibliography than in Firpo and more complete than in Mino Celsi, *In haereticis coercendis quatenus progredi liceat. Poems—Correspondence*, ed. Peter G. Bietenholz (Naples and Chicago: Prismi and the Newberry Library, 1982), 612. All references below are drawn from *Correspondance de Bèze*.

21. I argue here by analogy to Allan Megill's classification of historians' attitudes to grand narrative. "Grand Narrative and the Discipline of History," in Frank Ankersmit and Hans Kellner, eds., *A New Philosophy of History* (London and Chicago: Reaktion Books and University of Chicago Press, 1995), 151–73.

22. Alexius Horányi claimed that Dudic met Pole at Maguzzano in 1550. *Memoria Hungarorum et provincialium scriptis editis notorum* (Vienna: Anton Loew, 1775), 1: 550, apparently building on the contemporary life of Dudic by Quirinus Reuter. See Costil, *Dudith*, 64–65 and 71–73 for his time with Pole.

23. Costil, *Dudith*, 448.

24. For the date of composition of Dudic's and Binardi's adaptation, see

Gigliola Fragnito, "Gli 'spirituali' e la fuga di Bernardino Ochino," *Rivista Storica Italiana*, 84 (1972): 777–811, 803n.

25. Costil, *Dudith*, 448 citing a letter of Dudic to one Sylburg, dated Breslau, 25 February 1585.

26. Andras Dudic, *Vita Reginaldi Poli* (Venice: Domenico and Giovanni Battista Guerrei, 1563), sig. 4r.

27. Ludovico Castelvetro was one, serving up a fairly nasty life of Binardi in "Racconto delle vite d'alcuni letterati del suo tempo di M. L. C. Modenese scritte per suo piacere," printed in Giuseppe Cavazzuti, *Ludovico Castelvetro* (Modena: Società Tipografica Modenese, 1903), appendix, 7–8, and Alemanio Fino was the other, in a letter to Luca Michelonio, Crema, 29 November, probably 1565. Bergamo, Biblioteca Civica "Angelo Mai," Carte Stella in Archivio Silvestri 41/197 (hereafter Carte Stella); cf. Giuseppe Bonelli, "Un archivio privato del Cinquecento: Le Carte Stella," *Archivio Storico Lombardo* 34 (1907): 332–86, no. 346.

28. The only two manuscripts of "De sacramento" emanating from Pole's circle (London, British Library, Harl. 417, fols. 49r–68v [hereafter BL] and Città del Vaticano, Biblioteca Apostolica Vaticana [hereafter BAV], Vat. lat. 5967, fols. 141r–7v) are probably in the hand of Pole's principal secretary, Marcantonio Faita.

29. Castelvetro, "Racconto."

30. Carte Stella, 40/155 (Bonelli, no. 178).

31. See Thomas F. Mayer, "A Sticking-Plaster Saint? Autobiography and Hagiography in the Making of Reginald Pole," in Mayer and D. R. Woolf, eds., *The Rhetorics of Life-Writing in Early Modern Europe: Forms of Biography from Cassandra Fedele to Louis XIV* (Ann Arbor: University of Michigan Press, 1995), 205–22.

32. Andras Dudic, *Vita Reginaldi Poli*, in A. M. Querini, ed., *Epistolarum Reginaldi Poli*, 5 vols. (Brescia: Rizzardi, 1744–57), 1: 57.

33. Sebastian Merkle, ed., *Concilium Tridentinum Diariorum Pars Prima* (Freiburg: Herder, 1901), 82. Cf. Fenlon, *Heresy and Obedience*, 134.

34. *Reginaldi Poli ad Henricum octavum Britanniae regem, pro ecclesiasticae unitatis defensione* (Rome: Antonio Blado, [1539]), fols. VIr and XCIXr. Cf. also fol. CXIr–v, where in the midst of an exhortation to Charles V to invade England, Pole contrasted the tolerant attitude of the Turks to Christians with Henry's treatment of those who disagreed with him.

35. Some versions of the work begin with the expectation of a general council, which would seem to mean that it could have been begun as early as 1537, shortly after Pole became a cardinal, or at least in 1542 when Trent opened. The only dated manuscript (Naples, Biblioteca Nazionale, IX. A. 14) comes from 1556. It was not at all unusual for Pole to gestate a work over such a long time. The main collection of manuscripts is BAV Vat. lat. 5964, assembled in the volume backwards in terms of likely order of composition.

36. For discipline, see, e.g., fols. 105r/268r/336r. The bishops bore the brunt of Pole's displeasure at the beginning of the work, only to be replaced by the *populus*. See, e.g., fol. 146r for the bishops and fols. 50v/246v, the beginning of a lengthy treatment of the manifold faults of the *populus*.

37. BAV, Vat. lat. 5968, fols. lar–4v.

38. The text (BAV Vat. lat. 5968, fols. 227r–56v, headed "A fragment tow-

chinge the sacrament of the altare" and possibly related to the following section described as a sermon) was incorrectly identified by R. H. Pogson, "Cardinal Pole—Papal Legate to England in Mary Tudor's Reign" (PhD diss., University of Cambridge, 1972), 203 as being addressed to the synod. The person in question may well have been Pole's archdeacon (and part-time biographer) Nicholas Harpsfield. Bibliothèque Publique, Douai, MS 922, vol. 3, fols. 16r–17r (written in Calais, 22 May 1555) is Pole's appointment of Harpsfield and others as inquisitors in the city and diocese of Canterbury. For his contribution to Pole's myth, see "Sticking-Plaster Saint," 207–9.

39. BAV, Vat. lat. 5968, fols. 227r–29v.

40. Massimo Firpo, *Tra alumbrados e "spirituali." Studi su Juan de Valdés e il Valdesianesimo nella crisi religiosa del '500 italiano* (Florence: Leo S. Olschki, 1990), 132–38.

41. Massimo Firpo and Dario Marcatto, eds., *Il processo inquisitoriale del Cardinal Giovanni Morone*, 5 vols. (Rome: Istituto italiano per la storia dell'età moderna e contemporanea, 1981–89), passim, and Giacomo Manzoni, ed., "Il Processo Carnesecchi," *Miscellanea di Storia Italiana* 10 (1870): 189–573 passim. Cf. also Sergio Pagano, ed., *Il processo di Endimio Calandra e l'Inquisizione a Mantova nel 1567-1568*, Studi e Testi 339 (Città del Vaticano: Biblioteca apostolica vaticana, 1991) *ad indices*.

42. Pole offered that explanation of his relations with Flaminio to Carafa in 1553. G. B. Morandi, ed., *Monumenta di varia letteratura*, 2 vols. (Bologna: Istituto per le Scienze, 1797–1804), 1, part 2: 350. Ludovico Beccadelli, "Vita di Reginaldo Polo," in ibid., 326–27.

43. Benedetto da Mantova, *Il Beneficio di Cristo*, ed. Salvatore Caponetto, Corpus Reformatorum Italicorum, ed. Luigi Firpo and Giorgio Spini (Dekalb and Chicago: Northern Illinois University Press and Newberry Library, 1972), 478ff.

44. *Beneficio*, 454 for Morone's early opinion and Massimo Firpo, "Gli 'spirituali,' l'Accademia di Modena e il formulario di fede del 1542: controllo del dissenso religioso e nicodemismo," in Massimo Firpo, *Inquisizione romana e Controriforma. Studi sul cardinal Giovanni Morone e il suo processo d'eresia* (Bologna: Il Mulino, 1992), 29–118.

45. Simoncelli, *Caso*, 23–26.

46. Thomas F. Mayer, "Il fallimento di una candidatura: Reginald Pole, la 'reform tendency' e il conclave di Giulio III," *Annali dell'Istituto Storico Italo-Germanico in Trento* 21 (1995): 41–67.

47. Fenlon, *Heresy and Obedience*, 104–15.

48. Matthew Parker called Pole a *carnifex* for his treatment of Cranmer in *De antiquitate britannicae ecclesiae* (London: Bowyer, 1729), 533.

49. George Townshend and Stephen R. Catteley, eds., *The Acts and Monuments of John Foxe*, 8 vols. (London: Seeley and Burnside, 1837–41), 5: 308.

50. 26 December 1556, Bonner-Pole, in ibid., 8: 307.

51. Rawdon Brown, ed., *Calendar of State Papers and Manuscripts, Relating to English Affairs in the Archives and Collections of Venice*, 9 vols. (London: Routledge and Kegan Paul, 1873–86), vol. 6, no. 536 (hereafter *CSPV*).

52. 15 July 1556, Cheke-Pole, from the Tower of London. BL Add. MS 32091, fol. 149r–v; printed in John Strype, *Ecclesiastical Memorials Relating Chiefly to Religion, and its Reformation, under the Reigns of King Henry VIII, King Edward VI, and Queen Mary*, 7 vols. (Oxford: Clarendon Press, 1816), 3: 2, no. LIV, from a manuscript in his possession. See also the summary in John Strype, *The Life of the learned Sir John Cheke* (Oxford: Clarendon Press, 1821), 111–12. Cheke had been kidnapped and brought back to England for trial. D. M. Loades, *The Oxford Martyrs* (New York: Stein and Day, 1970), 258.

53. Jasper Ridley, *Thomas Cranmer* (Oxford: Clarendon Press, 1962), e.g., chap. 24 passim. Cf. Loades, *Martyrs*, 223 and A. G. Dickens, *The English Reformation*, 2d ed. (University Park: Pennsylvania State University Press, 1991), 294, who writes of Pole's "cold, official ferocity."

54. See note 24 for the manuscripts. The treatise was printed in Cremona by Cristofor Dracono in 1584, allegedly from a manuscript the editor's father had gotten from one of Pole's familiars in Rome. Ridley, *Cranmer*, 382 and Loades, *Martyrs*, 223 both date *De sacramento* 1554, but on unknown evidence. It probably was written before 26 October 1555, when Pole apparently referred to the work in a letter to the nuncio in Brussels (*CSPV*, vol. 6, no. 255). The second of Pole's letters, dated 6 November, is in BL Harl. 417, fols. 69r–78v; it is mutilated but still has his original signature. It is printed in John Strype, *Memorials of the Most Reverend Father in God Thomas Cranmer*, 2 vols. (Oxford: Clarendon Press, 1812), 2: 972–89.

55. 26 October 1555, BAV, Vat. lat. 6754, fols. 181r–2r; *CSPV* 6: 1, no. 255.

56. Vat. lat. 5968, fols. 227rff. A later set of sermon notes in the same volume (fols. 446r–82v) also merely blamed Cranmer in fairly mild terms for having led the English church astray.

57. Ridley, *Cranmer*, 379–80.

58. Carte Stella 40/145 (Bonelli, "Carte Stella," no. 168), Henry Pyning-Gianfrancesco Stella, London, 27 August 1559, which reported that Villagarcia had been seized in Zeeland on the orders of the Spanish Inquisition. For Villagarcia's close relations with Carranza (and hence by extension with Pole) and his time in Oxford, see J. I. Tellechea Idigoras, *Fray Bartolomé Carranza y el Cardenal Pole: Un navarro en la restauración católica (1554–1558)* (Pamplona: Institución Príncipe de Viana, 1977), 245ff. and James McConica, ed., *The History of the University of Oxford*, vol. 3, *The Collegiate University* (Oxford: Oxford University Press, 1986), 145, 325, and 353. Ridley, *Cranmer*, calls Villagarcia "Garcina" throughout.

59. John Calvin, *Selections from His Writings*, ed. John Dillenberger (Garden City, N.Y.: Doubleday, 1971), 301. Latin text in *Institutio religionis christianae (1536)*, *Opera Omnia*, vol. 2, cols. 76–77.

60. Steven M. Ozment, *The Age of Reform, 1250–1550: An Intellectual and Religious History of Late Medieval and Reformation Europe* (New Haven, Conn.: Yale University Press, 1980), 347, building on the work of James M. Stayer, *Anabaptists and the Sword* (Lawrence, Kan.: Coronado Press, 1976), esp. part 4.

61. Firpo, *Tolleranza*, 14–15 argues that toleration could only have arisen among Protestants.

62. Cf. Nancy S. Struever, *Theory as Practice: Ethical Inquiry in the Renaissance* (Chicago: University of Chicago Press, 1992).

63. R. G. Collingwood, *The Idea of History* (New York: Oxford University Press, 1956), 249–302. Megill, "Grand Narrative," 162 briefly summarizes Collingwood's argument and recasts it in terms of the imposition of coherence.

5

The Concept of Toleration in the *Colloquium Heptaplomeres* of Jean Bodin

Marion Leathers Kuntz

FOR THE MODERN READER the concept of toleration developed by Jean Bodin in his *Colloquium Heptaplomeres de rerum sublimium arcanis abditis* makes the work an important link with ideas of the Enlightenment. For our troubled modern age Bodin's dialogue may hold insights about toleration which are meaningful to us as we struggle with the questions of fragmentation and the resurgence of intolerance. Modern commentators have often mentioned tolerance as a significant aspect of the *Colloquium Heptaplomeres* but have seldom agreed on the nature of toleration expressed in the dialogue. Georg Roellenbleck has argued that Bodin reached no conclusion in regard to toleration, since the seven speakers maintained their own positions without change.[1] Mario Turchetti has recently published an important article on tolerance in the sixteenth century, although he surprisingly does not refer to Bodin's *Colloquium Heptaplomeres*.[2] He makes a strict distinction between tolerance and concord, arguing that for the most part Catholics and Protestants wanted concord, in which all would practice the same religion, instead of toleration.[3] Turchetti defined toleration in regard to its legal and psychological aspects, but no clear definition of concord emerges.[4] If Turchetti had considered Bodin's *Colloquium Heptaplomeres* in regard to the topic of toleration and concord, he would have perhaps arrived at a different conclusion.

The present discussion will attempt to demonstrate that harmony or *concordia* is the starting point for toleration, a by-product as it were, of harmony. The type of harmony or concord Bodin used as the underpinnings of his arguments did not demand unanimity of opinion. To make the point clear without being explicit, he framed his arguments around a *concordia discors* in God and nature. He also used discussions of musical harmonies to reinforce his theme. We shall demonstrate structural elements of the dialogue which elucidate Bodin's theme of harmony based on multiplicity, which in turn produces a tolerant attitude toward the opinions of others. Bodin's concept of toleration relies on the premise that all things are in all and share certain attributes in common. Toleration in the *Colloquium Heptaplomeres* is inclusive rather than exclusive.

Bodin does not develop an explicit theory of toleration in his dialogue. The major theme of the *Colloquium* is harmony,[5] from which toleration flows because variety adds to the harmony. Bodin's concept of toleration is not relativistic, exclusive, or disinterested. Toleration is inclusive, since it is based on knowledge of various opinions. Like harmony, it is inherent in the nature of things but must be sought out and understood by people. Bodin's concept of toleration does not imply cold sufferance but rather reveals a warm acceptance on a personal level and the ability to discuss differences on an intellectual level.[6] The interlocutors in Bodin's dialogue demonstrate civility and respect, common ground, and the many facets of truth as essential to the practice of toleration.

The *Colloquium Heptaplomeres* has had a checkered history. The manuscript circulated clandestinely in the sixteenth century.[7] Publication was announced in 1719; printing began in 1720, but, mysteriously, was forbidden by the civil officials of Leipzig. The manuscript was copied continuously, however, so that at the beginning of the eighteenth century almost every scholar of note had a copy. Queen Christina of Sweden commissioned the French erudite Claude Sarrau to secure a copy for her from the library of Henri de Même, who denied having one, as did Richelieu, Mazarin, and Guy Patin, although each did indeed possess it. Isaac Vossius aided in the search, and the Queen finally received her copy, which is now in the Vatican Library, Rome.[8] The *Colloquium Heptaplomeres* was written at least by 1588, since a manuscript at the Bibliothèque Mazarine carries that date.[9] Preachers declaimed against the work as soon as its existence was known, calling Bodin a Judaizer and an atheist. Its clandestine circulation added to its mystery in the sixteenth and seventeenth centuries. Bodin's fame in his lifetime and in later centuries, however, was a result of his *La République* and his *Methodus*.

The Latin reading public by the mid-nineteenth century was decidedly smaller, especially in America. A facsimile of the original printing of 1857 was published in 1966,[10] yet the *Colloquium Heptaplomeres* was only occasionally cited. In the twenty years since the *Colloquium* was published in English translation (the only complete, modern translation), Bodin's dialogue has finally come into its own. It was the subject of an international congress at Wolfenbüttel in 1994,[11] and scholars in various disciplines now consider it one of the most significant Renaissance texts.[12]

The *Colloquium Heptaplomeres* is a dialogue among men of seven different religious faiths or philosophic persuasions. The work contains six books in which the seven participants speak to each other about a variety of topics including nature, miracles, magicians, hidden meanings, divine law, truth and falsity, God, and which religion is the true and the best, to name only a few of the subjects of their conversations. The choice of Venice as the setting of the *Colloquium Heptaplomeres* was a significant aspect in the development of Bodin's concept of toleration. In the sixteenth century Venice was perhaps the most international city in Europe and represented the greatest blending of nationalities of East and West.[13] We know that Christians, Jews, Turks, Greeks, Armenians, Arabs, and others lived and worked side by side in the *Serenissima*. The participants in the dialogue also represent diverse beliefs and persuasions as well as different personality types. There is a trinity of Christians (Catholic, Lutheran, Calvinist), a duo of Jew and Arab, and another duo of natural philosopher and skeptic. One should note that, just as in Venice, where Christians had commerce with Jews, Arabs, and Turks, so in the dialogue the boundaries of religious persuasions were often crossed. This is an important structural element which will be discussed later. Bodin eulogized Venice in the first few lines of the dialogue:

Whereas other cities and districts are threatened by civil wars or fear of tyrants or either by exactions of taxes or the most annoying inquiries into one's activities, this seemed to me to be nearly the only city that offers immunity and freedom from all these kinds of servitude. This is the reason why people come here from everywhere, wishing to spend their lives in the greatest freedom and tranquillity of spirit, whether they are interested in commerce or craft or leisure pursuits as befit a free man. (Kuntz, *Colloquium*, 3)

Praise of Venice was common in the sixteenth century, not only among Venetians but among many Europeans. It has recently been noted that Bodin's description of Venice did not coincide with the reality of the Venetian Inquisition.[14] Yet one can argue that the Venetian Inquisition in the sixteenth century was relatively mild, according to recent opinions; at least one Inquisitor urged a young heretic to think of him as a *medicus* and as a father.[15] On certain occasions the Venetian Inquisition was open to the public during testimony and/or recantations. In the trial of Giacomo Callegaro, who made a long confession and denial of his former heresies, the doors of the Chapel of San Teodoro (the normal meeting place of the Inquisition), which was contiguous to the Basilica of San Marco, were left open for the large crowd gathered outside to witness the proceedings.[16] An open meeting of the Venetian Inquisition would demonstrate the tolerance practiced by the *Serenissima* and at the same time would serve as a warning to Venetians against the heresies of Anabaptists like Giacomo Callegaro. When Venice was compared in the Cinquecento with France, beset by civil strife and massive blood-letting, the *Serenissima* did indeed appear to be a haven of freedom and stability, as Bodin described. The Venetian Inquisition could be considered a mild instrument of punishment in comparison with the horrors of the wild passions unleashed in France from 1562–1593.[17]

Venice in the sixteenth century was home to numerous academies like that of Coronaeus, in whose home Bodin placed his dialogue of seven savants.[18] Many Venetian patricians frequented these gatherings, in which religion, philosophy, literature, and the arts were discussed. They were often investigated by the Venetian Inquisition. If an accused told the truth to the Inquisitor and indicated his contrition, his punishment was usually mild, no matter how heretical he may have previously been. This fact can be supported by a study of the *processi* in the records of the Holy Office of the Inquisition. When one considers life in the sixteenth century, Venice was certainly an appropriate setting for Bodin's dialogue.

The dialogue form seems especially appropriate for Bodin's presentation of his major themes. As we shall see, music is a central theme in the *Colloquium*, and through the poetry and songs in the dialogue Bodin's meaning is gradually revealed. Music is related to the dialogue form, since the *dialogo* is the term used to indicate all vocal compositions whose literary text reproduces the conversation of two or more speakers.[19] The musical dialogue was in vogue from around 1450 until 1638. The greatest variety of musical dialogues were composed in Italy, and especially in Venice. In 1559 Adrian Willaert published in Venice his *Musica Nova*, in which he included four compositions for seven voices entitled *Dialoghi*.[20] The musical dialogue is appropriately polyphonic in the most extended significance of the word, and it is a form considered typically Venetian. Because of the importance of the musical dialogues in Venice in the Cinquecento, especially those of Willaert, it is clearly no accident that Bodin used Venice as the setting of a written dialogue in which music pervades the discussions. Willaert used seven voices in his *Dialoghi* just as Bodin used seven speakers in his dialogue.

The Catholic Coronaeus had formed an intimate society of scholarly men in his home, "so that his home was considered a shrine of the Muses and virtues" (Kuntz, *Colloquium*, 3). Bodin writes that Coronaeus was an unusual scholar who had "an incredible desire to understand the language, inclinations, activities, customs, and virtues of different peoples." All the men he entertained as guests in his home were from abroad—not one was a Venetian or a Catholic. Coronaeus was not only tolerant of different opinions, but was especially disposed to men of disparate cultures and beliefs. Each man with his foreign sounding name—Fridericus Podamicus, Hieronymus Senamus, Diegus Toralba, Antonius Curtius, Salomon Barcassius, Octavius Fagnola—was warmly received as an equal in the home of Coronaeus. Each of the six guests represented a major religious persuasion or philosophical opinion in the sixteenth century: Lutheran, skeptic, natural philosopher, Calvinist, Jew, and Mohammedan.

Coronaeus, a Roman Catholic, set the tone for his guests and also the agenda for discussions. The guests, however, could pursue their own particular lines of inquiry as they developed the topics. The civility of Coronaeus as host was extraordinary, as was that of the guests to each other and to him. In spite of the fact that they had many conflicting views which they expounded with passion and conviction, they

lived not merely with sophistication of discourse and charming manners, but with such innocence and integrity that no one so much resembled himself as all resembled all; for they were not motivated by wrangling or jealousy but by a desire to learn; consequently they were displaying all their reflections and endeavours in true dignity. (4)

This description of the ambiance of Coronaeus's home and the diverse persons who lived there appears early in Bodin's dialogue and significantly establishes civility as an underlying principle of the tolerant attitudes of Coronaeus and his guests. Though all came from different backgrounds and culture, their civility of discourse and manners and their intelligence and desire to know made them a homogeneous body. Bodin emphasized this point by noting that each one was more like the others than like himself. The "all things in all" (*omnia in omnibus*) theme, expressed at the outset by the description of the members of Coronaeus's household as "all resembling all," lays the foundation for the theme of toleration in the *Colloquium Heptaplomeres*. This theme was to be repeated throughout the work.

Not only the speakers in the dialogue but even the furniture in the house represent the "all things in all" theme. The most impressive object in Coronaeus's home, which was filled "with an infinite variety and supply of books and old records . . . also instruments either for music or for all sorts of mathematical arts," was a grand *armadio* called a *pantotheca* (4). This veritable "theater of the world" was six feet square; each foot was divided into six square compartments so that the *pantotheca* held 1296 small boxes in which were displayed "likenesses of sixty fixed stars, then the replicas of planets, comets and similar phenomena, elements, bodies, stones, metals, fossils, plants, living things of every sort, . . . each in its own class." Since some things could not be acquired, they were represented by a drawing or description according to its classification. To illustrate the universe better, Coronaeus

had complete plants or roots displayed separately on rather large charts so that each box contained a particle of plant and animal life and in this arrangement: the last was connected to the first, the middle to the beginning and the end, and all to all in its appropriate class. (4–5)

Bodin's description of this fascinating object emphasizes the relationships of the parts of the universe to each other. The *pantotheca* allows him to demonstrate the "all things in all" theme in the natural world. Before the end of the first book, he has established a basis for toleration in the world without making the point explicit. If all parts of the universe are related to each other, and if all civilized men of good will resemble each other as do the guests of Coronaeus, one must surely ask at the outset how can men not be tolerant of each other?

Coronaeus had studied the contents in the little boxes of the *pantotheca* until he knew them all by heart. His knowledge of the universe and its interrelationships had obviously prepared him for his role as host of a disparate gathering of learned men. In the atmosphere of his home and under his subtle tutelage, his guests developed such an appreciation of each other that all seemed similar to each other, as Bodin clearly stated. The relationship of the interlocutors is illustrative of what I mean by Bodin's implicit theory of toleration. One should also note that no speaker ever refutes the other. This technique allows each speaker's opinion to have validity. In addition, each disparate opinion adds another dimension of truth to the subject under discussion. This method is essential to the seven savants, who are motivated by a great desire to know. Bodin is again implicitly indicating by the methodology he has chosen to use for the dialogue that only knowledge can help one understand human nature and the natural world. The men's conversations enhance the knowledge of each, since each man is expert in his given field. Knowledge opens windows and doors hitherto closed, and thereby renders accessible previously unknown ideas, customs, and beliefs as resources for all people. Knowledge puts man in closer touch with himself, with other men, and with nature.

Each day Coronaeus allowed ample time for the discussions, and each guest was well-qualified to participate in the conversations. Their various opinions had been carefully weighed before being spoken, and so were respected by the others even if not wholly accepted. When questions were raised for which preparation had not been made, discussion was delayed until the following day. Thus in the *Colloquium* knowledge is an essential facet of toleration. The vast knowledge of Coronaeus and his guests is a paradigm for the tolerant society in which they live.

The home of Coronaeus, a veritable "shrine of the Muses and Virtues," represented a microcosm of an ideal, tolerant society. If it represented the microcosm, Venice by analogy represented the macrocosm and served as a model for other cities and nations in the sixteenth century. Like the home of Coronaeus, Venice was home to people of numerous faiths and cultures from all over the world. This remarkable blend of manners, customs, languages, and beliefs produced an exotic mixture of opposites and contrasts, yet also a stable society in which all could enjoy its benefits. Sixteenth-century Venice represented the *concordia discors* that also defined Bodin's concept of harmony. One could ask where else in the world of the sixteenth century could such a dialogue as that described by Bodin in the *Colloquium Heptaplomeres* have taken place.

The number of interlocutors and also the number of books in the dialogue are significant structural aspects of the *Colloquium* that implicitly reveal the theme of harmony with its by-product, toleration. The number seven is appropriately chosen for the participants in the dialogue because the components of seven, namely three and four, have significance not only in Christianity and Judaism but also in the pagan world. In addition, the lyre or *lyra da braccio* of medieval and renaissance Italy and France usually had seven chords, though sometimes six. The lyre figures prominently in the music of the *Colloquium*, so the seven speakers in the dialogue perhaps represent the seven-chord lyre from which a complete harmony could evolve (la1–so2–fa3–mi4–re5–do6–si7).[21] Therefore the combination of three and four, and both three and four separately, would take into account priorities according to number of all the participants in the dialogue.

Bodin divided the *Colloquium* into six books. He noted in the first book that the number six was the perfect number among the digits. According to Bodin, the number six was represented most often in nature: "There are six perfect bodies, six simple colours, six harmonies, six simple metals, six regions, also six senses including common sense" (4). Furthermore, in Renaissance music theory the number six was considered the perfect number in which every musical consonance was found. In 1558 Gioseffo Zarlino da Chioggia published in Venice *Le istitutioni harmoniche*, in which he wrote of the number six:

There are also many properties of the number six; nonetheless, in order not to prolong the discussion, I shall recount only those things which apply to the topic: the first will be that, among the perfect numbers six is the first and contains in itself parts which are proportioned among themselves in such a way that, taking any two that one wishes, they have such a relation, that they give the reason, or form of one of the proportions of the musical consonances, either simple or composed as it is; . . . These then are the properties of the number six and of its parts; it is impossible to be able to find these in any other number whether it is less or greater.[22]

The citation from Zarlino is especially suggestive of the themes of the *Colloquium*. As we shall see, music becomes the medium through which each man in the dialogue becomes linked with the others. At the conclusion of each day's discussions, Coronaeus called in the choirboys, "who were accustomed to soothe everybody's spirits by sweetly singing divine praises with a harmony of lyres, flutes, and voices" (15).

Music is also used as a structural element to provide unity for the six books of the *Colloquium*. In the opening discussions of Book IV, music is the central theme. After the midday meal they all thank God and then sing hymns of praise. Coronaeus opens the afternoon conversations by asking "why there is such sweetness in a tone that has the full octave, the fifth and fourth blended at the same time." He noted that "although the highest tone is opposite to the lowest, why is it that harmonies in unison, in which no tone is opposite, are not pleasing to the trained ear?" (144). A learned conversation about musical harmonies develops, revealing the significance of music and musical discussions in the sixteenth century, especially in Venice.[23] Many different musical tastes are expressed by the participants in the dialogue, yet all agree with Toralba, who is a philosopher of nature, that

that pleasing delight of colors, tastes, odors, and harmonies depends on the harmony of the nature of each, a harmony which depends on the blended union of opposites. For example, something too hot or too cold offends the touch; likewise too much brightness or too much darkness offends the sight, and too much sweetness and too much bitterness offends the taste. But if these are blended by nature or art, they seem most pleasing. (145)

From the discussion of music the concept of the contrariety of opposites evolves as a principal basis, not only for harmony, but also for toleration. The participants in the dialogue agree that where there is no dissonance or opposite sounds, there can be no harmony. "Tones in unison would take away all sweetness and harmony," Toralba opines (146). Bodin allows each speaker to note in one way or another that contrarieties can be blended by nature or by art. Some things, however, can never be blended because their natures are completely different. Oil and vinegar, though pleasing to the taste, can never be mingled by any force, for example. When things cannot be blended in nature, when one pulls against the other, there can be no harmony. Octavius, a convert to Islam from Christianity, applies the point to music:

I think harmony is produced when many sounds can be blended; but when they cannot be blended, one conquers the other as the sound enters the ears, and the dissonance offends the delicate senses of wiser men. (145)

Toralba provides a summary of the topic that delineates the boundaries of *concordia discors*:

. . . things which are contrary to each other in nature herself cannot be mingled by design, but only blended, joined, or united so that they seem to be one. (146)

He uses as an example the syrup called oxymel, made from vinegar and honey, two contrary tastes. When cooked, however, bitter and sweet together, the taste thus blended becomes bittersweet or sweet and sour, "a flavor most pleasing to the palate." Bodin is making the point that even when things cannot be mingled by nature or design, a blending of opposites can take place so that the contraries *"seem to be one."* Even the appearance of union, the seeming to be one, as Bodin says, can be pleasing, as, for example, the taste of oxymel. This point is again reinforced by Fridericus, the Lutheran mathematician in the group, by a reference to musical modulations in which "contrariety does not seem to be destroyed, but extreme opposites are brought together by intermingling of the middle tones" (146).

This discussion of musical harmonies and the contrariety of opposites is an essential element in the structure of the *Colloquium*. These fascinating arguments are placed in the middle of Book IV, which is also the middle of the whole work. The question of contrariety with its central position in the structure of the work seems to be the hinge that holds the whole together. As previously pointed out, there are many statements made by the interlocutors about the relationship of the middle to the extremes. This is expressed in Book I in the "all things in all" theme and in the conclusion about enharmonics. The theme of *concordia discors* in the middle of Book IV is the center or middle that links the extremes.

The mean or middle is not easy to find, however, and when found always seems to have some hindrance, "as health with sickness, pleasure with pain, peace of mind with anxiety," according to the skeptic Senamus (147). A hindrance can be a blessing, however, for when the mean is found it is all the more appreciated. Impediments are even necessary, according to Bodin, "as a drainage ditch is in a city." The Calvinist Curtius illustrates the point:

Even that keenest sweetness of harmony which we have heard most eagerly just now would not have been so pleasing unless the musician had contrived some dissonant or harsh note for our sensitive ears, since the pleasure is not perceived without a pain that precedes it, and produces boredom when continued too long. (147)

In the lengthy discussion of musical harmonies Bodin indicates that God is the paradigm of *concordia discors* for man. He expresses poetically this idea, which is central to the concept of toleration in the *Colloquium*. We should also note that many important ideas are revealed through the poetry in the *Colloquium*. The poems are expressed in the various meters of Latin poetry, thereby enhancing the relationship of music and idea. This poem about God as the most perfect example of *concordia discors* is the most important poem in the *Colloquium* and is especially significant for our understanding of toleration in the work. It is worth citing in its entirety:

Creator of the world three times greatest of all,
Three times best parent of the heaven,
Who tempers the changes of the world,
Giving proper weight to all things,
And who measures each thing from His own ladle
In number, ratio, time,
Who with eternal chain joins with
remarkable wisdom two things,

opposite in every way, preparing
protection for each,
Who, moderating melody with different
sounds and voices
yet most satisfying to sensitive ears,
heals sickness,
has mingled cold with heat
and moisture with dryness,
the rough with the smooth,
sweetness with pain,
shadows with light, quiet with motion,
tribulation with prosperity,
Who directs the fixed courses of the heavenly stars
from east to west,
west to east
with contrary revolutions,
Who joins hatred with agreement,
a friend to hateful enemies.
This greatest harmony of the universe,
though discordant contains our safety. (147)

The problem of contrariety and the middle ground was also a significant aspect of political stability. Bodin advises through his interlocutors that it is wise to have more than two factions in a state lest there be continual strife. Three or more factions would provide a middle ground toward which two opposite factions could turn. Bodin presents here a strong argument for toleration based on pragmatism. For the stability of a state multiple parties are better than one or two, since one is normally in opposition to the other. Recalling the discussions of musical harmonies, one could say that one party, like a diatonic scale, tends to become boring. Two are in constant opposition, therefore too dissonant. Three or more provide the middle ground for a harmonious state, as in a musical harmony where dissonance is blended into the whole.

Since God alone is the only perfect contrariety of opposites, man has Him and nature as perennial models. Nature is the most ancient exemplar of a well-ordered state, since all elements which are contrary, even the stars themselves, are subject to divine majesty. Therefore God alone can be said "to reconcile peace in the lofty abodes" (150). Bodin's arguments about the well-ordered state are also applied to the appropriate number of religious persuasions in a state, and to which religion was best. This is perhaps the most difficult question argued in the *Colloquium*. Bodin allows the Lutheran Fridericus to joke about the difficulty of the task: "Would that now a certain Elias in sight of kings and people would prove by a heavenly sign which religion from so many is best" (173). On the particulars of this thorny problem the guests of Coronaeus can find no common ground; however, when general principles are presented, the middle ground is found. For example, principles which have been formulated with reason find acceptance with God. The Mohammedan Octavius cites St. Thomas Aquinas to prove the point: "When errant reason has established something as a precept of God, then it is the same thing to scorn the dictate of reason and the commands of God" (157–58). Knowledge is also presented as essential to the reasoning process. Bodin apparently wants to test his theory of *concordia discors*, as the principal aspect of toleration in regard to religious questions. Although several speakers agree that religious rites should not be blended, the question of contrariety is still significant. Bodin has Toralba present the argument that "it is certain that the best and most ancient religion of all was implanted in the human minds with right reason by eternal God, and this religion proposed the one eternal God as the object of man's worship" (185). God and the worship of Him should be the sole concern of man. God is also, according to Bodin, the exemplar of *concordia discors*. Therefore natural religion (which has God as its author) exemplifies the central principle of contrariety or *concordia discors*. In the complex problem of religious toleration, Bodin sees natural religion as the mean or middle ground between the extremes.

In a brilliant tour de foree Bodin allows Toralba and Salomon, the Jew, to dominate the discussions about religion, which is contrary to his usual practice in allotting speeches to his characters. By the preponderance of ideas about religion spoken by Toralba and Salomon, Bodin is implicitly designating the confession of God as Parent of the Universe and the worship of Him alone as the middle ground on which all men can agree. Natural reason given by God to every man equips him with the ability to worship God. Bodin had Toralba repeat many times that God had written the law of nature into the heart of every man. A philosophic argument from Simplicius is also introduced to support the primacy of natural philosophy: "As long as the human soul shall cling with deepest roots to its originator, it shall easily safeguard this integrity in which it was created; but if the soul is torn away from its source, it will languish and wither until it turns itself again to its origin and founder" (185). Bodin's citation from one of the last seven philosophers of Plato's Academy before it was closed in A.D. 529 by Justinian is typical of his method of linking "all things to all." Neo-Platonism, also an aspect of Bodin's *Colloquium*, continued to be an influence in Christian theology (208).

Bodin's method of expressing his concept of toleration based on *concordia discors* is to move away from the particular, which is often a point of disagreement, toward a general statement or principle to which most could adhere. The law of nature provides such a general principle. So also does the Decalogue. Salomon the Jew notes that "God surely ordered nothing in a loud voice except the Decalogue" (187). He also spoke at length about the moral law that oversees the worship of God and the mutual duties men have among themselves. Salomon quotes God's admonition to King Solomon to indicate the essence of the Ten Commandments: "Bind these upon your fingers; write them upon the tablets of your hearts" (188). Then he explains:

In this neat allegory of ten fingers He indicated the ten headings of the Decalogue, and by the double tablet of the heart He meant that the first tablet of the Decalogue pertains to the higher faculty of the soul which is the mind itself to which the laws of the first tablet about divine worship are related; the second tablet is related to the lower part of the soul by which we are taught to control anger, to restrain passion, to master desire, to keep our minds, eyes, and hands from another's possessions. (188)

The law of nature and the Decalogue reveal two general principles about which all agree. Bodin develops the interrelationship of natural law and the Decalogue through the discourses of Salomon. He has Salomon speak thus:

From these matters, you can know . . . that all the secrets of the highest matters and the hidden treasures of nature are concealed in the divine laws, that is, even in the records and books of our elders. Abraham Aben Esra considered this Decalogue to be the epitome of natural law. Since the latter seemed to be obliterated and violated by the greatest sins and crimes of men, the best and greatest God, having pity on the ruin of man, renewed the laws and prohibitions of nature with solemn covenant in the greatest assemblies of His people and incised on stone tablets with the clang of trumpets, with thunder, lightning and flames striking on Mount Horeb even to the midst of the heaven. (191)

When Salomon contemplates the Divine Goodness as exemplified in His Law, he breaks into a poetic song about the Decalogue, "as if struck by divine madness." Bodin reiterates and extends the relationship of the law of nature and the Decalogue by having Toralba, the natural philosopher, ask:

"What is this covenant which was perceived on two tablets and under ten headings except the very law of nature?" (192). Nature is the handmaiden of God and we have taken the law from nature, according to Toralba, who remarks that:

> In consequence of this law we were not instructed, but made, not taught, but imbued with the knowledge that eternal God, the first cause, is not only the effector of all things, but also the preserver. . . . Although there is no law which is not weakened by some limitation of time or place or person, still this one law is eternal. (192)

Because God is the first cause and preserver of all things, He must be "loved and honored with the complete power of our soul." Other laws are weakened by some limitation of time, place, or person. The Decalogue, however, is eternal. "With no exception is it violable, and it applies to all places, times, and persons: namely that God must be solely loved and followed" (192). The Law of God provides the general guide for life for all men everywhere, regardless of particular cultures or beliefs.

The moral principles expressed in God's Law universally direct the acts of rational men. All the participants in Bodin's dialogue with their different religious persuasions and various cultures found a common ground of agreement in the general moral principles of the Decalogue. To find *concordia* in the moral realm means that one can agree on general principles of moral prerogatives while at the same time respecting the particulars such as rites and dogma with which one may not agree. The particular can be called *discors*, while the general can be seen as *concordia*. This type of contrariety is a theme expressed throughout the *Colloquium*. Harmony in the state and harmony among religions depend on general principles that find the greatest common agreement and respect for the particular opinions and beliefs which are different from the majority. Bodin seems to be saying that for a society to be harmonious it must demonstrate a tolerance based on the principle of contrariety or *concordia discors*. Coronaeus, the host, notes that learned men have various opinions. In his home many divergent opinions are expressed, and Coronaeus respects all opinions even though he does not agree with all of them. The seven savants in Coronaeus's home exemplify the type of *concordia discors* Bodin believed was the foundation of toleration; they agree on general moral principles expressed in the Decalogue; they are always civil and courteous in spite of differing on particulars. Their respect for each other increases through knowledge gained from each other as well as from books, letters, the *pantotheca*, and instruments of music and science.

A few words should be said about Coronaeus, the Catholic host. Although Coronaeus holds firm to teachings of the Roman Church and believes its rites and practices are superior, he is the tolerant host who allows free argumentation to develop among his six guests. He treats all discourse with respect and courtesy. Coronaeus is the fulcrum that balances the disparate opinions. He opens his home to these men of various cultures, thereby demonstrating that he wants his own particular beliefs to be enriched by knowledge garnered from others. Coronaeus represents a truly catholic man, a paradigm for what a Roman Catholic should represent. Although Coronaeus was a devout Roman Catholic, his catholicity made him understanding when confronted with other beliefs. His knowledge made him tolerant, even as he clung to his own persuasion.

It has often been argued that one speaker or another represented the ideas of Bodin. Senamus the skeptic, Toralba the natural philosopher, and Salomon the Jew are often favored as the interlocutors who reveal Bodin's thought.[24] I believe these opinions are misguided, since his concept of harmony and toleration depends on *concordia discors*. All the speakers represent Bodin's opinions, and Coronaeus is representative not only of an ideal Catholic in the Cinquecento but of an ideal Catholicism that is truly catholic, being defined by *concordia discors*. This point is very important for an understanding of Bodin's religious views and his concept of toleration. Bodin was accused of being a Jew, a Protestant, and a heretic. My own opinion is that Bodin's religious views changed from time to time but that at least by 1588 he was a Catholic on the order of Coronaeus in the *Colloquium*.[25] Coronaeus's role in the dialogue gradually evolves, until he becomes the mediator between the non-Christians and the Christians. Coronaeus believes in the authority and magisterium of the Roman Church, but his belief does not hinder his appreciation of the non-Christians; in addition, his role as harmonizer also leads him to be tolerant of and even in agreement with some views of the non-Christians. Even if Bodin in his own life could not find the certainty of faith of Coronaeus, he was nevertheless inspired to describe the tolerance of an educated, loving Catholic like Coronaeus. All the speakers in Bodin's *Colloquium* taken together represent *concordia discors*,[26] and each separately represents *discors*. Therefore in Bodin's view of toleration each opinion must be blended with another to obtain a true harmony or contrariety as a foundation for a toleration which endures.

We have mentioned earlier the significance of music in the *Colloquium* in relation to the poetry in the dialogue and also in the discussions about musical harmonies. The conclusion returns to the theme of music and reinforces the theme of *concordia discors* as a basis for toleration in the *Colloquium*. At the end of a long discussion about harmony and toleration in society Coronaeus, as was the custom, has his amanuensis summon the choirboys to sing a song. This time, however, Coronaeus presents to the boys the song he wishes to be performed. The music requested represents the theme of *concordia discors* and also defines again the *persona* of Coronaeus. The song is as follows:

Lo, how good and pleasing it is for brothers to live in unity, arranged not in common diatonics or chromatics, but in enharmonics with a certain, more divine modulation. (471)

In my opinion, this song, the last in the *Colloquium Heptaplomeres*, contains the key for understanding the whole work. The first line in the song, "Lo, how good and pleasing it is for brothers to live in unity," is drawn from Psalm 132. The Psalms represent general moral principles and praise of God, to which all the participants in the dialogue adhere. This particular Psalm speaks, of course, of the joy of living in harmony with one's brother. The guests in the home of Coronaeus certainly share this view. According to the next words of the song provided by Coronaeus, the song, which was pleasing, is sung not in diatonics or chromatics but in enharmonics, whose modulation is more divine. The diatonic scale with its seven tones has the least variety, since this mode excludes the consecutive halftones. The chromatic scale is composed of twelve tones and provides more variety than the diatonic. However, neither the diatonic nor the chromatic scale is suitable for the song chosen by Coronaeus. Only the enharmonic mode provides the variety he believes fitting for the variety of his guests.

The enharmonic mode, according to Gioseffo Zarlino de Chioggia in his *Istitutioni harmoniche*, published in Venice in 1558, had often been misunderstood by the ancients and the moderns. He defines this mode as using intervals which are less "noble" and least in harmonic modulation. In other words, the intervals are smaller than the semitone intervals; that is, they are closer together. This, Zarlino says, is called "enharmonico," as if joined "excellently and appropriately, or as some say, as if inseparably."[27] In his book *L'Antica Musica*, published in Rome in 1555, Nicola Vicentini described the *genere enharmonico* as "much more sweet and soothing than the others." Vincentini also wrote that enharmonics, as practiced in the sixteenth century, allowed more division of interval than Boethius described; consequently "we have more richness of grades and consonances and of harmony" and "we have many divisions which generate more varied harmony."[28] Enharmonics produced a sweeter harmony because of its numerous divisions and variety of harmonies. Coronaeus and the other participants in the dialogue at the conclusion of the sixth day had learned to sing in enharmonic modulation, which was "more divine." All seven participants with all of their divisions (or intervals) are inseparably joined, forming one celestial *enharmonia*. The beauty of this sound with its multiple intervals and varied harmonies lifted the souls of the participants to a higher level of understanding. Since all the intervals and modulations in enharmonic mode, though multiple, are joined as if inseparably, we may say that "all are in all."

From the structure of the *Colloquium*, and especially from the use of the *pantotheca* and from the conclusion which introduces *enharmonia*, Bodin makes clear that the opinions of all speakers are necessary for understanding the various topics presented, especially in the discussions of true religion. All parts are joined together to form one enharmonic song, since each part is closely related to the other. Therefore, the structure of the *Colloquium* demonstrates that Bodin does not present a relativist concept of toleration, since the toleration epitomized in the *Colloquium* is not based upon indifference. The point is not that one view is as good as another so it does not matter which is expressed; rather, all views are important in arriving at the truth. The tolerance expressed in Bodin's great dialogue resulted from the mutual respect for the knowledge and opinions of each man in Coronaeus's home. This respect and knowledge in turn produced brotherly love among the men. The beauty of the enharmonic mode and the awe which it inspired leave the seven speakers with no need to discuss religion again. As Salomon and others said, man becomes silent when he contemplates the divine. Their souls were joined in the world of musical modulation which produced the most beautiful harmonies, based on the contrariety of tones in which dissonance is part of harmony. This realization led them to a more profound understanding of God, who in His multiplicity is the perfect Unity that reconciles in Himself and in nature all contrarieties. This was the great lesson learned from the discussions by each participant.

Bodin tells us that although "they nourished their piety in remarkable harmony and their integrity of life in common pursuits and intimacy," they had no more conversations about religion (*Colloquium*, 471). They did not need to have more conversations, since each had learned from the beliefs and knowledge of the others that God was the common ground of all thinking men, and in Him alone all find salvation. With this concept of toleration one did not need to give up his particular belief, since he could maintain his own personal faith and at the same time share in the general beliefs of all. For Bodin toleration was extended to all thinking men. An atheist would not be tolerated, however, because a rational man could not be an atheist, according to Bodin and most men in the Cinquecento. Atheism, as one understands the term in this century, had no meaning in the sixteenth century, as Paul Oskar Kristeller has carefully demonstrated.[29] The existence of God was a fact that was not denied by a thinking man in the sixteenth century. Beliefs about how one should worship God and about theological questions were hotly disputed, however; those who disagreed on the particulars called each other "atheists."

Concordia discors as a foundation for toleration is developed in the *Colloquium* through structural elements and themes presented in the conversations of the various speakers. The choice of Venice as a setting for the dialogue, the *pantotheca* with its 1296 little boxes, each containing a different part of the universe but each being related to the other, the "all things in all" theme used to describe the participants in the dialogue, the use of poetry and prose as vehicles for expression and especially the role of music in the dialogue, all reveal contrariety or *concordia discors* as the necessary underpinnings of toleration. The home of Coronaeus represented a microcosm of society and culture as a paradigm for the larger world. Bodin seems to be asking why, if seven men can live in harmony and appreciate each other and be tolerant of each other's differences, cannot all men practice toleration based on *concordia discors*? Only with this understanding can men become part of the macrocosm.

Notes

1. Georg Roellenbleck, "Der Schluss des «Heptaplomeres» und die Begründung der Toleranz bei Bodin," in *Münchener Studien zur Politik: Jean Bodin, Verhandlungen der internationalen Bodin Tagung in München*, Herausgegeben von Horst Denzer (München: Beck, 1973), 53–67.

2. Mario Turchetti, "Religious Concord and Political Tolerance in Sixteenth and Seventeenth Century France," *Sixteenth Century Journal* 22, 1 (1991): 15–25.

3. Ibid., 19.

4. Ibid., 18.

5. See Marion L. Kuntz, "Harmony and the *Heptaplomeres* of Jean Bodin," *Journal of the History of Philosophy* 12, 1 (1974): 31–41.

6. Ernst Benz's position that humanism is the common element for the interlocutors is close to my own. They have read the same books; they speak the same

language (Latin); they have visited the same places and enjoy the same culture. I do not agree with Benz, however, that the state should maintain tolerance and that religious and revelatory norms are consequently reduced in importance. See his "Der Toleranz-Gedanke in der Religionswissenschaft über den Heptaplomeres des Jean Bodin," *Deutsche Vierteljahrsschrift für Literaturwissenschaft und Geistesgeschichte* 12 (1934): 540–71. Note especially p. 569. Also see Theodore K. Rabb, "Religious Toleration During the Age of Reformation," in Malcolm R. Thorp and Arthur J. Slavin, eds., *Politics, Religion and Diplomacy in Early Modern Europe: Essays in Honor of DeLamar Jensen*, Sixteenth Century Essays and Studies 27 (Kirksville, Mo.: Sixteenth Century Journal Publishers, 1994), 305–20.

7. For an account of the transmission of the text, see Jean Bodin, *Colloquium of the Seven About Secrets of the Sublime*, trans., introduction, annotations, and critical readings by Marion Leathers Kuntz (Princeton, N.J.: Princeton University Press, 1975), xlvii–lxxii. All citations of my translation will be noted in the text as Kuntz, *Colloquium*. Also see Bodin, *Colloque entre sept scavans qui sont de differens sentimens des secrets cachez des choses relevées, traduction anonyme du Colloquium heptaplomeres de Jean Bodin*, texte présenté et établi par François Berriot (Genève: Droz, 1984), xv–lxvii.

8. See Kuntz, *Colloquium*, lxix–lxx. The shelfmark of the Queen's manuscript is Biblioteca Apostolica Vaticana, Regi. 1313.

9. I discovered this manuscript at the Bibliothèque Mazarine; the date 1588 is written on the title page.

10. A reprint of Noack's 1857 edition was published in Stuttgart, 1966. Guhrauer's very abridged edition of 1841 was reprinted in facsimile in Geneva in 1971.

11. The papers from this conference will be shortly published in Germany. The *Colloquium* was also the subject of several contributions at the International Congress on Jean Bodin at Angers in 1984. See *Jean Bodin: Actes du Colloque Interdisciplinaire d'Angers* (Angers: Presses de l'Université d'Angers, 1985).

12. See, e.g., Quentin Skinner, *The Foundations of Modern Political Thought* (Cambridge: Cambridge University Press, 1978), 2: 246–49.

13. See Marion Leathers Kuntz, "The Home of Coronaeus in Jean Bodin's *Colloquium Heptaplomeres*: An Example of a Venetian Academy" in Richard J. Schoeck, ed., *Acta Conventus Neo-Latini Bononiensis*, Medieval and Renaissance Texts and Studies 37 (Binghamton, N.Y.: Center for Medieval and Early Renaissance Studies, 1985), 277–83.

14. Silvana Seidel Menchi, "Protestantesimo a Venezia" in *La Chiesa di Venezia tra reforma protestante e riforma cattolica, a cura di Giuseppe Gullino* (Venezia: Edizioni Studium Cattolico Veneziano, 1990) Vol. 4, 131–154.

15. On the Venetian Inquisition see Paul F. Grendler, *The Roman Inquisition and the Venetian Press* (Princeton, N.J.: Princeton University Press, 1977), esp. 25–61; Ruth Martin, *Witchcraft and the Inquisition in Venice, 1500–1650* (Oxford: Oxford University Press, 1989); John Martin, *Venice's Hidden Enemies* (Berkeley: University of California Press, 1994); especially pertinent is the study of Andrea Del Col, "Organizzazione, composizione e giurisdizione dei tribunale dell'Inquizione romana nella repubblica di Venezia (1500–1550)," *Critica Storica* 25 (1988): 244–94.

The present author has recently tried to demonstrate that the Inquisitor who called himself a *medicus* was in fact using an appropriate designation for an Inquisitor in Venice, according to the accepted concept of the Venetian state.

16. See Archivio di Stato, Venezia, Santo Uffizio, Procesi, Busta 22, fascicolo 2, *costituito* Giacomo q. Luca da Sacil Callegaro.

17. The Venetian Inquisition was under the control of the state, and the Inquisitor, a Dominican after 1560 (previously a Franciscan), had to be a Venetian citizen.

18. Kuntz, "The Home of Coronaeus."

19. For an excellent and concise discussion of *dialogo* in music, see *Enciclopedia della Musica* (Milan: G. Ricordi, 1951), 48–51.

20. The *Musica Nova* was published by Antonio Gardano.

21. Apollo is represented in frescos from Pompeii and the Palatine with a seven-stringed lyre. In Christianity the number three represents the Trinity; in Judaism the unutterable name of God is represented by the number four. The numbers three and four also had significance for Islam.

22. Gioseffo Zarlino da Chioggia, *Le istitutioni harmoniche* (Venezia, 1558), prima parte, cap. 15, p. 25. English translation is my own.

23. See above, note 19.

24. See, e.g., George Holland Sabine, "The *Colloquium Heptaplomeres* of Jean Bodin" in *Persecution and Liberty: Essays in Honor of G. L. Burr* (New York: Century, 1931), 271–309.

25. I use the date 1588 since this date appears on one manuscript (see note 9).

26. In some ways Coronaeus reminds one of Gasparo Contarini. For the most recent work on Contarini see Elisabeth Gleason, *Gasparo Contarini* (Berkeley: University of California Press, 1994).

27. Zarlino da Chioggia, *Le istitutioni harmoniche* (see note 22), 4.

28. Nicola Vincentini, *L'Antica Musica* (Roma, 1555), libro primo, p. 15.

29. Paul Oskar Kristeller, "The Myth of Renaissance Atheism and the French Tradition of Free Thought," *Journal of the History of Philosophy* 6 (1968): 233–43.

6

Religious Coexistence and Confessional Conflict in the *Vier Dörfer*: Practices of Toleration in Eastern Switzerland, 1525–1615

Randolph C. Head

AFTER NEARLY A CENTURY of religious quiet, the prosperous villages of Undervaz, Trimmis, and Zizers outside the city of Chur, Switzerland experienced a series of conflicts about religious confession beginning in 1611 that rapidly escalated to riots, hostile raids from neighboring towns, and vandalism and harassment between the Catholic majority and a minority of Reformed Protestants. Although the villages enjoyed theoretical sovereignty and independence in religious matters, outside parties soon joined the fray, and the bitter dispute was still going more than thirty years later, despite war, plague, famine, and several shifts in the balance of power in the meantime. The villages had tolerated some kinds of religious diversity throughout most of the sixteenth century, and liberty of conscience and liberty of worship never became the key issue at stake during the troubles that followed at the end of the century. Instead, the inhabitants of Undervaz, Trimmis, and Zizers fought about which of several possible sets of social and institutional practices were most appropriate for regulating the terms of their religious coexistence.

Before 1600, the dominant pattern had combined local majority rule about which faith to profess with an individual right to abstain from collective worship, and even to attend church elsewhere. Starting after 1600, however, the minority Protestants demanded a proportional share of the material and social resources of the villages' churches, thus challenging the terms that had kept the villages peaceful for nearly a century. The final outcome was a bitter stalemate between Catholics and Protestants that continued well into the next century, in which each party tolerated the other in a narrowest sense of the word: each put up, legally and socially, with practices it felt to be an affront to God and an obstacle to desirable communal unity. The conflicts described here were thus not simply matters of tolerance versus intolerance, but rather show how crucial local context is for understanding the meaning of toleration as practiced in any particular society.

The study of religious toleration in pre-modern Europe often regards its subject in light of relationships between magistrates who are intent on religious orthodoxy, on the one hand, and dissident groups, whether a minority or a majority of the population, on the other. John Locke's *Letter on Toleration*, for example, which is sometimes seen as the first systematic defense of toleration in this context, takes it for granted that there is a civil magistrate whose duties are defined in such a way as to limit religiously motivated persecution.[1] Certainly the view that sees the main source of persecution in orthodox princes applies to much of early modern European history, both before and after the Reformation. The Spanish Inquisition's efforts to trace down alleged crypto-Judaism after the state-ordained expulsion of the Jews from Spain in 1492 is one clear example, as is the fining of recusants and the execution of priests in Elizabethan England or the expulsion of the Huguenots from France by Louis XIV. In such situations, any call for religious toleration had to explain to the prince why the imposition of religious uniformity was either unchristian, imprudent, or impossible.

In other parts of Europe, however, the problems of religious coexistence were more complicated. Despite the principle of *"cuius regio, eius religio"* that was enshrined at Augsburg in 1555, the Holy Roman Empire presents a quite different situation. Not only was official biconfessionalism established in certain Imperial cities by the ordinance of 1555, but many Catholic, Calvinist, and Lutheran princes had to cope with subject populations of mixed religious adherence, while cities sought to balance economic and political interests against the maintenance of religious uniformity, or at least harmony, at home.[2] On the margins of the Empire, from Poland to Switzerland, even more complex constellations developed in the absence of strong central governments and religiously homogeneous populations.[3]

A historical approach to the issue of toleration should not regard areas like Central Europe, where tolerance or intolerance had to be negotiated in light of local circumstances, as atypical or as deviations from the simple model of the orthodox magistrate and the persecuted minority. To the contrary, analyzing the historical complexities involved not only contributes to a deeper understanding of the real obstacles to both religious uniformity and religious peace during this period, but also adds a needed practical dimension to philosophically-based discussions of the very idea of toleration. Unless the theoretical central magistrate is imagined to have totalitarian powers far beyond the means of governments early modern or modern, after all, we must recognize that persecution or tolerance in any society is caught up in complex webs of political and economic relations, tied to competing conceptions of legitimacy and order, and thus inevitably historically contingent. It is to illustrate this point that this paper focuses on the course of religious coexistence between Catholics and Reformed Protestants in a few Swiss villages. The story told here is neither a tragedy of "rising intolerance" nor a guide to clear and simple definitions of what toleration might be, but rather an illustration of the locally determined contours of relations between individuals and groups who struggled to bring different identities, both shared and conflicting, into play in the course of managing their affairs from day to day.

The villages that are the subject of this paper, Igis, Zizers, Trimmis, and Undervaz, formed the commune of the *Vier Dörfer*, a member of the *Gotteshausbund* (League of the House of God), which was in turn a constituent of the Republic of the Three Leagues in Old Upper Rhaetia, equivalent to the modern Graubünden or Grisons. This confederated republic, located in the central Alps, took up most of the ancient episcopal see of Chur, and was firmly allied with the Swiss Confederation, although it was not itself a member. Well before the beginning of the Protestant movement, the Leagues and their member communes had purchased or seized most lordly prerogatives in the region, so that the communes were effectively self-governing. In 1499, the Bündner had joined with the Swiss to fight the house of Habsburg in the Swabian war; their victory had led to Switzerland's and Graubünden's effective separation from the Holy Roman Empire.[4] Although the Bishop of Chur remained the nominal sovereign over the *Gotteshausbund*, his subjects in the city of Chur and in the rural communes of the League paid less and less attention to his political prerogatives, and soon sought to limit his economic rights as well.

Early in the 1520s, the news of new reforming doctrines spread into the region from Zurich at the same time as struggles over political legitimacy and the distribution of economic resources were reaching a peak. Because of the autonomy and self-consciousness of the region's political communes and their leadership, moreover, the movement for religious change took on articulate form very early.[5] In 1524, the Leagues passed a new statute, the First Ilanz Articles, regulating the clergy: debts were no longer to be collected under threat of excommunication, priests should be able to absolve their parishioners for all sins, trials between clerics and laity should be held in a local court, and appeals to the Bishop's court should be prohibited except for matrimonial cases.[6] The erection of such reform statutes was accompanied by widespread unrest directed against ecclesiastical institutions, as more and more peasants withheld their tithes and dues from outside beneficiaries, and refused to acknowledge the bishop's lordship over them.[7]

The First Ilanz Articles did little to end the turmoil in the Republic in 1525 and 1526. Peasants in the *Vier Dörfer* continued withholding tithes and dues for years, convinced that the First Ilanz Articles justified their position.[8] In 1526, the Republic's magistrates decided to hold a religious disputation, thus allowing explicitly doctrinal questions to enter the political arena. The resulting disputation of Ilanz in 1526 resulted in victory for neither side. Instead, after an initial politically-motivated swing in the direction of traditional orthodoxy, the Republic's magistrates and communal delegates launched another set of articles regulating church-state relations, the Second Ilanz Articles, which were deliberated and ratified later in 1526.[9]

Although the assembled clerics in Ilanz had debated the scriptural foundation of the church and the role of the clergy, the new articles ignored such issues entirely. Instead, they specifically addressed the political activity of the higher clergy and the economic burdens imposed by the existing church, or legitimated by its doctrine. Sandwiched among the articles regulating tithes, dues, and land tenure was one giving every community the right to appoint or dismiss its own priest. This last provision provided an institutionally legitimate way to introduce Protestant worship into the Three Leagues, since the bishop was deprived of all means, spiritual or secular, of opposing or limiting the appointment of Reformed ministers.[10] It provided the cornerstone for the coexistence of two confessions in the Republic after that date, and its focus on the power of the *communes* to appoint or dismiss their clergy, moreover, set the terms of debate for decisions about religious adherence for the next century.

These terms of debate, with their focus on communal decision-making, were entirely consistent with political developments in the Republic during the same period. As the Bündner communes emancipated themselves from lordly control, they took over decision-making and distributive authority as well. Increasingly during the sixteenth century, communal majority votes at public assemblies became the most legitimate and authoritative way of reaching public decisions. The distribution of benefits and burdens of communal citizenship, and of membership in the Republic, meanwhile, became regulated by more and more complex mechanisms that either divided resources, rotated them if they could not be divided, or distributed them by lot.[11] In the 1520s, religious decisions about adherence to the old or new church were subjected to the same mechanisms. By making the selection of a clergyman the prerogative of the communes, where majority vote was the preferred method of deciding, the Ilanz Articles made the choice between Protestantism and Catholicism a matter of majority decision. During most of the sixteenth century, meanwhile, the material resources of each church were considered to be at the undivided disposal of the majority religion. Communes after 1526 often sold, divided, or leased their local church's property, but they did not partition it among members of the opposing faiths.

Communal decision-making about religious adherence, and the associated struggles about control over church resources, left open the question of *individual* rights with regard to religion. Over the course of the sixteenth century, the Bündner communes developed a new set of customary practices to cope with this issue as well. Older historiography has often seized on a document thought to have been promulgated in 1526, the "Recess of Davos" [*Davoser-Abschied*], as establishing the right of every individual to choose between Catholic and Protestant worship, thus establishing the freedom of religion, and implicitly that of worship. Unfortunately, no original of this document survives, and the earliest mention of it dates only to the late sixteenth century.[12] There, it is quoted as containing the following principle:

To every individual, of either sex and of whatever condition or estate of men, dwelling within the boundaries of our Rhaetian Leagues, it stands free as he wishes, and as he is admonished by his instinct of the good spirit, to choose, embrace, and confess either of the two religions, namely the Roman and the Evangelical.[13]

Whether an actual document to this effect was passed in 1526 is less important, however, than the process by which this principle, and the associated principle that individuals could go to neighboring communes if needed to worship, became established.

The first documented case to challenge the principle of communal authority over religious practice came from Chur in 1528. There the Dominican monks had continued to celebrate the Mass in their cloister despite the city's enthusiastic embrace of Protestantism. The mayor of Chur complained to a special arbitrational court set up by the Three Leagues, arguing that the city had not heard any effective defense of the Mass despite several disputations, and that moreover, "the Three Leagues had decided unanimously that what the majority in any commune decided, whether to have the Mass, or not, the minority should follow and accept the vote."[14] Interestingly, the monastery's defenders did not challenge this statement, but based their defense on another provision of the Second Ilanz Articles, which gave the Leagues rather than individual communes authority over all cloisters. "What the majority is in the Chur parish church is not the Leagues' business; nevertheless, there are still many pious people in Chur who would like to have the Mass, which had been practiced for so many years that they hoped it would not be rejected."[15] Clearly, the principle of individual religious choice was not yet well-established in 1528, although everyone agreed that communes should vote by majority what brand of preacher to appoint.[16]

The first solid evidence of efforts on the part of the Three Leagues to provide for the minority religion comes not from Graubünden itself, but from the Republic's subject territories in the Valtelline. There the population remained nearly exclusively Catholic even as more and more of the ruling communes in Graubünden became Protestant. After the Protestants gained a majority in the Republic in the 1550s, efforts began to convert the subject population, or at least to make proselytization by Reformed preachers easier. A law of 1557 illustrates this process. On first reading, the 1557 statute appears to be an effort to increase religious toleration in areas ruled by the Three Leagues. It opens with the demand that "ministers and Mass priests may teach in their churches, administer the sacrament, baptize children and bury the dead, each according to his practice" and ended with an exhortation that the subject population "should not insult or disrespect one another on account of their faith."[17] But the middle of the statute reveals that it was primarily an effort to gain entrance into Valtelline villages for the Protestants, even if they had no local support:

Where there are two churches in a village, one shall be given to the minister, the other to the Mass priest. And concerning the income that belongs to the church, the community shall vote which one to give it to. And where there is not more than one church in a village, then both parties shall use the church, but one party after the other.[18]

Since the vast majority of the Valtelline population was and remained Catholic, such a measure giving the Protestants presumptive rights to the use of churches represented a clear violation of majority rule in religious affairs.

Any notion that the Reformed majority was interested in promoting toleration through such legislation is dispelled by a tract composed in 1577 by a leader of the Reformed Synod, Ulrich Campell. Entitled "Concerning the Duty of Magistrates over their beloved Subjects in matters of Religion," the tract began by arguing that every magistrate was required by God to instruct his subjects in the Gospel. The Three Leagues, however, were ruled democratically, and a clear majority "both of communal votes and in the number of men" was Protestant. Therefore, Campell claimed, the Republic was a Protestant state, and was required to impose the Reformed religion on its subjects.[19] Clearly, the only toleration envisioned by these statues was that shown by the Catholic subjects, who were required to put up with Reformed ministers in their villages and in their churches.[20]

In the Republic's sovereign communes, in contrast, a functional balance between collective and individual religious conviction remained in place throughout the sixteenth century. In both Catholic and Protestant areas, local control over the church paralleled growing local political autonomy; both developments rested on the authority and legitimacy of majority decision at public assemblies.[21] At the end of the sixteenth century, individual dissent was acceptable only if confined to the private sphere, as illustrated in the village of Mulegns, where Christlj Buol moved and became a citizen in 1595. The village was Catholic but Buol was Protestant; when he became a citizen, therefore, he swore not to suggest any innovations or changes in religion at Mulegns. After being accepted as a citizen, he never went outside the village to practice his religion, but conformed outwardly by going to the Mass "on holidays and workdays."[22] His sons grew up Protestant, nevertheless, and after their father's death they helped support a Reformed minister in a neighboring village, and went there every two weeks to worship, which resulted in a lawsuit to withdraw their citizenship. Evidently, the commune accepted the Buols, known Protestants, as a citizens only as long as they kept their own religious convictions entirely to themselves in action as well as in thought.

As tension between the confessions rose toward the end of the century,[23] communes began taking measures to ensure the perpetuation of a solid confessional majority. As the Buol case showed, one way the religious balance within a village might change was if immigrants from other parts of Graubünden belonged to the minority religion. Rather than simply banning such immigration, however—which would have been difficult given the patchwork nature of confessional adherence in the Republic—villages after the mid-century began requiring new citizens to abstain from any votes on religious matters. In the *Vier Dörfer*, a relatively generous provision was made for new citizens who were Protestant, somewhere around 1567.[24] They merely needed to swear not to vote on religious affairs, and not to suggest innovations in worship within the villages where they lived. They were free, according to this oath, to go elsewhere for their own worship, as the Catholic party there pointed out during the religious disputes of the early seventeenth century.[25] Similarly, when the commune of Bergün converted to the Reformed camp in 1601, the agreement that regulated the matter specifically stated as its first point that "in our parish henceforth, in matters of faith, no one shall be forced."[26] That this statement was not a reflection of any belief in the general virtue of toleration is shown in the same document's preamble, however, which states that "in particular, we do not want to give any Mass priests place or tolerate them in our Reformed church: for it is altogether unfitting, according to God's word, that one should sow a field with two crops."[27] As late as 1601, then, Protestants were firmly proclaiming a by now traditional combination of communal majority decision about which of the two authorized religions a commune should accept, together with limits on how far any individual should be forced to conform to this communal decision. It was the breakdown of this pattern that led to the outbreak of violence in the *Vier Dörfer* after 1611.

Before we turn to the specific events in Undervaz, Trimmis, and Zizers, however, the situation in Bergün gives us a few more clues to the changing terms of confessional coexistence in the later sixteenth century. The village had been solidly Catholic until the 1560s, and Reformed adherence had spread only slowly among its population. Led by a few influential individuals, however, a Reformed minority was well-established by the late 1570s, and began agitating for a share of the local church and its resources.[28] At first these efforts were without effect, despite support from the Protestant majority of the *Gotteshausbund*. A month of stirring preaching by Ulrich Campell failed to move the Catholic majority, while the Bishop of Chur also bestirred himself to resist the efforts to divide the church in Bergün. Well aware of the threat of creeping Protestantism, in 1573 the bishop made what he hoped would be an effective appeal to the higher authorities of the republic:

You should consider carefully in this, dear loyal people of the *Gotteshausbund*, since you well know what the practice in Graubünden has been until now—that in all cases the minority has to follow the majority. . . . But if the opinion [that the Protestant minority was entitled to a minister at public expense] spread among the confederates, then it would be correspondingly legal and just that a Protestant commune be required to maintain a priest, if three or four Catholics were found there.[29]

By attacking the majority principle, the bishop argued, the Protestants opened themselves to similar claims by Catholic minorities. Whether because of this argument or otherwise, Bergün remained formally Catholic until at least 1592, and was not officially formally Reformed—again by majority vote—until the document of 1601 cited above.

The *Vier Dörfer* constituted a single unit in Bündner politics, but the villages also enjoyed considerable internal autonomy to manage their affairs.[30] In the central villages of Igis, Zizers, Trimmis, and Undervaz, political and economic issues provided the stimulus for early Reformation turmoil. After the passage of the two sets of Ilanz Articles in the 1520s, for example, the *Vier Dörfer*, like their neighbors, promptly put them into effect. In 1527 Zizers bought out the great tithe after the higher political authorities had ordered the See to negotiate with the villagers. Despite such moves, however, three of the four villages remained Catholic; only Igis and the Hintervalzeina became Reformed.

Religious conflict in the *Vier Dörfer* was muted throughout the rest of the sixteenth century.[31] The few relevant documents surviving in the communal archives have to do with the steady transfer of the bishop's holdings into communal control.[32] When voting on charges made against Bishop Thomas Planta in 1560, Reformed Igis and Catholic Zizers reached the same decisions,[33] nor was Igis treated differently in the distribution of communal offices when the four villages rearranged these in 1539.[34] Religious restrictions on new citizens, supposedly dating to 1567, indicated a rising awareness of confessional difference, but the archives are silent about any conflicts among or within the four villages over religious matters. Only when a small but influential Protestant minority began claiming a share of their village churches after 1611 did the chain of confrontations, riots, and lawsuits begin that would continue for the next thirty years. The particular shape of the conflicts in the *Vier Dörfer* rapidly uncovered the gaps and contradictions in the assumptions most Bündner held by this time about political authority and the proper arrangement of public life.

What the Protestant minorities in Undervaz, Trimmis, and Zizers needed was a principle that would help them undermine the authority of majority decisions about religion. They found two, at two different institutional levels. At the village level, they argued that the village churches and their property were in fact a communal good and ought to be distributed among the citizens like other communal goods, such as mountain pastures or bribes from foreign princes. In contrast, the standard view that majorities should decide religion implied that religious adherence was an indivisible marker of communal identity, and should therefore be subject to majority vote. But since the decision about how to define the church was itself subject to majority vote, the Protestants needed another lever to make their case stick; they found it not at the village or communal level but at the level of their League, the *Gotteshausbund*. The documents and traditions of the Republic generally recognized communal sovereignty over local affairs, but accepted the authority of the League or the entire Republic when local disputes proved intractable. This was just the opening the Protestants needed; it was attractive, moreover, because the *Gotteshausbund* had a strong Protestant majority, and even the Three Leagues as a whole were more Protestant than Catholic. This fact allowed the Protestants in the *Vier Dörfer* to claim that they too were following the rule of the majority, thus undermining the legitimacy of the Catholic position. More practically, the Protestant majority of the *Gotteshausbund* ensured that the arbitrational panels and courts appointed to adjudicate the matter would in fact be more favorable to Protestant than to Catholic appeals.[35]

In 1611, a few Protestants from Undervaz, including the deputy magistrate and the village scribe, appealed to the Republic's national assembly for the right to use their village church and to hire a Reformed minister.[36] That their appeal was not unpremeditated is suggested by the fact that the Reformed Synod of the Republic had discussed the situation of Protestant minorities only a month before, and that one of the Reformed delegation was the fiery minister Johann à Porta.[37] The Protestant majority at the Diet not only suspended the Undervaz citizenship oath, which had required immigrant Protestants not to suggest any innovations regarding the church, but also approved the Protestants' use of the church and the hiring of a minister. The citizens of Undervaz, still overwhelmingly Catholic, reacted quite moderately to this intervention. At a public assembly of the village, they rejected the demand that Protestants have access to the village church, but explicitly affirmed not only that they could worship elsewhere without hindrance, but also that they might invite a Reformed minister to preach in private houses in the village at their own cost.

The Reformed party seized this opportunity. On September 15, 1611, the pastor of Chur, Georg Saluz, came to Undervaz accompanied by the mayor of Chur and several hundred armed men. After a brief dispute on the bridge across the Rhine on the way to the village, he began preaching in an open meadow, but then moved into the village church, allegedly with the villagers' permission.[38] In subsequent weeks, Protestant services took place in a barn outside the village, accompanied by increasing anger from the population. When à Porta, among the most aggressive of the Reformed ministers, preached in early May, 1612, his beard was plucked by the village's women and he was thrown into the fountain.[39] Meanwhile, the Protestants also sued the village for the right to use the main church; by December 1611 a court of the *Gotteshausbund* had given a verdict that allowed the Protestants to use the village church after the Catholics, freed them from observing Catholic holidays in the village, and ordered the church endowment to be divided proportionally by the number of hearths. In addition, the court sentenced the commune to a stiff fine for "resisting" the authority of its League and for insulting à Porta. Meanwhile, the Undervazers appealed to the neighboring Gray League, which had a Catholic majority, and to the Catholic Swiss for support. The spiraling tension was damped in Undervaz only by the intervention of the French ambassador, who negotiated a compromise and convinced the Catholic majority in Undervaz to accept it, at least temporarily. It announced that "the two religions, namely the Catholic and the Evangelical, shall be free in Undervaz, and that each party may celebrate Divine services, with wives, children, servants, in safety without any obstruction" in the church. The Catholics were given the first use of the church, and the Protestants promised not to disturb the altar or decorations. As in the unilaterally imposed verdict of 1611, however, the church's income was divided proportionally according to the number of hearths adhering to each confession; similarly, Protestants were awarded one fourth of the seats on the village council, and the right to have a Protestant elected village magistrate [*Amman*] every third year, though election was to be by the entire commune.[40]

Before moving on to the conflicts that burst out in Trimmis and Zizers in the following years, a few key points should be noted here. First of all, the Reformed minority in Undervaz gained most of its goals by moving the debate from Undervaz itself to larger assemblies where Protestants predominated. Local-central relations in the Republic were still fluid at this time, and broadly-accepted principles such as majority rule did not necessarily provide unequivocal answers to disputes such as this one. The question, after all, was which majority was relevant. In addition, the Protestant case drew on an alternate model of legitimacy by claiming a *share* of the church. Bünder were used to dividing or alternating in their use of resources of many different kinds, making them more receptive to the argument that a church and its endowment, too, could be partitioned or rotated in a way that reflected the relative proportions of Catholics and Protestants in a commune. Finally, the compromise negotiated by the French ambassador repeatedly stressed public peace, and the responsibility that neighbors had not to "touch one another with disdainful or bothersome words, but to live in good peace according to our alliance."[41]

Although the general course of events in Trimmis resembled those in Undervaz, the intensity of the conflict rapidly spiraled higher. The Trimmiser had watched the failure of the relatively moderate stance taken by the Catholic majority in Undervaz and were apparently determined not to make the same mistake. Sometime around 1612 the village head (*Landamman*) of Trimmis, Oswald Gaudenz, and his brother made public their Reformed faith, and asked that the *larger* of Trimmis's two churches be handed over to them so that they could hear the "pure Gospel."[42] Even without the previous troubles in Undervaz, such a claim was sure to be rejected by the overwhelming Catholic majority, and like their brethren in Undervaz, the Protestants soon appealed to the Republic's Diet, late in 1613. Over Catholic protests, the court issued a "compromise" quite similar to the one in Undervaz. Both churches were declared to be communal property open to both confessions, although the majority confession was to have the first use. The majority was also to control the endowments (*Pfrunde*), but to divide the income proportionally according to the number of hearths belonging to each confession. Outvoted at the federal level, again, the Catholics from the entire Republic expressed their frustration at the way majority rule was being applied. They observed that their confederates "belonging to the opposite religion outvote us each time it comes to a dispute, establish a court and statutes as suits them, and then use violent means against those who do not want to obey and submit."[43] Yet this did not mean that the Catholic party wanted to give up the legitimacy that a majority offered them within the context of the Republic's political life. Instead, they offered an alternate proposal in January, 1614: in the future, each commune should decide for itself whether to employ a Catholic or Reformed clergyman by majority vote, and "the minority may then exercise its religion elsewhere wherever it wants."[44] Given the enormous legitimacy of communal autonomy, this was a clever move, and it forced the leaders of the Bündner Protestants to make the unpopular counter-argument that individual communes should not be given excessive authority.[45] In short, the Catholics now adopted the position that Protestants had advocated less than a generation earlier.

The court records that survive about Trimmis make it clear that things went from bad to worse during 1614. In May of that year, an armed band attacked the village from Chur: after they failed to gain entrance to the larger church, they broke into the smaller chapel of St. Emerita. In the following two years several attempts at compromise failed, even though they leaned further in the Catholic direction than the settlement in Undervaz had. Late in 1615, another court, this time appointed with equal numbers of Catholic and Protestant judges, met to settle the aftermath of a riot earlier that year.[46] The surviving depositions illustrate the high tension. Protestants complained that their hay and agricultural implements had been vandalized, and that they had heard threats that the Catholics "wanted to uproot and burn the Lutheran heretics within the week."[47] Another man reported that "he had heard the priest in his sermon say that there were three murderers, namely the Evil spirit, the Lutherans, and he couldn't remember the third one."[48] In testimony about a riot that the court was concerned with, Elsy Kochin declared that "she had seen Hartmann Hartmann running down with a naked sword, and when she asked him where he was going, he said he wanted to find the Reformed ministers."[49] Much of the testimony concentrated on the point that the Catholics had refused to stop when bidden to observe the peace—an action that was itself a serious violation of village statutes, and one which illustrates the intensity of passions aroused in Trimmis:

Hartmann Hartmann said, give us the old villain, and he [the witness] had also heard, that the Catholics had called out the Protestants. And the women confirmed the testimony, and more, saying that Hans Sch . . . had told them, when [the Protestants] spoke of the peace, [Hartmann] had answered that he sought no peace.[50]

In Trimmis as in Undervaz, then, we see the effort by a Protestant minority to redefine religious coexistence as a matter for partition and division of resources, rather than for majority decision. Sensitized by their setbacks in neighboring Undervaz, the Catholics fought back harder in Trimmis and worked to strengthen the majority principle locally. The compromises eventually imposed on Trimmis thus represented a victory for the Protestants, because they recognized Protestant claims to a share of their church in the first place. The solution that the Catholics suggested in 1614, although almost identical to the one the Protestants had imposed in Bergün in 1601, was no longer enough to satisfy the Protestant party. Under these circumstances, it is not surprising that any settlement imposed from outside remained unstable, and that Trimmis remained a site of considerable religious tension.

Zizers was the largest of the four villages, and the seat of the shared communal government. The struggles in Undervaz and Trimmis were bound to spread there as well, as soon as enough influential citizens of Zizers declared their adherence to the Reformed faith, which happened late in 1612. The majority in Zizers was accommodating at first: after a first refusal, the Protestants were given the use of the smaller church of St. Andrew, and the first Reformed services were held without causing disturbances. As Georg Saluz, the minister, put it, "the Undervaz affair taught them some manners."[51] Affairs proceeded without trouble for nearly a year, until the Protestant faction in Zizers, at the instigation of the Reformed Synod, gave their pastor Johann à Porta village citizenship without consulting their Catholic fellow citizens. In addition, the Protestants appealed to the *Gotteshausbund*—their favorite tactic—in order to gain control over the larger church of Sts. Peter and Paul and the church endowment. As they put it, "there are a substantial number of Evangelicals in the village now"—sufficient cause, they thought, to give them the preferred position. The Leagues decided to appoint a commission to investigate, with two Reformed and one Catholic member. Naturally, the Catholics refused to accept this arrangement, but the commission proceeded to craft an agreement similar to that in the other villages: both religions were to have use of the churches, the Catholics could keep the endowment as long as they were in the majority but had to share the income proportionally, and the Catholics were once again sentenced to pay significant court costs because of their "resistance." The pressure from the Reformed party continued, moreover, with the Protestants taking sole control of Sts. Peter and Paul after the Catholics refused to pay the costs and fines that had been assessed against them. In 1615 the Protestants forcibly dragged the Catholic priest, Oswald Carnutsch, out of the church after he attempted to preach there to the Catholic majority, and an armed confrontation was barely avoided.

To dampen the growing tension in the village, a new agreement was hammered out in November of 1616. Because it so vividly encapsulates the contradictory practices and principles that the opposing parties wanted to enforce, this document is particularly revealing. The preamble stressed the concrete harm that religious division was wreaking on all citizens of the village, "so that we must be concerned, unless God as the originator of peace should grant us by his grace the spirit of peace and love, further and greater inconveniences must await us." [52] The danger, the preamble argued, was the "spirit of disunity," and the first article of the agreement established that the exercise of both religions would be entirely free in the commune, for the explicit purpose that the inhabitants might be "not two communes, or parties, but rather one commune." [53] Since the rest of the document proceeded to divide the churches and their endowments, this sentiment appears to be more of a vain hope than a realistic conclusion; even so, it set this document apart from similar agreements in Trimmis and Undervaz. Whereas those compromises had turned to partitioning resources, either in proportion to the number of hearths involved or in equal part between the two parties, the Zizers document stressed the common ownership of the resources involved. Despite the various provisions regulating the use of the two churches and the division of the costs of maintenance and income, an article at the end carefully limited such division: "Everything shall belong to the entire commune undividedly, including both churches, the bells, the church decorations, to manage and control according to its wishes." [54] All in all, this effort differed markedly from the ever more detailed enumeration of the rights pertaining to the "Catholic community" and the "Evangelical community" that is found in the agreements negotiated or imposed in Undervaz and Trimmis. In Zizers in 1616, for a moment, a commune sought to concede as little as possible to the principles of proportional division or parity, even as they separated that part of their lives where coexistence was no longer possible.

The Zizers document of 1616 echoed contemporary documents from other parts of the Three Leagues that pointed toward an alternate solution. If Catholics and Protestants could remain "a single commune" even as they affirmed their religious convictions, this implied that the political commune was distinct from religious identity and not dependent on it. Such a position had not been possible under the older practice: as we saw with Christlj Buol in Mulegns, he could remain Protestant only in a purely private sense if he wanted to function as a citizen of his village. Membership in the village implied membership in the church, or at the very least, entirely private dissent. This was not a matter of identity only: the entire village supported the church through fees, dues imposed on common land, and through endowments made in the past. If the Zizers agreement had been followed in both spirit and letter, a new possibility would have appeared: a secular commune that ensured the support of both churches without giving sole authority to either one, and a village in which Catholics and Protestants "resided and lived next to one another as is fitting for honorable communal citizens and neighbors."[55]

What do the struggles in the *Vier Dörfer* and in the Republic of the Three Leagues tell us, either about the practice of religious coexistence during the long sixteenth century or about the idea of toleration more generally? First of all, they force us to recognize how much notions of toleration or religious liberty depend on local context. It was easy to say that religion was "free" in the Republic, at least to adherents of the two magisterial faiths, yet saying so meant nothing until that liberty was put into practice. It could mean the freedom to believe in one creed as long as one publicly followed the rules of the other, as in the case of Christlj Buol. It could mean the right to visit another village for religious services, or it could mean the right to use the same church for services of two different religions, and to divide the endowment that a village had built up over generations to support its church. Each of these alternatives also involved consequences for material resources, collective identity, and political procedure.

Consequently, defining the inhabitants of the *Vier Dörfer* as "tolerant" or "intolerant" appears to depend more on the viewer's perspective than on the course of events in the early seventeenth century. It appears equally plausible to say that the villages became more tolerant through allowing Protestants the right to use the village churches and giving them a share of the public funds used to support the clergy; or to say that by appealing to a sympathetic majority at a higher level the Reformed party was intolerantly depriving a Catholic majority of its property and the sanctity of its churches (given that the Catholics had at first been perfectly willing to allow the Protestants in Undervaz to worship and to support a minister at their own expense). One can agree that one result of the conflict was to make *each* party less willing to coexist with the other, although sentiments of communal unity and the fear of negative consequences led both parties to live with the uncomfortable compromises they had accepted.[56] Moreover, the fact that the physical church and its endowment were perceived as collective, public property meant that there could be no "neutral" or secular position about their disposition: the very decision whether to divide the church's resources, or to leave them to the majority—each a potentially legitimate solution in the political culture of the region—meant taking the side of the Catholics or the Protestants, as we have seen. In other words, the very conviction that the church *was* a public resource carried confessional overtones, and prevented any neutral separation of "church" from "state."

Second, working out the details of religious coexistence inevitably raised questions about which practices were both traditionally legitimate and also appropriate for managing the consequences of religious liberty. Rarely did either side in these conflicts appeal to novel or rational principles to bolster its position. Quite the contrary: each party sought to show that it was merely following well-established practices to reach the conclusions it desired. The result of this tendency was that conflicts over religion brought to the forefront the otherwise hidden conflicts among the practices by which the Bündner governed themselves. Was majority decision or proportional division the right response to two confessions in one village? Did a village, or a League, or the Three Leagues in common possess final jurisdiction over intractable local conflicts? Religious polarization put into stress the understandings that had held the Republic together for nearly a century.

Finally, we should note that the entire debate between Catholics and Protestants in the *Vier Dörfer* was carried out and resolved with scarcely any explicit references at all to toleration. In the few instances where *dulden* was discussed, as in Bergün in 1601, it was explicitly rejected as contrary to the will of God. Yet despite their lack of a positive theory of toleration the population of the *Vier Dörfer* in fact moved from one version of what modern analysts might call toleration to another. Certainly, religious practice was in fact considerably freer there, and throughout the Three Leagues, than in many other parts of Europe at this time. The shift in the terms of coexistence that took place between 1610 and 1620 was just that: a move from one version of religious coexistence to another. The regulation of what we would call toleration—the institutional framework for living with incommensurate convictions—was for the Bündner of this era above all a matter of conflict management. The people involved certainly argued from their values and principles (foremost among which was custom), but they did not need a theory of toleration to be tolerant, or to be intolerant.

Notes

1. John Locke, *A Letter Concerning Toleration, In Focus*, ed. John Horton and Susan Mendus (London and New York: Routledge, 1991), e.g., 17. In Locke's earlier writings on toleration, argues Robert Kraynak, he had used the same premise of a civil magistrate whose primary duty was to preserve public peace in order

to argue for the coercive imposition of religious unity: "John Locke: From Absolutism to Toleration," *American Political Science Review* 74, 1 (1980): 53–69.

2. Among the extensive literature note in particular: Paul Warmbrunn, *Zwei Konfessionen in Einer Stadt: Das Zusammenleben von Katholiken und Protestanten in den paritätischen Reichsstädten Augsburg, Biberbach, Ravensburg, und Dinkelsbühl von 1548 bis 1648*, Veröffentlichungen des Instituts für Europäische Geschichte Mainz, Abteilung für abendländische Religionsgeschichte 111 (Wiesbaden: Franz Steiner Verlag, 1983); and Joachim Whaley, *Religious Toleration and Social Change in Hamburg, 1529–1819* (Cambridge: Cambridge University Press, 1985).

3. On Poland, see Johannes Tazbir, *Geschichte der polnischen Toleranz* (Warsaw: Verlag Interpress, 1977). On Switzerland, Paul Steiner, *Die religiöse Freiheit und die Gründung des Schweizerischen Bundesstaates* (Bern and Stuttgart: Verlag Paul Haupt, 1976).

4. The most recent study of the political history of this region in the early modern period is my *Early Modern Democracy in the Grisons* (Cambridge: Cambridge University Press, 1995). The older standard histories with extensive narrative material are Friedrich Pieth, *Bündnergeschichte* (Chur: F. Schuler, 1945), and Conradin von Moor, *Geschichte von Currätien und der Republik "gemeiner drei Bünde" (Graubünden)*, 3 vols. (Chur: Verlag der Antiquariatsbuchhandlung, 1871).

5. On the secular commune in Graubünden, see Head, *Early Modern Democracy*, 73–89, and the literature cited there.

6. Oskar Vasella, "Zur Entstehungsgeschichte des 1. Ilanzer Artikelbriefes vom 4. April 1524 und des Eigenössischen Glaubenskonkordates von 1525," *Zeitschrift für Schweizerische Kirchengeschichte* 34, 3–4 (1940): 185–86.

7. Peasant actions and strategies after 1524 are described systematically in Oskar Vasella, "Der bäuerliche Wirtschaftskampf und die Reformation in Graubünden, 1526 bis etwa 1540," *Jahresbericht der Historisch-antiquitarische Gesellschaft von Graubünden* 73 (1943): 1–183.

8. Oskar Vasella, "Die Entstehung der bündnerischen Bauernartikeln vom 25. Juni 1526," *Zeitschrift für Schweizerische Geschichte* 21, 1 (1941): 58–78 and idem, "Bauernkrieg und Reformation in Graubünden," *Zeitschrift für Schweizerische Geschichte* 20, 1 (1940): 1–65, here 25–32.

9. Original text in Constanz Jecklin, *Urkunden zur Verfassungsgeschichte Graubündens, (Als Fortsetzung von Mohr's Codex Diplomaticus)* (Chur: Sprecher und Plattner, 1883), 89–95.

10. The article on the election of ministers did not take a particularly prominent place in the Second Ilanz Articles, appearing in the thirteenth place between provisions governing hunting and one establishing uniform weights and measures. The provision of reasonable support for pastors is the primary point, with the establishment of communal power to appoint or dismiss appearing almost as an afterthought. Jecklin, *Urkunden*, 92–93.

11. See Head, *Early Modern Democracy*, 73–89, for an overview.

12. This text first appears in Ulrich Campell's *Historia Raetica*, written in the 1570s, published as *Ulrici Campelli Historia Raetica*, ed. Placidus Plattner, Quellen zur Schweizer Geschichte, 8–9 (Basel: Felix Schneider, 1887–1890), 2: 161, dated to an assembly of March 15, 1526.

13. Cited from Petro Dominico Rosius à Porta, *Historia Reformationis Ecclesiarum Raeticarum* (Chur: Societatis Typographicae, 1771), 1: 146. The authenticity of this document is questionable, according to Oskar Vasella, *Abt Theodul Schlegel von Chur und seine Zeit, 1515–1529, Kritische Studien über Religion und Politik in der Zeit der Reformation*, Zeitschrift für Schweizerische Kirchengeschichte, Beihefte, 13 (Freiburg im. Ü: Universitätsverlag, 1954), 67, n. 1.

14. Cited in Fritz Jecklin, ed., "Beitrag zur Churer Reformationsgeschichte," *Anzeiger für schweizerische Geschichte* 3 (1895): 225–28.

15. Ibid.

16. There is almost no evidence and very little debate about the religious rights of minorities from this period. The only clear statement about minority religious views has to do with Anabaptists and other non-magisterial sects, which were banned in Graubünden as they were in the rest of Switzerland. Only the "two religions" enjoyed the privilege of communal choice.

17. The statute is cited in Fritz Jecklin, *Materialien zur Standes- und Landesgeschichte Gem. III Bünde (Graubünden), 1464–1803*, 2 vols. (Basel: Basler Buch- und Antiquariatshandlung, 1907), 2: 272 (No. 278, January 18, 1557).

18. Ibid.

19. In "De officio magistratus erga subiectos suos charissimos in religionis causa, in ipsorum salutem," Archiv der Evangelische Rhätischen Synode, Ms. B 3, pp. 27–35, here pp. 27–28. This tract was inserted into the protocol of the Rhaetian Synod during its meeting in 1577.

20. Campell did acknowledge that member communes of the Three Leagues should still be allowed to practice Catholicism, unlike the subjects. But he described this concession as a matter of "grace" in the interest of public peace. Ibid., 29.

21. Head, *Early Modern Democracy*, 75–82.

22. The conduct of Buol is described in a deposition in a lawsuit of 1645 concerning his heirs. Pfarrarchiv Mulegns, Urkunden, No. 12.

23. On the periodization and theoretical framework for understanding this tension, which appeared all over the German lands at this time, see esp. Heinrich Richard Schmidt, *Konfessionalisierung im 16. Jahrhundert*, Enzyklopädie der Deutscher Geschichte, vol. 12 (Munich: Oldenbourg, 1992).

24. The 1567 date is suspect because no original document survives. It is reported in Catholic sources from the 1640s, especially the sharply confessional "Historia Religionis" (Bischöfliches Archiv Chur, Historia Religionis B, p. 11).

25. See Berger, *Einführung*, 35, and below.

26. Gemeindearchiv Bergün, Urkunden, No. 46, July 5, 1601.

27. Ibid.

28. See Emil Camenisch, *Bündnerische Reformationsgeschichte* (Chur: Bischofsberger & Hotzenköcherle, 1920), 471–78.

29. Jecklin, *Materialien*, 2: 438 (No. 426, Aug. 17, 1573).

30. Each of the four main villages (Igis, Zizers, Trimmis, Untervaz) had its own parish church; Zizers also had a second, smaller chapel. The parish of Felsberg included the hamlet of Sais above Trimmis for some time, while the Valzeina was divided among the parishes of Zizers, Felsberg and Trimmis, and politically among the communes of the *Vier Dörfer*, Jenaz and Seewis. See *Helvetia Sacra*, ed. Albert

Bruckner (Bern: Francke Verlag, 1972–), I.i: 600–601, and Nicolin Sererhard, *Einfalte Delineation aller Gemeinden gemeiner dreyen Bünden*, ed. Oskar Vasella (Chur: Verein Bündner Kulturforschung, 1994), 201–2.

31. This is generally true across Graubünden, with the exception of times when individual communes experienced a Protestant movement to join the Reformed camp. Then, considerable violence could break out, until the final vote was taken. As a rule, however, once the (secular) commune had chosen its religious adherence, conflict waned immediately.

32. A general overview in Camenisch, *Bündnerische Reformationsgeschichte*, 514–16. Aside from the documents cited above, a document of 1539 (Gemeindearchiv Zizers, Urkunden, No. 54) regulated the appointment of criminal judges in rotation among the individual villages, since the bishop no longer had that right; one of 1554 from Zizers (Gemeindearchiv Zizers, Urkunden, No. 81) ordered the seizure of the *widdum*, because of the "decline" of the clergy, who refused to maintain their church's property; several from 1576 record the transfer of various pieces of land from the bishop or chapter in hereditary tenure (Gemeindearchiv Zizers, Urkunden, Nos. 93–98). Not until 1649 were the last episcopal property rights commuted.

33. Jecklin, *Materialien*, 2: 286–88 (No. 296).

34. Gemeindearchiv Zizers, Urkunden, No. 54.

35. The documents leave no doubt that this was the case, and in fact, the Catholic party in the *Vier Dörfer* complained loud and often that they were not receiving a fair hearing. See, e.g., STAGr AB IV 5/12, 375.

36. The narrative in this and the following paragraphs on Trimmis and Zizers relies primarily on Berger, *Einführung*, 3–52, although many of my conclusions differ sharply from his. See also J. F. Fetz, *Geschichte der kirchen-politische Wirren im Freistaate der III Bünde* (Chur: by the author, 1875).

37. Berger, *Einführung*, 4.

38. Saluz wrote a report for the Chur magistrates: Zivilstandsamt Chur, Kirchenbuch No. 2, cited by Berger, *Einführung*, 5.

39. The court of the *Gotteshausbund* used this incident to load more fines onto the commune and several individuals. Berger, *Einführung*, 10–11.

40. A copy of the accord in STAGr B 1538/15, 90–93.

41. STAGr B 1538/15, 92.

42. This first request is documented only in Bartholomäus Anhorn's *Palingenesia Rhaetica: Heilige Wiedergeburt der Evangelischen Kirchen/in den gmeinen dreyen Pündten* . . . (Brugg, 1680), without a specific date. Cited in Berger, *Einführung*, 32.

43. The word "übermehren" (outvoting) starts appearing only in the late sixteenth century in Graubünden, in order to describe the illegitimate use of majority power.

44. Bartholomäus Anhorn, "Chronick der statt Mainenfeld," Ms. in Stadtarchiv Maienfeld, cited in Berger, *Einführung*, 35.

45. Berger, *Einführung*, 36.

46. The documents from this court provide the most coherent set of images about Trimmis in this period. STAGr AB IV 5/12, 373–411. The Catholic judges

boycotted the court, with one exception, and the Trimmis Catholics disputed its jurisdiction.

47. STAGr AB IV 5/12, 407, testimony of Matheu Hartmann.

48. Ibid., testimony of Crista Schienne (the last name is poorly legible).

49. Ibid., 408.

50. Ibid., Testimony of Caspar Gadient, Eva Wincklerin, and Barbla Willi from Ems.

51. Cited in Berger, *Einführung*, 19. Nevertheless, it is worth noting that Saluz went to Zizers in the company of the Mayor of Chur and an armed guard.

52. STAGr B 1538/15, 95 (a copy from 1644).

53. Ibid.

54. Ibid., 96.

55. STAGr B 1538/15, 94 at the end of the preamble. For more discussion of this issue, see Randolph Head, "Rhaetian Ministers, from Shepherds to Citizens: Calvinism and Democracy in the Republic of the Three Leagues, 1550–1620," in W. Fred Graham, ed., *Later Calvinism: International Perspectives*, Sixteenth Century Essays and Studies 22 (Kirksville, Mo.: Sixteenth Century Journal Publishers, 1994), 55–69.

56. As the resumption of religious conflict in the Republic after 1639, and specifically in the *Vier Dörfer* in 1644, reveals, such acceptance did not come easily. See STAGr B 714/8 (letter from Zizers to the Swiss Catholics, 1644), and the arbitrational documents of that year in STAGr B 1538/15. For detailed analyses in a confessional vein, Felici Maissen, *Die Drei Bünde in der zweiten Hälfte des 17. Jahrhundert in politischer, kirchengeschichtlicher, und volkskündlicher Schau*, Vol. 1, 1647– (Aarau: Sauerländer, 1966).

PART III

THE SEVENTEENTH CENTURY

Introduction: Contexts and Paths to Toleration in the Seventeenth Century

John Christian Laursen

THE SHADOW OF THE SIXTEENTH century loomed large over the seventeenth century. The collective memory of the Reformation and its wars and persecutions was strong throughout Europe. Yet the seventeenth century also added its own influential historical events. Any division of the ideas and practices of the time by language and political boundary will inevitably be artificial, because the ideas washed back and forth throughout the known world and the practices in any one area served as examples in others. Nevertheless it is probably safe to say that the most influential political events for the purposes of toleration theory and practice were the Thirty Years' War (1618–1648), which took place mostly in Germany; the English Revolutions (1640 and 1689) and Restoration (1660); and the French Edict of Nantes (1598) followed by its Revocation (1685).

The Thirty Years' War broke out in Prague, which until a few years before had been the residence of the Habsburg King of Bohemia, who was also the Emperor of the "Holy Roman Empire of the German Nation." The war was caused by a mix of political and religious ambitions. It began in one of the regions that had the most relative religious freedom at the time: the religious settlement of Bohemia, issued by Rudolph II in 1609, was more tolerant of the Protestants than the Edict of Nantes, which regulated France, and the Peace of Augsburg, which regulated the rest of Germany. The problem, as might be expected, was that this settlement was unstable. When Rudolph died a few years later, Bohemian Protestants offered the crown to a Protestant prince and the Catholic Ferdinand II came to the imperial throne. War spread as Protestant powers intervened on behalf of the Protestants, and Catholics endeavored to bring Bohemia back into the Catholic fold.

Much of the course of the Thirty Years' War can be told as a tension between religious and political motivations. Chances for compromise were regularly missed by leaders who truly believed in their holy religious mission, and their intransigence and intolerance cost them dearly. Meanwhile, the more political and less single-mindedly religious rulers seemed to thrive. For example, the Catholic King of France came out ahead by siding with the German Protestants in order to counter-balance the growing power of Catholic Spain and Austria. One of the most tolerant rulers of the period, the Calvinist Elector of Brandenburg, consolidated his power by fully tolerating Catholics, Lutherans, and Calvinists in the different parts of his territories. This set the stage for Brandenburg's policy of repopulating devastated lands by inviting the Huguenots to settle there when they fled from France after the Revocation of the Edict of Nantes. The general tendency of the war was that political purposes prevailed as religious fervor died down.

The demonstration effect of the political benefits of toleration was matched by the example of the war as an object lesson in the desolation and devastation that intolerance could provoke. In some areas the population dropped by as much as two thirds as a result of marauding soldiers, disease, and dislocations in the economy. When rulers came to realize that neither side was likely to win a complete military and political victory and impose its religious settlement at will, the war was finally settled. The Peace of Westphalia of 1648 restored a Protestant-Catholic balance in some respects more favorable to the Protestants than the Peace of Augsburg of 1555.

If we are tempted to assume that contemporaries who lived through the Thirty Years' War drew the obvious (by modern standards) conclusion that religious persecution never paid, we would probably be wrong. One of the dominant myths about the age is that toleration was a matter of secularization, meaning that people began to accept a separation of their religious lives from a secular sphere, where reasons of state would reign supreme. But in fact, many of the greatest thinkers of the age never secularized in this sense. Samuel von Pufendorf, for example, was educated in Lutheran Leipzig not long after the end of the war, and spent most of his life in the Protestant countries that had fought in the war. It might be thought that he would have learned the merits of a broad toleration. And

indeed, the prevailing interpretation of his work takes his theory of separation of state and church as a substantial form of toleration. Detlef Döring's
contribution to this volume, however, shows that Pufendorf's toleration
was always a circumstantial toleration, tailored to specific cases, and sub-
ordinated to the general principle that the true religion should prevail. It
was a specifically Lutheran theory of toleration, and thus not fully tolerant
of Catholics or Calvinists.

This pattern of toleration driven by religious dogma was quite common. Frances Yates has shown, for example, how the mystical religious
movements spawned during the Thirty Years' War could lead to tolerance
of different religions in the name of religion.[1] Many religious leaders of the
century, such as Thomas Helwys and Leonard Busher for the Baptists, Jan
Comenius for the Moravians, Simon Episcopius and Hugo Grotius for the
Arminians, William Chillingworth and Jeremy Taylor for the Church of
England, and William Penn for the Quakers, demanded tolerance as a requirement of the truths of their religion. In my chapter on Pierre Bayle, toleration was a conclusion from Calvinist principles—and limited by those
principles.

The strongest legacy to toleration theory of the Thirty Years' War may
well have been in the writings of Gottfried Wilhelm Leibniz, who wrote
at the end of the seventeenth and beginning of the eighteenth centuries,
and pushed toleration theory well beyond anything Locke or Bayle could
manage. He is not discussed here because he is essentially an eighteenth-
century figure.

In France, the end of the Civil Wars and the Edict of Nantes of 1598
meant that the century opened with what was in principle a form of toleration. The Protestants, known as Huguenots, were permitted to retain
the churches they already had, but not to build new ones or proselytize.
It was clear that both the Protestants and the Catholics thought of it as
a temporary, tactical cease fire.[2] Henry IV was assassinated in 1610 by a
Catholic who thought he had been too generous to the Protestants. Low-
grade civil war between the two religions simmered. Occasional military
flare-ups ended with a victory for the Catholics in 1628 after a siege at La
Rochelle and another Peace signed at Alais in 1629.

From the 1670s the pressure on the Huguenots was ratcheted up-
ward with such measures as removal of children from Protestant families
in order to educate them as Catholics, quartering of troops in households
that refused to convert, prohibition of the exercise of many professions by
Protestants, and cash payments for conversion. In 1685, the Catholic king,

Louis XIV, felt strong enough to declare the legal fiction that there were no more Protestants in France so the Edict of Nantes could be revoked. Tens of thousands of Huguenots fled to the Netherlands, Brandenburg, England, and as far away as Russia and South Carolina, taking their skills with them and contributing to prosperity in their countries of refuge. This alone had a demonstration effect, but in addition, from their places of exile the Huguenots mounted a substantial propaganda campaign against French intolerance.[3] One of the key figures of that propaganda campaign was Pierre Bayle, discussed in my chapter in this volume.[4]

The Revocation of the Edict of Nantes was a monument to intolerance, but even Catholic France was never a monolith of intolerance of the Huguenots. One exemplar of toleration was François La Mothe Le Vayer, active in the middle of the century. His path to tolerance was through social and intellectual elitism: the mark of the Sage is not to get caught up in persecutory mob behavior and attitudes.[5]

In England, the century began with a strong memory of the English Reformation, and one of the dominant themes of the seventeenth century was the fear on the part of many Protestants of the return of England to Catholic "popery." The Civil War that broke out in 1640 was perceived by the rebellious Puritans as a defense of Protestantism against a monarchy and an ecclesiastical establishment under Archbishop Laud that were increasingly perceived as crypto-Catholic.[6]

As usual in the history of toleration debates, the Puritans who had united against persecution by the Church of England soon fell out among themselves. Once they took power as a majority in Parliament and were freed from persecution by others, the Presbyterians were not eager to turn around and grant toleration to the many new sects that were emerging. They began to seek a compulsory uniformity, and were opposed by the Independents, who called for toleration. Throughout the 1640s, toleration of the sects was understood to be associated with the breaking of social discipline and thus with social revolution. John Milton published his *Areopagitica* in 1643 as a contribution to these debates, which was also the first major defense of freedom of the press.[7] In this period the term "Erastianism" began to be used by the Presbyterians to describe those of their enemies who advocated state supremacy in matters of religion.

After the execution of the king in 1649, Oliver Cromwell consolidated power in the newly declared Commonwealth of England. In spite of the principles of many of his erstwhile supporters, he opted to maintain a state church, purging dissident ministers.

Shortly after Cromwell's death in 1658, General Monck offered the crown to the exiled heir to the throne, Charles II, and the monarchy was restored in 1660. The Church of England was effectively restored as well, with trappings such as church courts. Many Presbyterian and Independent clergymen were ejected from their pulpits, and members of all Protestant churches except the Church of England became known as Nonconformists. Efforts by the king to relieve pressure on Catholics were thwarted by Parliament with measures such as the Test Act of 1673, which required Church of England orthodoxy from all officeholders. Panics such as the Popish Plot of 1678 led to the execution of many Catholics. Much of the rest of this reign and that of James II, who came to the throne in 1685, was spent in jockeying for position between Protestants and Catholics.[8]

As in France, this period abounded with odd bedfellows on the issue of toleration. The chapter in this section by Richard Popkin (Chapter 10) shows how the deism that developed in this period could be taken to imply tolerance. Arlen Feldwick and Cary Nederman's chapter on Aphra Behn (Chapter 9) brings out the point that Royalists in the 1660s could base a policy of toleration on a range of commitments from Catholicism to deism. It also reveals something of the influence the wide dissemination of travel experiences could have on the theory and practice of toleration.

Then, in 1688–89 the question of James's Catholic sympathies was settled by the invasion of William of Orange. When James fled, Parliament declared the throne vacant and gave it to William and Mary. The status of toleration in England was determined for a long time to come by the Toleration Act of 1689, which excluded Catholics and anti-trinitarians from any toleration at all, and deprived the Nonconformists it ostensibly tolerated of any share in government offices.[9] It was at this time that Locke's first *Letter concerning Toleration*, written in 1685 while he was in the Netherlands, was published.[10]

Throughout the century, the English colonists in North America grappled with issues of toleration as well. The colonies had been founded under communal ideals, which militated against toleration of differences. But some of the colonists had also known persecution in England and had other reasons to be wary of it. There was much movement back and forth between England and the colonies, and sometimes they received royal advice to refrain from persecution. But, as Frank Way's essay in this volume (Chapter 11) demonstrates, much of the movement away from persecution and toward toleration seems to have been home-grown, a spontaneous reaction against persecution by local officials. Something like the routinization of charisma described by Max Weber[11] may have taken place, as local officials began to see that persecution did not achieve very much.

Until this point, we have reviewed major events such as wars and persecutions as spurs to thinking about and practicing toleration. But one of the most influential examples of the century was the non-events in the Netherlands. This was the most tolerant country, on the whole, in the century, and it prospered. This is not to say that the Netherlands was not involved in the wars, which it was, or that it did not persecute at all, which it did. But it did so much less than the other countries, and observers knew it. After a disruptive controversy in which Arminians and Gomarists persecuted each other in the first quarter of the century, and later controversies between Voetians and Cocceians, the Dutch settled into grudging toleration in practice of many religions and sects and got used to it.[12]

There were several reasons for Dutch toleration. One was the accidents of leadership personality. William the Silent, leader of the Dutch Revolt in the sixteenth century, had been averse to persecution for religious reasons. Although the Statholder Maurits (1585–1625) was more temperamentally inclined to persecute, his successors Frederik Hendrik (1625–1647) and William III (1672–1702) were not. Political leaders on both sides of the political divide between the House of Orange and the Regents thwarted religious persecution in many instances.

A second reason for the growth of toleration was the decentralized, federal nature of the political system. If a thinker or a book were prosecuted in one region, one had only to flee to another for safety. Only rarely could enough widespread indignation be stirred up to ban anything or anyone from all the provinces. A third reason for toleration was that the Dutch republic was above all a commercial republic, and many influential leaders were well aware of the benefits for trade that wide toleration meant.[13]

A fourth reason may be described as the development of intellectual justifications of toleration. It seems safe to say that the de facto toleration of a wide variety of religious sects led to the expression of a variety of reasons for toleration. Dirck Coornhert's Spiritualist *Synod of Freedom of Conscience* (1582) was a high point of toleration theory in the sixteenth century, followed in the seventeenth by a flowering of tolerationist calls from a wide variety of sectaries. The celebrated Hugo Grotius (1583–1645), associated with the Arminians, called only for toleration of liberty of conscience if kept to oneself; but his fellow Arminians Uytenbogaert (1557–1644) and Episcopius (1583–1643) called for full tolerance of expression as well, including Catholics. Although the Arminian theology on which the latter two rested was officially suppressed in 1618, enough of it remained in the hearts and minds of influential merchants and local leaders to justify calling the tolerationist political leaders of the rest of the century "Arminians."

These intellectual justifications of toleration seem to have been a natural outgrowth of the intellectual freedom that prevailed, willy-nilly, in the Netherlands. The key lesson of the Netherlands in this period may be the demonstration that, if intellectual freedom gets started, some of the strands of inquiry it opens up lead to toleration of an ever-widening range of ideas and practices. The technology of intellectual freedom, as Popkin's chapter shows, starts with the circulation of clandestine manuscripts, followed by publication in print. De facto freedom of the press was one key to toleration: the Dutch were the first to publish the writings of the Polish Socinians as well as those of other sects.

Popkin's chapter shows that theories and practices of toleration could grow out of either end of the spectrum between religious skepticism and dogmatism. On the one hand, skepticism about Christianity and Judaism could blunt the demand for persecution in their behalf: how could you justify persecution if you were not sure you were right? If religions were human creations to meet human needs, they should hardly be used to make people suffer. This sort of thinking was developed by Spinoza in his tolerationist *Tractatus Theologico-Politicus* of 1672. On the other hand, a number of Christian *dogmata* about the conversion of the Jews at the millennium required tolerance of the Jews until that time came. Isaac La Peyrère, Ana Maria van Schurman, Jean Labadie, and others promoted this stance in the Netherlands, and others did it elsewhere.

Popkin's case is only that both skepticism and dogmatism could be and were taken by *some* people to imply tolerance. Elsewhere, Richard Tuck has reminded us that skepticism does not necessarily imply toleration: Lipsius argued that if we cannot be sure of religious truth, then the persecuted have no claim to toleration based on the truth of their beliefs.[14] Popkin adds the example of Jurieu, who agreed with Bayle that there is no good evidence for the truth of any religion, but insisted that he could feel or sense the truth, and that his feeling justified intolerance. Popkin also reminds us that, although the flowering of millenarianism has been taken by some writers to imply persecution, many millenarians were broadly tolerant.

The upshot of this review is that the reader will find, in the following chapters, a wide variety of paths to tolerance and toleration in theory and practice in the seventeenth century. As Horst Dreitzel has put it, "it is always a sign of strength and not of weakness if political-social institutions can be supported by different theories, even if these theories partially or fully contradict each other." [15]

Notes

1. Frances A. Yates, *The Rosicrucian Enlightenment* (London: Routledge, 1972).

2. Elisabeth Labrousse, *La révocation de l'Edit de Nantes: Une foi, une loi, une roi?* (Paris: Payot, 1990 [orig. 1985]).

3. See John Christian Laursen, ed., *New Essays on the Political Thought of the Huguenots of the Refuge* (Leiden: Brill, 1995).

4. See also Guy Howard Dodge, *The Political Theory of the Huguenots of the Dispersion* (New York: Columbia University Press, 1947).

5. Ruth Whelan, "The Wisdom of Simonides: Bayle and La Mothe Le Vayer," in Richard Popkin and Arjo Vanderjagt, eds., *Scepticism and Irreligion in the Seventeenth and Eighteenth Centuries* (Leiden: Brill, 1993), 230–53.

6. For a grand survey of the English experience from 1550 to 1660, see William K. Jordan, *The Development of Religious Toleration in England*, 4 vols. (Cambridge, Mass.: Harvard University Press/London: Allen and Unwin, 1932–1940; reprint Gloucester, Mass.: Peter Smith, 1965).

7. Ernest Sirluck, "Introduction" to *Complete Prose Works of John Milton*, vol. 2 (New Haven, Conn.: Yale University Press, 1959), esp. 53–183.

8. See Mark Goldie, "The Huguenot Experience and the Problem of Toleration in Restoration England," in *The Huguenots and Ireland* (Dublin: Glendale Press, 1987), 175–203 and "The Theory of Religious Intolerance in Restoration England" in Ole Peter Grell, Jonathan Israel, and Nicholas Tyacke, eds., *From Persecution to Toleration: The Glorious Revolution in England* (Oxford: Clarendon Press, 1991), 331–68.

9. See David L. Wykes, "The Tercentenary of the Toleration Act of 1689: A Cause for Celebration?" in Edward J. Furcha, ed., *Truth and Tolerance* (Montreal: Faculty of Religious Studies, 1990), 60–82.

10. On Locke's later letters, see Mark Goldie, "John Locke, Jonas Proast and religious toleration, 1688–1692" in John Walsh, Colin Haydon, and Stephen Taylor, eds., *The Church of England c.1689–c.1833* (Cambridge: Cambridge University Press, 1993), 143–71.

11. Max Weber, *The Theory of Social and Economic Organization*, ed. and trans. Talcott Parsons (New York: Free Press, 1964 [orig. English edition, 1947]).

12. The best synthetic account is Jonathan Israel, *The Dutch Republic: Its Rise, Greatness, and Fall, 1477–1806* (Oxford: Oxford University Press, 1995).

13. This current of thought, justifying toleration on the ground that it was good for business, can also be found in French in Emeric Crucé, *The New Cyneas* (1623) and in English in Henry Robinson, *Brief considerations Concerning the Advancement of Trade and Commerce* (1641) and *Liberty of Conscience* (1644). Catholic natural lawyers from the time of Vitoria had written of a right to freedom of trade.

14. Richard Tuck, "Scepticism and Toleration in the Seventeenth Century" in Susan Mendus, ed., *Justifying Toleration: Conceptual and Historical Perspectives* (Cambridge: Cambridge University Press, 1988), 21–35.

15. Horst Dreitzel, "Gewissensfreiheit und soziale Ordnung. Religionstoleranz als Problem der politischen Theorie am Ausgang des 17. Jahrhunderts," *Politische Vierteljahresschrift* 36 (1995): 30.

7

Samuel von Pufendorf and Toleration

Detlef Döring

SAMUEL VON PUFENDORF'S WRITINGS contain many arguments for religious toleration in specific cases. In view of his position as one of the founders of the highly influential tradition of Protestant Natural Law, this places him at the origins of the modern theory and practice of toleration. However, his toleration was always a limited toleration, limited largely by Pufendorf's commitment in the long run to the unity of truth and to the eventual reunification of Christianity. In the last analysis, he never escaped from his Lutheran roots and thus his toleration was never more than a liberal Lutheranism.

The son of a Saxon pastor, Pufendorf emphasized that he was born and educated "in religione Lutherana" and would therefore profess that faith everywhere and at all times.[1] He concentrated specifically on theology during his student years at the University of Leipzig, second only to Wittenberg as a bastion of Lutheran orthodoxy.[2] Though he paid less attention to theological issues during the 1660s and 1670s, they remained relevant to his reflections on ecclesiastical politics, and played a considerable role in his defense against accusations that he was a destroyer of religion. In the 1680s, Pufendorf once again took up theology more directly: he wrote to his Leipzig friend Adam Rechenberg that he had resolved to spend the "horas subcisivas" of his old age on theological investigations, "so that successive generations may see that I did not think only about worldly intrigues, which disgust me since they are only *vanitas vanitatum*."[3] The weight of this resolution can be measured in his two late works,

Translated by Randolph C. Head

De habitu religionis christianae ad vitam civilem (*The Christian religion's attitude toward civil life*) of 1687 and *Jus feciale* (*The divine feudal law*) of 1695.

The fact that Pufendorf was consulted repeatedly by princely courts at Berlin and Stockholm on such matters as evaluating the Swedish Catechism and commenting on the "misguided teachings" of various individuals demonstrates the recognition he received as an expert in religious affairs, at least from the political authorities. Indeed, Pufendorf is an outstanding example of the tendency toward lay theology that became increasingly visible late in the seventeenth century, a tendency that turned against the clergy's claims to a monopoly over engagement with the Bible and with questions of faith. Consequently, the following discussion of Pufendorf's significance to the developing ideal of toleration must begin with an examination of Lutheranism's attitude toward tolerance, as well as with Pufendorf's own experience of relations among the religious confessions.

From its beginnings, Lutheranism had to confront a dilemma. On the one hand, it had begun entirely as a protest against the church of the Roman Popes, which was seen as having succumbed to the Antichrist, and in Martin Luther's personal experience of faith—that is, in a thoroughly individual apprehension of the facts of salvation. Thus the Lutheran church, like all the confessions that emerged in the Reformation era, was implicitly inclined toward toleration of varying religious understandings. On the other hand, Lutheranism remained unhesitatingly committed to the existence of a single true religion and church. Conscience and truth, according to Luther, forbade the toleration of erroneous doctrines in matters of faith.[4] Additionally, since it inherited from the Middle Ages the close connection between religious and sociopolitical affairs, the Lutheran church continued to perceive the existence of divergent religious conceptions within a single community as dangerous to the authorities and therefore unacceptable. In keeping with this conviction, religious ideas that deviated from the orthodox confessional documents were not tolerated in the German territorial states shaped by Lutheran influence. The best example of this appeared in Pufendorf's own Electoral Saxony, in the rigorous suppression of all so-called crypto-Calvinist tendencies during the second half of the sixteenth century.

At the level of the entire Empire, the stalemate between the confessional parties eventually forced mutual toleration sanctioned by Imperial Recess between Lutheranism and Catholicism (excluding the Calvinists), in the Religious Peace of Augsburg in 1555. Similarly, a strict policy of confessionalization could not always be enforced within the territories of the

Empire. In this context, the Lutheran theologians we shall concentrate on here also accepted the possibility of tolerating (in the sense of enduring) other religious groups. The influential *Loci theologici* (1610–22) of Johann Gerhard of Jena was particularly important for providing the appropriate justification.[5] He acknowledged that confessional unity represented an especially strong bond (*vinculum*) among citizens, but "in hac vita" this goal could not always be reached. Indeed, Gerhard generally rejected the imposition of a religion by force, although he immediately qualified this point, revealingly, by noting that coercion "ad veram religionem" was a rather minor sin. In the event that a substantial part of a state's population was devoted to a "false religion," one could tolerate this "ad evitandum majus malum," since repressive measures might put the state's very existence in danger. Moreover, laws, privileges, or agreements on the part of the ruler that admitted other confessions remained binding obligations. Such toleration should always be understood as a "pax politica," however, and never as approval (*approbatio*) of other views and thus as potential steps towards some "Syncretismus ecclesiae."

Resisting the latter became a central concern in the work of Lutheran theologians of the seventeenth century. The toleration of certain beliefs could also be linked with all sorts of limitations on actual practices, and Gerhard insisted that blasphemy could never be tolerated under any imaginable circumstances. The suppression of blasphemy was a ruler's duty, just as the ruler was positively responsible for the dissemination of the "true religion" among his subjects.

What were the concrete and personal experiences Pufendorf was able to gather about the relations between the confessions during his lifetime? The internal constitution of the "Holy Roman Empire of the German Nation" — Pufendorf's home in the broadest sense — rested after 1648 primarily on the Peace of Westphalia. The treaty also regulated confessional issues, and recognized the legality of the Catholic, Lutheran, and Calvinist confessions. Rulers of imperial territories were obliged to tolerate the presence of dissenters in their domains if such toleration had been conceded by privilege or treaty. Otherwise, the magistrate had the discretion either to tolerate the free exercise of religion or to allow dissenters to emigrate. Clearly, the terms of the 1648 treaty were still far removed from any recognition that the free exercise of religion might be a natural right of humankind. Limited toleration of other confessions, which might be accompanied by all sorts of discrimination, rested only on treaties or on exercises of grace that could not be required of the princes.

Pufendorf's career took him only through Lutheran (Saxony, Denmark, Sweden) and Calvinist (the Palatinate, the Netherlands, Brandenburg) territories. To our knowledge, he never visited a Catholic territory, nor was he ever in correspondence with any Catholics, with the exception of a few converts from Protestantism. His native Electoral Saxony was an exclusively Lutheran territory during his life, with the exception of Lausitz, annexed in 1635, and the not inconsiderable Catholic colony at court in Dresden.[6] Saxony was considered the strongest bastion of Lutheranism despite its pro-Habsburg policy during the Thirty Years' War, and despite recurring rumors about efforts from Rome and Vienna to convert the ruling house of Wettin. Catholicism was simply "the enemy" in Saxony. Fears about the Counter-Reformation remained virulent, and every convert who renounced "repulsive papistic abominations" strengthened the Saxons' self-consciousness. Such conversions were solemnly celebrated in Leipzig with the entire University in attendance. During his student years there (from 1650 to 1658, with an interruption of one year), Pufendorf had frequent opportunities to experience such dramas.[7]

Nevertheless the Saxon theologians saw their enemies not just in the Catholics but even more intensely in the representatives of their Reformed sister-church. Just as Pufendorf was scarcely likely to encounter any Catholics residing in Leipzig, so would he have been unable to make the acquaintance of any Calvinists, since these were found in the city only starting in the 1680s, and then in small numbers.[8] During his stay in Denmark, which was in any case strictly Lutheran, Pufendorf probably made no extended acquaintanceships, since his years there (1658–59) were spent mostly as a Swedish prisoner of war. Only in the Netherlands did he encounter a state that was not Lutheran in its orientation. Perhaps it was during his first visit to the Netherlands, which was followed by many more, that Pufendorf first developed his distaste, formulated in his later works, for the much too widely extended toleration that reigned there. All we know, however, is that he participated in the life of Leiden's Lutheran community during his student years in the city.[9]

In 1661 Pufendorf was called to the University of Heidelberg. The prince Palatine and his state were Reformed, although there was a substantial Lutheran population and some Catholics. At times, even a Socinian congregation existed. Elector Karl Ludwig exercised an unusual amount of toleration for his time, even though there was no lack of friction between Calvinists and Lutherans, for example. He also supported eirenic attempts to bring about closer contacts between the confessions; one symbol of this approach was the construction of the "Unity-Church" (*Eintrachtskirche*) in Mannheim, although this took place in 1680, long after Pufendorf's stay in the Palatinate.[10]

Later, Pufendorf's opponents were to claim that he had presented himself as a Calvinist while in Heidelberg, whereas Pufendorf emphasized that it was precisely in Heidelberg that anyone could profess his confession freely. He had simply maintained friendly relations with the Calvinists there: no conflicts over religion had broken out, and people did not attack one another as sons of the Devil on account of their differing religious ideas.[11] At the same time, as the relevant parts of his texts from those years about the constitution of the Empire demonstrate, he saw Calvinism as thoroughly problematic, primarily because it was superfluous.[12]

Sweden, where Pufendorf lived between 1667 and 1687, subscribed to the Formula of Concord only in 1663. This was the collection of confessional statements that had been accepted in the majority of Lutheran territories by 1580. Nevertheless the Scandinavian power's reputation as the "Spain of the North" was surely justified by the unwavering Lutheran position there. Pufendorf himself judged that the Swedish nation showed the greatest rigor in all matters pertaining to religion. This was why he had had to react with such sharpness to accusations that he was an injurer of true religion.[13]

The Swedish defense of religiosity was oriented most directly against any tendency that implied even the slightest hint of atheism. A dissertation that Pufendorf supervised in 1673, *De religione naturali*, expressed deep gratitude to King Charles X for an edict that harshly prohibited all forms of atheism.[14] By comparison, attitudes toward "atheism" in Electoral Saxony and in Brandenburg, Pufendorf's later home, appeared relatively lax. Nor is it necessary to point out that Sweden maintained a strong front against Catholicism as well. With regard to Calvinism, a similar distance was maintained in Sweden. In a letter from King Charles XI to the elector of Brandenburg, the king pointed out that any equality between Lutheranism and Calvinism comparable to that found in Germany could not exist in Sweden, because a "fundamental central statute" of his kingdom held that only the evangelical-Lutheran confession could be recognized.[15] Thus the Huguenots fleeing France found scarcely any acceptance in Sweden, since Charles prohibited the public exercise of worship on their part.[16] In 1687 he even issued a statute ordaining that the children of both Catholics *and* Calvinists were to be educated as Lutherans. The energetic protests of the Calvinists were met with the telling response that they "were viewed and treated in one and the same fashion" as the Catholics.[17]

Pufendorf spent the final six years of his life as court historian in the Electorate of Brandenburg. There confessional relations were unusual in that a nearly homogeneously Lutheran population was ruled by a Calvinist dynasty. Only in Brandenburg's Rhenish territories was the Calvinist confession predominant, while diplomatic agreements with Poland required the toleration of Catholic communities in East Prussia. The existence of Socinian congregations in Prussia, founded with the elector's approval after rising persecution of anti-Trinitarians in Poland, made the confessional situation more explosive. Although historiography has celebrated the myth of exemplary toleration in Brandenburg-Prussia, it is important to observe that the coexistence of multiple confessions gave rise to quite serious tensions.[18] It was above all Calvinists who were able to pursue careers in the court at Berlin and in the upper level of the government and administration. Reformed theologians were appointed pastors to Lutheran congregations, and the elector's efforts to abolish exorcism (expulsion of the Devil) at baptism—a practice long since eliminated from Calvinist ritual—caused storms of protest among the Lutherans. To all this was added a lively fear that Catholic missions were expanding their grasp, especially in East Prussia, and anger over the elector's approval of the immigration of anti-Trinitarians.

Pufendorf was drawn into such conflicts willy-nilly, for example as a member of several commissions appointed to investigate Catholic and anti-Trinitarian machinations.[19] Even more complicated was the course of controversies within the Protestant block. These flared again in the 1690s as a result of the Danish theologian Hektor Gottfried Masius's proposition that only accepting the Lutheran confession would guarantee the rights of the ruler. The administration in Berlin was outraged, and arranged for the distinguished theologian Johann Christoph Becmann to compose a refutation. Pufendorf also rejected the content of Masius's theory, and complained that it burdened relations between the electorate's Calvinist magistrates and their Lutheran subjects. Yet Pufendorf was also extremely displeased because the Privy Council had approved the publication of Becmann's text against his advice, since this amounted to pouring out poison "against our own" (the Lutherans),[20] and because Becmann himself was "in his heart a great enemy of the Lutherans."[21]

In short, the range of Pufendorf's own experiences covered the entire gamut of confessional relations: strictly confessional and intolerant states (Saxony and Sweden), the most tolerant public entity of the seventeenth century (the Netherlands), a state that tolerated religious minorities (the Palatinate), and a state in which the highest magistrates did not adhere to the religion of the population (Brandenburg).

As this short overview illustrates, Pufendorf spent most of his life in close contact with the princely courts that were the centers of political decision-making in the states of his era. He portrayed the history of these states in his voluminous published works, he justified their policies in his polemical writings, and, most important, the city (or state; *civitas*) took a central role in his legal philosophy as the institution that was capable of guiding human existence (*vita humana*) "ad maximum cultum, humanitatem et opulentiam."[22] How much importance, then, did religion—still a central reality of the era—have in this context? Pufendorf's seemingly paradoxical answer was that the state was separate from religion, or from the church, but that the two nevertheless should be closely linked to each other. Deciding the conceivable extent of and limits on the toleration of individual confessions was therefore a problem whose answer followed in the first line (though not exclusively) from his treatment of the relationship between state and church.

The following conclusion was decisive: just as science and philosophy were fundamentally independent from religion and theology, so the state did not exist for the sake of religion, but rather followed its own laws.[23] Pufendorf himself demonstrated the confusion of entirely different levels of analysis found among those who accused him of propounding a secularized natural law. Similarly, he maintained that the confessions or religious denominations should be evaluated according to the extent that they allowed the State to exist in its own sphere.

Most Pufendorf scholarship focuses primarily on his separation in principle of state and church. It leads to the conclusion that Pufendorf viewed toleration, understood as freedom of belief, to be a natural right that came to every human *eo ipso*.[24] However, since this interpretation projects the perspective of the nineteenth and twentieth centuries into the early modern period, it can be accepted only in part. Deeper understanding requires recognizing the often overlooked fact that Pufendorf's most revealing statements about toleration always reflected a background of specific events, and that his relevant publications therefore lacked an abstract, theoretical character. He wrote specifically about defending Protestantism against the Counter-Reformation that was making advances in France, England, and other countries. It is no coincidence that Pufendorf's late work *Jus feciale* ends with a fervent appeal to Protestant princes and theologians to set aside inter-Protestant disputes so as to turn all their energies against the common enemy, the papacy.[25]

However, Pufendorf also noticed an unacceptable effort on the part of Reformed polemicists to justify the suppression of the most widespread religion in a territory in favor of the prince's confession: it took no fine nose to sniff out the intentions of Becmann's thesis, *De religione praedominante*. Clearly, Pufendorf was referring to the pressure on Lutheranism in Brandenburg.[26]

Still, these were merely malformations of Protestantism, whereas Pufendorf considered the project of making the Pope the sole ruler of Christendom to be the central purpose of Catholicism. The boundaries Pufendorf established between church and state, and his exclusion of religion from the areas where a prince could demand obedience from a subject, served his eminently practical purpose of defending against the claims of the Roman clergy, whom he saw (especially through the Jesuit order) behind the persecution carried out in various Catholic states.[27] The state possessed no right to compel its citizens to any particular religion: "One should indeed observe in Romans 13:7 that Paul enumerates four things that subjects owe their magistrates: taxes, tolls, respect, and honor. Conscience and religion are not found among these things . . . and citizens are not obliged to defer to princes about them."[28] Therefore the "irresponsible" dogma, "quod Princeps possit cogere subditos ad suam religionem," should be rejected.[29] Pufendorf referred to the persecution of the Huguenots in France by observing that "among Christ's Apostles there was not a single dragoon."[30] Similarly, no magistracy in the present was permitted to use force in coercing its subjects towards a particular confession.[31]

The separation between church and state was by no means to be understood, however, as implying that the state should regard religion as a private matter for its citizens: indeed, religion possessed a constitutive role for the survival of any collectivity. Politics and religion, like state and church, also belonged together. At the most basic level, this implied for Pufendorf the entirely conventional conviction of his age, that no community could survive without religion.[32] No religion implied no conscience, consequently opening the door to every kind of crime—which meant, in turn, undermining the foundations of the state.[33] Religion thus became one of the very pillars of the state, since only the threat of eternal punishment could deter criminals from their misdeeds. It also followed from this view that anyone who spread the opinion that one could live without piety, faith, and religion should be prosecuted for a capital crime.[34] Pufendorf was again aiming at atheists, whose suppression had become an ever-increasing concern of his.[35]

Atheism did not represent the greatest danger, however, since it was relatively easy to recognize. But in addition to atheism, Pufendorf insisted, certain "dogmata moralia" violated natural law and transgressed upon wholesome politics [*sana politica*] under the cloak of religious justification [*sub religionis larva*], and thus threatened to undermine the state.[36] Such beliefs obstructed humans in the exercise of their obligations to God and undermined public morals.[37] In consequence, they were not to be tolerated, but should be persecuted and eradicated.[38] Which "dogmata moralia" Pufendorf had in mind became immediately clear. They involved the following assertions. There exists some priest outside the state, who deserves the obedience of all states, and who could release any subject from his obligations to his magistrates. All clergy in a state should enjoy immunity, and stand under the sole authority of this priest. The clergy are also authorized to heap up infinite wealth.[39] Also involved was the idea that one could placate God through money or other services, or be justified by the actions of another. One should not be obliged to hold one's oaths to those who had other beliefs, and one might encourage rebellion or civil war for the sake of religion.[40] The list goes on. In other words, it was the Catholic church and the Pope who pursued policies hostile to the state "sub religionis larva," and they should therefore be viewed in the harshest light.[41]

Pufendorf never tired of explaining the dangers that emanated from the Catholic church. The very first of his surviving texts, the lectures he held before the Leipzig learned society "Collegium Anthologicum" (1655– 58),[42] stress this theme to the same extent as the posthumously published late work, *Jus feciale*, which appeared only in 1695. The state that opened its borders to Roman priests would be materially weakened and would sink into dependency on persons who received their instructions from the outside—that is, from Rome.[43] Such a state therefore lost its most important feature, its sovereignty.

Moreover, it was not the responsibility of religion to take on the problems of governance. Christ "did not want to prescribe any laws to the regents, but rather wanted to leave them *principiis suis domesticis*." Consequently, neither could any theologian "write books *de jure Regio*, and impose these on all Christian Kingdoms *tanquam universalem regulam*."[44] All churches ran the danger of violating such boundaries, but the Catholic claim to dominion over the state was distinctive and unique: it rose and fell according to its program of accumulating the greatest possible power and wealth.[45] Therefore the Roman church did not actually represent a religion any more, or more precisely, it disseminated a false religion (*religio superficiaria*).[46]

There was also a second category of "dogmata moralia" that threatened the community despite its claim to religious value. Here Pufendorf had in mind the doctrines of the so-called Libertines, for example (although he did not actually name this sect by name). A man who had been freed from his sins by Christ could live according to his drives, and was not subject to any laws. Every citizen was entitled to act entirely according to his conscience, even against the laws of the state. Service to the state, moreover, was "per se" associated with guilt and impurity, since the true Christian need not contribute to the preservation of the state. Pufendorf categorized such views as the delusions (*deliria*) of fanatics.[47] Intended were the groups loosely described as *Schwärmer*, Anabaptists, Spiritualists, and so forth, who could expect no toleration from Pufendorf. Indeed, a central theme in Pufendorf's planned study of moral theology was to be the great dangers that "enthusiasm" and fanaticism represented to human society.[48] The views of these opponents threatened to turn Christianity into no more than "a clever moral philosophy," and to reduce it to no more than what could be grasped by reason. These new sects, especially the Anabaptists, also had "new policies in mind" and would therefore become "especially dangerous in that state where they took control."[49] This is why Pufendorf found it inconceivable why "circa tolerandas quasvis Religiones in excessu peccari" in the Netherlands.[50] To his mind, the Dutch tolerated groups that had scarcely anything to do with Christianity anymore.

Up to now, we have been speaking about Pufendorf's attacks on forms of untruth which, appearing under the cloak of religion, undermined the preservation of the state and which should not, therefore, be tolerated. The sign of true religion (*religio solida*), in contrast, was its contribution to the well-being of the state. True politics and true religion could never adopt contradictory postures; indeed, they positively depended on each other. Pufendorf's target here was explicitly any Machiavellian understanding of politics that allocated all political action to "sapientia hujus mundi," which stood in contrast to "sapientia divina." Politics that was in accord with its own true principles stood in harmony with Christian religion, rather, and reached its goals more easily, the more true religion was rooted in the hearts of mankind.[51]

If the citizen's loyalty to his religion was thus of fundamental importance for the cohesion of the state and beyond that, for fulfilling its final
goals, the next question that arose was whether one ought to favor the
domination of a single confession, or whether a plurality of confessions
could serve the same purpose. Pufendorf answered unambiguously that
confessional unity was desirable within any state.[52] Difference in religion,
in contrast, must be reckoned "among a state's weaknesses."[53] Pufendorf
responded to the Reformed theologian Jean Le Clerc, who had sharply
criticized this position of Pufendorf, by claiming that "in universum . . .
inter debilitates civitates referendum, si cives opinionibus circa sacra dis-
sideant."[54] Surely it was obvious that England or the Netherlands, for example, would enjoy greater internal security if their citizens shared a single
religious outlook. Likewise, the king of Sweden had no obligation to accept Huguenot refugees, since by admitting foreign rituals he might en-
danger the security of his state.[55]

Pufendorf saw the problem not so much in the differences between
confessions per se, but rather because the corruption of humankind would
turn confessional differences into occasions for tumults, polarization, and
finally for civil wars.[56] It was the magistrate's obligation, therefore, to ensure that the authorized persons produced a unified confession of faith,
which was then to be accepted by the individual citizens.[57]

This goal admittedly represented only an ideal to strive toward, and
which was rarely achieved in reality. Any number of reasons could result in
the necessity to tolerate the existence of various confessions within a state.
Above all, the relevant treaties and capitulations entered into by the ruler
could provide legal justification for persisting in a confession that diverged
from the state's. Such was the case above all in Germany.

Once accepted, moreover, a religion could no longer be banned at
will.[58] Equally, a prince who changed to a different religion (Pufendorf
had James II of England in mind) could not establish his new confession
as the national religion. The very fact that a majority (*magna pars*) of the
population adhered to a different religion, or even to a new religion, was
enough to create some legal protection for its exercise.[59] Nevertheless none
of these cases described by Pufendorf reflected our modern conception of
toleration. No legal grounds provided for tolerance of other confessions,
but rather irreversible historical antecedents or, above all, the "concessio"
of the prince, who had the power to permit adherents of other confessions
to sojourn in his territory.[60]

In this context Pufendorf again distinguished complete from limited toleration. His detailed discussions about toleration always resonated with the historical context of his writing. Thus, a prince should especially value those religiously dissident subjects who demonstrate particular fervor in conforming to his interests. Here Pufendorf was repeating an argument often used by the Huguenots who had been persecuted by Louis XIV. Pufendorf also warned repeatedly against tolerating groups who turned their dogmas against the state; the target here was naturally the Catholics. A state that attempted to overcome other states under the banner of religion should be opposed as an enemy of liberty. Here, Pufendorf was obviously thinking of France.[61]

These explanations might lead one to the impression that a state's confessional unity served primarily its reason of state, but Pufendorf's introduction of the concept of "true religion" at this point made a decisive difference. His claim that religions dangerous to the state should be forbidden by no means implied that every religion could be accepted, if only it did no political harm. A religion had to be judged further, to see if it resulted in good for the human soul. There was no question, therefore, of accepting the religion of the Muslims or of the Chinese.[62] It might well be that God conferred on non-Christian religions the responsibility to honor God and thus to ensure the survival of the state, but such religions could surely never provide the reconciliation with God that was necessary for salvation. Pufendorf vehemently rejected Thomas Hobbes's contention that every citizen had to accept entirely the religious ordinations of his state. If this were the case, Pufendorf claimed, then a prince would have the power to introduce the religion of the Brahmans or the Japanese, or to favor any group whatsoever "quae Christianum nomen prae se ferunt."[63] Under these circumstances, religion would be nothing more than a statute that any prince could alter at will. To avoid this, every religion should be confronted with the issue of its truth, since it was a crass falsehood to maintain, as Hobbes did, that religion served only to maintain tranquillity within the state.[64] Nor did the recognition of true religion pose a particularly difficult problem in Pufendorf's eyes: one had only to study the Holy Scripture, the infallible foundation of Christianity, and the solution to all confessional controversies would follow easily.[65]

In keeping with this precept, Pufendorf grounded the sketch of theology found in his *Jus feciale* entirely on the Bible. Studying scripture provided a number of irrefutable basic articles,[66] which were organized into a chain according to the model provided by Johann Coccejus's development of federal theology. Pufendorf's result conformed to the confessional statements of Lutheranism, which constituted the true religion in his eyes. Calvinism, too, ultimately rested on a true understanding of religion, but included a number of superfluous or even exceedingly harmful novelties like the doctrine of predestination.[67]

No prince could call upon the *jus territoriale* in order to force his subjects to abjure a true religion and accept a false one.[68] Thus the liberty of Protestantism rested not only on the separation of church from state, but also on the premise that true religion could not be repressed. No abstract liberty of conscience justified separation from the Roman church, but rather the demonstration that this church had fallen into error.

In Lessing's *Nathan the Wise*, Sultan Saladin asks what the true religion is. His interlocutor, the Jew Nathan, answers with the famous parable of the rings, which effectively rejects the Sultan's question as unanswerable. Every religion rests on faith, and no faith possesses more powerful means of proof compared to any other. What counts in the end is only the effect of any religion, since each makes its adherents comfortable before God and man.[69] When thinkers stopped taking for granted the existence of a single true religion, one of the theoretical bases for a modern understanding of toleration was laid. If no one can reach a decision about the truth of a religion, all religions stand in the same position when evaluated; from this fact, every religion gains a natural right to exist. But this was not Pufendorf's position. He would accept no doubt about the fact that there was but a single religion, which must be accepted as true. Lutheranism's legitimacy rested not on liberty of conscience, but on the fact that it represented the truth. Although no one could be forced to accept this religion for his own, natural law also provided no justified claim for the toleration of any "false" religion.

In addition to *Tolerantia Politica*, Pufendorf also considered *Tolerantia Ecclesiastica*, where he closely followed the position about this distinction that had already been laid out by J. Gerhard. Ecclesiastical toleration meant that people could mutually recognize one another as members of the same church, and admit one another to communion, even when they held differing views on particular dogmas.[70] Pufendorf took a relatively open position with regard to such ecclesiastical toleration, but he was much more restrictive about any potential unification (*conciliatio*) among different churches. Once again, the question of truth took a central position. There could be only one truth; consequently, one must declare a *single* doctrine to be correct, while rejecting all other interpretations. Doctrines not directly necessary to salvation left some room for differences of opinion, but when it came to fundamental issues, this was not possible.[71]

Our examination of Pufendorf's ideas has shown that he took an intermediate position on the question of tolerance. On the one hand his ideas led toward a modern understanding of toleration, but on the other hand he remained committed to inherited preconceptions to a considerable degree.[72] For him, the existence of multiple religions or confessions was a flaw that reflected human weakness, which one could scarcely expect to overcome in this world. Outside the sphere of Christianity, the obligation to participate in a natural religion had to suffice, provided it did not spread doctrines dangerous to the state under the mantle of religion. This at least secured the well-being of the community involved, although it did nothing for the salvation of the inhabitants. A Christian magistrate faced greater obligations. It was not enough that his subjects adhered to some kind of religion: the religion had to be Christian, which for Pufendorf meant Protestant, since Catholicism and the "sectarians" professed views that had little if anything to do with Christianity. Only reason of state could justify the toleration of these last two, since the goal was dominion by the one and specifically true religion.

When one compares this position with that of Gerhard, as described above, it becomes clear that despite substantial similarities, Pufendorf's Lutheran origins and his extensive experience living in a Lutheran world (47 of his 62 years) determined his position to a considerable degree. Some new elements were visible in his ideas, however, though they did not yet dominate the picture. For example, he ascribed considerable importance to the need for a state, whose duties went far beyond the mere material security of human existence. Thus religion often seemed to have an almost instrumental function, a view not inconsistent with Pufendorf's consistently critical attitude about the clergy of his own denomination. His criticism of the Catholic church started at the same point, emphasizing the dangers it posed to the state. This critique, pointing towards the Enlightenment, sounded a different note from traditional Protestant polemics, which concentrated on doctrinal differences. The idea that a contract provided a basis for the establishment of states, and a justification for the liberty of citizens from an imposed religious subjugation, was also foreign to Lutheran orthodoxy. Finally, Pufendorf's proclamation that the secular sciences should be free of influences from theology pointed the way to the future.

Comparing Pufendorf's position on the question of toleration to that of his great compatriot Leibniz reveals a number of shared features, such as the demand that the sciences be freed from the guardianship of theology, and above all their shared engagement in preserving Christian religion as the foundation of social life. Yet the crucial point is that Leibniz, despite his continuing personal adherence to the Lutheran confession, saw the entire Christian world as a unified entity. For him, what was shared outweighed what divided the confessions. He therefore concluded that all Christian denominations (with few exceptions) should mutually tolerate one another in the sense of mutual recognition with the hope of a later reunification.[73] This is a position that ultimately connects Leibniz to the ecumenical movements of the twentieth century, whatever the differences in historical context may be. Pufendorf, it is true, also spoke of a "Systema Theologiae" that was independent from the individual denominations, but for him such a system sought to define a *single* confession of faith as the only "true religion." Thus his encouragement of toleration was not a self-evident conclusion resulting from a fundamental sense of the unity of Christendom, but depended rather on calculations of political utility. Here we see the boundary between a modern concept of toleration and that of the early modern era.

Notes

1. Samuel Pufendorf, "Apologia," 9. Published as an appendix to Pufendorf's collection of polemical pieces, *Eris Scandica* (orig. 1686), cited here from the appendix to the 1706 Frankfurt am M. edition of *De jure naturae et gentium*.

2. Pufendorf's preoccupation with theology is denied by much of the earlier research. See Detlef Döring, *Pufendorf-Studien: Beiträge zur Biographie Samuel von Pufendorfs und zu seiner Entwicklung als Historiker und theologischer Schriftsteller* (Berlin: Duncker & Humblot, 1992), 55–142; and Leonard Krieger, *The Politics of Discretion: Pufendorf and the Acceptance of Natural Law* (Chicago: University of Chicago Press, 1965), 202–54.

3. From a letter to A. Rechenburg of Dec. 6, 1690 in Samuel Pufendorf, *Briefwechsel*, ed. Detlef Döring (Berlin: Akademie Verlag, 1996) (vol. 1 of *Gesammelte Werke*, ed. Wilhelm Schmidt-Biggemann), 298.

4. No doctrine in conflict with Holy Scripture was tolerable: Luther's "Preface" to Antonius Corvinus, *Quatenus expediat aeditam . . .*, published in M. Luther, WA, 38: 277.

5. *Ioannis Gerhardi Loci Theologici . . . denuo juxta editionem principem accurate typis excribendum curavit . . . Ed. Pruess.* (Berlin, 1868), 6: 362ff.

6. Cf. Siegfried Seifert, *Niedergang und Wiederaufstieg der katholischen Kirche in Sachsen 1517–1774* (Leipzig: Benno-Verlag, 1964).

7. Cf. the reports of Johann Jacob Vogel, published in *Leipziger Geschichtsbuch* (Leipzig, 1714). On Pufendorf's studies in Leipzig, Döring, *Samuel Pufendorf als Student in Leipzig* (Leipzig: Universitätsbibliothek, 1994).

8. See Paul Weinmeister, *Beiträge zur Geschichte der evangelish-reformierten Gemeinde zu Leipzig* (Leipzig: Johann Ambrosius Barth, 1900).

9. Ewert Wrangel, *Sveriges Litterära Förbindelser med Holland särdeles under 1600-Talet* (Lund, 1897), 127, note 1.

10. See Gustav Adolf Benrath, "Die konfessionellen Unions-bestrebungen des Kurfürsten Karl Ludwig von der Pfalz," *Zeitschrift für die Geschichte des Oberrheins* 116 (1968): 187–252.

11. Pufendorf, *Apologia*, 9.

12. Samuel Pufendorf (ed. Severinus de Monzambano), *De statu imperii Germanici*, chap. 8, § 7. The best text is now the German-Latin edition by Horst Denzer (Frankfurt am M. and Leipzig: Insel, 1994). There is no modern English translation.

13. From a letter from Pufendorf to Tobias Pfanner, Dec. 15, 1688, in *Briefwechsel*, 231.

14. *De religione naturali   sub Praesidio D. Samuelis Pufendorfii . . . publico bonorum examini subjecta a Nicolao Lundebergio* (Lund, 1673), esp. "Consectarium V: Etiam practice Athei e bene constituta Republica proscribendi."

15. Letter from Charles XI to Elector Frederick William, March 17, 1688, Hauptstaatsarchiv Dresden, Loc. 30103, "Bericht der holländischen Gesandtschaft."

16. Cf. Frank Puaux, *Histoire de l'établissement des Protestants Français en Suède* (Paris: Fischbacher and Stockholm: Giron, 1891), 55–72.

17. Hauptstaatsarchiv Dresden, Loc. 30103, "Bericht der holländischen Gesandtschaft."

18. On confessional relations in Brandenburg, see Detlef Döring, *Frühaufklärung und obrigkeitliche Zensur in Brandenburg. Friedrich Wilhelm Stosch und das Verfahren gegen sein Buch "Concordia rationis et fidei"* (Berlin: Duncker & Humblot, 1995), 38–60.

19. See Döring, *Pufendorf-Studien*, 115–29.

20. Letter to Adam Rechenberg, August 29, 1691, *Briefwechsel*, 320.

21. Letter to Adam Rechenberg, Oct. 24, 1691, *Briefwechsel*, 329.

22. *De civitate . . . Praeside Samuele Pufendorf . . . pro Gradu Magisterii . . . refert Andreas Helman* (Lund, 1676), Thesis XIV. See also *De officio hominis et civis*, II, 1, 9; and *De jure naturae et gentium*, II, 2, 2.

23. Samuel Pufendorf, *De habitu religionis christianae ad vitam civilem* (reprint Stuttgart and Bad Cannstatt: Frommann-Holzboog, 1972), §§ 32ff.

24. Heinrich von Treitschke was among the first to claim that Pufendorf had proposed the freedom of all confessions on the basis of the separation between church and state. "Samuel Pufendorf," in Heinrich von Treitschke, *Aufsätze. Reden und Briefe* (Meersburg: Hendel Verlag, 1929), 1: 315–99, here 378–83. Among newer studies, I mention only Simone Zurbuchen's work on the idea of toleration

in Pufendorf, *Naturrecht und natürlich Religion: Zur Geschichte des Toleranzbegriffs von Samuel Pufendorf bis Jean-Jacques Rousseau* (Würzburg: Königshausen und Neumann, 1991), according to which the liberty of belief and worship followed from the differentiation of church and state. Only atheism was excluded from this toleration, as all the scholarship has acknowledged (see the further comments in the main text above). One of the few exceptions to such views appears in Leonard Krieger's exposition, *The Politics of Discretion* (note 2 above), 240–43.

25. Samuel Pufendorf, *Jus feciale* (Lübeck, 1695), 393.

26. Letter to Christian Thomasius, Nov. 1, 1690, in *Briefwechsel*, 289.

27. Samuel Pufendorf, *Commentarii de rebus gestibus Friderici Wilhelmi Magni Electoris Brandenburgici* (Berlin, 1695), 1532.

28. Letter to A. Rechenberg, Nov. 18, 1690, in *Briefwechsel*, 292.

29. Letter to A. Rechenberg, May 2, 1691, in *Briefwechsel*, 313.

30. Letter to Landgrave Ernst of Hessen-Rheinfels, March 29, 1690 in *Briefwechsel*, 265.

31. *De habitu* (note 23 above), §6.

32. *De habitu*, §7.

33. Compare on this function of religion, e.g., *De officio hominis et civis*, I, 4; and *De habitu*, §48.

34. *De religione naturali* (note 14 above), Consectarium V.

35. See Döring, *Pufendorf-Studien*, 190–93.

36. *Apologia* (note 1 above), 7. Pufendorf expressed similar points in detail in his polemical text, "Specimen controversarium circa Jus Naturale ipsi nuper motarum," Ch. 6, §1.

37. *De jure naturae et gentium*, II, 4, 4.

38. Ibid.

39. *Apologia*, §6.

40. *De jure naturae et gentium*, II, 4, 4.

41. No clear demand to forbid Catholicism in Protestant states is found, to my knowledge, in Pufendorf's writings. Nevertheless, toleration of Catholicism appears extremely problematic. Catholic clergy would not refrain from any monstrosity (*immanitas*) to reach their goal. Pufendorf, *Epistolae duae super censura in Ephemeridibus Parisiensibus . . .* (Leipzig, 1688), cited here from the modern edition, Samuel von Pufendorf, *Kleine Vorträge und Schriften*, ed. Detlef Döring (Frankfurt: Vittorio Klostermann, 1995), 488–506.

42. These lectures now published in *Kleine Vorträge*, 21–78.

43. Pufendorf describes these dangers vividly in his little noted commentary on a Bull of Pope Clement IX ("Brevis commentatio super ordinum religiosorum suppressione ad Bullam Clementis IX . . . ," in *Kleine Vorträge*, 218–33).

44. Letter to A. Rechenberg, Nov. 18, 1690 (note 28, above). Pufendorf's target here is the Lutheran theologian Hektor Gottfried Masius.

45. Pufendorf, *Basilii Hyperetae, historische und politische Beschreibung der geistlichen Monarchie des Stuhls zu Rom* (Hamburg, 1679), cited here from the version in Pufendorf's *Einleitung zu der Historie der vornehmsten Reiche und Staaten* (Frankfurt am M., 1705), 815.

46. "De concordia verae politicae cum religione christiana," in Pufendorf, *Dissertationes academicae selectiores* (Lund, 1675), 543–82.

47. *De jure naturae et gentium*, II, 4, 4.

48. Letter from Pufendorf to J. Chr. Schomer, Oct. 6, 1690, in *Briefwechsel*, 286.

49. *Beschreibung der geistlichen Monarchie*, 870.

50. *Jus feciale*, 372.

51. "De concordia" (note 46, above), §1.

52. Ibid.

53. *Einleitung* (note 45, above), 528.

54. Compare Le Clerc's review of the *Einleitung* in the *Bibliothèque Universelle et Historique* 7 (1687): 205–11. Le Clerc responds by claiming that a diversity of confessions would never weaken a state. On the contrary, weakness resulted from confessional coercion. On this controversy see the detailed description in the edition of *Epistolae duae* in *Kleine Vorträge*, 469–87.

55. Nevertheless, he allowed freedom of conscience and the private exercise of religion (*Epistolae duae*, 505).

56. *Epistolae duae*, 503.

57. *De habitu*, §49.

58. *De habitu*, 170.

59. *Jus feciale*, 14f.

60. *Jus feciale*, 16.

61. *Jus feciale*, 16–18.

62. Pufendorf, *Spicilegium controversarium*, VI, 2, p. 275, cited from the edition in his *Eris Scandica* (see note 1).

63. Pufendorf did not address Hobbes directly, but rather the Dutch jurist Adriaan Houtuyn. In an appendix to *De habitu*, he accuses the Dutchman of reviving the doctrines of Hobbes.

64. *De habitu*, §49. Since there can only be one truth, he who "omnes dissentientes Religiones pari pretio aestimat" actually values no religion. *Jus feciale*, 12.

65. *Jus feciale*, 28. The result is a "vollkommen Systema Theologiae," which is joined "ad formam justae artis." *Basilii Hyberetae*, 869.

66. Such things are essential to salvation, and can therefore neither be ignored, nor denied, nor twisted, nor interpreted in another way. *Jus feciale*, 24–25.

67. Letter to A. Rechenberg, August 29, 1691, *Briefwechsel*, 320.

68. *De habitu*, 193.

69. G. E. Lessing, *Nathan der Weise*, Act III, Sc. 7.

70. *Jus feciale*, 20–21.

71. *Jus feciale*, 23.

72. Hans Guggisberg's observation about the sixteenth century applies equally, in my opinion, to the late seventeenth century: "But on the whole the period remains a period of beginnings, of collecting arguments, of temporary and provisional compromises and of many setbacks. In studying the toleration literature of the sixteenth century the modern historian is often confronted with allusions and arguments which require very careful reading because the theologi-

cal, political and philosophical reasoning does not reveal itself easily or directly to twentieth-century ways of thinking." "The Defence of Religious Toleration and Religious Liberty in Early Modern Europe: Arguments, Pressures, and Some Consequences," *History of European Ideas* 4 (1983): 35.

73. Leibniz's understanding is illustrated with special clarity by his attitude toward the "Glorious Revolution." He unambiguously condemned the deposition of James II. The king's goal, to help the English Catholics gain equal recognition, was entirely legitimate. See Leibniz's memorial to the Emperor of December, 1688, in G. W. Leibniz, *Sämtliche Schriften und Briefe*, 1st ser., vol. 5 (Berlin: Akademie Verlag, 1954), 333–39, esp. 336ff. For Pufendorf, in contrast, the expulsion of the king was *the* great blow for Protestant liberty against encirclement by the Catholics.

8

Baylean Liberalism: Tolerance Requires Nontolerance

John Christian Laursen

MANY OF PIERRE BAYLE'S WORKS contain arguments for freedom of conscience and of intellectual inquiry. They deepened and developed a strand of liberalism that has been largely overlooked in recent scholarly work on the history of political ideas. That strand can be reconstructed as an alternative to the prevailing view that liberalism has its deepest roots in one or more of the traditions of social contract, natural law, and civic republican theory. "Baylean liberalism," to coin a term, was fundamentally Calvinist and at the same time committed to the values of the cosmopolitan "republic of letters." It defended religious toleration by what Bayle described as "nontolerance" of what he considered superstition and enthusiasm when their effects carried over into politics.

Bayle's contribution to the history of political theory has been widely neglected. One reason for this may be that, on the litmus test of resistance theory, most readers have accepted Pierre Jurieu's charge that Bayle took the backward-looking position (from the Whig point of view) of passive obedience to absolutism.[1] Yet this would not account for the relative neglect of his treatment of toleration, more robust in some respects than almost any other of his time. Here a reason for neglect may be the Calvinist foundation of some of his ideas about toleration, no longer shared (or even understood) by many scholars. Nevertheless elements of his vision were shared, for example, by American public philosophy until quite recently.

Yet another reason for neglect of Bayle may be the practical difficulty of studying his political theory. One problem is that there is no one compact work on obligation or resistance or any other topic; no single *Essay concerning Toleration*. Rather, Bayle's style was to write and write and write, touching on many topics, returning to old topics again and again with different nuances, building up his case rather like a fugue with variations on a theme. Not only was this Bayle's style, but it can be read as a deliberate strategy. The medium is part of the message: toleration of many viewpoints is justified from many viewpoints. There is no single path of argument toward Bayle's sort of liberalism. There is no single theory of toleration, but rather a subtle and refined complex of recommended practices and justifying theories. The result is that each reader may have been massaged toward a belief in tolerance by a different set of arguments in Bayle's writings. Therefore the discussion below of his ideas will have to draw on many of his books and attempt to pull together a variety of strands. It is organized into sections dealing with several works at a time, in roughly chronological order.

One of the complexities of Bayle's treatment of toleration is that he was well aware that a simple theory of tolerance without an understanding of its proper limits might lead to an extreme position of tolerance of the intolerant, and thus of complicity with intolerance and persecution. But there were definite limits to Bayle's toleration. Although this point is much less discussed in the literature on Bayle on toleration, he could be vicious in his attacks on certain opponents. A special feature of this chapter will be an exploration of his intolerance of figures ranging from Savonarola through Jan Comenius to Pierre Jurieu, who came under fierce fire from our author. It will emerge that the chief reason for Bayle's intolerance was his belief that certain forms of superstition and enthusiasm threatened to blur the line between religion and politics and might lead to persecution. His intolerance can thus be explained as intolerance of intolerance.

Bayle is best understood as a controversialist, responding to particular issues of his day.[2] But he drew on virtually all the history of ideas available in Latin and French in response to those issues, and his responses often generated general arguments and theories of wider application than the crisis of the moment. For our purposes, the most important point for setting the context is that Bayle had plenty of personal and intellectual experience with persecution and intolerance.

Born in the south of France in 1647 into a Protestant family, he was persuaded by the Jesuits at school in Toulouse to convert to Catholicism in 1668, which resulted in a rupture with his family. Eighteen months later he abjured Catholicism, and as a "relapsed Protestant" subject to criminal penalties, had to flee to Geneva. He began to teach at the Protestant academy at Sedan in 1675, but it was closed by the authorities in 1681. He took up a new teaching job in Rotterdam in 1681, and was dismissed from that post in 1693 because of his controversial writings. In 1685 his brother Jacob was imprisoned in France in suspected retaliation for one of Pierre's books, and died in prison. Bayle knew what it meant to be persecuted for one's opinions.

But Bayle also knew what it was like to live in a relatively tolerant country. His residence for the last twenty-five years of his life, Rotterdam, was located in the most tolerant country in Europe. For a variety of reasons ranging from the history of the origins of the independence of the Netherlands in a war with persecuting Spain to the resistance of the merchant elite to the demands of the Calvinist clergy, Catholics and Jews and many varieties of millenarian Christians lived alongside Calvinist Protestants in relative peace.[3] This sort of observed experience clearly helped Bayle appreciate the benefits and discount the alleged dangers of toleration.

We have asserted above that Bayle's arguments for toleration were Calvinist, at least by his own lights. This may seem paradoxical in view of the fact that most Calvinists were quite willing to follow John Calvin in persecution of those with whom they disagreed. So it apparently was not pure Calvinist theology that determined Bayle's views; rather, the mixture of Calvinism with Bayle's social role was decisive. Probably the key to understanding Bayle on toleration in context is the point that he was first and foremost an independent intellectual.[4] As one of the most influential writers to become self-conscious of his social role and to promote the idea of the "Respublica Literaria," he institutionalized it in the title of one of the most widely read periodicals of the century, *News of the Republic of Letters*. The interplay between his Calvinism and his role as an intellectual seems to have led to his particular brand of toleration.

Some comparisons between Bayle's arguments for toleration and those of his contemporary, John Locke, will be briefly mentioned. Bayle's early writings on the issue preceded the writing and publication of Locke's *Letter concerning Toleration* and provide a more vigorous and thorough defense of toleration. Where Locke had a more insular perspective, concerned largely with England, Bayle ranged over the territory and issues of all of the francophone and Latin literature of the day. Nevertheless, like Locke, Bayle's strong principles of toleration virtually collapsed when politics became intertwined in certain ways with religion and, like Locke, Bayle could justify some kinds of persecution in the name of political stability.

Bayle's Arguments for Toleration in The Comet, Critique of Maimbourg, *and* New Critique of Maimbourg

Bayle's first major work was a critique of Catholic intolerance published in 1682 as *Letter on the Comet*, republished the next year as *Diverse Thoughts on the Comet* (hereafter *The Comet*).[5] His second major work was a response to the Jesuit Maimbourg's apology for persecution of the Huguenots, entitled *General Critique of the "History of Calvinism" of Maimbourg* (1682) (hereafter *Critique of Maimbourg*),[6] which was burned by the public hangman in Paris and led to Jacob Bayle's death. In *New Letters from the Author of the General Critique* of March 1685 (hereafter *New Critique of Maimbourg*),[7] Bayle expanded on ideas about the rights of conscience that he had mentioned in *The Comet* and *Critique of Maimbourg* and that he further elaborated in later writings. The core of Bayle's arguments for toleration can be found already in his writings before the Revocation of the Edict of Nantes in 1685.

Like all Bayle's works, *The Comet* contains a barrage of arguments, and delights in paradoxes. Bayle makes it clear that he will not be presenting a systematic case, a characteristic of all his writings. Nevertheless we can isolate a number of salient themes in this first major work that were to reappear in elaborated form in later works. Bayle attacked the authority of numbers, promoted a Biblical morality of peace and humility, contrasted atheism favorably to idolatry and superstition, insisted on the importance of reciprocity, justified intellectual freedom, and defended the conscience from government interference.

The chief aim of *The Comet*, Bayle writes, is to discredit the authority of numbers (*The Comet*, 1: 43, 62). Just because a lot of people think that comets are presages does not mean that they are. The larger implication in religious matters is that just because a majority (read: Catholics in France) believe in one religion does not mean that they are right. A second point is one that Bayle never abandons. It is the conclusion from the Bible that cruelty is evil[8] and that the hypocrisy of false conversions should never be rewarded. As a matter of theology, conversion for the sake of advantages and to avoid punishment is contrary to the spirit of the Gospel (*The Comet*,

1: 175–76), and violence has no place in religious matters (2: 490). Biblical morality is a matter of faith based on revelation, in Bayle's interpretation, and equally a conclusion from reason. It is the heart of Christianity for him, and requires moderation, forgiveness, and the abatement of pride (1: 116, 271). The paradox here is that Christianity is not a good religion for soldiers (1: 283–84).

In this early work Bayle introduced one of the theories that would gain him notoriety. He showed at length that a society of atheists can live by honor and civility, and even surpass idolatrous and superstitious nations in order and safety (1: 349–58). He stressed that idolatry and superstition (again, read: Catholicism) are either identical to or worse than atheism (1: 224, 233–40; 2: 397). One obvious implication was that toleration of atheists may cause less harm than toleration of these others.

Bayle also introduced a set of arguments that he was later to make much use of: reciprocity and *tu quoque* arguments that require the reader to take the point of view of other parties.[9] How could a comet have been a sign of the overthrow of the Persian empire without also being a sign of the overthrow of the Macedonians? (1: 143).

Some of Bayle's arguments promote intellectual freedom. Where it is said that the people do not need to know some truths, Bayle insists that it is lawful to promote the truth in all cases, provided that we observe the circumspection of Christian prudence (1: 188). It is men's actions that really count, and they are not based on general theories or printed works, but on particular judgments (1: 272–79). In addition, in a first suggestion of his theory of the erring conscience,[10] Bayle notes that skeptical doubts do not mean willful impiety (1: 324). Also to be developed later, he sketches the theory that conscience is not the business of the government (1: 314), claiming that it was the House of Austria's misguided effort to control consciences that provoked the Thirty Years' War (2: 485).

Bayle's answers to Maimbourg developed these points, with special attention to the reciprocity argument, more on the erring conscience, and a proposal for a law of nations among the religions. In *Critique of Maimbourg* he pointed out that the principle that "all those who are persuaded of the truth of their religion have the right to exterminate all others" is a sword that always cuts both ways. If it justifies the Catholics in France, it justifies the Protestants in England and the Japanese and Chinese in Asia (*Critique of Maimbourg*, 56–57). Catholics will say that they are right and Protestants are wrong, but Bayle argues that such logic simply justifies the

Protestants saying the reverse. Catholics who say they are saving infants taken from Protestant families from hell can be answered reciprocally by Protestants, Turks, or Jews who take Catholic infants in order to save them.

In this work Bayle also developed the implications of the distinction between good faith and willful errors from *The Comet*, arguing that a person has as much of a duty to obey an erroneous conscience as to obey an enlightened one, largely because by definition the person could not know which was which (*Critique of Maimbourg*, 86). A key to Bayle's analysis is that toleration is not a matter of giving rights to individuals, but is based on a theology in which "the empire of conscience belongs only to God" (91). In this theology, it is worse to live according to a true religion that one does not believe than to live by a false religion that one really believes.

In the case of a standoff between two or more religions that conscientiously believe that they are right and the others are wrong, one option is the war of all against all that Hobbes had described. The alternative solution that Bayle called for was "to establish a sort of law of nations among all the religions," in which each religion would have its rights and limits (*Critique of Maimbourg*, 88).[11] Reduction of two parties that claim to speak for God's truth to the status of nations in an international system was a brilliant borrowing from the Protestant natural law tradition of Grotius and Pufendorf.

In the *New Critique of Maimbourg* Bayle explained what he meant by the rights of an erroneous conscience. Both Catholics and Protestants consider themselves right and the others wrong. Taking a position from outside the fray, no more than one of them can be right and the other must be wrong. The key point, however, is that the rights of the truth are suspended so long as we do not know it. Again, Bayle's theory is based on a particular theology: "the rights that God has given the truth" apply only if we know it; put another way, "as long as the truth is unknown to us, it has no rights over us" (*New Critique of Maimbourg*, 219).

Bayle argues for this position with several points. To start with, a skeptical epistemology reminds us that "moral truths, as much as physical truths, are only revealed to us in a certain measure" (*New Critique of Maimbourg*, 221). Then Bayle focuses on what might now be called methodological individualism. "To speak reasonably about the rights of the truth over our souls, we must consider the truth not as a metaphysical idea, but as it is understood by each person." Attention must be drawn away from absolute truth to the truth as understood by "Jean, and Jacques, and the other individuals who exist" (221). So even if some people know the truth, they cannot assume that other people do, and they must judge those people by what those people know.

With these points in place, Bayle considers a variety of provocative analogies. One is the Oedipal dilemma of one who has killed his parent without knowing it; a second is a parallel between the concierge of a house and our conscience; a third is the case of a governor of a city receiving messages from the king; and a fourth is a woman's reception of a man she believes is her husband. In each case, Bayle asserts that ignorance of the truth after a conscientious effort to obtain it removes any blame for violating that truth. In each case, it would be worse if the people involved acted against their view of the truth, even if later it turned out that they did the right thing. By analogy, even if the Protestants are wrong, they should not act against their erring consciences as long as they are in good faith (227–28).

Up to this point, Bayle was content to take apart the Catholic charges one by one, to split hairs, draw numerous analogies, and generally argue as an advocate of the principles mentioned above. But the Revocation of the Edict of Nantes in 1685 raised the stakes and the level of stridency in the debate over toleration in Europe in Bayle's time.

News, France Wholly Catholic, and "Compel Them"

In 1684 Bayle began editing *News of the Republic of Letters* (hereafter *News*), a pioneer periodical of immense cultural influence that contained many reviews of books concerning questions of religious controversy and toleration. Typical of Bayle's work in this period was arranging for the publication in three languages of a letter on toleration by his friend and patron, Adrian Van Paets, and his own review of the letter in the *News* in October 1685.[12] Bayle agreed with Van Paets's call for a mutual tolerance on the contemporary English model between Catholics and Protestants which would only require that the Catholics abandon the theory and practice of persecution. Van Paets and Bayle may well have worked out the argument in mutual discussions over the previous years.[13]

Bayle's next two books were direct products of the Revocation of the Edict of Nantes and the violence of the ensuing persecution of Protestants, including the death of his brother. The strident *France Wholly Catholic* and indignant *Philosophical Commentary on the Words, "Compel Them to Come In"* (hereafter *"Compel Them"*) were published in 1686.[14]

In *France Wholly Catholic*, a Catholic canon sends a copy of a letter from an enraged Huguenot to another Huguenot, in hopes of converting him to Catholicism. The enraged Huguenot denounces in no uncertain terms the bad faith, lies, violence, cruelty, hypocrisy, cheats, crimes, murders, and scandals of the Catholics with respect to the Revocation of the Edict of Nantes. The style is both characteristic of Catholic polemics and uncharacteristic of Bayle. The second Huguenot replies in moderate and courteous terms that moderation and courtesy may well be more effective in reaching a compromise, and thus delivers a Baylean message. This seems to have enabled Bayle to vent his rage and indignation and at the same time to point toward the solution to all the trouble: civilized coexistence. Huguenots are shown that imitating the Catholic style is not likely to accomplish anything, and Catholics are shown that a more moderate stance may be more effective.

"Compel Them" consolidated the case for toleration that Bayle had been developing. It is a mature work, and coming after all the previously-mentioned works it demonstrates that Bayle's real forte was the dogged pursuit of the implications of a few principles, no matter where they would take him.

As far back as St. Augustine, Catholics (and, more recently, Protestants [15]) had found justification for conversion by force in a literal reading of a passage in the Bible in which Jesus tells his disciples a parable about a man whose guests do not come for dinner, so he orders his servants to go out into the streets and compel people to come in to eat. Although a single parable of dubious analogy may seem a weak reed on which to rest the theory and practice of organized conversion by force, its use demonstrates both the perceived need for and the difficulty of justifying such violence from the New Testament.

Bayle's strategy in answering Augustine and the persecutors was to emphasize the inconsistency of the literal reading of this parable both with reason, philosophy, and ethics, and with the spirit of the Gospel. Walter Rex has shown that the emphasis on reason was the culmination of developments within Calvinist theology, not a radical break from them.[16] The truths of reason and philosophy were not opposed to the truths of revelation, as they were to become in the eighteenth century. Rather, they were understood to confirm them under a theology according to which truth and reason are gifts from God and any reading of the Bible that does not accord with truth and reason is a false reading. Following Cartesian philosophy and especially Malebranche, Bayle's early work up to this point was founded on the idea that "elementary moral truths could be as evident to the human soul as the clearest mathematical postulates."[17] The inequity of persecution was one of these moral truths.

In addition, the literal reading of the parable was a violation of the revealed spirit of the Gospel in Bayle's reading. As we have already seen, Bayle's general understanding of the New Testament was as a call for gentleness and love. In *"Compel Them"* this was explained as a requirement to treat human beings with respect for their minds, such that they should be moved by enlightenment, not force. Thus toleration of diversity of opinion emerges from reason and is confirmed by a reading of revelation.

As Rex has described it, there is a polarity in *"Compel Them"* between the beginning, which is a defense of the intellectual truths of natural light, and the end, which is a defense of errors of conscience with a focus on the will. The second part reaffirms Bayle's methodological individualism, as sketched above. When Catholic authorities insist that failure to see the truth of their position is obstinacy, Bayle always counters that it is not obstinacy from the point of view of the individual involved, and that from his point of view the authorities are being obstinant.[18]

Taking stock of his arguments for toleration so far, we see that Bayle has gone quite far. At a time when most other theories of toleration attempted only to justify toleration among Protestants, or only among Christians, or only among the religious, Bayle's arguments called for toleration of Catholics, Protestant sects, Jews, Muslims, and even, in the texts we have reviewed above, Socinians and atheists. We shall return, below, to the limits of Bayle's case for toleration of diversity.

In much of the recent literature, Bayle's contributions to the political theory of toleration have been ignored or overlooked in favor of analysis of the work of John Locke. There is a tendency to play down the possible influence of Bayle on Locke, and to ignore the more robust defense of toleration of Bayle in comparison to Locke. This is despite the fact that we know Locke had made extracts[19] from the 1682 version of Bayle's *Letter on the Comet* in 1684 and that two of the other books reviewed above (*Critique of Maimbourg*[20] and *New Critique of Maimbourg*) had already been published before Locke drafted his own *Epistola de tolerantia* in the winter of 1685–86.

Raymond Klibansky writes of "a profound difference between Locke's and Bayle's approach"; "Undoubtedly Bayle's postulates were more universal and his conclusions more radical."[21] Sally Jenkinson concludes that Locke's was a backward-looking vindication of the older rights of community, where tolerance is limited to exemption from conformity, to be contrasted with Bayle's forward-looking claim to the new rights of individual liberty.[22] But it may have been more a matter of interpretation of specific cases than of principle when Bayle's theory called for toleration of Catholics and Locke's did not. Unlike Locke, Bayle was able to see that Catholics were not all necessarily superstitious or enthusiastic, and thus he did not call for a blanket persecution of Catholics. This was surely a result of his experience in the Netherlands where Catholics did not regularly betray their country for the sake of their religion.

Klibansky concludes that the reason Locke receives so much attention is that he wrote a short work, with simple, practical reasoning.[23] It is certainly possible that a combination of anglophone preoccupations and the greater difficulty of reading and understanding all of Bayle's discussions of toleration have led scholars of toleration theory to neglect his work. But that does not excuse such neglect. The proper relationship between Locke and Bayle is surely that both wrote Calvinist theories of toleration, of which Bayle's was the more tolerant in practice, and supplied the greater number of principles in defense of diversity. Only a careful reception history of the two theories of toleration in the eighteenth century could tease out the relative influences of these theories on modern and contemporary ideas about toleration. That remains to be done.

"Compel Them", Warning, Dictionary, *and the Limits of Bayle's Toleration*

Up until this point, we have focused on Bayle's arguments for toleration. There is another dimension to his writings, however, which requires attention: the limits to Bayle's toleration. As discussed above, Bayle was far too subtle and had explored far too many aspects of the subject to call for a simple, one-dimensional tolerance. At least three elements of Bayle's nontolerance in defense of toleration will be reviewed here. One is Bayle's treatment of the duties of conscientious persecutors; the second is his acceptance in at least one text of intolerance of atheists; and the third is his apparent approval of harsh measures against those he considered superstitious fanatics.

Bayle's analysis in *"Compel Them"* cut not only against Catholics but against Calvinist intolerance as well. It was a development of the theory of conscience adumbrated in the earlier writings. Squarely within the religious tradition, Bayle insisted that conscience was the voice of God. Then both persecutors and the persecuted would be sinning against God if they denied that voice. More sensationally than in the previous works, he demonstrates that a woman deceived by her conscience may commit adultery; that a misled servant may admit a thief into his master's house; that refraining from killing someone can be worse than murder. And finally, in chilling consistency with the logic of his position, the persecutor who persecutes in good conscience is justified in doing so.[24] Facing this last point, which could undercut much of his whole previous argument against persecution, Bayle answers that the best response to such persecutors is to try to change their consciences by persuasion. Thus if they read his book it will convince them not to persecute. We should "cry strongly against their false maxims, and try to supply better enlightenment for their spirit" (*"Compel Them"*, 430–31). But this is not much of a safeguard, and Rex laments that the upshot is that all is in ruins because toleration has been, to put it in recent jargon, deconstructed.[25]

In response to this, Rex returns to Bayle's Calvinist pessimism.[26] Calvinists believe that most of us are damned anyway, and it is simply a fact that only the elect *can* follow true consciences. So persecutors who conscientiously do the wrong thing are damned. Kings who do the wrong thing will be punished by God (*New Critique of Maimbourg*, 218)[27] and so, presumably, will persecutors. Meanwhile, we have to live with them.

However, Rex's position may be too pessimistic. Bayle himself insisted that his recognition of the duty of conscientious persecutors to try to persecute should not prevent the magistrate from stopping their violences, by force if necessary. As he used the terms, this would not be "intolerance" of the persecutors, but rather, "nontolerance." The absolute monarchy was justified in suppressing the Huguenots who burned Catholic churches in the sixteenth century and revolted against the king, and it was just as well justified in suppressing the (Catholic) persecuting conscience today. Thus, as a practical matter, depriving the persecutors of the aid of the secular arm and subjecting their violences to punishment by the secular arm would render their persecutory impulses relatively harmless.

Rex may be right in the sense that Bayle's position may justify persecution, but it is not persecution by religious fanatics that is to be feared here. Rather, Bayle seems to have been willing to give the authorities wide leeway to suppress would-be persecutors before they actually have the power to do anything. For example, Catholics could be prevented from seditious preaching and excluded from public office on the ground that if they ever did get a monopoly on power they would persecute (*"Compel Them"*, 411–12). If the state can punish anything it thinks smacks of proto-persecution, it can punish quite a bit, which may amount to persecution. But Bayle always insisted that nontolerance should not become persecution: no reprisals and no confiscations of property would be justified for such preventive purposes (361, 385).

On another important issue there is an apparent contradiction in *"Compel Them"* with Bayle's previous position. Faced with the objection that his theory would leave atheists free to declaim against God and religion, he denies it. Since magistrates are charged with maintaining the public peace, they may punish those who threaten the fundamental laws of the state, "among whom we are accustomed to include those who deny providence." A second reason why magistrates may punish them is that, since atheists deny the existence of God, they cannot use the argument that only God can judge their conscience (431).[28] This may be little more than a strategic concession to the spirit of the age which would prevent atheists from proselytizing,[29] but it suggests that Bayle's defense of toleration is not always as robust as it has sometimes been made out to be.[30] Nevertheless, at the very least, Bayle himself and other Calvinists would be estopped from persecuting atheists because they do believe that conscience is the voice of God, and if the atheists' consciences tell them to be atheists, the atheists should obey them. It does not seem relevant to inquire as to whether the atheist accepts this reason for tolerance.

Bayle's view of how the Huguenot refugees should respond to persecution was the subject of *Important Warning to the Refugees* of 1690. The importance of this text is largely in establishing beyond any doubt that Bayle's views of toleration should be understood in the context of a nonviolent political stance. His *magnum opus*, the *Historical and Critical Dictionary*, was published in 1696 with expanded editions in 1701 and posthumously in 1708.[31] Unlike our contemporary notion of a dictionary as a non-controversial reference work, Bayle's *Dictionary* was an extension of his polemical wars by other means. Again and again in the myriad of notes attached to the main articles, Bayle returns to his favorite themes, one of which is toleration and persecution, by and large confirming the theories we have reviewed above. However, as we shall see, the *Dictionary* also provides some of the best materials for understanding the limits of Bayle's spirit of toleration.

It emerges from numerous passages in this text that Bayle is constantly fighting against superstition and enthusiasm. Many elements of Catholicism are classified as superstition, and Jesuits like Maimbourg, among many others, are credited with creating the intellectual resources that justify the persecution of the Protestants by the superstitious Catholics. Given the historical circumstances, it is not hard to see how Bayle's position justified nontolerance of superstition. But the dangers of other forms of religious enthusiasm are perhaps not so obvious at first glance.

For a man who has been so tolerant of so many things in so many of the writings we have reviewed above, it comes as something of a surprise when Bayle is not sorry to see Savonarola tortured and burned at Florence, Simon Morin burned at Paris, Quirinus Kuhlman burned at Moscow, and Christopher Kotterus imprisoned, pilloried, and banished from the Austrian empire. Other "fanatics" who receive short shrift include Jakob Boehme, John Rothe, Serarius, Schwenkfeld, John des Marests, and Agreda. Jan Comenius is the target of many a barb, and Pierre Jurieu is clearly the target behind them all. It is important to note that Bayle does not positively recommend the burning and pillorying he reports, but it is clear that he thinks they were richly deserved. Bayle's attitude here can be interpreted as a fleshing out of the principles of nontolerance we have reviewed above.

We shall start with Jurieu. This Protestant divine had been a supporter of Bayle who arranged for the latter to teach at the École illustre in Rotterdam. But as Jurieu radicalized into a proponent of Huguenot resistance against the French monarchy, they became open enemies. Jurieu took Bayle's Important Warning and other writings as a complete betrayal of the Huguenot cause and lobbied for Bayle's dismissal from his teaching post. Each side wrote numerous polemical pieces against the other, and Bayle spread his diatribes against Jurieu throughout the Dictionary.[32]

One of Jurieu's chief arguments in favor of Huguenot resistance was prophecy. Both from his own reading of the Bible and from the prophecies of others, he expected an armed vindication of the Protestant cause in 1689. This gave Bayle the opportunity to skewer millenarianism, illuminism, prophecy, and the other elements of what he called fanaticism. But rather than direct his attack solely against Jurieu and his supporters, Bayle ransacked history for analogous cases, knowing that his readers would recognize the parallels.

In chronological order on a tour of selected targets of Bayle's ire, the Florentine priest Savonarola comes in for devastating criticism. Bayle suggests that the evidence convicts him of "an horrible and infamous imposture"; or, "if this Dominican was not an impostor, he must necessarily have been a prodigious Fanatic" (Dictionary, 5: "Savonarola," 65, 71[M]). His crime was not only that he "pretended to partake of divine revelations," but that he had a "factious spirit" and "concerned himself too much with political affairs" (57, 61).

One of Bayle's basic positions is that the clergy should not be involved with politics: "this is always blameable in persons who have dedicated themselves to the ministry of the word of God" (61). Such involvement is wrong on political and religious grounds. It subverts political stability: the letters Savonarola wrote to the King of France encouraging him to enter Italy would justify a conviction for treason (70[M]). The religious perspective is that it "profanes the name of GOD" when he "put off his particular opinions for immediate revelations" (69[M]). Bayle knew his readers would read "Jurieu" for "Savonarola."

Now, if Savonarola and his friends did something wrong but could be rehabilitated, there would be no justification for executing him. But, in Bayle's analysis, the infatuation of Savonarola's admirers is "an incurable disease" and "there is nothing that people will not do rather than own that they have been the dupes of an hypocrite" (66, 70[M]). Savonarola's fanaticism is "a virtue proceeding from vapours, an irregularity of the organs, a disorder in some fibres of the brain" (71[M]). This sort of thinking sets up the case for executing fanatics.

To the modern mind, perhaps the weakest link of the case for executing Savonarola is that his confession was obtained by torture. The otherwise "enlightened" Bayle[33] takes a hard line here: torture "is a legal [proof] in several countries, and it cannot be invalidated juridically under pretense that pain forces some people, of a delicate make, to accuse themselves of what they have not done" ("Savonarola," 69[M]). If proof by torture justifies religious persecution, Bayle's case for toleration in the earlier writings may be seriously compromised in practice.

The Moravian religious leader Jan Comenius is one of Bayle's chief bêtes noires, attacked not only in the eponymous article but in articles on Drabicius and Kotterus. The critique of Comenius follows the pattern of the critique of Savonarola. He is described as "infatuated with Prophecies, and Revolutions, the Fall of Antichrist, the Millennium and such like Whims of a dangerous Fanaticism: I say dangerous, not only in relation to orthodoxy, but also in relation to Princes and States" (*Dictionary*, 2: "Comenius," 537). Since Jurieu provoked and relied on Protestant prophecy inside France, Bayle knew his readers would recognize the analogy to the "knaveries, that have been discovered amongst the little prophets of the Dauphine" (*Dictionary*, 3: "Kotterus," 683[H]).

Again, part of the critique is religious and purports to come from inside Protestant belief. Bayle quotes a critic who accuses Comenius of "excessive pride . . . the general fault of those who pretend to be inspired," and then adds in his own voice that "if God did them that great Honour [of inspiring them], he would not refuse them the Spirit of Christian Humility" ("Comenius," 538[G]).

Part of the critique is for intellectual sophistry or chicanery. In his article on Drabicius, he describes the means by which Comenius and others who relied on this figure's prophecies managed to finesse the times prophecies did not turn out. If Drabicius prophesies something about Prince Ragotski, not knowing that the prince is dead, Comenius discovers that a previous prophecy forewarned of his death. "These are the Men for my Money: they are never at a loss . . . there is always some Clause which was not attended to." If "Ragotski's attempt had succeeded, no regard would have been had to the Non-observance of the Conditions . . . thus the same Clauses are Essential or Accidental to the Prophecies of those People, just as the Event pleases to determine. This is their Grand Key" (*Dictionary*, 2: "Drabicius," 692–93[E–F]). Reaffirming the psychology of his discussion of Savonarola, he writes that "Those, who had once believed him, contrived to do so still. . . . Thus it will always happen" (693). Back in the article on Comenius, he asserts that the failure of Comenius's prophecies never embarrassed him: "he always passed for a great Prophet; so true it is that Men are pleased to be deceived in some things!" ("Comenius," 539[I]).

Yet another charge against the enthusiasts is that of venality. Comenius is described as abandoning his cause after "finding a gold mine" in Amsterdam, and as spending a lot of his Maecenas's money without producing anything worthwhile (537). Kuhlman, too, "understood well enough how to trick people out of their money" (*Dictionary*, 3: "Kuhlman," 692).

But most of the critique is for political ambition and political errors. Bayle quotes with implied approval the charge that Comenius was responsible for the burning of the Moravian city of Lesno in Poland, on two counts. One, Comenius prevented the inhabitants from leaving while they still could by claiming that divine intervention would save them, and two, he rendered the Protestants odious to the Catholics "by reason of a Panegyric that he unseasonably made upon Charles Gustavus, King of Sweden, at the time of the Invasion of Poland" ("Comenius," 539[I]). Bayle's contemporaries would have recognized the parallel to Jurieu's panegyrics of William of Orange. The involvement of the clergy in politics is always suspect to Bayle. In another place, he remarks that "a divine, who travels as much as [Comenius] did, and who has such frequent business at the courts of princes, is a man, who is not much to be trusted" ("Kotterus," 682[F]).

In "Drabicius" Bayle makes the charge of political ambition, but this time it is to point to the dangers of manipulation of the prophets by political leaders: "it is very possible that a Prince, capable of laughing at these Chimera's, should form Projects, and great Designs, conformable to the Visions of these People: for they prepare the people by apocalyptical Explications, delivered with an Air of Inspiration, and Enthusiasm is a very powerful machine" ("Drabicius," 693[H]).

All these criticisms of the fanatics are presumably designed to justify strong measures against them, in the name of state security. As we have seen, this includes implied approval of torture, pillories, and burning. In his own work, it apparently justified biased reporting and the use of the same sort of selective interpretation he criticized in Maimbourg. Whelan and Knetsch have noted his selective use of sources in his articles on Agreda and Comenius respectively, violating all the canons of impartiality he stipulated in other texts.[34] He quotes uncritically from books by Arnoldus and Maresius against Comenius, with no attempt to balance the picture. Maresius's one-sided polemic is praised for his "zeal against the Enthusiasts, and the foretellers of great revolutions" (*Dictionary*, 4: "Maresius," 122). Guicciardini's balanced picture of Savonarola is roundly criticized ("Savonarola," 65). Anything goes against fanatics if they have become involved in politics.

This limitation of religious toleration to those who eschew politics means, on the one hand, that tolerance will be protected by the state from those who might be expected to violate it. On the other hand, it means that the resulting practice of toleration will not be very robust by modern standards. As soon as something is identified as political, toleration drops away. Bayle apparently realized that his polemics against the enthusiasts came close to contradicting his own calls for toleration. When he wrote that Comenius is "inexcusable" for printing the prophecies of Kotterus, he began a note as follows: "God forbid, I should pronounce judgment on what passes in the heart of my neighbor; those mysteries belong only to God." But then he immediately added: "on some occasions, one may speak one's thoughts upon appearances" ("Kotterus," 681[F]), and his view of the appearances of fanatics evidently justified persecution.

One likely interpretation of Bayle's hostility to what he called fanatics would explain it as a case of the general rule of the extremism often generated by fratricide. Bayle and his enemies were both, after all, children of the skeptical tradition. Since the time of Savonarola, as Richard Popkin has explained, that tradition had split into two factions.[35] Bayle followed the tradition that passed through Montaigne and concluded from our lack of knowledge that a certain liberal individualism was the best way of life.[36] Savonarola and his heirs down to Jurieu concluded that in the absence of scientific knowledge we should rely on prophecy. The two would naturally be more upset at each other's misunderstandings than at the dogmatists.

Bayle's view of toleration is complex, subtle, and balanced. While he does not positively recommend violence against fanatics, he does applaud it when it happens with the thinnest veneer of a public security justification. The upshot is that Bayle justifies toleration of religions when they are politically quietist, but not when they allow their religious enthusiasm to break out into political action. Then Bayle is ready to approve of torture, pillories, and burning.[37] A defender of intellectual freedom first and last, Bayle recognized that threats to a tolerant society must be responded to with firmness if that tolerant society is to be protected.

Notes

1. In her introductory essay to *Bayle: Political Writings from the Historical and Critical Dictionary* (Cambridge: Cambridge University Press, 1997), the editor and translator, Sally Jenkinson, draws attention to Bayle's remarks in praise of republican activism and of nonviolent resistance to unjust absolutism in the right times and places.

2. A good survey of the targets of Bayle's polemics can be found in Sally Jenkinson, "Rationality, Pluralism, and Reciprocal Tolerance: A Reappraisal of Pierre Bayle's Political Thought" in Iain Hampsher-Monk, ed., *Defending Politics: Bernard Crick and Pluralism* (London: British Academic Press, 1993), 22–45.

3. See Henri Méchoulan, *Amsterdam au temps de Spinoza* (Paris: Presses Universitaires de France, 1990) and *Etre juif à Amsterdam au temps de Spinoza* (Paris: Albin Michel, 1991); Jonathan Israel, *The Dutch Republic* (Oxford: Oxford University Press, 1995).

4. This is a point Elisabeth Labrousse has often made: see, e.g., her introduction to Bayle's *La France toute Catholique* (Paris: Vrin, 1973), 17–18.

5. In *Oeuvres Diverses*, ed. Elisabeth Labrousse, vol. 3 (Hildesheim: Georg Olms, 1966). Modern edition edited by André Prat and Pierre Rétat, *Pensées diverses sur la comète* (Paris: Société des Textes Français Modernes, 1994). Cited from the English translation, *Miscellaneous Reflections Occasion'd by the Comet*, 2 vols. (London, 1708). Typical of Bayle and the century, he added variations on the theme in *Addition to the Diverse Thoughts* (1684) and *Continuation of the Diverse Thoughts* (1704).

6. This was published just before the 1683 edition of *The Comet*. Cited from

the 1727 edition reprinted in *Oeuvres Diverses*, edited by E. Labrousse, vol. 2 (Hildesheim: Georg Olms, 1965).

7. Cited from the 1727 edition reprinted in *Oeuvres Diverses*, edited by E. Labrousse, vol. 2 (Hildesheim: Georg Olms, 1965).

8. In this, Bayle was following Montaigne and prefiguring Judith Shklar, *Ordinary Vices* (Cambridge, Mass.: Harvard University Press, 1984) and Richard Rorty, *Contingency, Irony, and Solidarity* (Cambridge: Cambridge University Press, 1989).

9. See John Kilcullen, *Sincerity and Truth* (Oxford: Oxford University Press, 1988), esp. chaps. 2 and 3.

10. See Walter Rex, *Essays on Pierre Bayle and Religious Controversy* (The Hague: Martinus Nijhoff, 1965), 115–19, 148–50, 168 for previous sources in Daillé and Jurieu of the erring conscience argument.

11. Cf. Elisabeth Labrousse, *Pierre Bayle* (The Hague: Martinus Nijhoff, 1965), 2: 526, and Kilcullen, *Sincerity and Truth*, 91.

12. *Oeuvres Diverses*, 1: 387.

13. This is suggested by E. Labrousse, *Pierre Bayle*, 2: pp. 553–54; at 543 she writes that the germ of the "erring conscience" argument can be found in Van Paets's letter.

14. Both in *Oeuvres Diverses*, vol. 2. These works spawned a large literature of answers. In 1687 Pierre Jurieu polemicized against Bayle's notion of toleration in *The Rights of the Two Sovereigns* and Bayle's friend Jacques Basnage dedicated a two-volume *Treatise on Conscience* (1696) to the issue, followed by Elie Saurin's *Reflections on the Rights of Conscience* (1697).

15. See Mark Goldie, "The Theory of Religious Intolerance in Restoration England" in Ole Peter Grell, Jonathan I. Israel, and Nicholas Tyacke, eds., *From Persecution to Toleration: The Glorious Revolution and Religion in England* (Oxford: Oxford University Press, 1991), 331–68.

16. Rex, *Essays* (note 10), 154–63.

17. Rex, *Essays*, 161–62.

18. Rex, *Essays*, 173–74.

19. Raymond Klibansky, "Preface" to John Locke, *Epistola de Tolerantia/A Letter on Toleration*, ed. Raymond Klibansky, trans. J. W. Gough (Oxford: Clarendon Press, 1968), xxxii–xxxiii.

20. David Wootton, "Introduction" to *Political Writings of John Locke* (New York: Penguin, 1994), 97, points out that "there is no evidence that [Locke] ever read the one that would be most relevant for our purposes, the *Critique générale* [*Critique of Maimbourg*]." But there is also no evidence that he did not.

21. Klibansky, "Preface," xxxiv. The author goes on to recommend a "detailed comparison between the English and French philosopher[s]" but does not provide one (xxxv). Klibansky's emphasis on differences can be contrasted with Kilcullen, who observes that "Mostly, Bayle's theory is like Locke's" (*Sincerity and Truth*, 96).

22. Sally Jenkinson, "Two Concepts of Tolerance: Or Why Bayle Is Not Locke," *Journal of Political Philosophy* 4 (1996): 302–22.

23. Klibansky, "Preface," xxxv.

24. Rex, *Essays*, 177–80; Kilcullen, *Sincerity and Truth*, 75–76.

25. Rex, *Essays*, 184–85.

26. Rex, *Essays*, 186.

27. See Elisabeth Labrousse, *Pierre Bayle*, 2: 584–86; Kilcullen, *Sincerity and Truth*, 100–101.

28. See Kilcullen, *Sincerity and Truth*, 100.

29. See Labrousse, *Pierre Bayle*, 2: 587, and Gianluca Mori, "Pierre Bayle, the Rights of Conscience, and the 'Remedy' of Toleration," *Ratio Juris* (1997), who calls it a provisional and tactical concession, perhaps designed to hide Bayle's authorship of *"Compel Them"*.

30. Michel Paradis asserts repeatedly that Bayle favored tolerating atheists, without mentioning the above-cited passage, in "Fondements de la tolérance chez Bayle," in Ethel Groffier and Paradis, eds., *The Notion of Tolerance and Human Rights* (Ottawa: Carleton University Press, 1991).

31. Cited from the English edition, *The Dictionary Historical and Critical of Mr. Peter Bayle*, 2d ed. (London, 1734–38).

32. The classic discussion of Jurieu is Guy Howard Dodge, *The Political Theory of the Huguenots of the Dispersion* (New York: Columbia University Press, 1947).

33. Elsewhere, he defends critics of torture: "Grevius" [B] Cited in Elisabeth Labrousse, "The Political Ideas of the Huguenot Diaspora (Bayle and Jurieu)," in Richard Golden, ed., *Church, State and Society Under the Bourbon Kings* (Lawrence, Kan.: Coronado Press, 1982), 265.

34. Ruth Whelan, *The Anatomy of Superstition: A Study of the Historical Theory and Practice of Pierre Bayle*, Studies on Voltaire and the Eighteenth Century 259 (Oxford: Voltaire Foundation, 1989), 9–30; F. R. J. Knetsch, *Bayle's oordeel over Comenius* (Groningen: Wolters-Noordhoff, 1970); Knetsch, "Le jugement de Bayle sur Comenius," *Bulletin de la Commission de l'Histoire des Eglises Wallones* (1969–71): 83–96.

35. See Richard Popkin, *The Third Force in Seventeenth-Century Thought* (Leiden: Brill, 1992), esp. chap. 6.

36. See John Christian Laursen, *The Politics of Skepticism in the Ancients, Montaigne, Hume, and Kant* (Leiden: Brill, 1992), chaps. 4–5.

37. Thus Ruth Whelan's claim that Bayle's position is "an undogmatic state of mind that pre-empts intolerance" must be qualified by recognition of his intolerance of religious enthusiasts. See Whelan, "The Wisdom of Simonides" in Richard H. Popkin and A. Vanderjagt, eds., *Scepticism and Irreligion in the Seventeenth and Eighteenth Centuries* (Leiden: Brill, 1993), 253.

9

"Religion Set the World at Odds": Deism and the Climate of Religious Tolerance in the Works of Aphra Behn

Arlen Feldwick and Cary J. Nederman

WHEN THE HISTORY OF TOLERATION is conventionally narrated, it is most often recounted in terms of a fundamental change either in the nature of the state (that is, as the process of secularization) or in the nature of the individual (recognition of liberty of conscience).[1] But another component of the rise of tolerance both in theory and in practice must surely be the spread of theological innovation and even religious skepticism in early modern Europe. By the seventeenth century, one commonly encounters deistic, naturalistic, and even atheistic teachings, especially in connection with new monistic and materialistic philosophies.[2] This seems especially true in England, where figures such as Edward Lord Herbert of Cherbury, Thomas Hobbes, Charles Blount, and John Toland (among many others) were at the forefront of European religious nonconformity and Freethought.[3]

Directly or indirectly, English nonconformism promoted tolerant attitudes by challenging central premises of enforced unity of belief: doubting the rational demonstrability of major tenets of theology; asserting the function performed by clerics and ecclesiastical institutions in the distortion and perversion of religious faith; and establishing the complicity between church authorities and secular rulers in maintaining religious conformity in the interests of the powerful. As a consequence, Freethinking, deism, and their ilk may be viewed as contributing noticeably to the growth of toleration as a political program as well as a philosophical principle in seventeenth-century England. In some cases the connection was explicit: Hobbes, for instance, is now often recognized as an advocate of toleration.[4] In other instances, tolerance remained an unstated (although obvious) conclusion to be drawn from the precepts of the nonconformists. As Richard Popkin has observed, deist views "play an important role in providing a basis for religious and political toleration in England, in the British American colonies, and later in Revolutionary France."[5]

It may still be wondered, however, whether the immediate influence of the nonconformists extended very far outside their circle or whether they were visible in their own day beyond the English literati. One figure associated with nonconformism who seems to have disseminated and popularized significant elements of its agenda was the English playwright and poet Aphra Behn (1640–1689). In matters of religion, as in so much else, Behn has long been an enigma. She was certainly implicated in the religious turmoil of her time. An ally of the Royalist cause, Behn sometimes evinces sympathy towards the Roman Church. Critics argue over whether Behn was merely sympathetic to the Catholic cause or was herself a Catholic, if a closet one.[6] Yet her name has also been invoked as a supporter of Anglicanism,[7] of various dissenting movements,[8] and of a kind of Epicurean-inspired libertinism.[9]

Given the diversity of positions that have been attributed to Behn, it is hardly surprising that some scholars have pronounced it impossible to ascribe to her any coherent religious doctrine. Surveying a range of Behn's writings, Sarah Mendelson concludes that her work refers "to so many pagan and Christian gods that she gives the impression of a befuddled polytheist."[10] Alternately, Janet Todd proposes that Behn's thought reflects concern less with religion on its own terms than with the practical consequences of religious faith.

Religion . . . often appears a matter of style as much as of content. Behn admired the baroque side of Catholicism and avoided much overt piety and concern with substance. Indeed in many works she puts forward a vigorous and sometimes skeptical rationalism and she rails against those who would unsettle the state with religious squabbling.[11]

But perhaps accusations of incoherence or disinterest in matters of religion are too harsh. The present paper argues that Behn did have an intelligible set of views regarding religion, derived from some of the leading themes propounded by the English deists. In particular, Behn's work consistently promotes a vision of orthodox, institutional (primarily Christian) belief as a corruption of the original purity of faith, and she couples this with a pronounced anticlericalism. As Justin Champion has recently demonstrated, these are exactly the topics prominent in the writings of leading English deists, such as Herbert and Blount, who were Behn's virtual contemporaries.[12] Moreover, Behn's associations with deism are not speculative. She is known to have been on friendly terms with Blount, as well as with leading nonconforming figures Buckingham and Rochester; and she translated two works by Bernard Fontenelle that were important for the development of deistic thinking.[13]

We assert, therefore, that Behn deserves recognition (previously denied her) as a force in extending the cause of deism. In part this explains her apparent attraction to a range of religious viewpoints. Deists starting with Herbert had argued for a set of natural and universal principles common to all religions; to the extent that any system of belief embodied these tenets, it had a presumptive claim to validity. Hence Behn could without contradiction praise Catholics such as Maitland and Stafford, consort with the Anglican divine Dr. Gilbert Burnet, and still laud the Anabaptist Tryon. Her pluralism was not "befuddled," but instead reflected her deistic readiness to embrace religion when it reflected those elements consonant with natural human worship of divinity. To connect her with deism is also to account for the repeated expression of anti-clerical sentiment that runs through her plays. Champion has shown that it is necessary to treat "the deist controversy not just as an argument in favour of the competence of human reason, but as an attack upon . . . the 'power' of the Church and priest."[14] To this end, the deists proclaimed the corruption of the priesthood and of organized worship, while identifying "the practice of true religion" with "morality and the rule of right reason."[15] Likewise, Behn's writings return time and again to the hypocrisy of various confessions, and in particular, to the follies and foibles of the priesthood; to these she juxtaposes natural goodness and rationality, which prove far more consistent with the fundamentals of religion than do the practices of adherents to organized faith. Hence Behn's work inevitably promotes a spirit of tolerance toward religious difference and nonconformity.

Before Religion—And After

One of the favorite themes of the seventeenth-century deists was the pos-
tulation of a sort of *ur*-religion, a primitive piety that had been erased
by the introduction of formal religious worship. In his *Antient Religion
of the Gentiles*, Herbert had declared that "before religion (i.e.) rites, ceremonies, pretended revelations, and the like were invented, there was no
worship of God but in a rational way." [16] For Herbert and his successors,
religion as presently practiced by human beings, burdened with unneces-
sary accretions, departs greatly from original, natural belief. Superstition
and idolatry, complex systems of guilt and its expiation, and the creation
of a professional priesthood, all mark religion's distance from true rever-
ence for the divine.

Aphra Behn clearly echoes the deist position on the nature of religion in a highly reflective 1684 poem (a loose adaptation of a French text)
entitled "The Golden Age," which contains her most cohesive remarks
on the subject. In this work she describes a primordial paradise in which
human beings were at peace with one another and with nature, a time without property, law, politics, and all the other manifestations of civilization.
These latter institutions Behn views as incompatible with purest human
nature, especially with human love. In Behn's primeval human state, the
amorous dimension of human experience, expressed without shame or re-
morse, takes precedence.

The main factor Behn blames for the erosion of idyllic human harmony and for the creation of contention is religion: ". . . the Gods / By
teaching us Religion first, first set the World at Odds: / Till then Ambition was not known, / That Poyson to Content, Bane to Repose; / Each
Swain was Lord o'er his own will alone, / His Innocence Religion was,
and Laws." [17] For Behn, religion breeds ambition, from which in turn derives human conflict and the abandonment of the principle of love. Prior
to the point at which formal religion was introduced, human beings were
autonomous, innocent and amorous creatures, living purely according to
their natural inclinations and desires.

The central problem with institutionalized religion, as Behn identifies it, is its imposition of norms that run counter to the goodness and
charitableness of human nature. Later in "The Golden Age," she remarks
that lovers met "uncontroul'd" and always maintained their vows to one
another, "Not kept in fear of Gods, no fond Religious cause, / Nor in obedience to the duller Laws. / Those Fopperies of the Gown were then not

known, / Those vain those Politik Curbs to keep man in, / Who by a fond mistake Created that a Sin; / Which freeborn we, by right of Nature claim our own."[18] Behn thus aligns herself with two important features of the deist case against religion: that priests have manipulated superstition and ritual to implant a fear of God in human beings; and that the authority of churches rests on a bogus claim that priests are uniquely competent to interpose themselves between human beings and divinity and to dictate to people (against their natural inclination and reason) how they shall live.[19] She seems to go so far as to equate religion with the creation of human misery, conflict, and immorality.

Behn concludes with a call for a return to the primitive condition: "Be gone! and let the Golden Age again, / Assume its Glorious Reign."[20] To achieve such a renewal, she says, would return human beings to closer contact with the divine: "But let the humble honest *Swain* go on, / in the blest paths of the first rate of man; / That nearest were to Gods Alli'd, / And form'd for love alone, disdained all other Pride."[21] "The Golden Age" thus contains a call for human liberation from the shackles of institutional religion, precisely in order that people may live more in accordance with their divinely-ordained natures. Her message is by no means impious or irreligious in a larger sense, but it does represent a direct challenge to the ecclesiastical monopoly of control over spiritual life. The return to the pure core of faith, to unsullied love, requires both the elimination of clerical domination and respect for human autonomy.

Cheats of Religion

The English deists explained the course of institutional religion (modern as well as ancient) in terms of "priestcraft," that is, the erection and dissemination of false ideas, practices, and superstitions in order to enhance the interests of priests themselves. As Blount asserted, "The original of sacrifices, seems to be as ancient as religion itself; for no sooner had man found out there was a God, but a priest stept up and said, that this God had taught them in what manner he should be worshipped."[22] Hence theological doctrines were propagated in the most mysterious and obscure manner not because truths about divinity were complex, but in order to confuse and therefore control the laity. A few years after Behn's death, John Toland went so far as to say that the distinction between religions resulted from the machinations of priests, designed to serve their baser worldly ambitions.[23]

Much of the substance of deistic anti-clericalism was directed toward debunking the trappings of priestly superiority that cloaked less esteemed motives.

In many of Behn's writings, too, we find a concerted effort to reveal to her audience the unsavory side of the clergy. Her disdain for the self-serving basis of clerical authority is perhaps most evident in her play, *The Roundheads; or, The Good Old Cause* (1681),[24] a political satire on the final days of the Commonwealth. One of the subplots involves the machinations of Lady Desbro, wife of a Commonwealth leader, to liberate her Cavalier lover Freeman from prison. In order to achieve the escape, she blackmails a pious elder, Ananias Goggle, into arranging Freeman's release. Lady Desbro is one of Behn's most sexually flamboyant characters, a kind of embodiment of the ideal of paradise sketched in "The Golden Age."[25] Goggle, by contrast, is first introduced as a self-righteous and pompous churchman:

Ah, the Children of the Elect have no Business but the great Work of Reformation: Yea verily, I say, all other Business is profane, and diabolical, and devilish; Yea, I say, these Dressings, Curls, and Shining Habilliments—which take so up your time, your precious time; I say, they are an Abomination, yea, an Abomination in the sight of the Righteous, and serve . . . to lead vain Man astray. (*Roundheads*, 384)

Of course, this "Head o' th' Church Militant, the very Pope of Presbytery" (as Lady Desbro facetiously calls him) (385), rapidly proves to be tempted himself by her sexual charms. Goggle suggests that Lady Desbro might prefer his favors to those of her aged husband: "There are Ladies of high Degree in the Commonwealth, to whom we find ourselves most comforting; why might not you be one?—for, alas, we are accounted as able Men in Ladies Chambers, as in our Pulpits: we serve both Functions—" (385). He even admits that the real "sin" is not in the act of adultery, but in the "scandal" of discovery.

Turning Goggle to her own ends, Lady Desbro threatens to reveal his advances to her husband if he does not cooperate in her conspiracy to release her lover Freeman from imprisonment. Lady Desbro berates the Protestant preacher for the fraudulence of his religion:

I'll set you out in your Colours: Your impudent and bloody Principles, your Cheats, your Rogueries on honest Men, thro their kind, deluded Wives, whom you cant and goggle into a Belief, 'tis a great work of Grace to steal, and beggar their whole Families, to contribute to your Gordmandizing, Lust and Laziness; Ye Locusts of the Land, preach Nonsense, Blasphemy, and Treason, till you sweat again, that the sanctify'd Sisters may rub you down, to comfort and console the Creature (386).

Behn's message is one befitting deist exposure of priestly self-interest. Goggle's dogma is revealed to be deceitful, designed to fleece and hoodwink his flock in order to aggrandize himself. What permits Lady Desbro to penetrate his deception, she claims, is only the fact that she is of like mind. "For know, Sir, I am as great a Hypocrite as you, and know the Cheats of your religion too; and since we know one another, 'tis like we shall be true" (388). Of course, Goggle becomes an accomplice in Lady Desbro's scheme, but not simply out of fear of being exposed; he also recognizes (and in some measure appreciates) the qualities he shares with her. Behn's portrayal of Goggle, in sum, seems intended as comment on the state of institutional religion itself, emphasizing perhaps that the more pious the principle, the more pronounced the self-interest lying behind it.

Characters similar to Ananias Goggle populate Behn's other writings and do not correspond to any particular confession. In her posthumously published prose tale, *The Wandering Beauty*, Behn berates the Anglican priesthood in the person of Mr. Prayfast, whose lust runs second only to his desire for social preferment.[26] Likewise, she derides the falsehoods of the Roman Church in her only tragedy, *Abdelezar; or, the Moor's Revenge* (1676), as well as in *History of the Nun; or, the Fair Vow-Breaker* (1689), both of which locate deceit and self-interest behind the pieties of Catholic worship.[27] In matter of fact, throughout Behn's corpus, we do not encounter a single portrayal of a clerical character who is sympathetic, let alone worthy of respect and veneration. She consistently unmasks the duplicity, hypocrisy, and self-serving motives of conventionally religious men and women. In her pronounced anticlericalism, then, Behn reflected and gave vent to the concerns of contemporary deists about the corruption endemic to all modern religions.

Virtue Contra Religion

In the place of organized and ritualized religious practices, the deists recommended natural worship best performed by sound moral action. Herbert asserted that "the Antients agree with us, who allow no means of salvation can befit or advantage us without the mind, vertue, piety and faith."[28] Or as Blount stated, "Vertue, goodness, and piety, accompanied with faith in, and love to God, are the best ways of worshipping."[29] Subsequent deists regarded this position not only as a defense of the "possibility of heathen virtue," but also as a commendation of "the pattern of virtue as a replacement for [modern] idolatry."[30] In the deist view, heathens were perhaps less encumbered by the cheats of religion than are latter-day Christians—and certainly no more so. Hence the practice of natural worship might be guided more by "heathen vertue" than by the more recent teachings of Christian (or Islamic or Judaic) religion.

It is precisely the failure of supposedly modern Christianity to serve as a practical source of virtue that also forms a central thread of Behn's widely acclaimed novel *Oroonoko* (1688). This work has been studied from a variety of perspectives: as evidence for Behn's political associations, as an expression of anti-slavery or anti-colonial sentiment, and as an early work of feminist fiction.[31] But although it contains considerable commentary on Christianity, *Oroonoko* has never received much attention for its hostile stance toward the tenets of Christian religion and its preference for "heathen vertue." The novel is broken into two main segments. The first takes place in the African nation of Coramantien. This small principality is ruled by an aging and impotent king whose only living heir is his grandson, Oroonoko, whom Behn praises effusively for his courage and beauty. Oroonoko is kidnapped by slave traders, who transport him to the English-controlled South American country of Surinam. The native population of Surinam has been left in peace by the Europeans: the indigenous peoples, says Behn's narrator, "we live with in perfect Amity, without daring to command 'em."[32] The reason for this policy is never further explained. Rather, Behn goes on to describe the pristine purity of the aboriginal tribes and to compare them to "our first Parents before the Fall" (3). In language clearly reminiscent of "The Golden Age," Behn says,

And these People represented to me an absolute *Idea* of the first State of Innocence, before *man* knew how to sin; and 'tis most evident and plain, that simple Nature is the most harmless, inoffensive and vertuous Mistress. 'Tis she alone, if she were permitted, that better instructs the World, than all the Inventions of Man: Religion wou'd here but destroy that Tranquillity they possess by Ignorance; and Laws wou'd but teach 'em to know Offence, of which they have no Notion (3–4).

Thus the natives of Surinam are neither compelled to labor for the Europeans nor subject to Christian conversion. Their presence instead seems to constitute a symbolic reminder of the possibility of the perfection human beings can achieve when ignorant of the devices of religion. The fact that Behn describes in great detail the qualities of the indigenous Surinamese in the very opening of *Oroonoko*, within a section that is otherwise set in Africa, is suggestive. Perhaps Behn regarded the natives as a sort of regulating principle of human nature, an untrammeled perfection, against which her readers are invited to judge the other characters—African as well as European—who follow thereafter. In any case, Behn's description of the Surinamese clearly introduces from the beginning of the novel the dual themes of religion as a corrupting force and of an irreligious stance as a sign of natural reason and virtue.

Because of their policy of living amiably with the natives, the English import black slaves into Surinam as workers. This is why Oroonoko is removed to South America, tricked into coming aboard a European boat by an unscrupulous captain. When he arrives in Surinam, however, he commands the respect of the English for his royal blood as well as his European education (the latter the result of a French tutor). He is not required to labor like his fellow Africans, but instead spends his days in relative luxury and idleness. Nevertheless he cannot ultimately stand to submit to the condition of his enslavement, and leads an unsuccessful slave revolt. As punishment for this insurrection, he is brutally tortured and killed at the hands of his European captors.

Some scholars have regarded the character of Oroonoko as a kind of "noble savage," a precursor of the Enlightenment image of the virtuous natural man, unencumbered by the conventions of social order.[33] But, as the contrast with the indigenous Surinamese makes evident, Oroonoko is in fact a highly civilized person, who lives not according to an intuitive moral code but rather in a manner consistent with a developed sense of honor and rectitude. What is significant about him, instead, is that his ethical precepts are grounded without reference to (indeed, in direct contrast with) Christian religion. His demeanor and learning, Behn relates, should be sufficient to convince people of the error "that all fine Wit is confined to the white Men, especially to those of Christendom" (*Oroonoko*, 8). Indeed, Oroonoko's refined Eurocentric education seems to have been the product of a rejection of orthodox Christian doctrine. The French royal tutor, who instructed him in "Morals, Language and Science," turns out to have been "banished out of his own Country, for some Heretical Notions he held: and tho he was a Man of very little Religion, he had admirable morals, and a brave soul" (7, 31). Behn thereby destabilizes any automatic connection between Christianity and moral goodness. This break is underscored by Behn's account of the African treatment of women: in Coramantien, she says, "the only Crime and Sin with Woman, is, to turn her out, to abandon her to want, shame and misery: such ill morals are only practised in *Christian* Countries, where they prefer the bare Name of Religion; and, without Vertue or Morality, think that sufficient" (10). Oroonoko's virtue, both as reflective of the customs of his native land and as inculcated by his tutor, derives from a standard which expressly deviates from the perceived dishonor of the Christian path.

In several of his speeches, Oroonoko explicitly contrasts the hypocrisy and self-interest that lie beneath Christianity with his own code of conduct. When he is first trapped aboard the European slave vessel, Oroonoko is given a solemn oath by the captain that he and his fellow countrypeople will be freed at next landfall. In exchange, Oroonoko promises on his honor—which "was such as he never had violated a Word in his Life himself, much less a solemn Asservation"—to do nothing to encourage the other Africans to disobey or disrupt the journey. The captain refuses to accept Oroonoko at his word, on the grounds that he finds it impossible "to trust a Heathen, he said, upon his Parole, a Man that had no sense or notion of the God that he worshipp'd" (34–35). The captain reasons that a non-Christian such as Oroonoko has nothing to fear from the breaking of a vow, whereas a devoted Christian who breaks his solemn word does. The lengthy response Behn places in the mouth of Oroonoko is a remarkable statement of the strengths of a deistic foundation for morality in comparison with the arguments of institutionalized religious superstition.

I swear by my Honour; which to violate, would not only render me comtemptible and despised by all brave and honest Men, and so give my self perpetual Pain, but it would be eternally offending and displeasing all Mankind. . . . But Punishments hereafter are suffer'd by one's self; and the World takes no Cognizance whether this GOD have reveng'd 'em, or not, 'tis done so secretly, and deferr'd so long: while the Man of no Honour suffers every moment the Scorn and Contempt of the honester World. . . . I speak this not to move Belief, but to shew how you mistake, when you imagine, That he who will violate his Honour, will keep his Word with his Gods. (35)

Note the beginning of the final sentence. Oroonoko's self-proclaimed purpose is not to alter the religious convictions of his interlocutor, but to demonstrate the error that infects Christian claims to be more trustworthy than "heathens." Both Christians and non-Christians are capable of honor, Oroonoko asserts, and it is this virtue that makes a person's word into a bond and an obligation. Religious belief is no guarantee of virtue; indeed, as Behn has already stated in *Oroonoko*, when religion is confused with moral goodness, human beings use holiness as a cloak to justify utterly self-interested and dishonorable behavior.

Oroonoko's maltreatment at the hands of successive Europeans, from the ship's captain and crew to the South American slave traders to the white inhabitants and governors of Surinam, provokes increasing doubts in his mind about so-called Christian virtue. Although well treated by the (female) narrator of the story—a character often, but not unproblematically, associated with Behn herself[34]—and some of the other Englishmen, he eventually resolves to stage a revolt out of a desire that his pregnant wife should not give birth to a child condemned to slavery. In this, he initially enjoys the support of the other enslaved Africans, who are shamelessly abused by their new European owners. The revolt fails, however, because the rest of the slaves back down and abandon Oroonoko to his fate.

Oroonoko initially refuses to surrender, but is once again made a promise by his white enslavers that, if he does so, he and his wife will be freed. His response reveals that he has learned much about the true value of oaths sworn in the name of the Christian God. He replies,

There was no Faith in the White Men, or the Gods they ador'd; who instructed them in Principles so false, that honest Men could not live amongst them; though no People profess'd so much, none performed so little: That he knew what he had to do when he dealt with Men of Honour; but with them a Man ought to be eternally on his guard, and never eat and drink with Christians, without his Weapon of Defence in his hand; and, for his own Security, never to credit one Word they spoke (66).

Nonetheless, Oroonoko permits himself to be talked into a surrender by one of the well-meaning members of the English establishment, who has been told that the conditions of manumission offered to the royal slave and his family will be honored. Of course, the reality turns out to be something horribly different. Despite the fact that the freedom of Oroonoko and his wife and unborn child have been guaranteed in writing, the Europeans set upon him and execute him, but not before they have mercilessly dismembered and mutilated his body. The cause of Oroonoko's ultimate downfall, one might say, is his inability to think so ill of his fellow human beings that he could not ultimately trust them to live by moral standards similar to his own.

There seems little doubt that Behn wants her reader to sympathize with Oroonoko and his plight at the hands of European civilization: she claims at the beginning of the novel that the incidents described are factual, and she declares in its final paragraph that she wishes "to make his [Oroonoko's] glorious Name to survive to all Ages" (78). *Oroonoko* represents itself as a chronicle of how supposedly "civilizing" colonial rule generates the height of barbaric brutality. But the natives of Surinam and, especially, the character Oroonoko also seem to embody elements of the deistic ideal of natural worship conducted through the exercise of virtue, in marked contrast with the self-consciously religious Europeans, many of whom demonstrate almost complete moral degeneracy. That Oroonoko professes no formal religion whatsoever only underscores a favorite deist point: it is by the light of natural reason, attuned to the practice of virtue, that the plan of a just and rational deity is best served. Inasmuch as the English deists had enjoined the worship of God by virtuous action rather than empty rite, Oroonoko seems to be the archetypical practitioner of deism.

Behn, Deism, and Toleration

Two further questions remain to be addressed before we can gain a full appreciation of Behn's religious views. First, can we extrapolate from the presence of deist themes in Behn's work to the claim that she was herself a committed deist? Second, how does Behn's treatment of religion impact on the history of toleration?

The first question raises a complex set of issues. Behn's business was not, of course, philosophy or theology; to make an adequate living, she had first of all to please her patrons and entertain her audience. But her repeated antipathy toward institutional religion and its priestcraft, as well as her praise of virtue uninformed by religious fervor, suggest that she was fundamentally in agreement with leading deists of her time in matters of basic principle. As has been pointed out, her known associates included prominent Freethinkers and Nonconformists, through whom she certainly gained familiarity with deist teachings. It thus seems plausible to regard her, at minimum, as a publicist of the deist position, bringing its anticlerical and naturalist doctrines to a wider and somewhat more diverse public than they might otherwise have achieved.

What makes it necessary to stop short of labeling Behn as a full-fledged adherent to deism—apart from the relatively unsystematic nature of her writings about religious topics—is an oft-ascribed connection between religious nonconformity and republican political conviction. Blair Worden counts as one "durable legacy of republicanism . . . the alliance it had formed with deism."[35] Likewise, Champion stresses the need to recognize the "historical link between religious skepticism and Republican political theory."[36] To the extent that the bond between the two is judged a necessary or inextricable one, Behn cannot be numbered among the true religious radicals. Her Toryism and royalism are too established in her life and writing, too pronounced a part of her ideological framework, for any other conclusion to be possible.[37] But, then, it may also be the case that the connection between deism and republicanism was in fact looser than current scholarship claims. After all, the same standard requires us to remove Hobbes—a central figure in English anticlericalism and nonconformism—from consideration as a "true" religious radical.[38] This is not the place where this issue may be given full airing. Suffice it to say that until scholars reach some sustainable conclusion about the relation between religious and political thought in seventeenth-century England, any final judgment about the extent of Behn's deism must be held in abeyance.

Behn's popularization of deist themes does seem to merit her a place in the history of religious toleration, however. As a point of biography, this should not surprise us. Given the number of years that she spent in the service of the English crown in the Low Countries, she obviously knew that a policy of broad tolerance toward religious diversity could work. Similarly, her association with the Duke of Buckingham, a longstanding and active advocate of toleration, lends credence to viewing her as sympathetic to religious tolerance.[39] Behn's plays and prose works seem bent on reminding her audience that any form of institutionalized sectarian religion is a danger to natural human freedom, virtue, and reason. True religion does not rely on strict adherence to a single body of religious doctrine guaranteed by a monopoly of sacerdotal authority (regardless of the particular confession). Inasmuch as Behn seems inclined to permit individuals to discover their own routes to beatitude, her fundamental stance proves inimical to persecution and enforced religious unity. Even if it is too much to expect the restoration of the vaunted Golden Age, where all people govern themselves solely according to their own natures, the force of her writing promotes human freedom and questions the beneficence of clerics and other holies who claim privileged access to religious truth. Thus, through both her anticlericalism and her vision of a world unencumbered by religious division and strife, Behn endorses a climate of toleration, as befits her deist predilections. To be accounted a proponent of a tolerant perspective, it is not necessary that Behn have authored a tract *de tolerantia* in the manner of John Locke. Indeed, when seen to be grounded in major elements of deism, Behn's spirit of toleration may ultimately have a more solid intellectual foundation than the equivocal and surprisingly narrow theory that one encounters in Locke.[40] And certainly the fact that Locke and so many other contributors to the toleration debates of the middle and late seventeenth century chose to express themselves in the esoteric language of Latin, whereas Behn wrote in the language of, and for, a less tutored audience, suggests that her ideas were more likely to penetrate and stimulate the popular consciousness than those of philosophers and churchmen.

Notes

1. The first position one might call the *"politique"* view, namely, that since the state's main role is to maintain public order, it should tolerate distinct confessions indifferently in the name of peace. The second position takes a "liberty of conscience" approach, which stresses that the individual has a fundamental or inalienable right to believe as she wishes. See Gordon J. Schochet, "John Locke and Religious Toleration," in Lois G. Schwoerer, ed., *The Revolution of 1688-1689: Changing Perspectives* (Cambridge: Cambridge University Press, 1992), 148–50.

2. These developments have been recently studied by Richard H. Popkin, *The History of Skepticism from Erasmus to Spinoza*, rev. ed. (Berkeley: University of California Press, 1979); Alan Charles Kors, *Atheism in France, 1650-1729*, 2 vols., Vol. 1, *The Orthodox Sources of Disbelief* (Princeton, N.J.: Princeton University Press, 1990); David Berman, *A History of Atheism in England* (London: Croom Helm, 1987); and Michael Hunter and David Wootton, eds., *Atheism from the Reformation to the Enlightenment* (Oxford: Clarendon Press, 1992).

3. The standard account is Don Cameron Allen, *Doubt's Boundless Sea: Skepticism and Faith in the Renaissance* (Baltimore: Johns Hopkins University Press, 1964). More recently, see Richard H. Popkin, "The Deist Challenge," in Ole Peter Grell, Jonathan I. Israel, and Nicholas Tyacke, eds., *From Persecution to Toleration: The Glorious Revolution and Religion in England* (Oxford: Clarendon Press, 1991), 195–215.

4. For example, see Alan Ryan, "A More Tolerant Hobbes?" in Susan Mendus, ed., *Justifying Toleration: Conceptual and Historical Perspectives* (Cambridge: Cambridge University Press, 1988), 37–59 and Richard Flathman, *Thomas Hobbes: Skepticism, Individuality and Chastened Politics* (Newbury Park, Calif.: Sage, 1993).

5. Popkin, "The Deist Challenge," 195.

6. See Mary Ann O'Donnell, "Introduction," *Aphra Behn: An Annotated Bibliography of Primary and Secondary Sources* (New York: Garland, 1986), 3, 93; Angeline Goreau, *Reconstructing Aphra: A Social Biography of Aphra Behn* (New York: Dial Press, 1980), 244; Sara H. Mendelson, *The Mental World of Stuart Women: Three Studies* (Amherst: University of Massachusetts Press, 1987), 117, 179–82; Robert Adams Day, "Aphra Behn and the Works of the Intellect," in Mary Anne Schofield and Cecilia Macheski, eds., *Fetter'd or Free? British Women Novelists, 1670-1815* (Athens: Ohio University Press, 1986), 374; George A. Starr, "Aphra Behn and the Genealogy of the Man of Feeling," *Modern Philology* 87 (May 1990): 362; and Gerald Duchovnay, "Aphra Behn's Religion," *Notes and Queries* 221 (May–June 1976): 236.

7. Maureen Duffy, *The Passionate Shepherdess: Aphra Behn, 1640–89* (London: Cape, 1977), 92, 239, 283, and passim.

8. See her poem, "On the Author of that Excellent Book Intituled *The Way to Health, on Life, and Happiness*," which praises the ascetic and vegetarian lifestyle of Anabaptist Thomas Tyron; Janet Todd, ed., *The Works of Aphra Behn*, vol. 1, *Poetry* (London: William Pickering, 1992), 180.

9. Mendelson, *The Mental World of Stuart Women*, 164; Janet Todd, "Introduction" to Aphra Behn, *Oroonoko, the Rover and Other Works* (London: Penguin, 1992), 17–18; Todd, *Poetry*, xxvi–xxvii; Day, "Aphra Behn and the Works of the Intellect," 379–80; Goreau, *Reconstructing Aphra*, 278.

10. Mendelson, *The Mental World of Stuart Women*, 173.

11. Todd, "Introduction," 3–4; see also Todd, *Poetry*, xiv.

12. J. A. I. Champion, *The Pillars of Priestcraft Shaken: The Church of England and Its Enemies, 1660–1730* (Cambridge: Cambridge University Press, 1992), 6–9.

13. Ibid., 158. On Buckingham, see Tim Harris, "Introduction: Revising the Restoration," in Harris, Paul Seaward and Mark Goldie, eds., *The Politics of Religion in Restoration England* (Oxford: Blackwell, 1990), 7, 11.

14. Champion, *The Pillars of Priestcraft Shaken*, 11.

15. Ibid., 143.

16. Edward Lord Herbert of Cherbury, *The Antient Religion of the Gentiles* (pub. 1705; first Latin ed. 1663), quoted in Champion, *The Pillars of Priestcraft Shaken*, 144.

17. Todd, *Poetry*, 31, ll. 53–58. The only thorough analysis of this poem, by Robert Markley and Molly Rothenberg ("Contestations of Nature: Aphra Behn's 'The Golden Age' and the Sexualizing of Politics," in Heidi Hutner, ed., *Rereading Aphra Behn: History, Theory, and Criticism* [Charlottesville: University Press of Virginia, 1994], 301–21), ignores entirely the religious dimension of Behn's statements. For them, the poem is an expression solely of her politics, a conclusion that is difficult to sustain in light of her attribution of human conflict and elimination of self-governance to the introduction of religion.

18. Todd, *Poetry*, 33, ll. 105, 109–14.

19. Champion, *The Pillars of Priestcraft Shaken*, 147, 160–61.

20. Todd, *Poetry*, 34, ll. 166–67.

21. Ibid., 34, ll. 162–65.

22. Charles Blount, *Great Is Diana of the Ephesians* (pub. 1680), quoted in Champion, *The Pillars of Priestcraft Shaken*, 147.

23. Ibid., 168.

24. Montague Summers, ed., *The Works of Aphra Behn*, 6 vols. (1915; reprinted New York: Benjamin Blom, 1967), 1: 384. This standard edition is in the process of being replaced by a new collection under the general editorship of Janet Todd; at the time of writing, only four volumes of the Todd edition (containing Behn's shorter works) have been published.

25. Speaking in the voice of an earlier generation, George Woodcock, *Aphra Behn: The English Sappho* (originally published in 1948 as *The Incomparable Aphra*) (Montrèal: Black Rose Books, 1989), 54, describes Lady Desbro as a "nymphomaniac." In more recent times, Behn scholars have recognized the importance, and also subversive character, of female desire in her writings. For further discussion of

the nature of female sexuality in Behn's work, see Arlen Feldwick, "Whigs, Wits and Women: Domestic Politics as Anti-Whig Rhetoric in Aphra Behn's Town Comedies," in C. Levin and P. A. Sullivan, eds., *Political Rhetoric, Power, and Renaissance Women* (Albany: SUNY Press, 1995), 223–40 and "Over the Body of a Wo/Man: Homosocial Bonding in Aphra Behn's *Oroonoko*," *Eighteenth Century: Theory and Interpretation* (forthcoming). Also helpful are articles in Hutner, *Rereading Aphra Behn*.

26. Summers, *Works*, 5: 455–56.

27. Summers, *Works*, 2: 6–98 and Janet Todd, ed., *The Works of Aphra Behn*, vol. 3, *The Fair Jilt and Other Short Stories* (London: William Pickering, 1995), 208–58.

28. Herbert, *The Antient Religion of the Gentiles* (note 16), 142.

29. Charles Blount, *Religio Laici* (1683), quoted in Champion, *The Pillars of Priestcraft Shaken*, 143.

30. Ibid., 148.

31. Research on *Oroonoko* has become a veritable cottage industry in the past two decades. For a sampling of published work, see George Guffey, "Aphra Behn's *Oroonoko*: Occasion and Accomplishment," in Guffey and Andrew Wright, *Two English Novelists* (Los Angeles: William Andrews Clark Memorial Library, 1975); Stephanie Athey and Daniel Cooper Alarcón, "*Oroonoko*'s Gendered Economies of Honor/Horror: Reframing Colonial Discourse Studies in the Americas," *American Literature* 65 (1993): 425–43; Charlotte Sussman, "The Other Problem with Women: Reproduction and Slave Culture in Aphra Behn's *Oroonoko*," in Hutner, ed., *Rereading Aphra Behn*, 212–33; Moira Ferguson, "*Oroonoko*: Birth of a Paradigm," *New Literary History* 23 (1992): 339–59; Robert A. Erickson, "Mrs A. Behn and the Myth of Oroonoko-Imoinda," *Eighteenth-Century Fiction* 5 (1993): 201–16; Jacqueline Pearson, "Gender and Narrative in the Fiction of Aphra Behn," *Review of English Studies* 42 (1991): 40–56, 179–90. For research on *Oroonoko* prior to the mid-1980s, O'Donnell's annotated bibliography is a standard resource.

32. Aphra Behn, *Oroonoko; or, the Royal Slave*, ed. L. Metzger (New York: Norton, 1973), 1–2.

33. See Lore Metzger's "Introduction" to *Oroonoko*, x.

34. See Martine W. Brownley, "The Narrator in *Oroonoko*," *Essays in Literature* 4 (1977), 174–81.

35. Blair Worden, "English Republicanism," in J. H. Burns and M. Goldie, eds., *The Cambridge History of Political Thought 1450–1700* (Cambridge: Cambridge University Press, 1991), 475.

36. Champion, *The Pillars of Priestcraft Shaken*, 170.

37. Feldwick, "Wits, Whigs and Women," 224–25.

38. Champion wrestles with this problem (unsuccessfully) in *The Pillars of Priestcraft Shaken*, 134–35.

39. Harris, "Introduction: Revising the Restoration," 11.

40. On some of the limitations of Locke's theory, see Jeremy Waldron, "Locke: Toleration and the Rationality of Persecution," in John Horton and Susan Mendus, eds., *John Locke: A Letter Concerning Toleration in Focus* (London and New York: Routledge, 1991), 98–124.

10

Skepticism About Religion and Millenarian Dogmatism: Two Sources of Toleration in the Seventeenth Century

Richard H. Popkin

IT IS A CURIOUS FACT THAT THE opposing positions of skepticism about religion and religious dogmatism provided two of the major roads to toleration in theory and practice in early modern Europe. The very idea that two such different positions could lead to the same outcome is surely part of the reason that toleration has triumphed in the modern West. This chapter will show how the two positions could and did lead to toleration, focusing largely on the seventeenth century. We will start with religious skepticism.

Skepticism About Religion: Jews, Deists, and Toleration

From the time of the Renaissance rediscovery of the major texts of ancient Greek skeptical thought, the writings of Sextus Empiricus, skeptical ideas were very much involved with the religious controversies that became known as the Reformation and the Counter-Reformation. Ancient Greek Pyrrhonism provided ammunition for both Catholics and Protestants, as well as providing a fideistic "defense" of religion. Since nothing can be known, one should *per non-sequitur* accept religion on faith alone,[1] a view offered around 1700 by both the Catholic Bishop Pierre-Daniel Huet, and the Protestant Pierre Bayle.

The seventeenth century saw a flowering of the application of skeptical analysis to the question of the truth of the Christian religion, or principal parts thereof, reaching the point of advocating disbelief in Christianity or in religion in general. This became a principal meaning of the word "skepticism." Several developments played a role in bringing this about: an intellectual crisis caused by the re-evaluation of ancient polytheism; the work of Bible critics Isaac La Peyrère, Baruch Spinoza, and Richard Simon; growing awareness of the criticisms of Christianity written by Jewish intellectuals in Amsterdam; and doubts about Judaism caused by the career of the false Messiah, Sabbatai Zevi, among others.

One of the most powerful attacks on the established religions, the notorious *Traité des Trois Imposteurs, Moses, Jesus et Mahomet, ou l'esprit de M. Spinoza*, probably written in its present form in the last decade of the seventeenth century and only printed in 1719,[2] is a good place to start our analysis. (A Latin work, *De Tribus Impostoribus*, written in the mid-sixteenth century with different content but similar purposes, was also part of the clandestine literature of the time.) *Les Trois Imposteurs* circulated widely in a great many manuscripts. It purports to be written by the secretary of Emperor Frederick II in the thirteenth century, but it appropriates passages about religion from Hobbes, Spinoza, Naudé, and La Mothe Le Vayer. It portrays the three great religious leaders as impostors, playing political roles for their own ends. It offers an explanation of how and why religions develop in terms of the psychological evaluations offered by Hobbes and Spinoza.

The possibility that such an attack on Judaism, Christianity, and Islam could be written is mentioned quite often in the seventeenth century, with discussion about whether such a work actually existed. Queen Christina of Sweden offered the equivalent of $1,000,000 for a copy.[3] Manuscripts of the work only surfaced at the end of the century, and were quickly copied and dispersed.

The same happened with the unpublished work of Jean Bodin, the *Colloquium Heptaplomeres*, purporting to be a discussion between believers in various religions, in which the Jewish participant wins the argument. The work surfaced in the mid-seventeenth century, and then manuscript copies were made. Leibniz and his associates prepared the text for publication, but it was not printed until the nineteenth century.[4]

The question of whether religious belief could be sustained in the light of modern knowledge appears in Bishop Edward Stillingfleet's attack on John Toland and John Locke. Stillingfleet feared that applying the empirical theory of knowledge to religious belief would just lead to no belief.[5] A similar problem seems to have been involved when the French Reformed Church in The Netherlands declared it a heresy to seek for clear and distinct evidence for religious belief.[6]

The actual content of religious belief came into question in the controversies between Jews and Christians of the time. In the seventeenth century some Jewish scholars who had been raised as forced converts to Christianity in Spain and Portugal and who escaped to the Netherlands presented forceful critiques of Christian beliefs using the dialectical techniques they had been taught at Iberian universities. In the tolerant atmosphere of seventeenth-century Holland, these Jewish thinkers could set forth their case without fear of punishment if they did not publish their work. Their attacks on Christianity circulated widely in manuscript.[7] Deists tried to obtain these manuscripts, and finally in 1715 a group of them were auctioned off in The Hague.[8] Their arguments were described without comment in the last edition of Jacques Basnage's *Histoire des juifs* of 1716.[9] Considering the Jewish views, Basnage concluded that Christians should give up trying to convert Jews by arguments, since the Jews knew the materials better and usually won the debates. Instead, one should leave the job of converting Jews to God and to God alone.[10]

The Jewish anti-Christian arguments became known to such figures as Anthony Collins, Voltaire, and d'Holbach, and were used as powerful ammunition against the Christian establishment. The arguments in these unpublished but widely circulated manuscripts[11] sought to show that there is no evidence that Christianity is the fulfillment of Judaism, and that there is no good evidence that the Messiah has already come. What is supposed to happen when the Messiah comes has not yet happened. But God or someone is still keeping the Jews in existence, so maybe there is still a major event to come.

D'Holbach published some of the arguments of seventeenth-century Jewish philosopher Isaac Orobio de Castro under the title *Israel vengé*,[12] thereby making them widely available. The power of this seventeenth-century argument can be demonstrated by some examples. Some of the manuscripts found their way across the Atlantic to the Harvard University Library, and a New England preacher, George Bethune English, came across them. His Christian beliefs were thoroughly shaken. He first consulted the rabbi of New York, and later converted to Islam.[13] These Jewish anti-Christian arguments played an important role in undermining intellectual conviction in Christianity elsewhere as well.[14] In a copy of *Israel vengé*, an unidentified reader wrote that Orobio proves by Sacred History that the Messiah has not yet come. A letter pasted in this volume states that Christians cannot answer Orobio's claims.[15] Zalkind Hourwitz, the French royal librarian of the Oriental collection in Paris at the time of the Revolution, asserted that one had to abandon Christian claims of superiority over Judaism, or else one would turn people into complete skeptics about religion.[16]

On the other hand, skepticism against Judaism also began to develop, first, from the intellectual debacle following the Jewish Messianic movement of 1666; and second, as a result of considering the Old Testament as just the secular history of a peculiar group of people of antiquity. Jews everywhere in the world became very excited when Sabbatai Zevi of Smyrna announced in late 1665 that he was the long awaited Messiah, and that the Messianic age was beginning. He then began acting the part, changing Jewish law and appointing new Kings of the World (his friends and relatives). It is estimated that at least 90 percent of the Jewish world at the time accepted him. A few months later the Turkish Sultan had Sabbatai Zevi arrested and threatened him with death. The "Messiah" quickly converted to Islam and lived out the rest of his life as a functionary of the Ottoman Empire.[17] The Jewish world was swept by doubt and dismay. Many Jews began to question whether the Messiah would be a man and whether the sacred texts had been misunderstood. This Jewish "skeptical crisis" has been going on ever since.

If the Jews developed doubts about their basic views, Christian opponents suggested that Jews lacked a trustworthy criterion for telling a true Messiah from a false one. If the Jews converted to Christianity, they suggested, they would be able to make proper judgments about such an important matter.[18] However, it did not take long before some free-thinking people suggested that the Christians had exactly the same problem as the Jews, and were no more able to justify their criteria for determining who was the Messiah. The critics thereby generated a skepticism about a central belief of both Judaism and Christianity.[19] They also generated a skepticism about theological and historical knowledge that was to have far-reaching effects from the eighteenth century onward. As part of this process, so-called revealed data were transformed into natural, secular data. The Scriptures were treated as just ordinary human writings, which can be best understood in the context of the human authors' milieu. Hobbes, Spinoza, and the early English deists are usually considered the ones who did the most to advance this view. Spinoza had written that the science of interpreting the Bible should be almost the same as the science of nature.[20]

La Peyrère, Hobbes, and Spinoza had all pointed out discrepancies, inconsistencies, and contradictions in the Biblical texts, and had maintained that Moses could not be the author of the entire work. They contended that much or all of it was a collection of writings by various people in and around ancient Palestine. We could not be sure that what we now possessed as the Bible was the same as the ancient texts, given all the transcriptions and transportations and transmutations that had taken place in the intervening centuries. The greatest seventeenth-century Bible scholar, Father Richard Simon, revealed the apparently endless historical and epistemological problems that lay between the present day reader and the original authors and texts.[21]

Spinoza claimed that we, with our later perspective, could understand the Biblical writings in terms of early Jewish history. The writings, according to Spinoza, did not and could not contain supernatural information, but rather contained data about secular affairs of the time. Spinoza developed a thorough-going skepticism about the possibility of humankind having any access to supernatural information. This then allowed him to see all historical claims, Biblical or other, as just claims about how human beings behaved at various times and places. The fact that some people said that they received messages from God, or had revelations, was interesting data about those people and their psychological states, rather than reports of genuine divine communications. Reading Scripture in this manner resulted in the Bible becoming an object *in* human history rather than a framework for explaining it.[22]

Drawing on this theory, one could conclude, as the *Traité des Trois Imposteurs* had it, that the three major religions were foisted on the human race by nasty priests and politicians in order to control people through fear and superstition. Churches and religious and political institutions were established to carry this on from generation to generation even though it was basically a fraud or hoax generated to gain and keep political power. This possibility was taken seriously enough that two leading English theologians of the seventeenth century, Ralph Cudworth and Edward Stillingfleet, tried valiantly to raise skeptical doubts about the very possibility of such a conspiracy having taken place. They sought to show the implausibility of so many people in so many times and places keeping up the imposture without anyone, in seventeen hundred years, catching on to the fraud.[23]

English deists, starting with Charles Blount, saw Spinoza's naturalistic reading of the Bible as supporting their own view that the Bible as we know it is only one of many human attempts to portray a natural religion in specific cultural terms,[24] an attempt open to comparison with that of many differing ancient and modern pagan versions from various parts of the planet.[25] This was coupled with Pierre Bayle's reading of the Biblical narrative (at least of the Old Testament) as comparable to any historical narrative, in which the characters, like the Patriarchs and King David, can be judged in the same way as any other moral or immoral actors on the human stage.[26] Bayle proceeded to show that the immoral, dishonest activities of the heroes and heroines of ancient Israel were as bad as those of pagan characters, of Europeans kings and queens and political leaders, as well as of religious leaders from post-Biblical times to the present. Bayle then contended that there is no relation between religion and morality, and that a society of atheists could be more moral than a society of Christians. He portrayed the "atheist" Spinoza as an almost saintly figure, while painting contemporary Catholic and Protestant leaders as liars, hypocrites, and cheats.

The story of Spinoza's own religious career, centering on his excommunication from the Amsterdam Synagogue, was symbolic of the malign power of priests and priestcraft. The first biography of Spinoza, *La Vie de Mr. Spinosa* by Jean-Maximilien Lucas[27] (often published with the *Traité des trois imposteurs*, or bound together with it in manuscripts), created the lasting picture of the saintly Spinoza, victim of the extreme religious intolerance of the priests of Judaism. The Amsterdam Jewish community was portrayed as a rigid, outmoded orthodoxy, unable to put up with a brave young truth-seeker. A horrendous excommunication service took place, and Spinoza had to flee. The chief rabbi was the epitome of the priestly tyrant. Although recent research has shown that this is a great misrepresentation of what the Amsterdam Jewish community and its leaders were like,[28] the legend has persisted, and is part of the hagiography of Spinoza, the sainted progenitor of the Enlightenment.

Added to this was the appearance of the autobiography of Uriel da Costa and the publication of the friendly debate between the very tolerant Remonstrant teacher, Philip van Limborch (a friend of John Locke), and Isaac Orobio de Castro.[29] Da Costa, a Portuguese priest of Jewish origins, fled the Inquisition for Amsterdam. There he offered his own version of Judaism, and was excommunicated. He finally recanted, was dreadfully punished, was readmitted, and soon after again was excommunicated. Finally he committed suicide around 1640 or 1647. His autobiography was unknown until Limborch published it.[30] It quickly was taken as more evidence of the horrible intolerance of religious groups. Bayle and many others wallowed in the pathos of da Costa's case.[31] He was made into the intellectual father of Spinoza. Near the end of his autobiography, da Costa cried out, "Don't be a Jew or a Christian. Be a man!"[32]

It was easy to use Spinoza and da Costa as symbolic victims of priest-craft since they came from a despised religion outside of established European Christianity. Their cases again showed why one should be skeptical about religious authority.

Another element of intellectual life in this period that led to both religious skepticism and tolerance was the rediscovery of many different religions in the ancient world and the present discovery of hitherto unknown religions all over the planet. These developments led to the comparative study of religion, partly to understand what it represented in different times, places, and cultures, and partly to try to find an inner core in all religions that might represent the "Ur-religion," the original and natural religion of humankind. John Toland's *Christianity not Mysterious* (1696) and Matthew Tindal's *Christianity as old as the Creation* (1730) sought pre-Christian or original Christian sources that constituted this basic religion, and explained contemporary Christianity as a disastrous deformation of natural religion that occurred when institutional priestcraft took over and controlled religion, supported by and allied with arbitrary political powers. Justin Champion and Mark Goldie have argued that the so-called "deist" movement in England was really a reform movement attempting to revive what they considered the ancient role of religion as a civic and moral religion, rather than the malevolent priestly monstrosity that had developed over the centuries.[33]

Bayle had claimed that the empirical evidence indicated that something like the Manichean hypothesis was the case, that there are two divine forces operating in the world, one good and one evil. Any attempt to explain how evil gets into the world on a monistic Christian hypothesis just leads to contradictions and implausible explanations. So, Bayle contended, whether sincerely or not, Christianity had to be accepted without reason, or against reason.[34] This kind of work culminated in seeing all religion as natural human developments. By the middle of the eighteenth century, David Hume could write a work entitled *The Natural History of Religion* in which polytheism was seen as the natural religion which, through psychological developments, ended up as the fractious splintered warring views of theologians of the present.

In France, where Catholicism was the official religion and rigid control was exercised to prevent the spread of heretical or unorthodox ideas, one finds a covert spread of skeptical irreligious ideas from the Netherlands and England. Spinoza's *Tractatus* appeared in French translation in 1678[35] and Bayle's *Dictionnaire* and French translations of Locke and the English deists were read by bright rebellious intellectuals like young Voltaire at the beginning of the eighteenth century.[36] From here two main trends developed. One was a "rational" scientific approach to natural knowledge and human knowledge within the bounds of a moderate skepticism, and the other was an almost rabid attack on religious institutions and practices.

The first was a distillation of what the French thinkers saw as the empirical fruits of modern science in Newton's accomplishments, the translation into French of Locke's *Essay concerning Human Understanding* by Bayle's friend Pierre Coste, who emphasized the skeptical themes in Locke's philosophy, and a moderate version of the total skepticism of Bayle and Pierre-Daniel Huet. The latter himself had said at the end of his *Traité* that the skeptic should follow the attitude and practice of the Royal Society of England, which combined an epistemological skepticism about ultimate knowledge with a practical way of gaining useful scientific knowledge.[37] In the French version this practical scientific knowledge would help explain natural phenomenon, and also would help to understand the problems of mankind *and* provide ways of solving them.

These thinkers, and their followers such as Condorcet, were deists rather than atheists, and saw a thoroughly secular world arising in which people would not have to believe anything in particular.[38] Theirs would be a completely tolerant world, in part because traditional religion was passé. It was an early superstitious way people *used* to think. Now, with enlightenment, one no longer needed churches and priestcraft. Their function could be replaced by secular academies and scientific organizations that would lead people to the most probable truths, and to the knowledge that could improve the human situation.

When the great influx of Huguenot refugees into the Netherlands took place late in the seventeenth century, the question of toleration came to the forefront. French Protestants fought over the issue of whether a variety of religious views could be permitted in their society. In France they had argued for tolerating Protestant views in a Catholic country. Now in the Netherlands they found a great variation in religious belief, from the rigid orthodoxy advocated by Pierre Jurieu to the almost Socinian views some French pastors had developed within the Protestant fold.

In the decades before 1700 a great battle of ideas between skepticism and dogmatism was fought between Bayle and Jurieu. The latter was most concerned to root out heresies that had crept into Protestant views during the persecutions in France, and to reveal the secret subversive atheism of his erstwhile colleague. And Jurieu was willing to justify total intolerance to guard people from false and dangerous views.

At the outset of his refugee life in Holland, Bayle published his *Commentaire philosophique sur les paroles de Jésus-Christ, contrain les d'entrer* (1686), attacking the intolerance of French Catholicism in its drive to force the Huguenots to convert to Catholicism. Bayle not only challenged any justification for forcing people to change religions, but extended his argument to Protestants compelling other Protestants to accept certain views. Bayle presented both a skepticism about whether one could be sure that any beliefs were the true ones, and a contention that belief per se could not be forced, only actions could be restrained or controlled. In advancing his skeptical outlook Bayle insisted that belief was a matter of conscience and that there was no way of distinguishing an erring conscience from an unerring one. Hence people with erring consciences had the same rights to believe what they will as others.[39]

Bayle also insisted that he was a true follower of John Calvin and that he and Jurieu shared the same skepticism, for the same reasons, about whether anybody could prove that his or her views were the right ones. Jurieu in exasperation agreed over and over that he and Bayle offered the same fideistic view, but Jurieu said that he, Jurieu, was serious, and Bayle was ironic or facetious.[40] They both agreed that there was no evidential basis for belief, and that true belief could only result from divine grace granting such belief to the believer.

Bayle and Jurieu agreed that there was no evidential way of determining whether one's beliefs were divinely given or just personal views. No matter how firmly one held one's beliefs, or how forceful one's convictions, they could be personal idiosyncrasies rather than the results of the actions of Holy Spirit on one's conscience. Then how could one be sure? Bayle said one could not. Jurieu insisted one could: one tasted the truth, one felt the truth, one sensed the truth. And this sufficed to give one sufficient assurance to damn other people's views.[41] Others, however, were not so sure.

During and after his slashing attacks on religious belief, Bayle always insisted he was not opposed to religion, but was just showing that religion is based only on faith, built only on the ruins of reason. Only by rejecting reason could one be a firm and true believer. Bayle's contemporary and erstwhile colleague and patron, Pierre Jurieu, insisted that Bayle was just ridiculing religion and was actually a secret atheist. For over twenty five years Bayle defended his "fideism" before the tribunal of the consistory of the French Reformed Church of Rotterdam, answering charges from Jurieu and other Calvinist ministers.[42]

Avant garde thinkers read Bayle as a severe, often devastating critic of religion, especially the Christian religion. But, surprisingly, as skeptical attacks undermined rational attempts to justify religious belief, some theologians, especially in France, began to see Bayle as an ally rather than an enemy precisely for showing that religion is not based on reason or reasonings, and that it is based solely on faith.[43] Later, David Hume ended his *Dialogues Concerning Natural Religion* with the ironic "fideist" observation, "To be a philosophical sceptic is, in a man of letters, the first and most essential step towards being a sound, believing *Christian*."[44] Hume's contemporaries, who called him "the great infidel," would not have seen him as a "sound, believing Christian." However, the German mystic J. G. Hamann read the passage in the *Dialogues* and proclaimed: "This is orthodoxy and a testimony to the truth from the mouth of an enemy and persecutor."[45] Bayle and Hume were transformed from heroes of the avant-garde thinkers to allies of the ancien régime. Taking up this Baylean motif, Hume became the prophet of the Counter-Revolution in France, admired by Louis XVI and later on by Joseph DeMaistre.[46]

The Netherlands in the seventeenth century was a deeply divided *religious* society that was often quite dogmatic and bigotted. Nevertheless, as we have already seen, toleration developed. The clash of religious views seemed to force a kind of truce in order for life to go on. The commercial heart of the Dutch economy depended upon working with peoples of all sorts of religious beliefs and practices. Méchoulan has argued that Dutch tolerance was a compromise with economic necessities and historical accidents.[47] The Dutch tolerance of the Jews, allowing them to live freely without ghettoes or restrictions, was an unexpected result of the Dutch rebellion against Spain. New Christians (forcibly converted Jews) from Belgium moved into the liberated territory of the northern Netherlands. At first the Dutch thought they were Catholics because of their Spanish and Portuguese names and language. When they realized that they were co-victims of Spanish Inquisitorial brutality, the Dutch allowed them to stay while the question of their status was investigated. Hugo Grotius drew up a less than friendly statement permitting the Jews to stay if they were supervised and were open to conversion. The fall of Grotius's party, the Arminians, left the matter to develop without legal decision. The Jews could stay if they would take care of their poor, and if they did not cause scandal.[48] So, without any real tolerance theory, Holland became the first place in Western Europe where Jews could practice their religion openly and live like anyone else. At the same time, the public practice of Catholicism was forbidden in Holland,[49] and the liberal Arminians had to flee or go into hiding for a while.

Religious Dogmatism: Millenarianism and Toleration

Why be tolerant if the truth is known? If the skepticism we have reviewed in the previous section is not accepted, people might be inclined to follow the Catholic authorities, Calvin, and Luther in persecuting those who are wrong on religious matters. But there was also a millenarian basis for toleration offered by dogmatic egalitarian chiliasts. These people took it as a truth that people had to be free and equal before the onset of the Millennium, free to choose for themselves the path to salvation.[50]

In *The Pursuit of the Millennium* and *Warrant for Genocide*, Norman Cohn attempted to link Millenarian activities with the worst kinds of intolerance starting from the medieval Peasant Revolts up to Nazism and Communism, seen as secular millenarian movements. Cohn examined groups of aggressive millenarians in the fifteenth and sixteenth centuries who felt it their divine given duty to prepare for the Millennium by scourging and eliminating the enemies of God, seen as the Jews, the Anti-Christ and his allies (the Pope and his officials), and other infidels, prior to the onset of the Millennium.[51] But a different kind of millenarianism played an important role in promoting tolerance from 1500 to 1830 in Europe and America: a benign egalitarian millenarianism.

We shall start with some developments in Spain after the establishment of the Inquisition and the expulsion of the Jews. Cardinal Ximines, the Primate of Spain and the most powerful figure in Iberia after 1492, devoted enormous energies and resources to preparing for the imminent expected return of Jesus and the onset of the Millennium. As part of this he founded the University of Alcala and established a project to publish the first Polyglot Bible, with the text in Hebrew, Greek, and Latin, plus the ancient Aramaic paraphrase of the Pentateuch. This required Aramaic studies (the language of Jesus), Hebrew studies, tolerance of reformed views, and tolerance for the New Christian (converted Jewish) scholars who did the work. Most of these were Erasmians, advocating a spiritualized non-doctrinal Christianity as opposed to the rigid formulation of the Inquisition. The editor of the Hebrew and Aramaic volumes was Alfonso de Zamora, a Jewish yeshiva student up to 1492, who only converted in 1506 when he was made professor at Alcala. Ximines's toleration was for an intellectual elite, who would accept a broad reformed Christianity. At the same he was extremely intolerant of Muslims, or backsliding Christians of Jewish ancestry.[52]

Ximines was the leader of the reformed Franciscans. He sent some of them to the New World around 1500 to establish a Millennial kingdom there in which there was complete toleration of Indian customs and beliefs and activities. The Indians were to be converted only by love, and were to be protected from the intolerance of the Conquistadores. The Indians, who fortunately had not yet been corrupted by European customs and decadent religion, had to be kept in an innocent situation from which they could freely accept God's message when it was presented to them from above.[53]

At the same time a Dominican, Bartolomé de Las Casas (from a converted Jewish family), who had gone on one of Columbus's voyages, also argued for complete toleration of the Indians. He managed to get the Pope to issue a Bull that began with the remarkable statement, "All peoples of the world are human."[54] Las Casas insisted on the possibility that some of the elect of God who will be recalled at the Second Coming, according to the Bible, could be Indians. Therefore they should *all* be tolerated and protected lest one or more of the elect be hurt or damaged. He sought to create such a tolerant kingdom in Chiapas, where he was the Bishop, and he barred Spaniards other than his followers from entering the territory.[55]

The toleration of the Franciscans and of Las Casas came with the expectation that the Indians would freely become Christians. They regarded forced conversions as had occurred en masse in Spain and Portugal as worse than useless, creating a more complete hostility toward accepting God's message.

Gregorio López, a mysterious Spaniard in mid-sixteenth-century Mexico, lived in a hut in Mexico while helping Indians by improving their health and general conditions. He devoted himself to love of Indians. He was described by his disciple, the Bishop of Mexico, as the perfect man—God and Jesus, he said, could find a home in his soul![56] His only writing was a commentary on *Revelation*.[57] There is no indication that Lopez sought to make the Indians into Christians, but he tried to create a better physical and spiritual world for them from which they could make their own choice.

Another set of seventeenth-century millenarian tolerant views were presented by Antonio de Vieira, a Portuguese Jesuit who was the apostle to the Indians in Brazil. In his *History of the Future*, he foresaw the Jews returning soon to Portugal as free citizens. The Second Coming of Jesus would take place first in Portugal. Then the Jews would be taken to rebuild Jerusalem, and everybody would be saved in the ensuing Millennium. Everyone would become pure Christians by free choice.[58]

Miguel de Molinos, a seventeenth-century Spanish priest, went to Rome to have Gregorio López canonized (which did not happen after Molinos was condemned). Molinos's mystical millenarian quietism proclaimed that all persons should quiet their souls and allow God to perform all their actions. God-ordained actions could not be bad. Hence all behavior was to be tolerated. There was no need for an institutional church, or for intercession of Jesus or Mary.[59] Molinos's opponents claimed that he was not a Christian and that his views would turn people away from Christianity. The Jesuits in Italy, who managed to have him arrested and his views condemned, claimed that he was Jewish and had never been baptized.

Two important Protestant quietists, active in the Netherlands and northern Germany in the latter part of seventeenth century, Jean Labadie and Anna Maria van Schurman, formed spiritual millennial communal societies without any creeds, in which all activity of anyone was regarded as holy. They denied the need for any Sabbath observances, and insisted that from the human point of view all days are equal. They rejected all existing Christian churches as degenerate and irrelevant to the spiritual life, though they saw themselves as ardent, pious Christians.[60] Instead they set up a communist community, where all members' lives were dominated by the immediate action of the Holy Spirit upon them. Two Labadist colonies were set up in the New World, perhaps the first utopian communist communities in America.[61] Their societies were the beginning of religious communist groups in Europe and America, in which there was complete toleration of beliefs and practices (for a while).[62]

Isaac La Peyrère (1596–1677) was the secretary of the Prince of Condè.[63] In his millenarian scenario, there would be universal toleration all over the world. To prepare for the Millennium, he claimed in his *Du Rappel des Juifs* (1643), first the Jews should be readmitted to France, anti-Semitism should be legally banned, and a Jewish-Christian church should be established (with no doctrines or practices repugnant to Jews). Then the Jewish Messiah would come to France and take the Jews and the King of France to rebuild Jerusalem. The millennial world would be ruled by the Messiah, the King of France as his regent, and the Jews and all the peoples of the world will be saved regardless of their origins, creed, or nation. This includes all the descendants of Adam as well as the pre-Adamites outside the Biblical world, which for him included most of the people on the planet. La Peyrere's vision includes a tolerance for everyone.[64] This was a view shared at the time by the Quaker Samuel Fisher, who asked, "Is the Light in *America* then any more insufficient to lead its Followers to God, than the Light in *Europe*, *Asia*, *Africa*, the other three parts of the World? I have ever lookt upon the Light in all men (since I began to look to it in my self) as one and the self-same Light in all where it is."[65]

Some radical English and Dutch millenarians such as Henry Jessey, Peter Serrarius, and John Dury, as well as their friend, rabbi Nathan Shapira of Jerusalem, developed the tolerant view that one can be a Jewish Christian or Christian Jew.[66] The question was posed to Dury: can one be a faithful follower of the Law of Moses and a true and believing Christian? He carefully considered the matter and concluded that the answer was "yes," but that it would be best to practice this in Amsterdam, not in Germany.[67]

In his forty-five years of trying to unite all the Christian churches, Dury evolved a doctrineless, creedless Christianity, a moral view rather than a theological one that could be accepted by everyone.[68] He was in the forefront of pressing for the readmission of the Jews to England, without requiring their conversion. However, he did insist on some restrictions on their business activities and on their being willing to consider Christian views. This, he believed, would lead to their conversion as they came to appreciate the "pure Christianity" of Puritan England.

The millennial tolerationists covered above almost all expected the end result of their toleration policies would be to make everybody pure and true Christians if God so willed. In the interim (which they did not think would be too long), a legally tolerant world had to be created in order to prepare for this. Their advocacy and action to create such a world probably did at least as much to create modern tolerant societies as the deist and nonreligious groups in Europe and America in the seventeenth and eighteenth centuries. The abbé Henri Grégoire and the deist Condorcet joined in leading the Société des Amis des Noirs in fighting for the end of slavery in France, the American colonies, and the new United States of America, and for the public equality of blacks.[69] In the American colonies and in the early United States of America, millenarians like Elias Boudinot, leader of the Continental Congress during the Revolution; Ezra Stiles, President of Yale; and Joseph Priestley, who had recently fled from England to Pennsylvania, all played significant roles in developing a new republic striving for liberty and justice for all.

Perhaps, in the years immediately before or after the year 2000, other egalitarian millenarian movements may emerge as ways of dealing with the disasters of the so-called scientific age of our present, and may bring us back to searching for the bases of human equality in our world community. They may again provide some of the needed energy and outlook to make us join with all of humanity in trying to make a better world.

Notes

1. On this, see Richard H. Popkin, *The History of Scepticism from Erasmus to Spinoza* (Berkeley: University of California Press, 1979), esp. chaps. 1 and 2.

2. *Trattato dei Tre Impostori, La vita e lo spirito del Signor Benedetto de Spinoza*, a cura di Silvia Berti, prefazione de Richard H. Popkin (Torino: Einaudi, 1994). Much of the pre-history of this book appears in Berti's introduction, and in her article, "Jan Vroesen, autore del Traité des Trois Imposteurs," *Rivista Storica Italiana* 103 (1991). See Silvia Berti, Françoise Charles-Daubert, and Richard H. Popkin, eds., *Heterodoxy, Spinozism, and Free Thought in Early Eighteenth-Century Europe* (Dordrecht: Kluwer, 1996).

3. Gilles Ménage, *Ménagiana* IV (Paris, 1754): 397–98.

4. Cf. Richard H. Popkin, "The Dispersion of Bodin's Dialogues in England, Holland and Germany," *Journal of the History of Ideas* 49 (1988): 157–60. See also Marion Leathers Kuntz's chapter in this volume (Chapter 5).

5. On this see Robert S. Carroll, *The Commonsense Philosophy of Bishop Edward Stillingfleet* (The Hague: Nijhoff, 1975); and Richard H. Popkin, "The Philosophy of Bishop Stillingfleet," *Journal of the History of Philosophy* 9 (1971): 303–31.

6. This happened at the synod meeting on Dec. 18, 1694. See Pierre Jurieu, *La religion du latitudinaire, avec l'apologie pour la Sainte Trinité, appellée l'heresie des trois Dieux* (Rotterdam, 1696), 331–66; and Richard H. Popkin, "Hume and Jurieu: Possible Calvinist Origins of Hume's Theory of Belief," in *The High Road to Pyrrhonism* (Indianapolis: Hackett, 1993), 164–66.

7. For a general description of these manuscripts, see Yosef Kaplan, *From Christianity to Judaism: The Story of Isaac Orobio de Castro* (Oxford: Oxford University Press, 1989), esp. chaps. 9 and 10.

8. Cf. Richard H. Popkin, "Jacques Basnage's *Histoire des juifs* and the *Bibliotheca Sarraziana*," *Studia Rosenthaliana* 21 (1987): 154–62.

9. Basnage wrote the first history of the Jews since Josephus in ancient times. It first appeared in 1706, was translated into English in 1708, and the much enlarged last edition was in 1716. Basnage, a Huguenot, was a close friend of Pierre Bayle.

10. Jacques Basnage, *Histoire des juifs* (1715 ed.), last chapter of vol. 15.

11. A catalogue of 1811 from Amsterdam lists many copies of various of the items for sale (250 of them), indicating that a great many must have existed at the time. See the catalogue of Solomon Jessurum, Amsterdam 1811, which is in the collection of the University of Amsterdam Library, Nv.837.

12. Isaac Orobio de Castro, *Israel vengé, ou Exposition naturelle des prophéties hébraiques ques les chrétiens appliquent à Jesus leur prétendu Messie* (n.p., 1770).

13. See George Bethune English, *Grounds of Christianity Examined* (Boston, 1813). On English's career, see Walter L. Wright, Jr., "English, George Bethune," *Dictionary of American Bibliography* (1928–36), 3: 165.

14. See Richard H. Popkin, "Jewish Anti-Christian Arguments as a Source of Irreligion from the Seventeenth to the Early Nineteenth Century," in Michael Hunter and David Wootton, eds., *Atheism from the Reformation to the Enlightenment* (Oxford: Oxford University Press, 1992), 159–81; and "The Image of the Jew in Clandestine Literature circa 1700" in Guido Canziani, ed., *Filosofia e Religione nella Letteratura Clandestina Secoli XVII e XVIII* (Milan: Francoagnelli, 1994), 13–34.

15. See Orobio, *Israel vengé*, Bibliothèque Nationale, Paris, Rés. D2.5193.

16. Zalkind Hourwitz, *Apologie des Juifs* (Paris, 1789), 59.

17. On his case, see Gershom Scholem, *Sabbatai Sevi, the Mystical Messiah, 1626–1676*, Bollingen Series 93 (Princeton, N.J.: Princeton University Press, 1973).

18. See, e.g., John Evelyn, *The History of the Three Late Famous Imposters* (London, 1669). The text is actually by Paul Rycaut, the English consul at Smyrna at the time. See also Charles Leslie, *A Short and Easy Method with the Jews*, in his *Theological Works* (London, 1721), 1: 52; and J. P. Marana, *Letters Writ by a Turkish Spy* (London, 1692), 4: letters 5 and 11.

19. See, e.g., Voltaire's article, "Messie," in the *Dictionnaire philosophique*.

20. Benedict de Spinoza, *Tractatus Theologico-Politicus*, chap. 7.

21. On these matters, see Richard H. Popkin, *Isaac La Peyrère (1596–1676): His Life, Work and Influence* (Leiden: Brill, 1987).

22. This thesis is developed in the first seven chapters of Spinoza's *Tractatus*, and the appendix to Book I of his *Ethics*.

23. This is discussed at great length in Edward Stillingfleet, *Origines Sacrae*, and Ralph Cudworth, *The True Intellectual System of the Universe*.

24. Blount published the first English translation of any of Spinoza's writings, the chapter from the *Tractatus* on why miracles are impossible, *Miracles No Violations of the Laws of Nature* (London, 1683). He may also be the as yet unknown translator of the whole of the *Tractatus*, Benedictus de Spinoza, *A Treatise Partly Theological, and Partly Political, Translated out of the Latin* (London, 1689; republished 1739). On this see Richard H. Popkin, "The Deist Challenge," in Ole Peter Grell, Jonathan I. Israel, and Nicholas Tyacke, eds., *From Persecution to Toleration: The Glorious Revolution and Religion in England* (Oxford: Clarendon Press, 1991), 205–7.

25. See Justin Champion, *The Pillars of Priestcraft Shaken: The Church of England and Its Enemies, 1660–1730* (Cambridge: Cambridge University Press, 1992).

26. Bayle's articles on Old Testament figures in the *Dictionnaire* include "Aaron," "Abimelech," "David," "Ham," "Sarah," and many others. The only article on anyone in the New Testament is a brief one on St. John the Evangelist.

27. Not much is known about Lucas except that he was a French Protestant in the circle of radical followers of Spinoza in the Netherlands at the end of the seventeenth century.

28. As shown in the many studies of Yosef Kaplan; in Henri Méchoulan's *Etre Juif à Amsterdam au temps de Spinoza* (Paris: Albin Michel, 1991); Jonathan I. Israel, *European Jewry in the Age of Mercantilism, 1550–1750* (Oxford: Clarendon

Press, 1985); and H. P. Salomon's introduction to his edition of chief rabbi Saul Levi Morteira's *Tratado do verdade da lei de Moises* (Braga, 1988); Richard H. Popkin, "The Historical Significance of Sephardic Judaism in 17th Century Amsterdam," *American Sephardi* 5 (1971–72): 18–32, and "The Jewish Community of Amsterdam" in D. Frank, ed., *Routledge History of Jewish Philosophy*, forthcoming.

29. Part of van Limborch's claim to fame at the time was his authorship of the *History of the Inquisition* in which he showed how awful and intolerant both the medieval and Spanish Inquisitions were. His major case history for the Spanish one was the account Orobio de Castro had told him of how he was tortured. The debate with Orobio was published by van Limborch under the title *De Veritate Christianae: Amica collatio cum erudito Judaeo* (Gouda, 1687). The review of this in the *Bibliothèque Universelle* 7 (1687): 289–330, is probably by John Locke, who may have been present at the actual debate.

30. There is some question whether the text that was printed is complete or even authentic. Limborch took it from a manuscript that his father-in-law possessed, in Latin. The original presumably would have been in Portuguese. Nothing that has surfaced corroborates the events described. Until recently da Costa's main theological writing was unknown, but a copy was discovered by Herman P. Salomon a few years ago and published by him with an English translation: Uriel da Costa, *Examination of Pharisaic Traditions* (Leiden: Brill, 1993).

31. See Bayle's article "Acosta" in the *Dictionnaire*.

32. Uriel da Costa, *Examination*.

33. Justin Champion, "Europe's Enlightenment and National Historiographies: Rethinking Religion and Revolution (1649–1789)," *Europa* (1993): 73–93, and *The Pillars of Priestcraft Shaken*; and Tim Harris, Paul Seaward, and Mark Goldie, eds., *The Politics of Religion in Restoration England* (Oxford: Oxford University Press, 1990).

34. Bayle, *Dictionnaire*, "Manichéens," "Pauliciens," "Eclaircissement sur les Manichéens," and "Eclaircissement sur les Pyrrhoniens."

35. It was translated by Gabriel de Saint Glain and appeared under three different false titles. Spinoza had a great influence in France. See Paul Vernière, *Spinoza et la pensée française avant la Révolution* (Paris: Presses Universitaires de France, 1954).

36. C. J. Betts, *Early Deism in France* (The Hague: Nijhoff, 1984), and Champion, "Europe's Enlightenment and National Historiographies."

37. Huet, *Traité* (1723 ed.), Livre II, chap. 10, 221.

38. This comes out forcibly in the anonymous pamphlet Condorcet wrote in 1786, "On the Influence of the American Revolution on Europe," printed in Condorcet, *Selected Writings*, ed. Keith Michael Baker (Indianapolis: Bobbs Merrill, 1976), 71–83.

39. This view is developed forcefully in Bayle's *Commentaire philosophique* and in most of his subsequent writings. See also Labrousse, *Pierre Bayle*, Vol. 2, *Heterodoxie et Rigorisme* (The Hague: Nijhoff, 1964), chaps. 18 and 19.

40. See especially Pierre Jurieu's last attack on Bayle, published right after Bayle's death, *Le Philosophe de Rotterdam, accusé, atteint, et convaincu* (Amsterdam, 1706).

41. Cf. Popkin, "Hume and Jurieu," where many sources in Jurieu for this theory are cited.

42. Cf. Elisabeth Labrousse, *Pierre Bayle*, Vol. 1, *Du Pays de Foix à la cité d'Erasme*, 2d ed. (The Hague: Nijhoff, 1985), chaps. 7–9, and *Heterodoxie et Rigorisme*; and Popkin, "Introduction" to Pierre Bayle, *Historical and Critical Dictionary: Selections* (Indianapolis: Hackett, 1991).

43. Pierre Rétat, *Le Dictionnaire de Bayle et la lutte philosophique au XVIIIe siècle* (Paris: Les Belles Lettres, 1971). See also Alan C. Kors, *Atheism in France, 1650–1729* (Princeton, N.J.: Princeton University Press, 1990), chap. 7.

44. David Hume, *Dialogues Concerning Natural Religion*, ed. R. H. Popkin (Indianapolis: Hackett, 1980), 89.

45. Johann G. Hamann, *Schriften*, Theil I (Berlin, 1821), 406.

46. Cf. Rétat, *Dictionnaire*, and Laurence Bongie, *David Hume, Prophet of the Counter-Revolution* (Oxford: Oxford University Press, 1965).

47. Henri Méchoulan, *Amsterdam au temps de Spinoza: Argent et liberté* (Paris: Presses Universitaires de France, 1990).

48. See H. Méchoulan, *Etre Juif à Amsterdam au temps de Spinoza*.

49. The not-so-secret practice of Catholicism was accepted and tolerated.

50. On this see my paper on "Millenarianism and Toleration," Conference on Toleration, Clark Library, May 1994.

51. Norman Cohn, *The Pursuit of the Millennium: Revolutionary Messianism in Medieval and Reformation Europe and Its Bearing on Modern Totalitarian Movements* (New York: Harper Torchbooks, 1961; first ed. 1957) and *Warrant for Genocide* (London: Penguin, 1970; first ed. 1967).

52. See Richard H. Popkin, "Christian Jews and Jewish Christians in Spain, 1492 and After," *Judaism* 41 (1992): 248–67.

53. On the Reformed Franciscans in America, see John Leddy Phelan, *The Millennial Kingdom of the Franciscans in the New World* (Berkeley: University of California Press, 1956).

54. This appears in a Papal Bull dated June 9, 1537. See Lewis Hanke, *The Spanish Struggle for Justice in the Conquest of America* (Philadelphia: University of Pennsylvania Press, 1949); and Richard H. Popkin, "The Philosophical Bases of Modern Racism," in *The High Road to Pyrrhonism*, 81.

55. Bartholomé de las Casas, *A Selection of His Writings*, trans. and ed. by George Sanderlin (New York, 1972), Part IV.

56. See *Vida, y Escritos del venerable Varon Gregorio Lopez* (Madrid, 1678). It appeared in English, first printed in Paris in 1638, and last as *The Life of Gregory Lopez* (Boston: Henry Dager, 1857). See also Fernando Ocaranza, *Gregorio Lopez, el hombre celestial* (México: Ediciones Xochitl, 1944).

57. Gregorio López, *Tratado del Apocalipsi* (Madrid, 1678).

58. On Vieira see R. Cantel, *Prophétisme et Mèssianisme dans l'oeuvre du Pere Vieira* (Paris: Ediciones Hispano Americano, 1960); and A. J. Saraiva, "Antonio Vieira, Menasseh ben Israel et le Cinquiéme Empire," *Studia Rosenthaliana* 6 (1972): 26–32.

59. On the biography of Molinos, see E. Pacho, article "Molinos," *Dictionnaire de spiritualité ascétique et mystique* (Paris: Beauchesne & fils, 1977–80), 10, part

2: 1486–1514; José Angel Valente, "Ensayo sobre Miguel de Molinos," in Miguel Molinos, *Guia Espiritual* (Barcelona: Ediciones Jucar 1974), 28–40; and P. Dudon, S.J., *Le Quietiste espagnol Michel Molinos (1628–1696)* (Paris: Beauchesne, 1921).

60. See T. J. Saxby, *The Quest for the New Jerusalem: Jean de Labadie and the Labadists, 1610–1744* (Dordrecht: Martinus Nijhoff, 1987) and Mirjam de Baar, M. Lowensteyn, M. Monteiro, and A. A. Sneller, eds., *Choosing the Better Part: Anna Maria van Schurman (1607–1678)* (Dordrecht: Kluwer, 1996).

61. Saxby, *Quest*, chaps. 12 and 13.

62. On the quietism of Labadie and van Schurman, see Richard H. Popkin, "Fideism, Quietism and Unbelief: Scepticism for and Against Religion in the 17th and 18th Centuries," in Marcus Hester, ed., *Faith, Reason, and Skepticism* (Philadelphia: Temple University Press, 1992), 121–54, 169–74.

63. On La Peyrère, see Richard H. Popkin, *Isaac La Peyrère (1596–1676). His Life, Work and Influence* (Leiden: Brill, 1987).

64. Isaac La Peyrère, *Du Rappel des Juifs*, Livres I–V (n.p., 1643); and Popkin, *La Peyrère*, chap. 4, 53–59.

65. Samuel Fisher, *Rusticos ad Academicos [The Rustick's Alarm to the Rabbies]* (London, 1660), in *The Testimony of Truth Exalted* (n.p., 1679), 696.

66. Cf. Richard H. Popkin, "Jewish Christians and Christian Jews in the 17th Century," in Popkin and Gordon M. Weiner, eds., *Jewish Christians and Christian Jews from the Renaissance to the Enlightenment* (Dordrecht: Kluwer, 1994), 57–72.

67. This appears in an unpublished writing in the *Hartlib Papers* at the University of Sheffield, Ms. 25/4/1–7.

68. Richard H. Popkin, "The End of the Career of a Great 17th Century Millenarian: John Dury," *Pietismus und Neuzeit* 14 (1988): 203–20.

69. On this see Popkin, "Condorcet, Abolitionist," in Leonora C. Rosenfield, ed., *Condorcet Studies I* (Atlantic Highlands, N.J.: Humanities Press, 1984), 35–47.

11

The Problem of Toleration in the New Israel: Religious Communalism in Seventeenth-Century Massachusetts

H. Frank Way

THE EARLY EFFORTS TO ESTABLISH the Massachusetts Bay Colony as a Christian community present in microcosm one of the more enduring issues in Western history. A vision of a religiously based community is deeply rooted in Christian history. In Acts 13:47, St. Paul reported that the Lord said to him, "I have set thee to be a light of the Gentiles, that thou shouldest be for salvation unto the ends of the earth." Eventually, the Roman Catholic Church's hope for a universal Christian community approached a degree of reality. Increasingly, however, the Catholic Church faced a host of countermoves to restore the less centralized primitive Christian communities of the early church. This thirst for Christian community exploded in the Protestant Reformation of the sixteenth century. Yet the Reformation could never completely fulfill this dream, if for no other reason than that Protestanism is based on a dynamic that is unable to put a period to religious individualism. The Bay Colony thus presents us with an opportunity to examine the dynamics and social statics of religious communalism: Protestant pluralism and dissent, religious individualism, and religious coercion.

In the centuries following the founding of the Bay Colony (1630), countless closed religious communities, such as the Shakers and the early Mormons, acted on their dreams of community. But even the broader

based religious groups of the early nineteenth century, such as Presbyterians, Congregationalists, and Baptists, all shared a dream of building
a Protestant Christian nation. The ideal of Christian community or even
a Christian nation remains a part of the social and political agenda of
America. This study will allow us to see something of the complexities of
this ceaseless quest for Christian community, for a religiously united social
and civil order in which individuals find their release by submission to
norms thought to be derived from the Bible.[1]

The most expeditious route to unraveling religious communalism in
the Bay Colony is to focus on the leadership of the colony as revealed
through the views of its Puritan ministers and the religious activities of the
governing body of the colony, the Massachusetts General Court. In the
course of this study, we will look at the support for and the role of coercion
in maintaining religious unity in the early Bay Colony, and the contextual
factors that help to explain the shift toward toleration that occurred by the
early 1690s.

Religious communalism and the preservation of religious truth were
central to the founding of the Bay Colony. Puritan leaders such as Governor John Winthrop and the Rev. John Cotton viewed the colonization
of Massachusetts as an opportunity to establish a pristine Bible-centered
community. The unsettled wilderness coupled with the vast Atlantic Ocean
offered the founders protection against the contamination of what they
considered to be an increasingly Catholic-leaning Anglican church. In the
wilderness they could restart the Reformation by ridding themselves of the
Romanish rituals of the Anglican church and the interference of its bishops. Calvinism could once again triumph over the corrupting doctrines
of the English church and religious truth be fostered and preserved. They
would build a community infused with Christian love, piety, and truth; a
community based on self-discipline, personal sacrifice, brotherhood, and
respect for the social order. In short, Winthrop and his company would
build a New Zion.

John Winthrop was elected governor of the Massachusetts Bay Company in London by the other merchant investors in 1629, several months
before he led a fleet of ships to the recently established colony. He justified the founding of the new colony by, among other reasons, arguing
that "It wilbe a service to the Church of Great Consequence to carry the
Gospel into those parts of the world, and to raise a bullwarke against
the kingdom of Antichrist which Jesuits labour to rear up in all places of
the world."[2] On the other hand, a reading of the transactions of the Bay

Company while it was still situated in London during 1629 suggests that provisioning the expedition, raising money, and establishing a basis for the future allotment of Massachusetts land were among the Company's most pressing concerns. Provision was made, however, to send over ministers to Salem and among the provisions purchased were Bibles, Calvin's *Institutes*, tracts against separatists, atheists, and Catholics, and various catechisms and works of piety.[3] Indeed, once Winthrop's fleet arrived in Boston, the first order of business of the governing body was establishing how to provide for two of the ministers.[4]

The Ideal of Community: The Modell of Christian Charity

It was not an early minister, however, who left us the most enduring image of the ideal of a New Zion these settlers hoped to plant in Massachusetts. Rather, it was Governor John Winthrop who gave a lay sermon on the flagship *Arbella* sometime prior to the fleet's arrival in the summer of 1630.[5] We know the sermon by the title "A Modell of Christian Charity."[6] In his sermon Winthrop offered a powerful vision of a new structured community, one in which the rich would possess the virtues of mercy, gentleness, and temperance and the poor the virtues of patience, faith, and obedience. In his community, one built on mercy and justice, all would be knit together by love in a bond of brotherly affection. It would be a community bound by the moral law and by the law of the Gospels, one in which individuals would heed one another in distress or want, for all were brothers in Christ, all created in the image of God. Furthermore, for Winthrop, to be a member of a Christian community carried great charitable responsibilities. He wrote:

wee are a company professing our selves fellow members of Christ, in which respect onely though wee were absent from each other many miles, and had our imployments as farre distant, yet wee ought to account our selves knitt together by this bond of love.

In his community, then, the "care of the publique must oversway all private respects." To these ends Winthrop suggested that in their new home his fellow passengers must redouble their efforts at Christian living and put into Christian practice that which heretofore was "maineteine as a truthe in profession only." In short, New England would be a community held together in meekness, gentleness, patience, and liberality; one where all "must delight in each other, make others condicions our owne, rejoyce together, mourne together, labour and suffer together, allwayes having before our eyes our commission and community."

In concluding his sermon, Winthrop noted that the passengers had entered into a covenant with God; it was their duty to succeed so that subsequent settlers would look to New England as their model, "for wee must consider that wee shall be as a city upon a hill, the eies of all people are upon us." In summary, for Winthrop community and Christianity were inseparable. The moral law and the Bible, especially the Gospels, provided the framework for a new community in the wilderness in which the public good would prevail over private interest.

Over three hundred years after Winthrop gave his sermon, it remains one of the more memorable public addresses in the annals of American history. It breathes the air of charity, love, self sacrifice, and community, values that transcend generations and cults. Was the sermon, however, a herald of the immediate future of the Bay Colony? In a limited sense the sermon seems not to have been a harbinger. The overwhelming focus of the sermon was on Christian love as the bond of perfection and yet the fact that Massachusetts quickly took on a persecuting spirit seems, at first glance, to be inconsistent with this message of love and brotherly affection. If the community was to be knit together by love and affection, then why did community come to be defined as order, even as a coercive order? Certainly one explanation is simply that, while Winthrop's use of the term love included human affection, its broader compass was theological. He argued that love was the fruit of a new spiritual birth; that none could have love except they become "a new Creature." Only through this new birth could an individual see Christ's love in himself and thus see Christ's love in others who were his elect.[7] In short, Winthrop's vision of a new community infused with Christian love was firmly rooted in Calvinist theology. While it called for "the care of the Publique" that must "oversway all private" interest, still the care of the public was not simply a material charge, but also a spiritual responsibility, for "the end is to improve our lives to do more service to the Lord . . . and . . . to be better preserved from the common corruptions of this evill world." And in warding off the "common corruptions" the Puritans would find that it would take state coercion as well as the bond of brotherly love.

Preserving the Christian Community

There was little that was novel in Winthrop's vision. The emphasis in "A Modell of Christian Charity" on a social life that was interdependent and interconnected, on the importance of order, structure, and unity to society, on the need to sublimate individuals to the public good, were all part of traditional sixteenth-century English culture.[8] What was arresting, however, about Winthrop and the other early leaders of the Bay Colony was their conviction that New England would be a New Zion, that the Reformation could be restarted in the wilderness. Furthermore, Winthrop and others thought that the centrality of their religion was tied to its purity, and they made a commitment that their communities would be free of religious contamination. Thus in 1629, months before Winthrop's fleet departed, the Bay Colony had established an outpost in Salem and the London investors discovered that they had agreed to allow one Ralph Smith to take passage on one of their chartered ships. But Smith was a minister who "had a difference of judgment in some things from or ministers." In April 1629 the Company instructed the resident governor in Salem "that unless hee wilbe conformable to or government, you suffer him not to remaine within the limits of or graunt."

Here, then, we see early evidence that the Bay Colony intended to form not just a Godly society but a true and pure one based on a social covenant that would bond all to religious unity and conformity. As the Dedham Covenant (1636) recorded, "we shall by all means labor to keep off from us all such as are contrary minded, and receive only such unto us as may be of one heart with us."[9] And in their early church covenants the settlers bound themselves into a company of saints, gathered out of the world.

The View of the Puritan Ministers

It would have been surprising, even revolutionary, for the Bay Colony to have viewed religious dissent as no threat to community. When the Dedham town covenant pledged to "profess and practice one truth according to that most perfect rule," it was simply reflecting an elite consensus that there was an orthodoxy or truth and that it should be maintained. As the Rev. Thomas Shepard wrote to a friend, "There is but one truth, you know."[10] Indeed, there was an almost circular quality to this commitment.

The town would profess and practice one truth and the churches would help to maintain a united and morally based community. It would not be surprising, then, to see that religious dissent would be responded to with the same vehemence and fear that earlier had characterized Christianity's response to heresy in Europe.

We begin our survey of the response to dissent with one of Massachusetts Bay's early ministers, the witty Rev. Nathaniel Ward (1578–1652). In the *Simple Cobler of Aggawam* (1645–1647) he wrote:

> If the devill might have his free option, I beleeve he would ask nothing else, but liberty to enfranchize all other Religions, and to embondage the true; nor should he need: It is much to be feared that laxe Tolerations upon State-pretences and planting necessities, will be the next subtle Stratagem he will spread, to distate the Truth of God . . . and supplant the peace of the Churches.
>
> He that is willing to tolerate any unsound Opinion, that his owne may also be tolerated, though never so sound, will for a need have Gods Bible at the Devills girdle.[11]

It was not just that Ward saw that dissenters imperiled Christian truth, but rather what he saw lurking on the horizon. Some of the closest supporters of the Bay Colony ministers in England were the Independents within the broader grouping of English Puritans. At the time Ward was writing, the Independents, such as John Goodwin, were arguing for toleration.[12] Ward apparently viewed calls for toleration as mere expediency for reasons of state and argued that on the contrary, a religiously united state was far better than one in which religious truth survived only in a part of the nation.

Ward wrote *The Simple Cobler of Aggawam* in 1645, almost a decade after the Antinomian crisis had been successfully ended with the 1637 banishment of the Rev. John Wheelwright and the 1638 banishment of Anne Hutchinson. It was, however, written at a time that Baptists were establishing churches in Rhode Island and when occasional Baptist opinions were heard in Massachusetts. At this point, however, the Baptist threat to unity was minor. What seemed to loom as a greater threat by the 1650s was the arrival of Quaker missionaries.[13] In the late 1650s the Rev. Mr. John Norton was commissioned by the General Court to write a response to the Quaker threat. In 1659 his tract entitled *The Heart of New England Rent* appeared. While Norton acknowledged that the civil authority had no coercive power over the conscience of the heterodox, that was true only so long as the heterodox kept a low profile, or what Norton referred to as "quiet or heresy alone."[14] Quiet heresy, uttered and not retracted but without an effort to induce others to accept the error or without disturbing the public order, was not subject to punishment. But "turbulent" heresy was quite another matter. Turbulent heretics, or Quakers, tried to persuade others to accept their blasphemies. Norton was torn by the issue of liberty of conscience in the treatment of Quakers and annoyed at English reaction to how the Bay Colony was treating Quakers. But Norton's only concession to conscience was to the conscience that did not or could not persuade, that is, to the silent conscience.

Civil Magistrates, Separation, and the Voluntary Principle

The ministers did not hesitate to enlist the magistrates in the cause of orthodoxy; the magistrates would be the "nursing fathers" of the churches. Thus, the Rev. Thomas Shepard, writing in 1652, argued that Christian magistrates had the power to preserve the moral laws; "I conceive it is casting off Christ's power to take away power from magistrates to punish sins against the first table, of which errors and heresies in religion are part."[15] For Shepard, the end of government was spiritual. Therefore the state had the duty to see that God's ordinances were enforced. However, for Shepard and the New England ministry this was a two-way relationship. It was also a sin to cast off deliberately made and prudently published civil orders. In short, the ministers seemed willing to play a role in keeping individuals from breaking their bonds to society and in the 1630s civil leaders such as John Winthrop understood that the loving bond between the ministers and the people could be used to preserve the community.[16]

The clear implication of the Bay Colony as a "city on a hill," a New Zion, was that this chosen land would be exceptional, not merely a replication of old England. It was to be an apostolic order in which love would link all; there would be voluntary obedience to a new godly order, to a renewed religious life. Yet the records suggest that the religious life was troubled and that government needed to use its coercive powers to infuse obedience into the new order of saints. For example, in March 1634 the General Court passed an act imposing a fine of up to five shillings for not attending Sabbath services, and in March 1635 an act was passed to prohibit the establishment of a church without the prior approval of the majority of the churches and without prior notification to the government, an apparent contradiction of the congregational view of church independence. In September 1638 the General Court passed the first compulsory law ordering every inhabitant of the towns to contribute to church support, "proportionably to his ability"; and failure to do so would result in an individual assessment. By the 1650s most Bay Colony towns had adopted compulsory maintenance.[17]

The comfortable working relationship between the churches and the government that had developed in the 1630s continued in the next decades. Between 1633 and 1649 the ministers and magistrates met on over seventy occasions, and gradually the ministers and ruling magistrates formed an alliance as against freemen and the new deputies to the general court.[18] The reward for the ministers was additional protective legislation. In May 1642 the churches and the government agreed that only church members could become freemen, that is, citizens with voting rights. This was followed on November 4, 1646 by an act requiring *all* inhabitants to attend religious services—Sabbath, and days of thanksgiving and fast—on pain of a fine of five shillings for every such absence. And on the same day the Court made it an offense, punishable by a fine of forty shillings, for anyone who renounced their "church estate or ministry" upon such "groundles conceite" that church ordinances apply only to "carnall Christians" and not to "spirituall or illuminated persons."

These last two acts are particularly revealing. Together they imply that the religious community may have faced an indifferent population among non-church members and furthermore that the hoped for unity was under attack. Indeed, from the outset there was no monolithic religious order, no single unity in the Bay Colony. The very nature of congregationalism, with its emphasis on church autonomy, prevented a tightly centralized Christian order. While Puritans had a moral vision of community based on self-discipline and self-denial, Puritan communities were not necessarily harmonious,[19] and some degree of religious pluralism and religious disagreement quickly became a hallmark of a New England community.[20] Yet the ministers and magistrates did not live comfortably with religious disagreements, especially where the disagreements gave rise to "dangerous" doctrinal views.

Early Religious Dissent: Roger Williams and Anne Hutchinson

Just over seven months after the Winthrop fleet began arriving in the late spring of 1630, the ship Lyon arrived with twenty passengers, including the Reverend Roger Williams and his wife Mary. In many respects this man of "devers dangerous" opinions was well within the mainstream of Puritanism, at least in 1631 when he arrived. He was a Calvinist, committed to the depravity of man, predestination, and the centrality of the Scriptures. He was also, however, a separatist, rejecting the Anglican church as a true church and calling on the nonseparating congregationalists to end all ties with the Church of England.[21] This man, who was to become a seeker and was to be subsequently viewed as a religious liberal, had some rather stiff-necked views about the unregenerate. These views were to alienate him from the ministry of the Bay Colony. At this point he was religiously exclusive rather than inclusive, holding that churches could not allow the unregenerate to attend nor could there be communion or prayer with those who had not the saving grace.[22] The political overtones of his religious views were equally difficult for the magistrates and ministers to accept. Williams repudiated the Old Testament acceptance of a binding relationship between civil and spiritual powers. States were not Christian communities and, while people created states, they could not baptize them; God redeemed individuals, not nations. The only holy community was a company of the regenerate who had been gathered out of the world and into a church. Thus magistrates had no religious powers, no power to enforce the First Table, nor power to correct the erring conscience.

The core of this argument was that the conscience erred, often, frequently, and even generally. For that reason it was important not to allow the civil authority, men most likely of erring consciences, to coerce the conscience, because they would likely coerce those few whose consciences were pure.[23] Finally, in the full logic of the early Reformation Williams argued that "In vaene have *English Parliaments* permitted *English Bibles* in the poorest *English* houses, and the simplest man or woman to search the scriptures, if yet against their soules persuasion from the scripture, they should be forced . . . to believe as the church believes."[24] Still, it was an unconvincing argument for those committed to orthodoxy. By September 1635, the ministers and magistrates concluded that his views were unacceptable to both church and state for he "hath broached and divulged dyvers newe and dangerous opinions against the authorities of magestrates as also writt letters of defamation both against the magestrates and the churches" (*Records*, 1: 160–61). He was banished from the colony.

The banishment of Roger Williams was but one of several early cases where individuals of some distinction were sentenced to banishment rather than to imprisonment or death. The Antinomian crisis of 1637, in which Anne Hutchinson and the Rev. John Wheelwright were banished, presented a far more serious threat to both the churches and civil authority. She became a "prophetess" of spiritism; it was not good works and a pious life that marked a saint but only the presence of the holy spirit, a presence that had nothing to do with the will or works of ministers. In short neither the churches nor civil society could do anything to hasten grace or assure it and once grace was received nothing could change it.[25] For thus "troubling the peace of the churches and commonwealth" Hutchinson and several of her friends, in November 1637, were excommunicated and banished and over seventy of her followers disarmed.

As one scholar has suggested, the Antinomian or Anne Hutchinson crisis is instructive about the fundamental divisions within Puritanism that colonial leaders would need to paper over.[26] Stephen Foster has argued that conventional ideas of what constituted heresy, when placed in the unsettled doctrinal context of transplanted Puritanism, easily resulted in viewing any differences as apostasy. In short, American Puritanism was a far from coherent and settled theology. Indeed, that unsettled theology allowed for a degree of doctrinal heterogeneity that belied the idea of orthodoxy.[27]

Building a Cordon Sanitaire

The banishments of Williams and Hutchinson indicate that the magistrates thought they could draw a *cordon sanitaire* around the Bay Colony. In November 1644 the Court passed a banishment act aimed at expelling Anabaptists and others who questioned the lawfulness of war and the right of the magistrates to enforce breaches of the First Table. We capture a sense of the urgency of the act in the following:

It is ordered and agreed, that if any person or persons within this jurisdiction shall either openly condemne or oppose the baptizing of infants, or go about secretly to seduce others from the approbation or use thereof, or shall purposely depart the congregation at the administration of the ordinance, or shall deny the ordinance of magistracy, or their lawful right or authority to make warr, or to punish the outward breaches of the first table, and shall appear to the court willfully and obstinately to continue therein after due time and meanes of conviction, every such person or persons shall be sentenced to banishment. (*Records*, 2: 85)

It was a law that one Massachusetts man said "makes us stinke everywheare."[28] But Massachusetts would continue on the same path, adding other measures to keep it free of the errors of the world.

In fact, the "errors of the world" were long since a part of Massachusetts. No *cordon sanitaire* would keep the Baptists or Quakers out, nor was there a safe and sure way to maintain total religious conformity, even in the congregational churches. In May 1646 the General Court passed a particularly interesting piece of legislation. It had provisions on blasphemy, heresy, compulsory church attendance, rash and vain swearing, and the reproaching of a sermon, and a provision penalizing those who renounced their ministers, churches, and the ordinances of the churches. What the act reveals is that there was some tension between the religious order they aspired to and the liberty of conscience they acknowledged. Throughout the various parts of the act the General Court professed liberty of conscience, professing that "faith be not wrought by the sword but by the word" and that they could not compel the Christian faith by force of arms or penal laws nor could any "humane power be Lord over the faith and consciences of men and therefore may not constrain them to believe or profess against their conscience." Still the General Court found ample justification to pass "necessary and holesome lawes," to restrain religiously offensive conduct and, in the interests of state prosperity and the faith, to compel all to attend religious services, and to prohibit Indians at anytime to "pawwaw or performe outward worship to their false gods or to the devill." In short, liberty of conscience was no excuse against "damnable heresees, tending to the subversion of the Christian faith and destruction of the soules of men."

The acts of 1644 and 1646 offer early evidence that the General Court had adopted something approaching a siege mentality. The intent was to warn dissenters away from the colony, but should dissent appear then it would face the coercive power of the state. Finally the act of 1646, when coupled with the call to the Cambridge Synod, suggests that it was not just external threats that the colony faced but also dissent within the established churches. The local population was not always faithful in Sabbath attendance and some were even inclined to swear, to "curse and smite" their parents, to play games for money, or to be "idle and unprofitable." In short, the community that was to be knit by love seemed to need the coercive power of the state to maintain a pious and faithful religious order.

Raising Needless Questions

Given the wide range of religious beliefs encompassed by English Puritanism, it was surely unrealistic for Winthrop and the early ministers to think that they could build a singular religious community in the Bay Colony.

Certainly it was clear from the outset that the General Court would need to be active in suppressing dissenters. In a letter dated from London in April 1629, the Governor of the Bay Company wrote to Captain John Endecott, who was then acting as the leader of the first settlers in Salem, Massachusetts, that the ministers were "of one judgment and bee fully agreed on the manner how to exercise their ministry." Not only does this seem unlikely, but the next sentence in the letter speaks volumes about English Puritanism. Governor Cradock warned Endecott that,

because it is often found that some busie persons (led more by their will than any good warrant out of Gods word) take opportunitie [of] moving needless questions to stirr up strife, and by that [meanes] to begett a question, and bring men to declare some different judgment, . . . wee pray you that if any such disputes shall happen among you, that you suppress them, and bee carefull to maintaine peace and unitie. (*Records*, 1: 394)

Undoubtedly the Antinomian crisis was the greatest "mischief" that beset the early period of the Bay Colony, yet the General Court was ever vigilant against "busie persons" moving "needless questions." From 1630 through 1649 the General Court's records reveal that 192 individuals received, either singly or in groups, some form of penalty, punishment, or other negative action for their violations of approved religious conduct or beliefs. Not just prominent people like Hutchinson and Roger Williams but also their followers and a host of obscure dissenters were hailed before the General Court.

The point here is simply that "busy persons" raised "needless" religious questions throughout the seventeenth century in Massachusetts. This is given some additional confirmation when we examine the public rhetoric of the General Court, that is, proclamations of days of public humiliation, thanksgiving, and of fast. By the 1650s it was common to request public prayers to heal "the sad divisions" in the churches (*Records*, 4, part 1: 347) or to justify the need for public humiliation because of the "irreparable vents and divisions in sundry churches." By 1660, the General Court was proclaiming that the colony was beset by horrid blasphemies, wickedness, and "great declensions" (*Records*, 4: 417–18).

Until the Restoration in 1660, the evidence drawn from the records of the General Court suggests that the Court had an active and aggressive religious policy aimed at maintaining one faith and one religious order. On the other hand, it is equally clear from these records that the Court recognized, and perhaps exaggerated, the presence of dissent, not only outside congregational societies, but also within the churches. Thus in May 1646 the Court in requesting the elders to assemble in a church synod gave as one example of the need for the synod the substantial disagreements within the churches over infant baptism. Furthermore, the Court found it necessary to be increasingly intrusive into the internal affairs of local churches. For example, in 1651 the Court found the minister at the Malden Church to have made errors and unsafe expressions, and the church was censured and fined (*Records*, 4, part 1: 70–71). Two years later, the Court enjoined the new Boston church from ordaining a minister that the Court concluded was unfit (*Records*, 4, part 1: 177). In May 1660 the goal of orthodoxy was given further administrative support when the Court delegated to the various county courts the power to purge the towns of heterodox ministers.

The Court reserved its high dudgeon, however, for the external threats to the congregational way: the Anabaptists (Baptists) and the Quakers. The Court in November 1644 passed its first and only punitive act against the "turbulent" Baptists, making it an offense subject to banishment for anyone to oppose infant baptism or to deny the right of the state to wage war. While the Court continued to characterize the Baptists as "turbulent," by the 1660s it had toned down its language. Baptists were no longer referred to as heretics but rather as "schismatics." This somewhat relaxed position toward Baptists can be explained, at least in part, because many Baptists were theologically Calvinists, and indeed the early English Baptists were identified with the Puritan movement. On the other hand, Quakers were outside the mainstream of Puritanism and the Court reserved its greatest fury for these "holy imbeciles."[29]

The "Holy Imbeciles": The Persecution of Quakers

The reaction of the Massachusetts authorities to the first Quaker missionaries once again demonstrates that coercion, not persuasion, would be the first line of defense against dissent. The first Quaker missionaries arrived in the summer of 1656 and were immediately arrested, questioned, and ordered banished.

Quakers were unquestionably the most hated and feared religious group in seventeenth-century New England. It was not simply that Quakers were heterodox, but this was accompanied by an enthusiasm for individual acts of zealotry—marching into a religious service and interrupting it by calling the minister the devil's mouthpiece or walking naked through a town to protest civil conformity.[30] They were deeply spiritual, holding that the Holy Spirit dwells in all, not just in the Saints; one simply had to accept its presence. Their doctrine of the Inner Light, however, was seen as an attack not only on the authority of Scriptures but also on the value of the organized ministry. Their disapproval of war and oaths coupled with their rejection of parental authority would have made a reasonable seventeenth-century magistrate fear their presence in the community. Furthermore, their spirit of infallibility coupled with a penchant for martyrdom placed them on a collision course with the Bay Colony.

In July 1656 two Quaker women, Mary Fisher and Ann Austin, arrived in Boston from the West Indies. They were seized, their "heretical and blasphemous" books were burned in the marketplace, and they were imprisoned for five weeks and then transported back to Barbados.[31] While Massachusetts would not prove to be as fertile ground for Quaker missionaries as Rhode Island or parts of Long Island, it would, however, prove to be fertile soil for Quaker martyrs. Guided by the Inner Light, enthusiastic Quakers would risk death to bring their truth to the Bay Colony.

Fisher and Austin had been banished only two days when eight more Quakers arrived in Boston, and they, too, were imprisoned and banished to England. Six of these eight would, at their peril, return again. As the Quaker martyr Mary Dyer warned the Bay Colony authorities:

Do you think you can restrain those whom you call "cursed Quakers" from coming among you, by anything you can do to them![32]

Dyer and three Quaker men were executed between 1659 and 1661 for returning from banishment. In a letter of December 1660 to Charles II, the General Court justified the first of these executions by arguing that the Quakers had their own blood on their heads because of "theire super-added presumptuous and incorrigible contempt of authority by breaking in upon us, notwithstanding theire sentence of banishment" (*Records*, 4, part 1: 451).

Even if the religious community of the late 1650s was rather more complex and layered than the word orthodox implies, still the leadership had shaped and molded a community, and experience suggested to them that coercion, not just persuasion, would help to preserve their "congregational way." While coercion helped preserve a substantial measure of the monopoly status enjoyed by congregational churches until well into the nineteenth century, still it was a case of winning the battle and losing the war. In the last analysis the Quakers won, and they did so at least in part because they provided so many ready martyrs.

The General Court was quick to engage in the battle against those "capitall blasphemers," those "malignant and assiduous" promoters of false doctrines, who through "dangerous, impetuous and desperate turbulency" threatened "our churches and state" (ibid.). By the fall of 1656, the Court had written its first anti-Quaker law, which placed a fine of one hundred pounds on any ship master who brought a known Quaker into the Colony (*Records*, 4, part 1: 277–78). One year later another act was passed, which placed a large fine on anyone who helped to bring a Quaker into the colony and a lesser fine on anyone who sheltered or concealed a Quaker. The act also provided that any banished Quaker male who returned to the colony could have his ear cut off, or both ears for the second offense; for the third return the tongue of the offender could be bored with a hot iron. Women could be severely whipped for the same offenses (*Records*, 4, part 1: 308–9). One year later, in October 1658, the court added death as the possible punishment for Quakers who returned from banishment (*Records*, 4, part 1: 346–47).

After the executions of Mary Dyer (1660), William Robinson (1659), and Marmadake Stephenson (1659), and before that of William Leddra (1661), the Bay Colony came under pressure from the new government in London. No longer could Boston count on the sympathy and/or administrative neglect that had characterized the period of the Civil War and the Cromwell government. In October 1660 the Boston government allowed all imprisoned Quakers to return to England. Yet in the following year, on May 22, 1661, the Court passed the Vagabond Quaker or Cart and Whip Act. Passed under a claim of leniency towards the intruding Quakers, the act characterized Quakers as rogues and vagabonds, and provided that any Quaker, on conviction of being a vagabond, could be stripped to the waist and tied to the tail of a cart and whipped from town to town until out of the Colony (*Records*, 4, part 2: 2–4). On the third return they would be branded with an **R** on their shoulder; if they returned again, death was to follow. Six days later, on May 28, 1661, the Court, in a seemingly contradictory gesture, ordered the release of all Quakers then in prison but ordered them to be banished. The community would be purged of its invaders.

Through the end of the charter government, the Court continued to pass an occasional anti-Quaker act. The articulated premise of these acts was that Quakers were heretics and enemies of the community, civil and religious. An act of 1663 denied Quakers who refused to attend "established" churches the right to vote in all civil elections. After the usual heated language, the Court made this revealing observation: Quakers "combine together in some tounes and make partjes suiteable to their designes in election of such persons according to theire ends" (*Records*, 4, part 2: 88). Here the Court effectively recognized that Quakers had made inroads in some orthodox communities. An act of November 1675 may reveal something about perceptions of these inroads. This act prohibited Quaker meetings, an admission that Quakers were now of sufficient strength to organize regular meetings. Even more revealing was the provision that a constable who did not enforce this law would be subject to a fine. Two years later, in May 1677, the Court expanded the power of constables to prevent Quakers from meeting by allowing them to break down doors of houses where there was suspicion that Quakers were holding a meeting. Once again the Court imposed a fine on any constable who neglected to enforce the act, although the Court reduced the fine by half, from four pounds to forty shillings. These coercive measures seemed ineffective in the face of the religious zeal displayed by the early Quakers. Coercion undoubtedly slowed their success and may have tempered their conduct, but it could not stop those who believed that walking in harm's way was a service to God. And in some hard to measure way these early Quakers helped shift Massachusetts toward toleration.

Shifting Priorities

As measured by twentieth-century standards, the final decades of the colonial government from 1660 to 1689 were far from tolerant; indeed the colony did not abandon the centrality of religion as an organizing force in society. Still, in the last decades of this government the Colony's priorities shifted, at least as measured by attention paid to religious matters by the General Court. The Court continued until the end to pass legislation governing the relations between the state and the churches; it still passed laws governing religious conduct and religious beliefs; and it still took time out to hear cases of individuals charged with violations of the various religious statutes. Yet as Table 1 indicates, in all these areas the activity level fell significantly in the final decades of the colonial government. Indeed, in only one area did the Court's output of religious legislation increase. Religious rhetoric, as measured by the number of Court proclamations of days of humiliation and days of thanksgiving, rose by 44 percent in the final years.

TABLE 1.   Religious activity by the Massachusetts General Court

| | Number of actions passed | |
Category	1628–1659	1660–1686
Church-state[1]	52	38 (−27%)
Religious conduct and beliefs[2]	36	16 (−56%)
Individual violations of religious laws[3]	192	43 (−78%)
Religious rhetoric[4]	25	36 (+44%)

[1] Category includes all laws passed regarding ministerial maintenance, laws regarding building of meeting houses and actions taken to call church synods, actions to discipline churches or ministers, and arbitrations of church disputes.
[2] Category includes sabbath, blasphemy, witchcraft, heresy laws; laws against contempt of ministers or churches; laws regarding religious conduct of Indians.
[3] Category includes any trial, sentencing, appeal, or order pertaining to an individual accused of violating a religious law.
[4] Category includes all proclamations of days of thanksgiving or of humiliation.

This is a marked difference, for example, from the 78 percent decline of the Court's attention to cases involving individual violators of religious laws or the 56 percent decline in the number of laws passed governing religious conduct and religious beliefs. Even in the area of church-state relations, an area in which the legislature would remain active throughout most of the eighteenth century, there was a marked decline of 27 percent in the number of laws passed in the final decades of the charter government.

It would be hazardous to place much value on the language or number of legislative proclamations of days of thanksgiving or days of humiliation. These proclamations were intended to be either expressions of worshipful thanksgiving or intended by a sinful people to placate an angry God; they were not necessarily designed to reveal the policy views of the Court. Prayers for good harvests or to give thanks for being spared a flood or prayers for the victims of smallpox reveal little about the General Court. Still, the rhetoric occasionally revealed other concerns. During the height of the "Quaker invasion," the Court recommended a day of humiliation in part because God had turned "our sweete union to much division" (*Records*, 4, part 2: 44). It also asked that the people pray that God spare the colony the "impetuous and restless intrusions of haereticks and enemies and the cursed combination of the Antichrist and his adherents" (*Records*, 4, part 2: 34–35). From the mid-1660s until 1689, the General Court did not again, in its public proclamations, address the issue of religious disunity, although that topic continued to be occasionally addressed in legislation.

A theme emerged in subsequent proclamations that tells us something of the Court's concerns in the religious arena. Undoubtedly in response to the questions pressed on the colony by the Royal Commissioners in the middle 1660s, the Court frequently asked the people and elders to pray for the preservation of the colony's civil and ecclesiastical liberties.[33] By ecclesiastical liberty the Court meant church liberty, not individual liberty, and the Court thought that church liberty was threatened by the London government. In short, there is some evidence that pressure from London was now of greater concern than the former priority of preserving religious unity. This seems consistent with the overall trend of government priorities, at least as measured by the published work product of the General Court. The marked decline in religious and church legislation after 1659 and the even more pronounced decline in the Court's hearing cases of individuals charged under religious laws is one indication of the Court's shifting priorities. Massachusetts was becoming a more complex colony, expanding its land frontiers, incorporating new towns, and regulating the economy. And by the end of the first charter government the religious scene had changed, particularly insofar as it affected Quakers and religious liberty. By the 1680s a Quaker correspondent could write, "We enjoy outward Peace at present. The parsecuting spirits be under contempt themselves and much awed by the present Power in England, so that we enjoy our Meetings Peaceably."[34] As Governor Simon Bradstreet said in a letter to the Reverend Increase Mather, "that cursed brat toleration" had gained a foothold.[35]

The First Stage of Toleration

By the early 1690s there was some evidence of movement away from persecution and toward a policy of grudging toleration. Quaker agitation played a role in this shift. The new Massachusetts Charter of 1691 contained a provision guaranteeing liberty of conscience. The new monarchs, William and Mary, specified in the charter that:

> Wee doe by these presents for Our heires and Successors Grant Establish and Ordain that for ever hereafter there shall be a liberty of Conscience allowed in the Worshipp of God to all Christians (Except Papists) Inhabiting or which shall inhabit or be resident within our said Province or Territory.[36]

The Rev. Increase Mather, the one largely responsible for obtaining the new charter, announced to the Quakers in 1693:

Your religion is secured to you. Now you need not fear being sent to Prison (as some of you were under a late Government) because you scruple Swearing by a Book. You may Worship God in the greatest Purity, and no one may disturb you.[37]

For Mather that was a significant shift in opinion. In the late 1670s, Mather referred to the toleration of Quakers as sinful and wrote that "indeed the Toleration of all Religions and Persuasions, is the way to have no true Religion at all left."[38]

That toleration was gaining acceptance in Massachusetts by the late seventeenth and early eighteenth centuries is beyond much doubt. By 1708 the Massachusetts government was openly acknowledging that conditions had changed, and in particular that Quakers had changed. Placing the problems of the Quakers in the past tense, the government noted that there

are those that go Under the Denomination of Quakers now such as were then [seventeenth-century], who were some of them Open bold Disturbers of the Publick Peace and their Principles notoriously known to be Heretical, but are much refined both in principles and Conversation.[39]

Philip Gura has argued that persecution of radical Puritans, such as the early Baptists and Quakers, served a larger ideological purpose; their punishments were a part of a social ritual which helped New Englanders to renew their belief in their special destiny, their communal purpose.[40] Religious persecution thus became a kind of ritual terrorism that served the purpose of maintaining traditional social values. In modern jargon, persecution became a form of pattern maintenance. New England historians may well be correct in arguing that seventeenth-century Massachusetts successfully countered the attacks of radical dissenters, that is, Baptists and Quakers.[41] It is not being suggested here that by the end of the seventeenth century Massachusetts was a scene of rapid social change. It is contended, however, that the Quakers and to a lesser extent the Baptists did play a significant role in altering one social pattern: the public acceptance of the persecution of those who attempted to worship outside an authorized congregational society.[42] In that limited sense the "brat toleration" won. But it was not a social change that had a single cause.

Contextual Factors in the Shift to Toleration

It seems reasonably clear that no single social, economic, or political factor either caused the shift toward toleration or loomed so large that without it the shift would have been problematic. For example, it might be tempting to conclude that the Quaker factor in this shift should be accorded a weight beyond all other forces. Indeed, Quaker and to a lesser extent Baptist agitation coupled with Quaker influence in powerful circles in London was a significant factor in bringing magistrates and ministers to adjust their policies of intolerance. The usable martyrology created by Quaker pamphleteers may well have helped to create a climate of doubt about the policy of persecution. On the other hand the excesses of early Quaker missionaries gave way to more acceptable conduct. The "cursed sect of haereticks" began to lose its turbulent spirit, such that the "ranterism" that had characterized some early missionaries and converts became less acceptable within the circle of Friends.[43]

Thus it was not just adjustment to the Quakers by the dominant culture, but also adjustment by Quakers to the majority that made the transition to toleration more probable. Yet would there have been such a factor had it not been for a geographical-political reality, that is, the open border with Rhode Island, the sixteenth-century haven for dissenters? Although Massachusetts occasionally tried to influence the course of events in Rhode Island and in Plymouth Colony, the fact remains that the border areas of Plymouth and Rhode Island were open highways for dissenters.

Plymouth Colony and Rhode Island were not, however, the only sources of religious diversity. As Massachusetts reached out to enlarge its borders it threatened the religious cohesiveness that had been established at the outset of the colony. From 1643 until 1677 parts of New Hampshire were annexed, and in the southern areas in and around the towns of Portsmouth and Dover and Exeter there were Antinomian and Anglican communities. Similarly, when Massachusetts assumed control over the southern portion of Maine it again confounded the problem of religious uniformity. The southern Maine towns of Kittery and York had well-established communities of dissenters.

Nor was it just religious diversity in adjoining colonies or agitation by dissenters or Quaker links to powerful merchant families in England that alone pressed forward the claims of toleration. Changes in the English government after the Restoration of Charles II, and especially the changes that accompanied the Glorious Revolution and the coming of Whig governments, made it imperative that Massachusetts adjust to the new political context of English government. Whig governments and English dissenters made common cause on toleration, and in this they had the support of William and Mary, foreshadowing the Whig and Quaker alliance under the leadership of Robert Walpole in the 1720s.

It is impossible, of course, to give precise weights to the factors that influenced the shift toward toleration in late seventeenth-century Massachusetts. The newly felt presence of the London government in colonial affairs, open borders, and Quaker and Baptist agitation may all have been successfully countered had it not been for a structural problem inherent in the civil and ecclesiastical policies of the Bay Colony, as we shall see. Furthermore, the preservation of religious community was made problematic by the decentralized nature of both congregationalism and the Massachusetts civil government.

Congregationalism sought church or ecclesiastical liberty, which meant the right of each congregation to elect its own officers, select its minister and teacher, and manage its own affairs. Voluntary membership and church independence had been cornerstones of English congregationalism, and Massachusetts churches resisted the centralizing features of Presbyterianism and episcopacy. Respect for church autonomy found its way into seventeenth-century Massachusetts law, which provided for a wide measure of church liberty.[44] Thus to concede the right of a synod or a legislature to prescribe religious duties and beliefs was for congregationalism a troubling inconsistency. In effect, a congregational establishment was a contradiction in terms. The tradition of "Independency" in congregationalism made uniformity a sometimes distant goal.[45] Decentralization of church life became a pronounced feature of New England congregationalism. Even when synods were recognized in the Bay Colony, the continuing power of church localism provided an opportunity, in the right circumstances, for pluralism. Church localism did not mean that the local meeting house did not constitute a cohesive religious community. All that is being suggested here is that the larger vision of Winthrop's Modell of Christian Charity was made problematic by a central feature of congregationalism.

If congregationalism held that church independence was scriptural, then New Englanders held that local government was a birthright of Englishmen. The General Court, the principal governing body of the colonial period, organized the colony around units of government familiar to them, towns and counties, and these units became the principal administrative units of government. The General Court was thus dependent on local officials—sheriffs, constables, assessors, selectmen—to enforce the laws. When, however, certain towns or even whole areas began to have significant numbers of Quakers and Baptists, enforcement of some of the religious laws, such as laws for ministerial maintenance or prohibitions against unauthorized religious meetings, became problematic. For example, the problem of tax delinquent towns that either failed to set a rate to support an orthodox minister or to collect an established rate forced the General Court to provide penalties against non-compliant local officials or to take matters into their own hands and establish a rate and assess a delinquent town. The problem was particularly acute in the areas formerly a part of Plymouth Colony, such as Bristol and Barnstable counties, where the towns of Swansea, Dartmouth, Freetown, Tiverton, Rehoboth, and Attleboro had significant numbers of dissenters who resisted religious taxation and were apparently influential in discouraging local officials from assessing or collecting the ministerial rates.[46] Local opposition to forced maintenance, when coupled with the growing, albeit small, numbers of dissenters, forced some towns to agree to voluntary maintenance and in the case of the town of Swansea, a Baptist elder became the town minister in 1699.[47] In effect, in some areas of Massachusetts the established church and the community ceased to have common boundaries. Clearly by this point Winthrop's sense of community, of the common identity of a town and a church, was being challenged.

In noting the importance of localism in the rise of toleration, we should, however, be careful not to underestimate the significance of the coercive measures passed by the General Court. Local acceptance of dissenting churches may well have contributed to the rise of toleration, yet the General Court acted as a brake on such liberalizing tendencies. If, however, local communities generally were in advance of the Court on issues of toleration, then surely it would not have taken so long for this social change to be reflected in state policy. The process may have been dialectical, but other factors beyond localism were at work in pushing the Bay Colony toward toleration.

Jon Butler has argued that from 1630 through the 1660s New England sacralized the landscape in ways that thoroughly outstripped religious life in old England.[48] Rates of church membership, attendance, and baptism reached levels rarely attained in the home country. Spiritual reform, the hope of rekindling the Reformation, was the goal of many of the early immigrants. But apparently the religious motivation of the third and fourth waves of immigrants was less evident. Indeed, loss of religious zeal or the rhetoric of decline were common themes of ministers in the late seventeenth century.[49] After 1650, Butler argues, the new immigrants were less likely to join churches and less likely to have ties to English congregational groups. While the new immigration helped to create a more secular society,[50] it also brought greater religious diversity.[51] In these circumstances the singular Christian community envisioned by the Mathers, Winthrops, Endecotts, and Shepards faced internal threats to its homogeneity and external pressures to accept some measure of diversity.

In the search for possible causes of the gradual movement toward toleration, one final factor needs to be briefly explored and that factor has to do with the internal dynamics of Protestantism and congregationalism. In general, Protestantism as it developed through the end of the sixteenth century was a Bible-centered religion in which religious truth was revealed through Scripture. Liberty of conscience came to be understood as the right and obligation individuals had to obey the truth as revealed to them through the Scriptures. This created a dilemma for Protestants. By thus encouraging a degree of religious individualism Protestantism could give no clear answer to the question of who was to be the final arbiter of religious truth and error. While Congregationalists rejected the papacy, episcopacy, and to some extent the quasi-hierarchical structure of Presbyterianism as means to the end of defining and preserving religious truth, Puritanism still had about it a high degree of communalism. While religious uniformity was clearly the early ideal in Massachusetts, Puritanism often rejected the organizational means to that end. The ideal of maintaining religious truth thus conflicted with the role that Protestantism gave to the individual in preparing for his or her own salvation. From the Antinomian controversy through the Quakers' assertion of the "inner light" to the "new lights" of the religious revivals of the early eighteenth century, Puritanism in particular and Protestantism in general were placed under the cross pressures of religious individualism, which needed and demanded a wide measure of religious freedom, and religious communalism, which needed and demanded a wide measure of uniformity and discipline. As Alan Simpson has written, religious individualism proved to be more central to Protestantism than did the collective impulse of Puritanism.[52]

Conclusion

Our fascination with seventeenth-century Massachusetts must in part be attributed to the constant iteration by the clergy and civil authorities of ideals that still have wide currency—of a morally based community in which the public good is made paramount over self-interest, where self-sacrifice, self-denial, and brotherly and sisterly love infuse the social order. Even in the secular world of the late twentieth century the rejection of worldliness has more than the ring of quaint charm. But to have cast our examination of religious communalism and toleration against the backdrop of Winthrop's famous "Modell of Christian Charity" and the writings and sermons of the early clergy may have placed a larger burden on New England Puritans than they ever intended to place on themselves. The purpose, however, has been to highlight the tension between the ideals of religious communalism and the practical problems of adjusting to social conditions that made the realization of some, but not all, of these ideals either impractical or impossible.

Unquestionably, the leaders of Massachusetts Bay were successful in establishing a Christian/Protestant order. However, it was neither a tightly centralized order nor one that was completely uniform in church practices or beliefs. Doubtless the Bay leaders—clergy and magistrates—had an initial vision of a community withdrawn out of the world, one that separated saints and sinners, the servants of God from the profane world. Yet for at least two immediate reasons there was a degree of unreality to this. Given the many issues—theological as well as those concerning church polity—that remained unresolved within the broad family that constituted English Puritanism, it was most unrealistic to think that a policy of religious uniformity could be maintained successfully. The second and equally compelling problem was that not even the Atlantic Ocean or the great wilderness could separate the Puritans from the world they rejected. The most that could be done was to gather a church out of the world and try to preserve some measure of the religious truth the congregation accepted at first. Yet here was the dilemma faced by these Puritans, for if, as they did in the Cambridge Platform, they restricted full church membership to those who could demonstrate through a "relation" their experience in receiving the Holy Spirit, to that extent the profane world around them grew larger while the visible saints who qualified for membership were proportionally reduced. In this sense, there was a loss of religious and social communion.

It may well be true, as some have suggested, that part of the durability of the Congregational Way was due to its willingness to assimilate some of the positions of the dissenters, especially the Antinomians. Yet it seems dubious to assert that a Christian social order could have been maintained by measures that restricted the reality of a Christian community. If the meeting house was no longer conterminous with community, as increasingly in some areas it was not, then the options to restore community were restricted. The state chose coercive measures, which had some degree of initial success, in that it temporarily deprived some dissenting groups, such as the Baptists, of leaders like Obadiah Holmes. No one needs to doubt the efficacy of coercive measures in the broad arsenal of means to social control. Yet the implications of this study suggest how problematic coercion can be in the world of religious beliefs and how chimerical the world of orthodoxy can become.

Notes

1. Christian and religious communalism as used in this essay denotes ethnocentric alliance of local communities based on a common acceptance of Christian social and religious norms; it assumed the superiority of its culture and often pressed alien cultures to adopt it.

2. Darrett Rutman, *John Winthrop's Decision for America, 1629* (Philadelphia: Lippincott, 1975), 87; Perry Miller, in assessing the Puritans, wrote that in their eyes the struggle between Catholicism and Protestantism was the most important issue in the Western world. Perry Miller and Thomas Johnson, *The Puritans* (New York: American Book Co., 1938), 8.

3. *Records of the Governor and Company of Massachusetts Bay* (Boston, 1853), 1: 23–24, 37, 55, 66. Hereafter cited as *Records*.

4. *Records*, 1: 73. At least four ministers accompanied the Winthrop fleet and four had preceded it. For a number of years the colony had a fairly heavy concentration of practicing ministers.

5. The foregoing is not intended to suggest that the clergy were without an expansive ethical view of community. Knight has argued persuasively that the New England followers of the English Puritan Richard Sibbes, such as John Cotton, preached that the fruit of grace was the love of God and man. Janice Knight, *Orthodoxies In Massachusetts: Reading American Puritanism* (Cambridge, Mass.: Harvard University Press, 1994).

6. Reprinted in Miller and Johnson, *The Puritans*, 195–99.

7. *Winthrop Papers* (Boston: Massachusetts Historical Society, 1947), 2: 290.

8. Darrett Rutman, *American Puritan* (Philadelphia: Lippincott, 1970), 47–51. Rutman does suggest, however, that the intensity of adherence to traditional culture in early New England may have been a deviation from the norm of tradition (51); see also Michael Zuckerman, *Peaceable Kingdoms: New England Towns in the Eighteenth Century* (New York: Alfred Knopf, 1970), 70.

9. Quoted in Avihu Zakai, *Exile and Kingdom: History and the Apocalypse in the Puritan Migration to America* (Cambridge: Cambridge University Press, 1992).

10. Quoted in Samuel E. Morison, *Builders of the Bay Colony* (Boston: Houghton Mifflin, 1930), 123.

11. Nathaniel Ward, *The Simple Cobler of Aggawam in America*, ed. P. M. Zall (Lincoln: University of Nebraska Press, 1969), 7.

12. Perry Miller, *Orthodoxy in Massachusetts, 1630–1650* (Gloucester, Mass.: Peter Smith, 1965), 271–72, and Robert E. Wall, *Massachusetts Bay: The Crucial Decade, 1640–1650* (New Haven, Conn.: Yale University Press, 1972), 19.

13. Some scholars conclude that neither Baptist nor Quaker missionaries were particularly successful in winning converts. See David Hall, *Worlds of Wonder, Days of Judgment* (New York: Alfred Knopf, 1989), 7.

14. John Norton, *The Heart of New England Rent at the Blasphemies of the Present Generation* (Cambridge in New England: Samuel Gordon Publisher, 1659).

15. *The Works of Thomas Shepard* (New York: AMS Press, 1967), 3: 34.

16. David Hall, *The Faithful Shepherd* (Chapel Hill: University of North Carolina Press, 1972), 152–53.

17. Hall, *Faithful Shepherd*, 146–47.

18. Ibid., 145.

19. Sumner Chilton Powell, *Puritan Village: The Formation of a New England Town* (Middletown, Conn.: Wesleyan University Press, 1963).

20. Hall, *Worlds of Wonder*, 8–10; and Jon Butler, *Awash in a Sea of Faith: Christianizing the American People* (Cambridge, Mass.: Harvard University Press, 1990), 59.

21. The Bay Colony was nonconforming and nonseparating, whereas Plymouth Colony was nonconforming and separatist.

22. For a general treatment of Williams and his views see Edwin S. Gaustad, *Liberty of Conscience: Roger Williams in America* (Grand Rapids, Mich.: Eerdmans, 1991).

23. *The Bloudy Tennent Yet More Bloudy* (1652), *Complete Writings of Roger Williams* (New York: Russell and Russell, 1963), 4: 313–14. Williams, however, did think the civil authorities could coerce conscientiously motivated conduct that endangered public safety and welfare. See Edmund Morgan, *Roger Williams: The Church and the State* (New York: Harcourt Brace and World, 1967), 134.

24. "To Every Courteous Reader," Prefatory to *The Bloudy Tenent of Persecution* (1644), *Complete Writings*, 3: 13.

25. Charles L. Cohen, *God's Caress: The Psychology of Puritan Religious Experience* (New York: Oxford University Press, 1986), 262–65.

26. Stephen Foster, "New England and the Challenge of Heresy, 1630–1660: The Puritan Crisis in Transatlantic Perspective," *William and Mary Quarterly* 38 3d ser. (October 1981): 642.

27. Butler, *Awash in a Sea of Faith*, 59.

28. Miller, *Orthodoxy in Massachusetts*, 281.

29. Alan Simpson, *Puritanism in Old and New England* (Chicago: University of Chicago Press, 1955). He argues that Quakers were in fact the final thrust of Puritanism.

30. Jonathan Chu, *Neighbors, Friends, or Madmen: The Puritan Adjustment to Quakerism* (Westport, Conn.: Greenwood Press, 1985), 20–21.

31. Rufus M. Jones, *Quakers in the American Colonies* (London: Macmillan, 1911), 26–29.

32. Ibid., 84.

33. E.g., 1666, 1678, 1680, 1684.

34. Quoted in Susan Reed, *Church and State in Massachusetts, 1691–1740* (Urbana: University of Illinois Press, 1914), 20.

35. Phillip Gura, *A Glimpse of Sion's Glory: Puritan Radicalism in New England* (Middletown, Conn.: Wesleyan University Press, 1984), 324.

36. Quoted in Reed, *Church and State*, 21. The English Toleration Act of 1689 effectively granted the right of worship to dissenters, requiring only that they subscribe to most of the Thirty-Nine Articles and continue support of the established church. It gave special recognition to Baptists and Quakers, exempting the latter from the required oath to the crown and allowing them to declare their belief in a short profession of Christian faith.

37. Quoted in Reed, *Church and State*, 22.

38. "Danger of Apostasy," 1679, quoted in Michael Hall, *The Last American Puritan: The Life of Increase Mather* (Middletown, Conn.: Wesleyan University Press, 1988), 130.

39. Reed, *Church and State*, 48.

40. Gura, *Glimpse of Sion's Glory*, 227–28.

41. E.g., Foster, "New England," 660; Gura, *Glimpse of Sion's Glory*, 325–26.

42. There was no movement toward toleration of Catholics, and Massachusetts passed anti-Catholic legislation as early as 1646.

43. Jones, *Quakers in the American Colonies*, 1: 301.

44. See generally, *Records*, 4, part 2: 221; the General Court was not always respectful of church liberty and noted in 1665 that "subjection to ecclesiastical discipline is necessary for the well-being of any Christian society" (222).

45. Keith Stavely, *Puritan Legacies* (Ithaca, N.Y.: Cornell University Press, 1987), 116–18.

46. William McLoughlin, *New England Dissent, 1630–1833* (Cambridge, Mass.: Harvard University Press, 1971), 1: 113–225.

47. Ibid., 1: 136.

48. Butler, *Awash in a Sea of Faith*, 57.

49. Hall, *Faithful Shepherd*, 140–41.

50. A note of caution about seventeenth-century immigration is in order; the immigrants were overwhelmingly English, and Massachusetts authorities remained hostile to other groups, including the Scotch-Irish. This exclusivity may have contributed to more stable social behavior and a predictable social outlook. See Michael Zuckerman, *Peacable Kingdoms*, 107–8.

51. David Allen, *In English Ways: The Movement of Societies and the Transferral of English Local Law and Custom to Massachusetts Bay in the Seventeenth Century* (Chapel Hill: University of North Carolina Press, 1981), 11–12.

52. Simpson, *Puritanism in Old and New England*, 109.

Index

Contributors

Detlef Döring of the Saxon Academy of Sciences in Leipzig, Germany is the author of *Pufendorf-Studien* (1992) and *Frühaufklärung und obrigkeitliche Zensur in Brandenburg* (1995) and editor of Samuel von Pufendorf: *Kleine Vorträge und Schriften* (1995) and Samuel Pufendorf: *Briefwechsel* (1996).

Arlen Feldwick is pursuing graduate studies in the Department of English at the University of Arizona. She is the author of several published papers on Aphra Behn, and her research also encompasses modern British fiction, multicultural literature (especially of the South Pacific), and film.

Randolph C. Head is Associate Professor of History at the University of California, Riverside. He is the author of *Early Modern Democracy in the Grisons: Social Order and Political Language in a Swiss Mountain Canton, 1470–1620* (1995) and a number of articles.

Marion Leathers Kuntz is Fuller E. Callaway Distinguished Professor in the Department of Modern and Classical Languages at Georgia State University in Atlanta. She is the editor and translator of Jean Bodin's *Colloquium of the Seven About Secrets of the Sublime* (1975) and author of *Guillaume Postel, Prophet of the Restitution of All Things* (1981) as well as numerous articles and book chapters.

John Christian Laursen is Associate Professor of Political Science at the University of California, Riverside. He is the author of *The Politics of Skepticism in the Ancients, Montaigne, Hume, and Kant* (1992) and editor of *New Essays on the Political Thought of the Huguenots of the Refuge* (1995) as well as articles and book chapters published in several languages.

Thomas F. Mayer is Associate Professor and Chair of History at Augustana College. He is the author of *Thomas Starkey and the Commonweal* (1989) and many articles, and the editor of Starkey's *Dialogue between Pole and Lupset* (1989). He is the co-editor of *Political Thought and the Tudor Commonwealth* (1992) and *The Rhetorics of Life-Writing in Early Modern Europe* (1995).

Constant J. Mews is Senior Lecturer in History and Director of the Centre for Studies in Religion and Theology at Monash University, Clayton, Victoria, Australia. He is co-editor of *Petri Abaelardi Opera Theologica III* (1985) and author of *Peter Abelard* (1994) for the Variorum series, Authors of the Middle Ages, as well as of numerous articles relating to twelfth-century intellectual and religious history.

Cary J. Nederman is Associate Professor of Political Science at the University of Arizona. His recent books include *Community and Consent: The Secular Political Theory of Marsiglio of Padua's Defensor Pacis* (1995) and *Medieval Aristotelianism and Its Limits: Classical Traditions in Moral and Political Philosophy, 12th–15th Centuries* (1997). He is presently at work on a study of the medieval roots of political economy.

Richard H. Popkin is Professor Emeritus at Washington University and Adjunct Professor at U.C.L.A. He is the author of *The History of Scepticism from Erasmus to Spinoza* (3rd edition, 1979), *Isaac La Peyrère (1596–1676)* (1989), and *The Third Force in Seventeenth Century Thought* (1992), and co-editor of *Heterodoxy, Spinozism and Free Thought in Early-Eighteenth-Century Europe* (1996). He is also the author of over 200 articles and editor of numerous other books.

Gary Remer is Associate Professor of Political Science at Tulane University in New Orleans. He is the author of *Humanism and the Rhetoric of Toleration* (1996) as well as many articles on toleration themes.

H. Frank Way is Professor Emeritus of Political Science at the University of California, Riverside. He is the author of *Liberty in the Balance* (5th edition, 1981), "Religious Marginality and the Free Exercise Clause," *American Political Science Review* (1983) and "The Death of the Christian Nation," *Journal of Church and State* (1987).